Kiss,
Bow,
OR
Shake
Hands

Kiss, Bow, *or* Shake Hands

How to Do Business in Sixty Countries

**Terri Morrison,
Wayne A. Conaway, &
George A. Borden, Ph.D.**

BOB ADAMS, INC.
Holbrook, Massachusetts

Published by Bob Adams, Inc.
260 Center Street, Holbrook, MA 02343

ISBN: 1-55850-444-3

Printed in the United States of America.

J I H G F E D C B

Library of Congress Cataloging-in-Publication Data
Morrison, Terri
    Kiss, Bow, or Shake Hands : how to do business in sixty countries / Terri Morrison, Wayne A. Conaway and George A. Borden.
       p. cm.
    Includes bibliographical references and index.
    ISBN 1-55850-444-3 (pbk.)
    1. Business etiquette. 2. Corporate culture. 3. Business communication.
4. Negotiation in business. I. Conaway, Wayne A. II. Borden, George A. III. Title.
    HF5389.M67   1994
    395'.22—dc20
                               94-24754
                                CIP

This publication is designed to provide accurate and authoritative information with regard to the subject matter covered. It is sold with the understanding that the publisher is not engaged in rendering legal, accounting, or other professional advice. If legal advice or other expert assistance is required, the services of a competent professional person should be sought.
— From a *Declaration of Principles* jointly adopted by a Committee of the American Bar Association and a Committee of Publishers and Associations

This book is available at quantity discounts for bulk purchases.
For information, call 1-800-872-5627.

A Stella, Wayne, y la familia

*"I am not an Athenian or a Greek,
but a citizen of the world."*

—*Socrates*

Contents

Preface

Hans Koehler,
Director, Wharton Export Network

The prosperity of modern business is contingent upon successful globalization. Reject the opportunities of foreign markets and you reject the very future of business.

Globalization, by definition, requires you to deal with, sell to, and/or buy from people in other countries. These people probably speak different languages, have different cultural attitudes, and have different historical backgrounds. They cannot be dealt with, sold to, or bought from in the same way as a domestic company.

Multicultural awareness is a vital component of any global marketing strategy. This book addresses that challenge.

Naturally, one book cannot contain all the knowledge a U.S. executive needs in order to operate overseas. That would require multiple volumes. However, it does contain the minimum required information to be successful abroad.

To put it another way, you may know your particular industry inside and out, forward and backward, better than anyone else. Yet when you step off that plane in a foreign country, that expertise is not enough. If you do not have the knowledge of foreign business practices, negotiation techniques, cognitive styles, and social customs compiled here, the odds are that you will fail.

In effect, trying to do business overseas without this information is like skiing without poles. You might get lucky: The slopes may be smooth for a while, but eventually, as you pick up speed, you will fall. At the least, you have put yourself at a disadvantage before you have even begun.

Give yourself an advantage. Do not start to globalize until you've read *Kiss, Bow, or Shake Hands.*

Introduction

So you've decided to go global!

That's a wise decision. No matter how large your domestic market is, it is dwarfed by the global marketplace.

Most progressive U.S. companies have come to the same decision. However, problems often occur in efforts at globalization. For example:

- The Thom McAn Company traditionally sells shoes with a nearly-illegible "Thom McAn" signature printed inside the shoe. But when it tried to sell footwear in Bangladesh, a riot ensued in which more than fifty people were injured. It seems that the "Thom McAn" signature looked like Arabic script for "Allah." Outraged Muslims decided that Thom McAn was trying to get Bangladeshis to desecrate the name of God by walking on it—an insult in any culture, but especially in Bangladesh, where the foot is considered unclean.
- The Ford Motor Company was unsuccessful at marketing the Ford Pinto in Brazil. Ford had not realized that "Pinto" is a slang term in Portuguese for "small penis." Not surprisingly, few Brazilian men were willing to be associated with a Pinto. (Ford managed to save its investment by changing the name of the car to *Corcel*, Portuguese for "horse.")

As these examples show, a small misstep can threaten or even destroy your marketing efforts in a foreign country. This book will allow you to avoid many of the errors made by others abroad.

Each chapter in this book focuses on a single country. Every chapter is broken down into four areas. "Country Background" covers the basics: where the country is, a brief history, the language, the religion, the population, etc. The "Business Practices" section tells you exactly what to expect when you do business in that country: concepts of time and punctuality, making appointments, how to negotiate, etc. "Protocol" will be useful anytime you deal with a native of that country, whether you are traveling to the foreign country or hosting visitors. This section includes such information as greetings (do you *Kiss, Bow, or Shake Hands?*), forms of address, gestures, and gift giving. Finally, the "Cultural Orientation" portion takes a scholarly approach to intercultural communications; this is explained in the next chapter.

Remember that you will deal with individuals, and there are always exceptions to every rule. For example, the book states that most Japanese executives are reserved, polite, quiet, and rarely display emotion. Somewhere there is probably a loud, boisterous, gesticulating Japanese executive who is as emotional and imperious as any prima donna. Just because we haven't met him (or her) doesn't mean that no such person exists.

The process of communication is fluid, not static. The success of your intercultural interactions depends upon you, and the quality of your information. *Kiss, Bow, or Shake Hands* provides you with the best and most current data possible on what foreign business and social practices to expect in your efforts at globalization.

"The most universal quality is diversity."

—*Montaigne, 1580*

Cultural Orientation

For each of the sixty countries in *Kiss, Bow, or Shake Hands*? there is a cultural orientation section. Cultural orientation is a field of study that gives us a model for understanding and predicting the results of intercultural encounters. It is, however, a model—a theory. New discoveries continue to be made about why we act the way we do.

Furthermore, communication always takes place between individuals, not cultures. Few individuals are perfect representations of their culture. Citizens of the United States of America are generally known for addressing one another by first names, a habit that most of the world does not follow. However, there are many U.S. citizens who are more comfortable with formality, and prefer to use last names and titles. This does not make them any less of a U.S. citizen. It just makes them individuals.

What can our model of cultural orientation do for you?

It can help you predict how people in certain cultures will speak, act, negotiate, and make decisions. Since in reality we deal with individuals, there is a margin of error. For example, a German who would be addressed by his German colleagues as *Herr Doktor Schmidt* might tell a U.S. consultant, "Just call me Ernst." This is certainly not standard practice in Germany. However, Dr. Ernst Schmidt may work constantly with U.S. executives, and be trying to adapt to them to make them more comfortable.

Since some foreigners may adopt U.S. manners, why does the U.S. executive need to study foreign ways? There are many reasons. First of all, many foreign business people often can not or will not imitate U.S. mannerisms. Can you afford to leave them out of your plans for globalization? Second, you may wish to sell to the general public in a foreign market. The average foreign consumer is certainly not going to have the same habits or tastes as consumers in the United States. Third, although Good Old Ernst may act and sound like one of us, he isn't. He probably is not even thinking in English; he is thinking in German. Knowing how Germans tend to arrive at decisions gives you an edge. And don't we all need every business advantage we can get?

Here is a breakdown of the information in the cultural orientation section.

Cognitive Styles: How We Organize and Process Information

The word cognitive refers to thought, so "cognitive styles" refers to thought patterns. We take in data every conscious moment. Some of it is just noise, and we ignore it. Some of it is of no interest, and we forget it as soon as we see/hear/feel/smell/taste it. Some data, however, we choose to accept or ignore.

1) Studies of cognitive styles suggest that people fall into open-minded and closed-minded categories. The open-minded person seeks out more information before making a decision. The closed-minded person has tunnel vision—he or she sees only a narrow range of data and ignores the rest.

Something that may surprise you is that most experts in cultural orientation consider the citizens of the United States and Canada to be closed-minded.

Open-minded people are more apt to see the relativity of issues. They admit that they don't have all the answers, and that they need to learn before they can come to a proper conclusion. Frankly, there are not many cultures like that on this planet. Most cultures produce closed-minded citizens.

Here's an example: Most theocratic (governed by religious leaders) cultures are closed-minded. That's one of the characteristics of such a culture: God tells you what is important. Anything outside of those parameters can be ignored. From a business point of view, that can be a weakness. For example, Islam prohibits charging interest on a loan. There can be no argument and no appeal: Charging interest is wrong. Obviously, running a modern banking system without charging interest is difficult.

So why are Canada and the United States closed-minded?

Assume that someone from an Islamic country tells a North American that the United States is evil and should become a theocracy. The North American is likely to scoff. The United States a theocracy? Nonsense! Why, the separation of church and state is one of the most sacred precepts established by the founding fathers of the United States of America.

That North American is being closed-minded. He or she is refusing to even consider the Muslim's reasoning. A truly open-minded person would consider the proposition. He or she might reject the possibility after due thought, but not without a complete evaluation.

In fact, a person who wants to study cultural orientation should consider such questions. Granted, most business people would probably decide that the United States should not become a theocracy. But considering the topic can lead to some useful insights. Perhaps most important is the concept that most of the world does not share the United States' predilection for the separation of church and state. This separation is a specifically Western notion, which evolved out of the hundreds of years of European religious wars that followed the Protestant Reformation.

In point of fact, most cultures tend to produce closed-minded citizens as long as things are working fairly well. It often takes a major disaster to make people open-minded. For example, the citizens of many former Communist nations are now becoming open-minded. Their old Communist ideology has fallen apart, and they realize they need new answers.

2) Another aspect of cognitive styles is how people process information. We divide such processing into associative and abstractive characteristics.

A person who thinks associatively is filtering new data through the screen of personal experience. New data (we'll call it X) can be understood only in terms of similar past experience (Is this new X more like A or B, or maybe C?). What if X is not like anything ever encountered before? The associative thinker is still going to pigeonhole that new data in with something else (X is just another B). On the other hand, the abstractive thinker can deal with something genuinely new. When the abstractive person encounters new data, he or she doesn't have to lump it in with past experiences (It's not A, it's not B or C—it's new! It's X!). The abstractive person is more able to extrapolate data and consider hypothetical situations ("I've never experienced X, but I've read about how such things might occur").

3) Now, no culture has more than its share of smart (or dull) people. However, some cultures have come to value abstractive thinking, whereas others encourage associative patterns. Much of this has to do with the educational system. A system that teaches by rote tends to produce associative thinkers. An educational system which teaches problem-solving develops abstractive thinking. The scientific method is very much a product of abstractive thinking. Both the United States and Canada produce a lot of abstractive thinkers.

One final category has to do with how thinking and behavior are focused. People are divided into particular versus universal thinkers. The particularistic person feels that a personal relationship is more important than obeying rules or laws. On the other hand, the univeralistic person tends to obey rule and laws; relationships are less important than one's duty to the company, society, and authority in general.

Not surprisingly, these categories tend to go together in certain patterns. Abstractive thinkers often display univeralistic behavior: It requires abstractive thought to see beyond one's personal relationships and consider "the good of society" (which is a very abstract concept).

Negotiation Strategies: What We Accept as Evidence

In general, let us assume that everyone acts on the basis of his or her own best interests. (Anyone who rejects a contract because he or she believes it is a good deal belongs in an entirely different book—on psychology!) The question becomes: How do I decide if this is a good deal or not? Or, in a broader sense, what is the truth?

Different cultures arrive at truth in different ways. These ways can be boiled down to faith, fact, and feeling.

The person who acts on the basis of faith is using a belief system which can be a religion or political ideology. For example, many small nations believe in self-sufficiency. They may reject a deal that is overwhelmingly advantageous simply because they want their own people to do it. It doesn't matter that you can provide a better-quality product at a much lower price; they believe it is better that their fellow citizens produce the product, even if they do it badly and at a higher cost. Presenting facts to such a person is a waste of time. His or her faith operates independently from facts.

Obviously, people who believe in facts want to see evidence to support your position. They can be the most predictable to deal with. If you offer the low bid, you get the job.

People who believe in feelings are the most common throughout the world. These are the people who "go with their gut instincts." They need to like you in order to do business with you. It can take a long time to build up a relationship with them. However, once that relationship is established, it is very strong. They aren't going to run to the first company that undercuts your offer.

Value Systems: The Basis for Behavior

Each culture has a system for dividing right from wrong, or good from evil. After a general statement concerning the values of the culture, this section identifies the culture's three value systems (Locus of Decision Making, Sources of Anxiety Reduction, and Issues of Equality/Inequality). The following three sections identify the Value Systems in the predominant culture—their methods of dividing right from wrong, good from evil, etc.

Locus of Decision Making

This section explores how much a culture prizes individualism as opposed to collectivism. Some countries, such as the United States, are very individualistic, while others, such as China, are very collectivistic. A person in the United States may consider only himself or herself when making a decision, while a person in China must abide by the consensus of the collective group.

Such pure individualism and collectivism is rare. In most countries people consider more than just themselves, but are not bound by the desires of the group.

It is possible to consider the loci of decision making as a series of concentric circles. In the center, in the smallest circle, is the individual. The next circle, slightly larger, is usually the family. Many cultures expect each individual to consider "What is best for my family?" in each decision. The next circle represents a larger group. It could be an ethnic group, a religion, or even the individual's country. Some cultures expect individuals to consider the best interests of the entire, expansive group.

Of course, when a person is acting as representative for a company, the best interests of the company are paramount.

Sources of Anxiety Reduction

Every human being on this planet is subject to stress. How do we handle it? How do we reduce anxiety?

We can identify four basic sources of security and stability that people turn to: interpersonal relationships, religion, technology, and the law. Frequently, a combination of sources is used.

A person who must decide on an important business deal is under stress. If this person is your client, it may help you to know where he or she will turn for help and advice. This is especially true when the person turns to interpersonal relationships. If an executive is going to ask his or her spouse for advice, you had better make sure that you have made a good impression on that spouse.

Issues of Equality/Inequality

An important characteristic of all cultures is the division of power. Who controls the government, and who controls the business resources?

"All men are created equal" is a sacred tenet of the United States of America. Despite this, prejudice against many groups still exists in the United States.

All cultures have disadvantaged groups. This section identifies some sectors that have unequal status. These can be defined by economic status as well as by race or gender. Only the most industrialized nations tend to have a large, stable middle class. Many countries have a small, rich elite and a huge, poverty-stricken underclass.

Issues of male-female equality are also analyzed in this section. It is useful for a female business executive to know how women are regarded in a foreign country.

Never forget that this model represents cultural patterns that may or may not apply to each individual you work with. Utilize this information as a guideline and remain open to the new experiences we all encounter abroad.

"There is no conceivable human action which custom has not at one time justified and at another condemned."

—Joseph Wood Crutch (1929)

BUENOS
AIRES

Argentina

Country Background

History

The original Indian inhabitants of Argentina were nomadic hunters and gatherers, more similar to the majority of U.S. plains Indians than to the agricultural Inca Empire of Peru. They were warlike, and killed the first Spanish explorers who landed in Argentina in 1516. They even forced the abandonment of the first Buenos Aires settlement some twenty years later. Their ultimate fate was similar to that of their North American brethren: They were defeated and hunted down.

The Spanish considered Argentina to be useless grassland, with insufficient mineral wealth and populated by hostile Indians. Most of Spain's attention was focused northward, toward Mexico and Peru, where the agricultural Indians made more tractable slaves, and gold and silver were abundant.

Argentina developed slowly, utilizing the grasslands for cattle and mules. The cities in northwest Argentina developed first, since they were closest to the phenomenally wealthy mines of Bolivia. Buenos Aires, far to the south, was ignored, which accounts for the lack of Spanish colonial architecture in Buenos Aires.

Buenos Aires gained importance late during the Spanish reign, when it was designated as the capital of the new Viceroyalty of Río de la Plata in 1776. This Spanish viceroyalty lasted for scarcely four decades.

Napoleon's conquest of Spain prompted the Argentines to declare temporary self-rule in 1810. This led to a full declaration of independence in 1816, under the grandiose title of the United Provinces of Río de la Plata.

Fighting quickly broke out, as many provinces refused to be ruled by Buenos Aires. The territory of Río de la Plata divided into modern Argentina, Bolivia, Paraguay, Uruguay, and southern Chile. Even the old, established cities of northern

Argentina resisted domination by the upstart port of Buenos Aires. Not until 1880 was Argentina fully united.

Given such an uncertain start, it is not surprising that Argentina has suffered from political turmoil. For much of its history, Argentina has swung between elected governments and military dictators.

In 1976, threatened by terrorism and hyperinflation, most Argentines were relieved when the military seized power. Stability was restored at the cost of human rights. But after a few years, brutality, corruption, and bad monetary policy made the junta unpopular. The junta decided to distract the populace by invading the British-held Falkland Islands in 1982. To the junta's surprise, the United Kingdom fought to hold these essentially useless islands. Argentina lost the Falkland War, and the junta was humbled.

The junta ceded power to an elected government in 1983.

Type of Government

a————————————————**CULTURAL NOTE**
common Argentine saying is that Argentina has always been "blessed by resources but cursed by politics." Despite its turbulent political history, Argentina has remained one of Latin America's most prosperous nations.

Today the Republic of Argentina is once again a democracy. Its military junta stepped down after the country's loss to Great Britain in the 1982 Falkland Islands War. But the military remains in the background, and several unsuccessful coup attempts have been staged.

In September 1990, Argentina was the first Latin American country to send a contingent to the Middle East during the Persian Gulf War.

Language

Spanish is the official language, although many people speak English, Italian, or other languages. Argentine Spanish is heavily influenced by Italian and is unlike Spanish spoken anywhere else on the continent.

Religion

Church and state are officially separate, but about 90 percent of the population considers itself Roman Catholic. Jews and Protestants account for 2 percent each.

Demographics

About 85 percent of Argentines are of European descent, primarily Spanish or Italian. Indians, mestizos (people of mixed Indian and Spanish ancestry), and blacks together make up only 15 percent of Argentina's 33 million people. There are also significant numbers of French, English, and German immigrants. Buenos Aires boasts the largest number of Jews in Latin America; they are commonly referred to as *los rusos* (the Russians) because most of the early Jewish settlers emigrated from Czarist Russia.

Cultural Orientation

Cognitive Styles: How Argentines Organize and Process Information

Strong European influences make Argentines less open to discussion of new ideas than the citizens of most other Latin American countries. Those with higher educations are more apt to be abstractive in their thinking, although associative, experiential thinking is the rule of thumb. Strong personal relationships make Argentines more concerned about the consequences of an action than about the action itself.

Negotiation Strategies: What Argentines Accept as Evidence

There is a decided conflict among the forces of feeling, faith, and facts. Argentines look at problems from a subjective perspective, but these feelings are usually influenced by faith in some ideology (primarily the Catholic church, a political party, or ethnocentrism). Facts are always acceptable as long as they do not contradict either feeling or faith. However, an outsider may never realize this, since it is difficult for Argentines to openly disagree with someone they like.

Value Systems: The Basis for Behavior

Humanitarian values are strong, but consumerism is resulting in a more materialistic society. The following three sections identify the Value Systems in the predominant culture—their methods of dividing right from wrong, good from evil, and so forth.

Locus of Decision Making

Decisions are usually made by an individual, but they are always made with the best interest of a larger group in mind. The most honored group is the extended family, from which one gains his or her self-identity. Kinships and friendships play major roles in decision making.

Sources of Anxiety Reduction

Although the older generations are still attached to the church and the extended family for their security, the younger generation is putting more faith in the social structure. This sometimes leads to unrealistic allegiance to a strong political figure or ideology.

Issues of Equality/Inequality

Those who are in power consider themselves entitled to the privileges that come with the office. Although *machismo* is still very strong, it is being challenged on all fronts. There are now more women than men in school, and women are taking a leading role in both politics and business.

Business Practices

Appointments

PUNCTUALITY

♦ Visitors are expected to be punctual. However, do not be surprised if your Argentine counterpart is late. In general, the more important the person, the more likely it is that he or she will keep you waiting.

♦ Note that social occasions have different rules. Even North Americans are expected to be thirty to sixty minutes late for dinner or parties; to show up on time would be impolite. But be on time for lunch and for events with a scheduled starting time, such as the theater.

♦ When it is important to know if your Argentine counterpart expects promptness, you can ask, "¿En punto?" (on the dot?).

- Remember that many Europeans and South Americans write the day first, then the month, then the year (e.g. December 3, 1999, is written 3-12-99). This is the case in Argentina.
- It is wise to make your first appointment in Argentina with an *enchufado*—an individual who has high-level contacts in your industry segment. This person opens the doors, and can greatly facilitate the process of doing business. Get a list of potential *enchufados* or local representatives through the U.S. Embassy or your company's legal or accounting firm.
- Because the telephone system is undependable, it is often easier to make appointments by mail than by phone. Having lived for years with poor phone service, Argentines are also used to people dropping in without phoning first. If the person isn't in, a note can be left.
- Argentine executives may put in a very long day, often lasting until 10:00 P.M. An 8:00 P.M. business meeting is not at all unusual.

 Negotiating

- The pace of business negotiations is usually slower than in the United States. Do not be surprised if it takes you several trips to accomplish your goal.
- One reason business moves slowly is that Argentina is a highly bureaucratic and litigious country. Each decision must be approved by many people.
- Personal relationships are far more important than corporate ones. Each time your company changes its representative, you will virtually be starting from scratch. A new relationship must be built up before business can proceed.
- Any time you want to deal with the Argentine government, it is vital to have an Argentine contact to act as an intermediary. Without one, you probably won't even get an appointment.
- Don't assume that each portion of a contract is finalized once agreement on that portion has been reached. Until the entire contract is signed, each portion is subject to renegotiation.

 Business Entertaining

- Business meals are popular and are usually held in restaurants; offers to dine in Argentine homes are relatively infrequent.
- To summon a waiter, raise your hand with your index finger extended or call out *mozo* (waiter) or *moza* (waitress). Don't adopt the local habit of making a kissing noise to attract a waiter; although common, it is considered impolite.
- Business lunches are uncommon outside of Buenos Aires, since most people go home to eat lunch.
- Argentines do not usually discuss business over meals; meals are considered social occasions.
- As dinner does not begin until 10:00 P.M. (or later on weekends), Argentines have tea or coffee and pastries between 4:00 and 6:00 P.M. If you are in a meeting during that time, you will be offered something. Accept something to drink, even if you don't want it. Argentines do not put milk in their coffee, so it will probably not be available.
- When dining, keep your hands on the table, not in your lap.

*a*void pouring wine, if possible. There are several complex taboos about wine pouring, which a foreigner can unknowingly violate. For example, pouring with the left hand is a major insult, pouring wine backwards into a glass indicates hostility, and so on.

- Remember that the taxes on imported liquors are enormous. When you are invited out, your host will be paying, so don't order imported liquors unless your host does so first. Try a local drink instead; most types of liquor are produced in local versions.
- To indicate that you are finished eating and have had enough, cross your knife and fork (with the prongs down) on your dinner plate.
- Argentina serves some of the best beef in the world; expect to see a lot of it at meals.

Time

- Argentina is three hours behind Greenwich Mean Time (G.M.T.-3), making it two hours ahead of U.S. Eastern Standard Time (E.S.T.+2).

Protocol

 Greetings

- Except when greeting close friends, it is traditional to shake hands briefly and nod to both men and women.
- Close male friends shake hands or embrace upon meeting; men kiss close female friends. Close female friends usually kiss each other. The full embrace (*abrazo*) may entail a hug, a handshake, and several thumps on the shoulder, ending with another handshake.

 Titles/Forms of Address

- While many languages will be heard on the streets of Argentina (English, French, German, Italian, and several Indian languages), all the businesspeople you meet will be fluent in Spanish, so Spanish titles may be used.
- Note that Argentine Spanish has many unique features not found in other Spanish-speaking countries; it is highly influenced by Italian.
- Most people you meet should be addressed with a title and their surname. Only children, family members, and close friends address each other by their first names.
- Persons who do not have professional titles should be addressed as Mr., Mrs., Miss, plus their surname. In Spanish, these are
    - Mr. = *Señor*
    - Mrs. = *Señora*
    - Miss – *Señorita*
- Most Hispanics have two surnames: one from their father, which is listed first, followed by one from their mother. Only the father's surname is commonly used when addressing someone; e.g., Señor Juan Antonio Martinez García is addressed as Señor Martinez, and Señorita Ana María Gutierrez Herrera is addressed as Señorita Gutierrez. When a woman marries, she usually adds her

husband's surname and goes by that surname. If the two people in the above example married, she would be known as Señora Ana Maria Gutierrez Herrera de Martinez. Most people would refer to her as Señora de Martinez or, less formally, Señora Martinez.

- When a person has a title, it is important to address him or her with that title followed by the surname. A Ph.D. or a physician is called *Doctor*. Teachers prefer the title *Profesor*, engineers go by *Ingeniero*, architects are *Arquitecto*, and lawyers are *Abogado*.

Gestures

- The Argentine people converse at a closer distance than U.S. citizens are used to—often with a hand on the other person's lapel or shoulder. Restrain yourself from trying to back away; an Argentine will probably step forward to close the distance.
- Maintaining eye contact is very important—something that North Americans may find difficult while speaking to a person at such close quarters.
- A pat on the shoulder is a sign of friendship.
- The gesture that some North Americans use to mean "so-so" (twisting the flat, open hand from side to side) is common in Argentina. The meaning is the same.
- A sweeping gesture beginning under the chin and continuing up over the top of the head is used to mean "I don't know" or "I don't care."
- With thumb and middle finger touching (as if holding a pinch of salt), one taps them with the index finger to indicate "hurry up" or "a lot."
- Avoid placing your hands on your hips while speaking.
- Make sure to cover your mouth when either yawning or coughing.
- Sit only on chairs, not on a ledge, box, or table.
- Don't rest your feet on anything other than a footstool or rail; it is very impolite to place them upon a table.
- Eating in the street or on public transportation is considered impolite.

CULTURAL NOTE

- Try to avoid offering any political opinions. Be especially cautious about praising Argentina's neighbors (notably Chile). Argentina has fought wars with all of them.
- Most Argentines are anxious to put the Falkland Islands War behind them, so avoid bringing the subject up. However, if it is discussed, remember to refer to the islands by their Argentine name, the Malvinas Islands.
- The Argentine style of banter may seem odd, as it may include mildly derogatory comments about your wardrobe or your weight. Don't take it seriously; indeed, it is a sign that your Argentine colleague is getting comfortable around you.
- Argentines are great sports fans. Talking about sports is always a good way to open a conversation. Soccer (called *futbol*) is the most popular sport. U.S.-style football is *futbol americano*.
- Most Argentines love opera, so this is a good topic to discuss. Restaurants and sightseeing are also fine topics.

Dress

- Dress is very important for making a good impression in Argentina. Your entire wardrobe will be scrutinized.

- While Argentines are more in touch with European clothing styles than many Latin Americans, they tend towards the modest and the subdued. The provocative clothing popular in Brazil, for example, is rarely seen in Argentina.
- Business dress in Argentina is fairly conservative: dark suits and ties for men; white blouses and dark suits or skirts for women.
- Men may wear the same dark suit for evening wear, but may substitute an ascot for their tie. Women should wear a dress or skirt.
- Both men and women wear pants as casual wear. If you are meeting business associates (outdoor barbecues, called *asado*, are popular), avoid jeans and wear a jacket or blazer. Women should not wear shorts, except when invited to a swimming pool.
- Indian clothing is for Indians; don't adopt any native costumes, no matter how attractive. The same goes for *gaucho* outfits.
- Bring lightweight clothing for the summer, topcoats and sweaters for the winter (especially as central heating is not universal). Don't forget that the seasons in South America are the reverse of those in North America.
- Don't wear anything outside that can be damaged by water during Carnival time. Drenching pedestrians is a favorite Carnival pastime of the young.

 Gifts

- High taxes on imported liquor makes this a highly appreciated gift. The most popular types are scotch and French champagne. Don't bring wine; the Southern Cone produces plenty of good-quality wines.
- As in any country, any gift given should be of high quality. If the item is produced by your corporation, the corporate name or logo should appear discreetly, not be emblazoned over the whole surface.
- Avoid giving knives; they symbolize the severing of a friendship.
- Electronic gadgets like pocket calculators are popular
- Argentina is a major cattle producer, and thus a major leather producer. Avoid bringing leather gifts.
- If you are invited to an Argentine home, bring a gift of flowers, imported chocolates, or whiskey. Bird-of-paradise flowers are highly prized.

CANBERRA

Australia

CULTURAL NOTE

Country Background

History

The original inhabitants of the continent, the aborigines, were hunters and gathers who arrived at least 38,000 years ago. Many of these people retain their traditional culture and live separately from the rest of the population. In recent decades, efforts have been made by the Australian government to be more responsive to aboriginal rights.

In 1770, Captain Cook took formal control of Australia for Britain. Soon after, Australian penal colonies were established; thus the first settlers in the country were convicts and soldiers. Free settlers arrived later when word spread of the opportunities available "down under." The numbers greatly increased when gold was discovered in 1851.

Australia became a member of the British Commonwealth in 1901. In 1942, the Statute of Westminster Adoption Act was passed, which officially gave Australia complete autonomy in both internal and external affairs. British authority was finally removed in 1986.

CULTURAL NOTE

Type of Government

The Commonwealth of Australia is a democratic federal state system that recognizes the British monarch as the chief of state (represented nationally by a governor general and in each state by a governor). However, Australia is an independent nation and does not consider itself a constitutional monarchy.

The legislative branch of the government is a federal parliament, composed of the Senate and the House of Representatives. The prime minister heads the executive branch and is the head of the government. An independent high court heads the judicial branch. There are three major political parties: Labor, Liberal, and Australian Democrat.

Australia is known for offering extensive social welfare programs to its citizens. It is active in the United Nations and is particularly involved in assisting its developing neighbors in Asia and the Pacific. At present eighty countries receive aid from Australia.

Language

English is the official language of Australia; it is spoken by 95 percent of the population. Australian grammar and spelling are a mix of British and American patterns. For example, the Australian majority party is spelled "Labor" (American spelling), not "Labour" (British spelling).

a————————————**CULTURAL NOTE**

lthough most Australians speak English, communication problems can—and do—exist with foreign English speakers. An extensive accent and slang have developed that make spoken Australian English quite unique. Some idiomatic differences in "Strine" (Australian) include

"Full bottle" = fully informed, knowledgeable

"No worries" = no problem

"Fair dinkum" = true, genuine

"Bludioth!" (Bloody oath!) = yes (emphatically)

Australians tend to shorten words to one syllable, then add a long e sound to the end. Therefore, a barbecue becomes a "barbie," a mosquito becomes a "mozzi," and the people are known as "Auzzies" rather than Australians. Avoid the terms "stuffed" (which is said in the United States after one eats too much) and "rooting" (which those in the United States do for their favorite team); both these terms have vulgar connotations in Australia.

Religion

Christians, divided equally between Anglicans and Roman Catholics, make up 76 percent of the population. Jews, Muslims, and Buddhists are also present. A significant proportion of Australians (almost 13 percent) claim no religious affiliation.

Demographics

Australia has a population of 17.5 million, concentrated mainly on the southern and eastern coasts. (This is approximately the population of the state of Texas, in a nation the size of the lower forty-eight United States.)

The 206,000 aboriginals constitute only 1.2 percent of the Australian population. Immigration continues to be largely from Europe (Europeans still make up 93 percent of the population), although significant numbers are arriving from Asia (some 5 percent of the population) and other world regions.

Australia has one of the world's highest urbanization rates, with 85 percent of its population living in cities.

Cultural Orientation

Cognitive Styles: How Australians Organize and Process Information
Australians are individually open-minded and trusting of equals until given reason not to be. They are quite analytical and conceptual in their thinking. Rules and laws almost always take precedence over personal or emotional feelings about an issue. Company policy is followed regardless of who is doing the negotiating.

Negotiation Strategies: What Australians Accept as Evidence
Facts are given the highest validity, since Australians tend to reason from an objective perspective. Little credence is given to feelings, as personal emotions are untrustworthy. Australians are highly ethnocentric, so a basic faith in their nation may underlie some of their arguments.

Value Systems: The Basis for Behavior
The Judeo-Christian ethic pervades all behavior, but material progress is more important than humanistic progress. The following three sections identify the Value Systems in the predominant culture—their methods of dividing right from wrong, good from evil, and so forth.

Locus of Decision Making
Individualism is very important in decision making, but it is subject to company policy. Australians do not find it difficult to say "no." One's life is private and not to be discussed in business negotiations. Friendships are few and specific to needs.

Sources of Anxiety Reduction
There is low anxiety about life, since external structures (democracy, organizations, scientific method) provide stability and insulation from life. The nuclear family is the rule and is the strongest socializing force. There are established rules for everything. Anxieties are developed over deadlines and results.

Issues of Equality/Inequality
Egalitarianism stresses a high minimum standard of well-being for the whole of society and an outward show of equality that minimizes privileges associated with formal rank. Emphasis is on one's ability. Traditional sex roles are changing rapidly, but women are still fighting for equality in pay and power.

Business Practices

Appointments

 _____ **PUNCTUALITY**

♦ Be punctual at meetings. To Australian business people, tardiness signals a careless business attitude.

♦ As an employer, however, it is not always easy to get punctuality out of the traditionally antiauthoritarian Australian employees. It's not enough to demand that people arrive on time; you have to prove that their tardiness causes harm.

■ Appointments are relatively easy to schedule at all corporate levels. Most executives are friendly and easy to approach; they will be glad to meet to discuss business. Make arrangements for meetings one month in advance by telephone or telex.

- Business hours are 9:00 A.M. to 5:00 P.M., Monday through Friday and 9:00 A.M. to noon, Saturday.
- The best time to visit is from March through November, since the peak tourist season is December through February. Christmas and Easter are especially hectic; many executives will be on vacation.

 Negotiating

- Australians generally do not like negotiating or high-pressure sales. They value directness. Therefore, present your case in a forthright manner, articulating both the good and the bad.
- Modesty and casualness are Australian characteristics. A business presentation filled with hype and excitement will not impress Australians; instead, it will inspire them to deflate the presenter with caustic humor.
- Australians may emphasize profit over market share.
- Do not digress or go into too much detail. Laconic Australians consider brevity a virtue.
- Decision making takes place with the consultation of top management. This takes time and will generally be slower than in the United States. Be patient.
- Australians are very direct and love to banter. If you are teased, take it in good humor and tease back without insulting anyone.
- Australians are wary of authority and of those who consider themselves "better" than others. Be modest in interactions, and downplay your knowledge and expertise. Let your accomplishments speak for themselves.
- Before beginning business meetings, spend a brief period of time in small talk. This social time will be short but will establish a familiar rapport, which is important to Australians.
- If you are invited out for a drink to establish a friendly relationship, don't talk about business unless your host brings it up. Work and play are taken equally seriously in Australia, and are not to be confused.

 Business Entertaining

- Australians do not make unannounced visits; always call ahead.
- In an Australian pub, it is vital to remember that each person pays for a round of drinks. Missing your turn to "shout for a round" is a sure way to make a bad impression.
- Australians don't invite strangers into their homes right away. They take their time getting to know someone before an invitation is made. Barbecues are a favorite reason for gathering.
- To avoid confusion, remember that "afternoon tea" is around 4:00 P.M., "tea" is the evening meal served between 6:00 and 8:00 P.M., and "supper" is a late-night snack.
- Good conversation topics are sports, which are very popular, and sightseeing, since Australians are very proud of their country. Politics and religion are taken very seriously, so expect some strong opinions if you discuss these topics.
- Remember that Australians respect people with opinions, even if those opinions conflict with their own. Arguments are considered entertaining, so do not be shy about espousing any truly held beliefs.

- Do not bring up Australia's treatment of the aborigines. (The situation is not unlike the way Native American tribes have been treated in the United States.)
- Allegations exist that U.S. intelligence services intervened covertly in the 1980 Australian national elections. Whether this is true or not, many Australians believe it. It is a toss-up which they resent more: CIA interference in their elections or the implication that Australia is in the same league as so-called banana republics where the United States has toppled governments with impunity.

Time

- Australia has three time zones. The easternmost zone, which includes the city of Perth, is eight hours ahead of Greenwich Mean Time (G.M.T. + 8). The central zone, which encompasses Adelaide, Alice Springs, and Darwin, is 9 1/2 hours ahead of G.M.T. (G.M.T. + 9 1/2). The westernmost zone (the closest to the Americas) is ten hours ahead of G.M.T. (G.M.T. + 10). Most of the big cities are in this zone, including Sydney, Melbourne, and Canberra (the national capital). The Australians name these time zones Eastern, Central, and Western Standard Time, respectively.
- All of Australia practices daylight saving time except Queensland and Western Australia, which remain on standard time throughout the year. Since the seasons are opposite, when the United States is on daylight saving time (April through October), Australia is usually on standard time.
- When traveling to Australia from the Americas, remember that one crosses the International Date Line: When flying westward (United States to Australia), one "loses" a day; flying eastward (Australia to United States), one "gains" a day.

CULTURAL NOTE

*a*ustralians demonstrate their disdain of class by sitting up front with their drivers, both in taxis and in limousines. If a single passenger goes to sit in the back seat, he or she will be seen as putting on airs.

Protocol

Greetings

- Australians are friendly and easy to get to know. They do not have the British reserve of their ancestors. It is acceptable for visitors to introduce themselves in social situations.
- Australians greet each other with "Hello" or an informal "G'day," but they tire of hearing tourists overusing the latter.
- It is the custom to shake hands at the beginning and end of a meeting. Women don't usually shake hands with one another, but will often give a kiss on the cheek in greeting.
- It is appropriate to present a business card at an introduction, but don't be surprised if you do not get one in return since many Australians do not have them.

y————————————————**CULTURAL NOTE**

our best approach is to be friendly, relaxed, modest, and unpretentious. Australians find it amusing how hard foreigners (especially North Americans) try to make a good impression. Australians are very difficult to impress . . . and if you did impress them, they wouldn't admit it.

The usual advice is "just be yourself" in dealing with Australians. However, if your usual demeanor is wired, nervous, officious, or self-important, you should downplay those aspects of your personality.

 Titles/Forms of Address

- Full names are used for initial greetings, and "Sir" is an address of respect. Australians are quick to go to a first-name basis. Wait for them to initiate this as a cue for you to do the same.
- "Mate" will be heard far more often than "sir." It refers to anyone of one's own sex, but when used with the pronoun "my" (e.g., "my mates"), it refers to one's friends. Women also refer to other women as "mate."
- As part of Australia's classless society, academic qualifications are downplayed—in public. Australians will make sport of anyone who sounds like a resume, quoting his or her qualifications and experience.
- Follow the lead of others in using titles. In Australia, a title—whether academic or job-related—does not command respect in and of itself. The individual must still win the respect of others.

 Gestures

- The thumbs-up sign, which in the United States signifies hitchhiking or "O.K.," is considered rude.
- For a man to wink at a woman, even when being friendly, is inappropriate.
- Men should not be too physically demonstrative with other men.

 Dress

- Dress is generally informal. Fashions follow North American trends, although women wear pants much less than in the United States.
- Australia is in the Southern Hemisphere, so the seasons are opposite to those of North America. Most of the country is tropical, but with Australia's great size, this varies greatly. Southern Australia has warm summers and mild winters, so light clothing is best. During winter months, warmer clothes and rain gear are needed.
- Business dress is conservative. Men may wear a dark suit and tie (the jacket can be left off in the summer). Women may wear a skirt and blouse or a dress.

 Gifts

- Australians do not generally give gifts in a business context. If you are invited to a home for dinner, however, you may want to bring a small gift of flowers, wine, chocolates, or folk crafts from home.
- As a foreigner, an illustrated book from your home area makes a good gift. You may also bring a preserved food product from your home area, but it will be confiscated by Australian customs unless it is in a can or bottle.

MINSK

Belarus

t ———————————————————CULTURAL NOTE
his nation has been known in the West under several different names: White Russia, Byelorussia, Belorussia, and others. Its current official name is the Republic of Belarus.

Country Background

History
Belarus declared its independence from the U.S.S.R. on July 27, 1991, and is a parliamentary republic within the Commonwealth of Independent States (C.I.S.).

t ———————————————————CULTURAL NOTE
he Republic of Belarus was one of the three founders of the C.I.S. (the others were Russia and Ukraine). The leaders of these three Slavic countries held a meeting in Belarus, in *Bulorusskaya Pushcha* (Belarussian woodland), and put an end to the former U.S.S.R.

The selection of Belarus for this meeting had symbolic significance. Historically, Russia and Ukraine were rivals, while Belarus was known for its traditional calmness, tolerance, and neutrality. When the C.I.S. was created, everyone agreed that many of its international bodies would be situated in Minsk, the capital of Belarus. Minsk was even considered as a possible C.I.S. capital. That dream has not become a reality, yet the economic and political role of Belarus in the C.I.S. is still significant.

Belarus has no substantial history as an independent nation. Its flat terrain provides no defensible frontier, and it has been ruled by neighboring nations for the past seven hundred years. For most of the last century, its territory was divided between Poland, Lithuania, and Russia. In fact, the current Lithuanian capital of Vilnius was formerly the Belarussian city of Vilno. After the defeat of the Russian Empire in World War I, Belarus became an independent nation in March 1918. However, in 1922, the Belarus People's Republic became one of the first nations to join the new Union of Soviet Socialist Republics.

Minsk, now the capital, is not the historical capital of the Belarus nation. Nevertheless, it does have an impressive history that is eight centuries long.

Type of Government
The newly-independent Republic of Belarus was the only nonpresidential parliamentary republic among the C.I.S. countries. Belarus was headed by the chair-

man of the Supreme Council. Executive power was represented by the cabinet ministers and the prime minister. Recently, the office of president was created.

One of the three founders of the C.I.S., Belarus was third (after Kazakhstan and Uzbekistan) to join the new ruble union in August 1993 following Russia's monetary reform. In July 1994, the Belarussians elected Alexander Lukashenka as President; he favors closer relations with Russia.

Language

The official language is Belarussian, which is a Slavic language closely related to Russian and Ukrainian. Belarussian is written in the Cyrillic alphabet. Most of the population also speaks Russian.

Religion

The majority of believers follow the Belarussian Orthodox Church. Church and state are still separated. A substantial part of the population considers itself nonreligious. Still, the church is in fashion now, and nineteen religious denominations are registered. In addition to the Orthodox, there are Catholics, Lithuanian Protestants, and Jews.

Demographics

Native Belarussians now form 78 percent of the population. Russians constitute 13 percent, and the remainder are Poles, Jews, and Lithuanians. The population of Belarus is 10.4 million (including 1.7 million in the capital, Minsk).

Cultural Orientation

Cognitive Styles: How the Belarussians Organize and Process Information

The Belarussians have a great desire for independence and autonomy, but they are steeped in tradition and tend to follow powerful leaders without question. Most education is skill-oriented; it is practical rather than conceptual. Belarussians' concerns are for the immediate, particular situation.

Negotiation Strategies: What the Belarussians Accept as Evidence

Truth is found in the immediate, personal feelings of the participant. It is often enhanced by faith in an ideology or a strong leader, but seldom by the accumulation of objective facts.

Value Systems: The Basis for Behavior

Although the name of this country means "White Russia," the people are more similar to the Ukrainians in their values than they are to the Russians. The following three sections identify the Value Systems in the predominant culture—their methods of dividing right from wrong, good from evil, and so forth.

Locus of Decision Making

There is a continual struggle between individual freedom and obligations to the collective unit. Traditionally the extended family is the basic unit for decision making, but this unit includes persons other than blood kin that are accepted into the family. Although all members have a strong need to contribute to the welfare of the collective unit, decisions are made by the head of the family or unit.

Sources of Anxiety Reduction

Because Belarus has been dominated by Poland, Lithuania, and Russia, there is considerable national uncertainty stemming from the controversies over its name, language, traditions, and national heritage. Loyalty to an employer or local leader provides a sense of security. This makes the extended family or collective unit essential in avoiding uncertainty. Religious Belarussians are primarily Belarussian Orthodox Christians, and the church puts a great deal of structure into their lives.

Issues of Equality/Inequality

There is a strong desire for autonomy, individual freedom, and private property, but both tradition and Communism have taught Belarussians to accept and respect collectivism. Power is vested in the leader, and he or she is responsible for the behavior of subordinates. For example, disobedience among children is considered the fault of the parents. Men and women have strict sex roles that are not to be confused, but each has an autonomy that is respected by the other. There is a strong sense of equality between husbands and wives.

Business Practices

Appointments

PUNCTUALITY

+ Belarussians (as well as Russians and Ukrainians) believe that punctuality is the hallmark of foreign business practice. Therefore, your image as a typical Western business executive depends on your punctuality. Lateness could even make them think you are an impostor!
+ Don't be surprised if high-ranking Belarussians are late. Punctuality is your image, not theirs.

- As in Russia and other C.I.S. countries, the day is written first, then the month, and then the year. You will find 4.11.99 or 4.11.1999, and both mean November 4, 1999—not April 11, 1999.
- Getting a positive response at every bureaucratic level requires solid groundwork and help from an intermediary.
- Before your first meeting, the company's top executive should know who you are, what you are interested in, what your project is, and (most importantly) which other Belarus bureaucrats have agreed to it or are supportive.
- This data is usually transmitted most effectively through your hired intermediary. Your contact can be a medium-level executive, but he or she should be respected and known by top management.
- At the first meeting, Belarussian bureaucrats will appreciate a written, straightforward outline of the project under discussion. Your intermediary should be prepared to expand on details when necessary.
- The intermediary should not only promote your project but follow up as well. A good intermediary verifies that faxes and telexes on both sides are properly prepared, translated, transmitted, and received. Equipment and delivery can be frustratingly inefficient.
- Further meetings should be planned immediately and the dates fixed; the names of people to be involved (plus their fax numbers) should also be deter-

mined. If this meeting is to be a month later, send follow-up messages with copies to your intermediary.

- Business hours are usually from 9 A.M. to 6 P.M., with lunch from 12 or 12:30 to 1:30 or 2 P.M. Generally the last hour of a day is not the best time for a top-level appointment. Note that for official business, Belarus uses the twenty four-hour clock (as used by the U.S. military).
- Food stores are usually open from 8 A.M. to 8 P.M., nonfood stores from 9 or 11 A.M. to 7 P.M., department stores from 9 A.M. to 8 P.M. Some nonfood stores close for lunch from 1 to 2 P.M., and food stores close from 2 to 3 P.M.

Negotiating

- Take extra business cards. There are only a few telephone books available, and they are of limited scope and circulation. Western-style directories are rare, and people depend on keeping a file of business cards. You may not get a card in exchange for yours, so try to get all the phone numbers you need before leaving.
- Basically, bureaucrats tend to answer "no" to a proposal if they have nothing to bargain with by agreeing. Indeed, the ability to say "no" is their only real power.
- The higher the executive level, the easier it seems to be able to get a "yes." But this does not guarantee an affirmative on lower levels. Even routine Western business practices are unknown, and every aspect must be explained at all levels.
- Currently, the rate of exchange for the national currency is so low that a relatively small investment in U.S. dollars could be worth a very, very great deal.
- At this time there are very few experts in Belarus business and legal regulations. Even Belarus business people will not have a full grasp of the legal issues. Hire a local lawyer who is an expert in Belarussian law to monitor the entire business environment and report to you independently. Keep in mind that local and federal laws and interests may not always coincide with one another at this time of political and economic change.

- Belarussian negotiators will probably walk out of the talks at least twice. While this tactic often alarms Westerners, it is one that Belarussians use and expect. A deal would not be considered well made if its discussion and details went smoothly.
- Your Belarussian partners are expecting concessions, so go to the talks with a private list, made in advance, of items on which you are prepared to bargain. Concede one item at a time, so that your partners feel that such benefits are a result of their efforts. Once a deal is final, Belarussians usually consider renegotiation impossible.

- At the appropriate time, make certain that all sides completely understand any legal regulations from your home country that are involved in the deal.

 Business Entertaining

CULTURAL NOTE

*M*ost Belarussians will think you know a great deal about them and will enjoy talking about their political and economic prospects. The United States is a source of constant interest. Remember that Russian propaganda against the West was intense (and sometimes bizarre), so their questions about the United States may seem extraordinarily strange and their knowledge of the West astonishingly limited.

- Belarussians like to invite business partners to restaurants or to their homes. They have a strong tradition of hospitality that was strictly restrained during the Communist years, when every foreigner was considered a spy.
- Accept their invitations. Be aware that the food will be rich and the drinks strong. In fact, Belarussians feel that business arrangements go more smoothly when their business partner is more relaxed through convivial drinking. Belarussian men are proudly confident of their own drinking ability, and a man may drink half a liter of vodka in an evening without any obvious effect.
- It is gracious to learn a few toasts. The most common are *na zdo ro vie* (your health) and an ancient Polish toast, *sto-lyat* (a hundred years).
- When hosting a meeting, be certain to use china, not plastic, for serving refreshments. Also have a supply of cigarettes, lighters, calculators, and so forth. Belarussians usually have a variety of refreshments when conducting meetings and appreciate reciprocity.
- Restaurant tables are usually for four or six. If your party has only two or three, you may have to share a table with strangers. The maitre d' will not understand your efforts to either be alone or maintain your private party of two or three.
- Bottles are often on the table when you are seated. Once you open one, you must pay for the entire bottle, no matter how little of it you drink. Many restaurants and cafes accept only hard currency.
- An invitation to a Belarussian home is an honor for you and a tradition-bound event for the host. The host will prepare three or four times as much food and drink as the guests can possibly consume, because it is traditional to present an atmosphere of comfortable abundance. Choices of sodas, wines, cocktails, brandy, and "the best Belarus vodka in the world" will be served at the dinner.
- In a home situation you will probably find that the children are included.
- Dinner invitations are usually for Saturdays at six, but guests take up to an hour to gather.

CULTURAL NOTE

*W*hen entering a hotel, the doorman will ask to see your guest card identification. Most doormen are retired police or security officers, and cordiality is not in their nature. If there is some misunderstanding, speak in English, and be forceful, persistent, and firm. In most cases, you will be successful.

Remember that it is usually to your advantage to look and sound like a foreigner, since foreigners get preferential treatment and help almost everywhere.

In general, the more powerful your home country, the more deference you will be accorded (as natives of small or poor nations have discovered to their dismay). If a New Zealander is mistaken for a citizen of the United States, he or she may want to think twice before correcting that mistake.

Time

- Belarus is in the western part of the C.I.S. time zones and is three hours ahead of Greenwich Mean Time (G.M.T. + 3). This makes Belarus eight hours ahead of U.S. Eastern Standard Time (E.S.T. + 8).
- Belarus undergoes a form of daylight saving time, with the switch usually occurring around the end of March and October. The exact dates of time changes are announced from year to year and generally differ from the schedule used in Western Europe.

Protocol

 ### Greetings

- Belarussians are not demonstrative in public. Only relatives, very good friends, or well-known business friends of long standing are greeted cheerfully with an embrace and a kiss on each cheek.
- Except at formal or state affairs, Belarussians usually shake hands and state their own last name to a stranger instead of using a phrase like "How do you do?" Answer the same way.
- Men and women readily shake hands with each other.

 ### Titles/Forms of Address

- Belarussian names are written in the same order as in the West. The middle name is a patronymic (a name derived from the father's first name). In the example Svyatoslav Alesevich Bryl, Svyatoslav is the first name, the patronymic means "son of Ales," and the surname is Bryl.
- Women often add an "a" to their surname; some will even add an "a" to their husband's last name.
- Be careful not to confuse the order of names. It is now acceptable to use only the last name for a person of slight acquaintance; for example, Bryl, Gospodin Bryl (the polite method), or even Mr. Bryl is appropriate. His wife would be Gospozha Bryl or Mrs. Bryl. Never use both, as in Gozpozha Mrs. Bryl.
- The only title of respect traditionally used in Belarus is Professor. It is used when addressing a doctor of science, an elderly scientist, or a schoolteacher beyond the elementary level.
- There are few variations of first names and surnames. Some are so often used (e.g., Vasil, Vasilievich, and Vasiliev) that confusion is inevitable. Furthermore, if you are invited to address a person by his or her first name, remember that all first names have diminutives, nicknames, and pet names. Which you will use depends on the depth of your acquaintance. The best advice is to ask; he or she will be happy to explain.

Gestures

- Belorussian is a language that is abundant in curses, and there are a number of obscene gestures. The North American "O.K." sign (thumb and forefinger touching in a circle) and any shaken-fist gestures are interpreted as vulgar.
- It is impolite to sit with your legs spread apart or with your feet propped up on a table.
- The thumb between the forefinger and middle finger means "you'll get nothing."
- Whistling is not a sign of approval at a concert or sporting event. It means that you strongly disapprove.
- Whistling inside a building is also inappropriate because of a superstition that it will cause one to lose money.
- Sitting a minute before leaving home brings good luck, as does knocking three times on wood.
- "Thumbs up" means "good" or "O.K.," as in the United States.
- *Nyekulturny* is a Russian word that is used the same way in Belarus. It means that something is "just not done," or is ill-mannered.
- Some *nyekulturny* behaviors include
  - Wearing an overcoat in a public building, concert hall, or restaurant, and particularly the theater. Leave your coat in the *garderob* (cloakroom). Many office buildings have them too.
  - Sitting on your coat at a concert or restaurant (but it is acceptable at the cinema).
  - Standing with your hands in your pockets, raising your voice, or laughing loudly in public buildings, subways, or on the street.
- Spitting in public is commonly done, and it is not unusual to see Belarussian men urinating in the street. (Public facilities are rare.)
- Belarussians often wander comfortably through the halls of their hotels wearing only pajamas or bathrobes. You are welcome to do this as well.

Dress

- Do not wear unconventional clothes to business meetings. Belarussians dress conservatively for the office and are years behind Western styles.
- Some buildings may not be well heated in winter, so a layered dress style will be more comfortable.
- Dress for a dinner invitation can be anything from black tie to blue jeans. Hosts may offer slippers, but guests sometimes bring extra footwear, especially in winter, when overshoes are often left at the door.

Gifts

- Belarussians appreciate small gifts—pens, business card holders, rock or country-and-western cassettes, picture or art books, fine bars of soap, calendars, Walkman tape recorders, American cigarettes, inexpensive solar calculators, inexpensive gold or silver jewelry, or small household appliances. Perfume is a prized gift for women, while electronic specialties (especially cameras) are best for men. Baseball caps are also popular. Blue jeans, formerly in short supply, are now readily available in Belarus.

- Note that some visitors may give expensive, prestigious watches, pens, lighters, and so forth. You are not expected to compete in gift giving. Flowers are always proper to give to a lady or your host's wife.
- Western alcohol, especially a high-quality, expensive one, is not necessarily a good gift. Belarus cities now have commercial kiosks that are full of different kinds of Western drinks. Most are cheap and of poor quality, but very few Belarussians would notice or understand the difference between twelve-year-old Johnny Walker Black Label and the offerings in the kiosks. Only if you know that your contact appreciates good liquor does an expensive brand become a good gift.
- Exotic food, especially seafood, could be a good gift, but avoid caviar, salmon, sturgeon, and shrimp, all of which are abundant in the area.

Belgium

BRUSSELS

CULTURAL NOTE

*b*elgium has the most complex legislation regarding language in Europe. Three languages are recognized by the constitution: French, Flemish (a variety of Dutch), and German. Brussels is officially bilingual, although the French-speaking Walloons outnumber the Flemish. The northern part of the country is Flemish, while the southern part is Walloon. In the east, German is spoken. Operations need to be conducted in both Flemish (Dutch) and French.

Country Background

History

Julius Caesar conquered what is now Belgium in 50 B.C. Roman rule faded, and Belgium came under the domination of the Franks in the fifth century. After Charlemagne's empire broke up, Belgium was attached to one duchy after another.

In 1516, through marriage and inheritance, Belgium and the Netherlands came under the rule of Spain (the whole area was then called the Spanish Netherlands). The Protestant Dutch resented being ruled by the Catholic Spanish king. With some help from Protestant England, the Dutch successfully broke away and formed the Dutch Republic. Catholic Belgium did not revolt, but it was hard-pressed to survive, trapped between two aggressive nations—the Dutch in the north and the French in the south. After the War of the Spanish Succession, control of Belgium passed to Austria, and then to Napoleonic France. When the map of Europe was redrawn by the Congress of Vienna in 1815, the Netherlands were given control of Belgium. The Belgians did not want to be ruled by the Dutch, and just as the Dutch had done before them, the Belgians successfully broke away (with help from Britain and France) in 1830. The independent Kingdom of Belgium dates from this revolt.

Belgium was occupied by the Germans in both world wars.

Type of Government

Belgium is a constitutional monarchy with two legislative houses. The king is the chief of state, and the prime minister is the head of the government. Elections to the parliament occur every four years, and voting is compulsory. There is a 185-seat Senate and a 212-seat House of Representatives. Local communities and regions have been granted the authority to make decisions regarding education, welfare, public works, and investment.

Language
(See the Cultural Note at the beginning of this chapter.) Three languages are recognized by the Belgian constitution: French, Flemish (a variety of Dutch), and German.

Religion
Although all the major world religions are represented in Belgium, the country is overwhelmingly Roman Catholic. Holidays and cultural festivals are determined by the Catholic church calendar.

Demographics
Belgium has a population of 9.9 million; it is the second most densely populated country in Europe. Its capital is Brussels.

Cultural Orientation

Cognitive Styles: How Belgians Organize and Process Information
In general, the Belgians are open-minded to outside information and will engage anyone in a discussion of facts, principles, or theories. Information is generally processed from a conceptual perspective. They are proud of their intellectual heritage. The German speakers tend to follow abstract codes of behavior while the Dutch and French speakers are more apt to emphasize interpersonal relationships. In all three groups friendships are particular and deep.

Negotiation Strategies: What Belgians Accept as Evidence
Although facts are the most valid form of evidence, the Belgians' strong humanitarian perspective makes feelings important in any negotiation situation. Belgians also have a strong faith in the perspectives of their religious ideologies.

Value Systems: The Basis for Behavior
There are three major cultural value systems in Belgium: German, French, and Dutch. Knowing the cultural orientations of these three cultures may help someone who goes to Belgium. The following three sections identify the Value Systems in the predominant culture—their methods of dividing right from wrong, good from evil, and so forth.

Locus of Decision Making
The individual is responsible for his or her decisions. Although ethnocentric values are adhered to, the relationship between the participants is a major variable in the decision-making process. Decision making is slow and involved, as all peripheral concerns must be taken care of in the process. Belgians hold to the principles of common sense and compromise.

Sources of Anxiety Reduction
The nuclear family remains the basic unit, but the extended family is the primary focus all through life, bringing structure and stability. One of three social units shapes a person's life: He or she is born into the Catholic, socialist, or liberal group. This then supplies the agencies in which the person participates socially. Belgians are joiners, so there is an organization for every kind of need.

Issues of Equality/Inequality
Although most Belgians are Catholic and bi- or trilingual, they have not come to terms with the religious and linguistic cleavages. There is still considerable

group and ethnic bias. The French speakers feel that they are of a higher class, and the Walloons feel that they are superior to the Flemish. Women still play an inferior role to men, but this is changing.

Business Practices

Appointments

────────────────────────────────── **PUNCTUALITY**

◆ Always be punctual for business appointments in Belgium.

- Remember that many Europeans and South Americans write the day first, then the month, then the year (e.g. December 3, 1999, is written 3.12.99). This is the case in Belgium.
- At 35.8 hours, the Belgian work week is one of the shortest in the world.
- Businesses open at 8:30 A.M. and close at 5:30 P.M. for most of the week, although some stay open until 9:00 P.M. on Fridays.
- Stores are generally open from 9:00 A.M. to 6:00 P.M., Monday through Saturday.
- Most Belgians take a one-month vacation each year.
- Phone or write for an appointment at least a week in advance.
- The Belgian company will set the time of your appointment. An 11:30 A.M. appointment is a lunch appointment.
- Expect the first appointment to be social. Most Belgians must get to know you before they decide whether they want to do business with you.

 ### Negotiating

- Belgians vary. Some will get down to business right away, while others insist on an extended period of socializing first.
- Be modest about talents and about wealth.
- Mutual trust is highly valued by Belgian business people.
- Senior executives arrive at the office later than subordinates. Don't try to "get in good" with the staff by going early, because Belgians are very aware of status and will feel uncomfortable.
- The Belgians respect privacy; knock and wait for an answer, and keep doors closed in the office.
- It is important to reply promptly to any request from a Belgian office.
- Assure clients that you will be available and will meet all deadlines.
- Exchanging business cards is standard practice.
- It is good to have your business card translated; one side can be in English and the other in French or Flemish, depending on the dominant language in your region.
- Present the card with the language of your colleague facing him or her.
- The cultural and linguistic divisions of the country are a sensitive subject. Do not confuse the three cultural groups and their languages.

- In general, Belgians do not discuss personal subjects. The U.S. conversation starter "What do you do?" is not appropriate.
- Religion is not a good topic of conversation.
- When with a Flemish speaker, speak English, not French (unless you are fluent in Flemish).

Business Entertaining

- Dinner is usually at 7:00 or 8:00 P.M.
- Allow the Belgians to be the first to bring up business at the dining table.
- Belgians are very proud of their food, so compliments are in order.
- Belgium's most famous culinary items are mussels, chocolates, waffles, 300 types of beer, and french fries (which the Belgians claim to have invented).
- As in most of Europe, the knife should be held in the right hand and the fork in the left, and never switched.
- It is a great compliment to be invited to a Belgian home.
- Don't help yourself to food at a party until it is offered.
- Don't drink until the toast is made.
- Among the Flemish, glasses are raised twice during a toast: you raise glasses during the verbal toast, then you exchange glances and raise the glasses again. Only then is it permissible to drink.
- Belgians are known for their frugality, so it is best to finish what you are given or have ordered.
- If you travel to rural areas, it is polite to remove one's shoes, if they are dirty, before entering a home.

Time

- Belgium is one hour ahead of Greenwich Mean Time (G.M.T. + 1) or six hours ahead of U.S. Eastern Standard Time (E.S.T. + 6).

Protocol

Greetings

- Belgians shake hands with everyone in the room or office upon meeting and upon leaving.
- Among friends, Belgians touch cheeks and kiss the air three times, alternating cheeks. Men will do this as well.

Titles/Forms of Address

- Remember that there are three linguistic groups in Belgium: German, French, and Flemish (which is a variant of Dutch).
- With German or Flemish speakers, you should use the English terms Mr. and Miss, Mrs., or Ms.
- With French speakers, use *Monsieur* and *Madame* or *Mademoiselle*.
- Never use *Madame* or *Monsieur* with a Flemish speaker; use Mr., Ms., Miss, or Mrs.

- As in all of Europe, first names are not appropriate except among close friends.
- The order of names is the same as in the United States: first name followed by surname.

Gestures

- In general, avoid gesturing. It is better to be exceedingly formal and restrained than to be perceived as a wildly gesticulating American.
- Snapping the fingers of both hands is a vulgar gesture.
- Talking with one's hands in one's pants pockets is rude.
- Belgians do not use toothpicks in public.
- It is rude to point with the index finger.

Dress

- Conservative dress is best.
- Slip-on shoes such as loafers are not appropriate for men. Shoes should be well polished.
- Belgians dress in their finest clothes on Sundays, whether they intend to go visiting or just take a stroll.

Gifts

- Gift giving is not normally a part of business relationships in Belgium.
- If you wish to give a gift to a close business associate, do not include your business card with it, and do not give a gift that is a vehicle for your company logo.
- If you are invited to a Belgian home, bring flowers (not chrysanthemums, which signify death) or chocolates for the hostess. Do not bring 13 of any flower. Red roses are only for lovers.
- Present any gift before, not after, the meal.

LA PAZ

Bolivia

CULTURAL NOTE

*b*olivia is perhaps best known for its isolation. It is certainly the most remote, insular country on the continent. Queen Victoria once wished to punish Bolivia after her ambassador had been publicly humiliated. (The Bolivian dictator Mariano Melgarejo is alleged to have had the British ambassador stripped, tied to a donkey, and run out of town.) After being informed that Bolivia was too far inland for British gunboats to shell, the queen supposedly took her pen to a map of South America and struck Bolivia out of existence. Whether the story is true or not, the outside world has frequently ignored Bolivia. The country has made the news only when outsiders died there, such as Butch Cassidy and the Sundance Kid in 1911 or Che Guevara in 1967.

Country Background

History

Bolivia, once part of the powerful Inca Empire, was conquered by the Spanish in 1538. Naming the area Upper Peru, the Spanish found that Bolivia possessed the mineral wealth they so avidly sought. The huge silver mines at Potosí, discovered in 1545, were the richest in the world. Until the silver was depleted, Potosí was one of the biggest and wealthiest cities in North or South America. Thousands of Indians were forced to work the mines. The silver ran out after two centuries, but the mines still produce great quantities of tin.

In 1809 Bolivia rebelled against Spanish rule, a revolt that inspired independence movements throughout the entire Southern Cone. But unlike the other countries, Bolivia was known to contain great mineral wealth. The Spanish fought for sixteen years to keep Bolivia a colony. Bolivia finally gained its independence in 1825. The country was named after its liberator, Simón Bolívar.

At the time of its independence, Bolivia was much larger; it even had a seacoast and a port on the Pacific. Unfortunately, a quarter of this land was lost in several wars with neighboring nations (except for its war of independence from Spain, Bolivia has never won a war). The War of the Pacific (1879-1883) resulted in the loss of Bolivia's seaport of Antofagasta to Chile. Bolivians have never reconciled themselves to this loss, and to this day they maintain a small navy—just in case they ever get the coast back (meanwhile, the navy patrols Lake Titicaca, the world's highest large body of water). Indeed, the loss of its only access to the Pacific has been blamed for many of Bolivia's problems. Unlike neighboring landlocked Paraguay, Bolivia even lacks large navigable rivers to connect it with the outside world.

Despite its mineral wealth, Bolivia has the lowest per capita income of any country in South America.

b ─────────────────────────────────**CULTURAL NOTE**
olivia has not been known for political stability. Since independence in 1825, it has had sixteen constitutions and almost 250 governments. Its presidents have ranged from a woman (Lidia Gueiler Tejada, elected in 1980 and ousted by a coup the same year) to a brutal lunatic (Mariano Melgarejo) who, during the 1870 Franco-Prussian War, decided to march the Bolivian army eastward to aid France. (He turned back when it began to rain.)

The past few decades have been turbulent for Bolivia. The violent narco-regime of General Luis García Meza ended in a coup in 1981. Unable to maintain a stable government, the military recalled the Congress, and a civil government was installed in 1982. Since that time the military has eschewed direct political involvement. Bolivia's economy subsequently suffered hyperinflation, which by 1985 had reached 24,000 percent a year. Great sacrifices were made to stabilize the economy.

Type of Government
The Republic of Bolivia is a multiparty republic with two legislative houses, the 27-seat Chamber of Senators and the 130-seat Chamber of Deputies. The president is both the chief of state and the head of the government.

For over ten years now, the Republic of Bolivia has had a peaceful transfer of power between civilian governments.

Language
Bolivia now has three official languages: Spanish, Aymara, and Quechua. While all businesspeople speak Spanish, many of the Indians speak only their native Aymara or Quechua.

Religion
Although Protestantism has been making some gains, about 93 percent of the people are Roman Catholics. Catholicism is the official religion, but freedom of worship is guaranteed by law.

Demographics
Almost half of Bolivia's 7 million population is involved in agriculture. Mining now occupies only some 3 percent of the workforce. A full two-thirds of the population lives outside urban areas.

Full-blood Indians (Quechua and Aymara) account for over half of the Bolivian populace. About 30 percent are mestizo (mixed Indian and European heritage), and 15 percent are of European descent.

Cultural Orientation

Cognitive Styles: How Bolivians Organize and Process Information
The basic tendency of the Bolivians is to be open to discussion of new ideas, but this is tempered by a strong ethnocentrism in each of the several ethnic groups. Those with higher educations have learned to think abstractively, but associative, experiential thinking is the rule. Very strong kinship ties make Bolivians more concerned about the consequences of an action than about the action itself.

Negotiation Strategies: What Bolivians Accept as Evidence

There is much conflict between the forces of feeling, faith, and facts. Basically, Bolivians look at problems from a subjective perspective. The word of a friend or family member (feelings) has the highest validity, but a strong faith in an ideology (e.g., the Catholic church, a political party, or ethnocentrism) may override one's feelings. Facts are always acceptable as long as they do not contradict the other two forces. Note that it is difficult for Bolivians to disagree with someone they like. Their true opinion might not be evident.

Value Systems: The Basis for Behavior

The four ethnic groups—Quechua, Aymara, mestizos, and whites—have very different value systems. Consumerism is found primarily among the whites.

The following three sections identify the Value Systems in the dominant white culture—their methods of dividing right from wrong, good from evil, and so forth.

Locus of Decision Making

Decisions are usually made by an individual, but always with the best interests of a larger group in mind. Self-identity is based on the social system and the history of the extended family. Consensus forms the basis of community decision making, with kinships and friendships playing major roles.

Sources of Anxiety Reduction

The church has a great moral influence and gives a sense of stability to life. The nuclear family is extremely stable. Kin and family are the core of social structure, and great stress is placed on the bonds of responsibility among kin. There is a laid-back view of life that always allows time to talk with a friend. Deadlines are not considered important.

Issues of Equality/Inequality

Ethnicity is the focus of much of national life and there is a strong bias by the white elite against all others. There are extreme contrasts between rich and poor. Machismo is very strong with women considered subordinate and inferior to men. This puts severe restrictions on their social and work behavior.

Business Practices

Appointments

PUNCTUALITY

- ◆ Punctuality is not a high priority in Bolivia. However, a North American is expected to be punctual.
- ◆ Bolivian business meetings rarely start on time. Anticipate that your Bolivian counterparts will be late.
- ◆ Note that social occasions have different rules. Even North Americans are expected to be fifteen to thirty minutes late for dinner or parties; to show up on time would be impolite. But be on time for lunch and for events with a scheduled starting time, such as the theater.
- ◆ When it is important to know if your Bolivian counterpart expects promptness, you can ask, "¿En punto?" (on the dot?).

- Remember that many European and South Americans write the day first, then the month, then the year (e.g. December 3, 1999, is written 3.12.99). This is the case in Bolivia.
- Mornings are best for appointments.
- Make appointments two to three weeks in advance.
- Try to arrive in Bolivia a day early, to allow yourself to get acclimated to the high altitude.
- Business hours are generally 9:00 A.M. to 12 noon and 2:00 to 6:00 P.M., Monday through Friday. Some business people keep office hours on Saturday mornings as well.
- Government offices are open six days a week, as follows: 9:00 A.M. to 12 noon and 2:00 to 6:30 P.M., Monday through Friday, and 9:00 A.M. to 12 noon, Saturday.
- Shop hours, in general, are 9:00 A.M. to 12 noon and 2:00 to 6:00 P.M., Monday through Friday. Some shops keep Saturday hours as well.
- The best months of the year to conduct business in Bolivia are April and May, and September and October. Little business is accomplished in the two weeks before and after Christmas and Easter, and during Carnival week (the week before Ash Wednesday) and Independence Week (the first week in August). January through March is typically vacation time in Bolivia.

 Negotiating

- The pace of business negotiations in Latin America is usually much slower than in the United States. This is especially true in Bolivia, where trying to rush a deal by applying pressure will probably fail.
- Do not be surprised if it takes you several trips to Bolivia to accomplish your goal. Bolivians respond best to low-key, slow-paced negotiations.
- Colorful visual aids, such as charts and models, are well received by Bolivian business people.
- Personal relationships are far more important than corporate ones in Bolivia. Each time your company changes its representative in Bolivia, you will virtually be starting from scratch. A new relationship must be built up before business can proceed.
- Don't assume that each portion of a contract is settled once an agreement on that portion has been reached. Until the entire contract is signed, each portion is subject to renegotiation.
- Bolivians will doubt your importance unless you stay at the most prestigious international hotels.
- Direct eye contact is very important in Bolivia. Failure to meet someone's gaze is interpreted as untrustworthiness.
- Bolivians converse much closer together than do North Americans. If you instinctively back away, a Bolivian will probably move forward to close up the space. This closeness makes maintaining eye contact more difficult for U.S. natives.
- At a gathering such as a party, you may have to introduce yourself. Only at a formal party (or one hosted by a older person) can you expect that someone else will introduce you.
- Eating in the street is not considered proper.
- Avoid whispering; it is impolite to anyone out of earshot and arouses suspicion. Wait until you can talk to the person in private.

- Try to avoid offering any political opinions. Be cautious about praising Bolivia's neighbors (especially Chile). Bolivia has lost wars with all of its neighboring countries.

f—————————————————————**CULTURAL NOTE**

ew executives are Indians or of Indian blood. Indeed, most people in Bolivian business classes identify with their European heritage and will be insulted if you assume that they are Indian. Do not be surprised if a dark-complexioned Bolivian explains to you that he or she is Spanish, not Indian.

The current polite term for Indians is not *indios* but *campesinos*.

There are so few African-Americans in Bolivia that people have the superstition that seeing one is good luck. Do not be surprised if, upon seeing a black person, a Bolivian chants, *"¡Negro, negro, buena suerte!"*

- While many of the executives you meet will speak English, check beforehand as to whether or not you need an interpreter.
- All printed material you hand out should be translated into Spanish. This goes for everything from business cards to reports to brochures.
- Bolivians often have trouble with North American names, so hand out your business card to everyone you are introduced to.
- Bolivians are great sports fans. Talking about sports is always a good way to open a conversation. Soccer, which is called *fútbol* (U.S.-style football is *fútbol americano*), is the most popular sport.
- Families and food are also good topics of conversation. Bolivians also appreciate visitors who know something about their country.

 Business Entertaining

- Business meals are popular in Bolivia. They are usually held in restaurants; offers to dine in a Bolivian home are relatively infrequent.
- While one can discuss business over lunch, dinner is considered a social occasion. Do not bring up business over dinner unless your Bolivian counterpart does so first.
- Lunch is usually the largest meal of the day. Dinner may start anytime from 7:30 to 9:30 P.M. A formal dinner usually begins at 9:00 P.M.

w—————————————————————**CULTURAL NOTE**

ives are not usually asked to attend business meals in restaurants—especially not on Friday night, which is called *viernes de soltero* (bachelor Friday), when men go out dining and drinking without their spouses.

- When dining, keep your hands on the table, not in your lap.
- Never eat with your fingers; there are utensils for everything. Even fruits such as bananas are eaten with a fruit knife and fork.
- Avoid pouring wine, if possible. There are several complex taboos about wine pouring (e.g., pouring with the left hand is a major insult, pouring wine backwards into a glass indicates hostility, and so forth.).
- Be warned that Bolivian food may contain very hot peppers.
- When eating at a Bolivian home, understand that everyone—including the guest—is expected to eat everything on their plate. Your hosts will encourage you to eat, and it is traditional for you to decline the first time your hostess asks

if you want more. Wait until they insist, or you may be deluged with food. A compliment is taken as a request for more food, so hold your compliments until after the meal.
- Stay at the table until everyone is finished eating. It is polite to leave a home about thirty minutes after dinner is concluded.

Time
- Bolivia is four hours behind Greenwich Mean Time (G.M.T. - 4), making it one hour ahead of U.S. Eastern Standard Time (E.S.T. + 1).

Protocol

Greetings
- Except when greeting close friends, it is traditional to shake hands firmly with both men and women.
- Close male friends shake hands or embrace upon meeting; men kiss close female friends. Close female friends usually kiss each other. The full embrace (*abrazo*) may entail a hug, a handshake, and several thumps on the shoulder, ending with another handshake.
- Close friends of either sex may walk arm in arm. Women often hold hands.
- Good friends will greet each other at each encounter, even if they have greeted each other already that day.

Titles/Forms of Address
- While the Indian languages of Aymara and Quechua are (along with Spanish) official languages in Bolivia, all the business people you meet will be fluent in Spanish, so Spanish titles may be used.
- Most people you meet should be addressed with a title and their surname. Only children, family members, and close friends address each other by their first names.
- Persons who do not have professional titles should be addressed as Mr., Mrs., or Miss, plus their surname. In Spanish, these are
    - Mr. = *Señor*
    - Mrs. = *Señora*
    - Miss = *Señorita*
- Most Hispanics have two surnames: one from their father, which is listed first, followed by one from their mother. Only the father's surname is commonly used when addressing someone; e.g., Señor Juan Antonio Martinez García is addressed as Señor Martinez and Señorita Ana María Gutierrez Herrera is addressed as Señorita Gutierrez. When a woman marries, she usually adds her husband's surname and goes by that surname. If the two people in the above example married, she would be known as Señora Ana María Gutierrez Herrera de Martinez. Most people would refer to her as Señora de Martinez or, less formally, Señora Martinez.

- When a person has a title, it is important to address him or her with that title followed by the surname. A Ph.D. or a physician is called *Doctor.* Teachers prefer the title *Profesor,* engineers go by *Ingeniero,* architects are *Arquitecto,* and lawyers are *Abogado.*

Gestures

- A pat on the shoulder is a sign of friendship.
- The gesture that some North Americans use to mean "so-so" (twisting the flat, open hand from side to side) indicates "no" in Bolivia. Bus and taxi drivers use this gesture to indicate that their vehicles are full. Street vendors use it to indicate that they have no more of something.
- Another gesture for "no" is a wave of the index finger.
- Beckon using a scooping motion with the palm down. Children can be summoned in this way, but adults may find it demeaning.
- Make sure to cover your mouth when either yawning or coughing.
- Sit only on chairs, not on a ledge, box, or table. Manners dictate an erect sitting posture; don't slump.

Dress

- Business dress in Bolivia is conservative: dark suits and ties for men; white blouses and dark suits or skirts for women. Women are not required to wear nylons during the summer. Men should follow their Bolivian colleagues' lead with regard to wearing ties and removing jackets in the summer.
- The formality of dress varies in different cities. La Paz will be very formal, and three-piece suits are common there (of course, the altitude of La Paz often makes it very chilly). In Cochabamba a two-piece suit is usual; and in freewheeling, tropical Santa Cruz, businessmen wear lightweight suits or go without a jacket.
- Dress to handle the weather in Bolivia. The lowlands are subject to great heat and humidity in summers. Most local people wear cotton in such weather. Don't forget that the seasons in South America are the reverse of those in North America.
- Sweaters are recommended during the winter or at night in high-altitude cities.
- Whatever the season, be prepared for sudden changes in weather and temperature.
- Men may wear the same dark suit for formal occasions (such as the theater, a formal dinner party, and so forth), but women are expected to wear an evening gown. The invitation will specify that the affair is formal. Tuxedos are rarely worn.
- Both men and women wear pants as casual wear. If you are meeting business associates, avoid jeans and wear a jacket or blazer. Women should not wear shorts.

CULTURAL NOTE

i ndian clothing is for Indians; don't adopt any native costumes, no matter how attractive.

Wearing a bowler hat will make you a laughing stock; Indian women wear a hat that looks just like a bowler.

- Don't wear anything outside that can be damaged by water during Carnival time. Drenching pedestrians is a favorite Carnival pastime of the young.

Gifts

- Bolivians are favorably impressed by any gift. The intention is more important than the gift itself.
- As in any country, a gift should be of high quality. If the item is produced by your corporation, the corporate name or logo should appear discreetly, not be emblazoned over the whole surface.
- As the United States is currently popular, gifts with "U.S.A." on them are prized.
- Avoid giving knives; they symbolize the severing of a friendship.

> **CULTURAL NOTE**
>
> *R*ealize that Bolivia is a major trading center with plenty of well-off consumers. Everything finds its way to the markets of La Paz. You may have to search to find something from the United States that isn't for sale in Bolivia. In fact, the same gifts can often be bought at a cheaper price in Bolivia if you are prepared to bargain with the merchants. This is especially true of electronic gadgets.

- Popular gifts are fine leather briefcases, well-made chess and backgammon sets, and linen items such as towels. Kitchen gadgets are popular for cooks and women.
- When invited to a Bolivian home, bring a gift of flowers, chocolates, wine, or whiskey. Avoid purple flowers, which are used for funerals, or yellow flowers, which signify contempt.

BRASILIA

Brazil

Country Background

History

In 1500 the first European, Pedro Alvares Cabral, reached Brazil. Brazil was colonized by Portugal and became one of its most important, and by far the largest, colonies. When Portugal was occupied by Napoleon, members of the Portuguese royal family fled to Brazil. Rio de Janeiro was the seat of the entire Portuguese Empire from 1808 to 1821, but the Portuguese emperor became increasingly unpopular. After the emperor returned to Lisbon in 1822, Brazil declared independence. The new Brazilian Empire experienced instability until its second emperor, Dom Pedro II, came of age. Ruling from 1840 to 1889, Dom Pedro II proved to be a dedicated, enlightened and modest ruler. He was also the final emperor; the military overthrew him and proclaimed Brazil a republic in 1889. Subsequently, there was a succession of presidents and military coups until the 1980s. Ex-president Fernando Collor de Mello, who was impeached, became the first directly elected president in twenty-nine years.

Type of Government

Brazil is a multiparty federal republic. The president is both the chief of state and the head of the government. There are two legislative houses: an 81-member Senate and a 503-member Chamber of Deputies.

Language

Portuguese is the official language. Some segments of the population speak Spanish, Italian, or various Amerindian languages.

Religion

There is no official religion. The predominant religion in Brazil is still Roman Catholicism, espoused by 90 percent of the population. Within that group are various Catholic sects. Some 16 percent of Brazilians practice Afro-Brazilian religions that combine tribal and Catholic beliefs (they are sometimes known as Spiritist Catholics). Evangelical Catholics make up 9 percent. Protestant sects have been making many converts in Brazil, although they still account for less than 9 percent. Judaism, Buddhism, and other religions exist in Brazil as well.

Demographics

Brazil's population of approximately 146 million is concentrated on its two hundred miles of east coast. Over 90 percent of the people live on 10 percent of the land, and over 15 million live in São Paulo and Rio de Janeiro. Brazilians' cultural heritage is rich and varied, with 55 percent of European descent (primarily Portuguese), 38 percent a mixture of cultures (African, German, Japanese, Amerindian, and so forth), 6 percent African, and only 1 percent Amerindian (about 150,000). Nearly 50% of the population is under twenty years of age.

*d*espite massive economic problems, Brazil is often regarded as a potentially rich country with a strong industrial sector, large agricultural production, and rich natural resources. An example of its potential for efficient utilization of resources is its processing of sugarcane into ethyl alcohol for fueling 1.5 million Brazilian cars. Its natural resources include gold, nickel, tin, oil, and timber taken from its tropical rain forest in the Amazon River basin—a practice now regarded as controversial and cause for international concern.

Cultural Orientation

Cognitive Styles: How Brazilians Organize and Process Information

Brazilians are open to discussions of most subjects, but home and family are very private matters and are not a topic for acquaintances. Brazilians tend to be more analytical and abstractive than other Latin Americans. They look at the particulars of each situation rather than looking to universal rules or laws.

Negotiation Strategies: What Brazilians Accept as Evidence

Brazilians tend to approach problems indirectly, allowing their feelings to dictate the solution. Facts are admissible as evidence, but they may change with the needs of the negotiator, and they seldom overrule subjective feelings.

Value System: The Basis for Behavior

There are large groups of Germans (who kept their own language) and Japanese (who learned Portuguese) who have their own value systems, which differ somewhat from the Brazilians'. The following three sections identify the Value Systems in the predominant culture—their methods of dividing right from wrong, good from evil, and so forth.

Locus of Decision Making

The individual is responsible for his or her decisions, but family loyalty is the individual's highest duty. Nepotism is the influential family member's first obligation. The family is more important in Brazil than in any other Latin American country. It has been the single most important institution in the formation of Brazilian society.

Sources of Anxiety Reduction

The most significant kin group is the *parentela*—the relatives one recognizes from both families—which may include hundreds of individuals, all related to an illustrious ancestor. This creates a social structure that gives the individual a great sense of stability. The Catholic church is an essential part of the culture and social life. Although most Brazilians are only nominal Catholics, the church gives structure to their lives.

Issues of Equality/Inequality

The concepts of class and status are strong and may determine what job a person will have. Class is described in economic terms. There is a strong color bias. There are extreme contrasts between rich and poor, but the concept that powerful people are entitled to special privileges of office is being questioned. The macho male image prevails, and Brazilian men continue to expect women to be subordinate.

Business Practices

Appointments

 —————————————————————————————**PUNCTUALITY**

* The lack of punctuality is a fact of life in Brazil. Become accustomed to waiting for your Brazilian counterpart.

- Avoid any business transactions around Carneval, which always precedes Ash Wednesday, the beginning of Lent.
- Make appointments at least two weeks in advance. Never try to make impromptu calls at business or government offices.
- Business hours are generally advertised as 8:30 A.M. to 5:30 P.M., but decision makers usually begin work later in the morning and stay later in the evening. Try making appointments between 10:00 A.M. and noon, and 3:00 and 5:00 P.M. If your business runs into lunch, be prepared to spend at least two hours.
- Be prepared to commit long-term resources (both in time and money) toward establishing strong relationships in Brazil. Without such commitments, there is no point attempting to do business there at all.
- Brazilians conduct business through personal connections and expect long-term relationships. Before you invest in a trip, hire an appropriate Brazilian contact in your industry to help you meet the right people. Your Brazilian contact (called a *despechante* in Portuguese) will be invaluable. Contacts can be found through the U.S. Department of Commerce, the American Chamber of Commerce in Brazil, or international organizations to which you may belong.

 Negotiating
- Be patient. It will usually require several trips to get through a bargaining process.
- During negotiations, be prepared to discuss all aspects of the contract simultaneously rather than sequentially.
- Seemingly extraneous data may be reviewed and re-reviewed. Try to be as flexible as possible without making definite commitments.
- Sometimes Brazilians find U.S. aggressive business attitudes offensive—do not expect to get right to the point. Avoid confrontations, and hide any frustrations.

- If you change your negotiating team, you may undermine the entire contract. Brazilians value the person they do business with more than the firm name.
- Make sure you have a local accountant and *notario* (similar to a lawyer) or lawyer for contract issues. Brazilians may resent an outside legal presence.
- It is normal for a conversation to be highly animated, with many interruptions, many statements of "no" being interjected, and a great deal of physical contact.
- Brazilians are enthusiastic soccer (called *futbol*) fans, and soccer provides a lively topic for conversation.
- Avoid deep discussions of politics and any topics relating to Argentina (Brazil's traditional rival).
- Brazilians use periods to punctuate thousands, and use commas to delineate fractions.
- Be aware that Brazilians consider themselves Americans also. Do not use the phrase "in America" when referring to the United States.

 Business Entertaining

- Ask your prospect's secretary to recommend a prestigious restaurant.
- Do not expect to discuss business during a meal. You should participate in the conversation, but not try to direct it too much. Wait until coffee is served to begin any business.
- Stay at a first-class hotel, and entertain there if the hotel has an excellent restaurant.
- If you are invited to a party, it will probably be given at a private club rather than at a home. Arrive at least fifteen minutes late.
- A snack consisting of cookies, cake, and beverages is usually served at 4:00 or 5:00 P.M.
- Brazilian dinners take place any time from 7:00 to 10:00 P.M. Dinner parties can easily continue until 2:00 A.M., but it is not unheard of for dinner parties to break up as late as 7:00 A.M. the next morning!

Time

- Most of Brazil is three hours behind Greenwich Mean Time (G.M.T. - 3), or two hours ahead of U.S. Eastern Standard Time (E.S.T. + 2). Western Brazil is four hours behind G.M.T., or one hour ahead of U.S. Eastern Standard Time.

Protocol

 Greetings

- Greetings can be effusive, with extended handshakes common during the first encounter, progressing to embraces once a friendship has been established. Women often kiss each other on alternating cheeks: twice if they are married, three times if single. The third kiss is supposed to indicate "good luck" for finding a spouse.
- It is polite to shake hands with everyone present in a group, both upon arrival and upon departure.

Titles/Forms of Address

- When available, titles such as *Doctor* or *Professor,* and so forth, are used to address business acquaintances, or the term *Senhor* (Mister) or *Senhora* (Mrs.) is used to precede the surname. Be aware that people may sometimes introduce themselves using their titles and their first names (e.g., Doctor John).

Gestures

- Brazilians communicate in extremely close proximity. They may keep in physical contact by touching arms, hands, or shoulders during the entire conversation. They are friendly and outgoing, and physical interaction is simply an extension of the Brazilian persona—do not back away.
- The sign for "O.K." in the United States (a circle of first finger and thumb) is totally unacceptable in Brazil. It is considered vulgar.
- To signal "come here," extend your palm face down and wave your fingers toward your body.
- Snapping your fingers while whipping your hand up and down adds emphasis to a statement, or can indicate "long ago."
- To invoke good luck, place your thumb between your index and middle fingers while making a fist. This is also known as the "fig."
- Flicking the fingertips underneath the chin indicates that you do not know the answer to a question.

Dress

- Brazil is a tropical country, so expect the weather to be hot. Clothing made of natural fibers will be cooler and more comfortable. (The seasons in Brazil are opposite to those in North America—July is midwinter, and January is summertime.)
- Sometimes three-piece suits carry an "executive" connotation, whereas two-piece suits are associated with office workers.
- The colors of the Brazilian flag are green and yellow, so avoid wearing this combination in any fashion.
- Conservative attire for women is very important in business. Any misstep in clothing or behavior will reflect upon your firm, and may even determine whether or not anyone will do business with you. Also make sure your nails are manicured.
- Only young people wear jeans (always clean and pressed). Men should wear slacks and long sleeved shirts for casual attire.

Gifts

- Avoid giving anything black or purple, since these are colors of mourning.
- Avoid giving knives, which symbolize cutting off a relationship, or handkerchiefs, which connote grief.
- Giving a gift is not required at the first meeting. Instead, buy lunch or dinner, and then consider the individual's tastes for future gift giving.

- Wait until after the formal meeting is over to present a gift. A relaxed social situation is the best time.
- Small electronic gadgets are appreciated—for example, calculators (scientific calculators for important clients), electronic address books and day-timers, pocket CD players, and so forth.
- Tapes and CDs of popular U.S. entertainers are expensive in Brazil and make good gifts.
- Inexpensive cameras and name-brand pens are appropriate.
- When invited to a home (an important occurrence), bring candy, champagne, or scotch. Also bring something for the children—U.S. university T-shirts, and so forth.

Canada

Country Background

History

Like the United States, Canada is a former British colony. Now a self-governing member of the British Commonwealth, Canada achieved its independence from the United Kingdom in a series of gradual treaties rather than via a war of independence. Indeed, after the U.S. War of Independence, many British Loyalists left the United States to live in Canada. The only foreign invaders that British-controlled Canada has ever had to repel were from the United States. The last official U.S. invasion occurred during the War of 1812, when U.S. troops tried to annex Canada and "throw the British out of North America." The outmanned Canadians managed to hold off U.S. forces until British naval power forced an end to the war.

The original inhabitants of Canada were Inuits (the acceptable term for Eskimos) and Native Americans (Indians). The first European claim to Canada was made by French explorers in 1534, who established the colony of New France in what is now Québec. The British followed with a colony in Newfoundland in 1583, and for almost two hundred years France and England ruled competing colonies in Canada. The colonies were sustained by the fur trade with the Indians, and only in missionary work did the French outpace the British. European conflicts between France and England often led to fighting in Canada as well. Finally, during the course of the European Seven Years' War, the British forces in Canada overwhelmed the French. The French troops abandoned the unprofitable New France colony in 1760, and Canada became a British possession.

Like the original thirteen colonies of the United States, Canada was divided into separate colonies under British rule. However, in part because of the historical animosity between the French and the English, there was far less unity among the Canadian colonies. After the grievances of the American colonies incited the United States to fight for its independence, Britain tried to avoid the same mistakes with Canada. The Canadian provinces were given a considerable amount of self-government, and most Canadians generally found Britain's rule acceptable.

It took further threats from the United States to convince the colonies of British Canada to unite in a defensive confederation. After the U.S. Civil War, thousands of Irish soldiers were discharged from the Union Army. Many of these armed, trained men joined the Fenian Brotherhood, a society dedicated to freeing Ireland from British rule. The Fenians hatched a lunatic scheme: They would invade the Canadian colonies and hold them for ransom, demanding freedom for Ireland. In 1866, Fenian forces invaded Canada at three separate border crossings. Their incursions posed little threat, and the Fenians were soon repulsed. However, they did frighten the recalcitrant colonies into accepting unification. Under the British North America Act, most of the colonies were united on July 1, 1867. Canada dates its origin as a country from this event. Since the United States objected to the title "Kingdom of Canada," the new country was given the less imperial, biblically-inspired name "Dominion of Canada."

Like the United States, Canada expanded westward in the nineteenth century, and new provinces were added. The Canadian frontier expansion is remembered as a fairly peaceful process, unlike the violent American "winning of the West." Rather than gunslingers, outlaws, and Indian fighters, Canadians glorified the builders of their transcontinental railroad, which was completed in 1885. Canada followed Britain into both world wars, providing soldiers, food, and manufactured goods. The 1931 Statute of Westminster granted Canada full independence from the United Kingdom, and the postwar NATO alliance brought the United States and Canada closer together. Canada reached its current configuration in 1949, when the last remaining colony, Newfoundland, finally joined the Canadian confederation.

Type of Government

Canada is a federal multiparty parliamentary democracy, with the provinces holding more power than do states in the U.S.A.

The titular head of state of Canada is the British monarch, represented by the governor general. The head of government in Canada is the prime minister. The Canadian parliament has two houses: a 104-seat Senate and a 295-seat House of Commons.

t——————————————————————**CULTURAL NOTE**

here has been friction between the French-speaking Québecois and the English-speaking peoples who have surrounded them for centuries, long before Canada existed as a nation. The Quebecois have seen French speakers in other provinces become assimilated, and they are determined not to let that happen in Québec. They have insisted upon changes in the Canadian constitution, including recognition as a "distinct society" within Canada. The constitutional changes were considered in 1990 at Meech Lake. The provinces could not come to an agreement, in part because some Native American tribes were also demanding recognition as "distinct societies." Quebec's independence party, the Parti Québecois, continues to advocate sovereignty, and it remains to be seen if a compromise can be reached.

Language

English and French are the official languages, with French predominating only in Québec.

Religion

The traditional division of Canada between Roman Catholic (46 percent) and Protestant (41 percent) remains; Jews and Eastern Orthodox each constitute less than 2 percent.

Demographics

The current population of Canada is about 27 million. The traditional French and British lineage of Canadians has been changed by immigration and intermarriage. Twentieth-century immigrants were likely to be German, Italian, or Ukrainian. Recently, the pending return of the British Hong Kong colony to mainland Chinese control in 1997 has prompted many Hong Kong Chinese to come to Canada.

Native Americans and Inuits constitute only 1.5 percent of Canada's population.

Cultural Orientation

Cognitive Styles: How Canadians Organize and Process Information

Canadians in general are well informed and open to reasonable discussions. The French province of Quebec is less open. They are quite analytical and prefer objective information over subjective. They act on problems more from the perspective of universal rules than from the particular perspectives of the people involved.

Negotiation Strategies: What Canadians Accept as Evidence

Facts are accepted as the primary evidence in negotiations, with little credence given to feelings. There is a strong ethnocentrism within the provinces, especially in Québec. This leads to a faith in self-determination that may underlie their behavior in negotiations.

Value Systems: The Basis for Behavior

The French province of Quebec has quite a different value system from the rest of Canada. Consumerism is well developed in all provinces. The following three sections identify the Value Systems in the predominant culture—their methods of dividing right from wrong, good from evil, and so forth.

Locus of Decision Making

There is extremely high individualism in decision making, but one must follow company policy. Therefore, one person can be exchanged for another without disrupting negotiations. Canadians do not find it difficult to say "no." A need for privacy prohibits discussing one's family and personal affairs in business negotiations. Friendships are few and specific to needs.

Sources of Anxiety Reduction

An objective approach to life allows the use of social organizations and other external structures to provide stability and insulation from life. Emotion is not to be shown in public. Competitive behavior is expected, since recognition is one's greatest reward. Time is money. Experts are relied upon at all levels.

Issues of Equality/Inequality

Emphasis is on one's ability, but considerable tension exists between the provinces, particularly with Quebec. Although there are inequalities in roles, equal rights should be guaranteed to all, as superiors and subordinates are "people like me." Material progress is as important as humanistic progress. Traditional sex roles are changing rapidly, but women are still fighting for equality in pay and power.

Business Practices

Appointments

————————————————————————PUNCTUALITY

♦ Punctuality is considered important. Be on time for all business-related meetings.

♦ French-speaking areas of Canada may have a somewhat more casual attitude toward time, but individual business people vary. As a foreigner, you will be expected to be prompt, even if your Canadian counterpart is not.

♦ In general, it is acceptable to be fifteen minutes late for evening social occasions.

- Remember that people in many countries write the day first, then the month, then the year (e.g. December 3, 1999, is written 3.12.99). This is usually the case in Canada.
- Mornings tend to be preferred for appointments.
- Business hours are generally 9:00 A.M. to 5:00 P.M., Monday through Friday.
- Shop hours are generally 10 A.M. to 6 P.M., Monday through Saturday, but many shops are open to 9 P.M. Sunday shopping was prohibited under The Lord's Day Act, but some provinces have changed the law, allowing local municipalities to decide if they want Sunday shopping.

 Negotiating

- Negotiating styles tend to be very similar to those in the United States, although the pace may be slightly slower.
- Canadians associate the United States with self-promotion and "hype." Never inflate a product's benefits; it could generate claims of illegal promotion.
- When dealing with French Canadians, it is important to have all material written in French as well as English.

————————————————————————CULTURAL NOTE

*i*n Québec, there are very stringent French-language requirements for all commercial endeavors. French is the only legal language in which to conduct business, and all signs must be posted in French only. However, English phrases that have no French equivalents (such as "happy hour" or "bargain basement") are allowed.

- In general, the manners of English-speaking Canadians are similar to those of English-speaking U.S. citizens. Canadian business people expect a firm handshake, direct eye contact, and an open, friendly manner.
- Despite these similarities, English-speaking Canadians are closer to the reserved traditions of the British than U.S. citizens. It is important not to come off as an overbearing boor from the United States.

- While many Canadians quickly address others by their first names, it is safest to wait for your Canadian counterpart to suggest it.
- One "un-American" habit that the Canadians have inherited from the British is a disdain for new clothing. Old clothes that are neat, clean, and "broken in" are respected among business people; new, trendy clothes may not be.
- Acknowledge Canadians' desire for a "Canadian identity."
- French Canadians generally exhibit less reserve than English-speaking Canadians. Their gestures will be more expansive, they may stand closer while talking, and they are more likely to touch during a conversation.
- Canada is a multiethnic nation—British, French, Inuit, Indian, German, and so forth—and the etiquette of business people may reflect their ethnic background. For example, many wealthy Hong Kong Chinese have acquired Canadian citizenship; their habits may be quite different from those of other Canadians.

 Business Entertaining

- Business meals are popular in Canada, although the concept of the breakfast meeting is only now gaining acceptance.
- Most entertaining is done in public establishments, such as restaurants or nightclubs. (Contrary to popular belief, most Canadian cities do have an active nightlife.)
- Traditionally, dinners were considered social occasions—if business was discussed at all, it was at the end of the meal. While this is changing, it is safest to allow your Canadian counterpart to bring up business first.
- Invitations to dine at a Canadian home are relatively infrequent, except in the western provinces, where outdoor barbecues have become popular.

Time

- Canada spans six time zones. Most of Quebec and Ontario are on Eastern Standard Time [five hours behind Greenwich Mean Time (G.M.T. - 5)]. Western Ontario, Manitoba, and eastern Saskatchewan (including Regina) are on Central Standard Time. Western Saskatchewan, Alberta, and easternmost British Columbia are on Mountain Standard Time. Most of British Columbia is on Pacific Standard Time (eight hours behind G.M.T.). All of these correspond to time zones in the United States.
- Atlantic Standard Time (four hours behind G.M.T.) is one hour ahead of Eastern Standard Time. All the Maritime Provinces are on Atlantic Standard Time except for Newfoundland Island, which reminds the world of its separate identity by maintaining a separate time zone that is thirty minutes ahead of Atlantic Standard Time (3 1/2 hours behind G.M.T.). Note that this thirty-minute difference applies only to Newfoundland Island; Labrador, which is the mainland part of Newfoundland Province, is on Atlantic Standard Time.
- From the end of April through late October, most of Canada is on daylight saving time.

Protocol

Greetings

- The standard greeting is a smile, often accompanied by a nod, wave, and/or verbal greeting.
- In business situations, a handshake is used upon greetings or introductions.
- Among Canadians of British descent, the handshake tends to be firm, and a weak handshake may be taken as a sign of weakness. Men usually wait for women to offer their hand before shaking.
- French Canadians also have a fairly firm handshake. And they shake hands more often: upon greetings, introductions, and departures, even if the person has been greeted earlier that day.
- Good friends and family members sometimes embrace, especially among the French. A kissing of cheeks may occur as well. Note that the French do not finish an embrace with a pat or two on the back, as many U.S. citizens do.
- If you see an acquaintance at a distance, a wave is appropriate.
- The greeting "How are you?" is not an inquiry about your health. The best response is a short one, such as "Fine, thanks."

Titles/Forms of Address

- The order of most Canadian names is first name, middle name, last name.
- To show respect, use a title such as Dr., Ms., Miss, Mrs., or Mr. with the last name.
- When you meet someone for the first time, use the person's title and surname until you are told to do otherwise (this may happen immediately).
- Note that although they often use first names over the telephone, French Canadians may revert to using surnames in person.

Gestures

- The standard space between you and your conversation partner should be two feet. British Canadians are uncomfortable standing any closer to another person. French Canadians may stand slightly closer.
- Canadians, especially those of British descent, do not tend toward frequent or expansive gesturing.
- In general, friends of the same sex do not hold hands. Only French Canadians commonly touch during conversation.
- To point, you can use the index finger, although it is not polite to point at a person.
- To beckon someone, wave all the fingers in a scooping motion with the palm facing up.
- To show approval, there are two typical gestures. One is the "O.K." sign, done by making a circle of the thumb and index finger. The other is the "thumbs up" sign, done by making a fist and pointing the thumb upward.
- The "V-for-victory" sign is done with the palm facing out. It can be taken as an insult when done with the palm inward.

- The backslap is a sign of close friendship among British Canadians. It is rarely used among the French.
- To wave good-bye, move your entire hand, facing outward.

CULTURAL NOTE

*i*n most of Canada, to call the waiter or waitress over, briefly wave to get his or her attention. To call for the check, make a writing gesture. In Québec, it is only necessary to nod the head backwards or to make a discreet wave of the hand.

- Direct eye contact shows that you are sincere, although it should not be too intense. Some minorities look away to show respect.
- When sitting, Canadians often look very relaxed. They may sit with the ankle of one leg on the knee of the other or prop their feet up on chairs or desks.
- In business situations, maintain good posture and a less casual pose.

Dress

- In cities, conservative business attire is best.
- In rural areas and small towns, clothing is less formal and less fashionable.
- When not working, Canadians dress casually.
- Canadian winters can be quite cold. Dress warmly.

Gifts

- Business gifts should be modest. Ostentation tends to be frowned upon by Canadians.
- When you visit a home, it is customary to take a gift. Flowers, candy, or alcohol are common gifts.

CULTURAL NOTE

*w*hen visiting a French-Canadian family, be aware that houses are divided into "public" rooms (which visitors may enter) and "private" rooms (which they may enter only when asked). The kitchen is often a private room; do not enter unless asked.

- At Christmastime gifts are exchanged. To your business associates, you can give gifts that are helpful at the office, or liquor or wine. Most stores gift-wrap at Christmas.
- A good time to give a gift is when you arrive or when you leave. The best gifts are those that come from your country.
- Business gifts are given after you close a deal. Unless the giver specifies a time at which the gift is to be opened, as may happen with a gift at Christmastime, gifts are usually unwrapped immediately and shown to everyone.
- Taking someone out for a meal or other entertainment is a common gift.

SANTIAGO

Chile

Country Background

History

The first European settlers in Chile were Spanish explorers in search of gold and silver, following the defeat of the Inca Empire in 1533. What they found instead was a fertile valley, and Chile quickly became part of the Spanish Empire, governed from Peru. Immigration from Spain, however, was limited because of the ferocity of the local Araucanian Indians, who remained a threat as late as 1883.

Bernardo O'Higgins, Chile's renowned patriot, led a struggle for independence against the Spanish from 1810 to 1818. Helped by an army trained by Argentine patriot José de San Martín, Chilean independence was formally declared on February 12, 1818.

During the nineteenth century, Chile expanded its territories. A treaty with Argentina gave Chile control of the Strait of Magellan and a stretch of land facing the Atlantic (although most of Patagonia went to Argentina). Chile then won the War of the Pacific in 1883 against Peru and Bolivia, expanding Chile's territory northward to an area rich in natural resources. But relations with Bolivia remain difficult to this day, as the now-landlocked Bolivia has never reconciled itself to the loss of its entire Pacific seaboard.

In the beginning of the twentieth century, Chile's emerging representative government degenerated as the ruling oligarchy struggled to retain control over the working class. By 1932, a strong middle class party, the Radicals, emerged as the key influence in government, and remained so until 1965. During this time, the state nurtured industrial development and improved and expanded social welfare and educational systems.

In 1964, Eduardo Frei, a Christian Democrat, was elected to the presidency. His program was marked by the slogan "Revolution in Liberty" and consisted of far-reaching social programs. But the radicals felt that these reforms were insufficient, while conservatives saw them as excessive. In the next election, in 1970, Dr. Salvador

Allende won with 36 percent of the votes over two other candidates, becoming the first freely-elected Marxist leader in this hemisphere. He initiated programs of massive land redistribution and nationalized many private industries and banks—including U.S. interests in copper mines. But he did not have majority support in the Chilean Congress, and discontent grew as a result of shortages of food and consumer goods. Furthermore, in the United States, the Nixon administration decided that the presence of a new Marxist regime in the Americas was unacceptable.

On September 11, 1973, a bloody, CIA-backed military coup overthrew Allende, abolished the Congress, and banned political parties. Allende was killed. A four-man military junta (known as *los Generales*) instituted a repressive regime. Thousands of people were imprisoned, and several hundred disappeared altogether. The leading general, Augusto Pinochet Ugarte, ruled as president and commander of the army.

In 1980, a new constitution was approved in a national plebiscite. Under it, General Pinochet was elected to an eight-year term, with the military junta acting as the legislature. At the end of that term, Pinochet allowed another plebiscite to decide if he should continue for another eight years. When he lost the plebiscite, he called for free elections in December 1989. As a result of that election, President Patricio Aylwin Azocar took office in March 1990 as the first elected president since 1970. Since then, political power has passed peacefully from one elected government to the next.

Type of Government

The Republic of Chile is a multiparty republic with two legislative houses, the 48-seat Senate and the 120-seat Chamber of Deputies. The president is the chief of state as well as the head of the government.

Suffrage is universal and compulsory at age eighteen.

While the current government is considered stable, the civilian leaders must deal with both the still-influential military and a rising tide of leftist terrorism. Although the president is technically the "supreme commander" of the armed forces, he has little practical control over the military, and the possibility of another coup always exists.

Language

The official language of Chile is Spanish, although English is spoken by well-educated business people and in tourist centers.

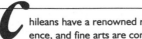

CULTURAL NOTE

Chileans have a renowned reputation for achievement in many cultural fields. Literature, social science, and fine arts are considered prestigious areas of study.

Religion

There is no official religion in Chile, but over 78 percent of the population identify themselves as Roman Catholics. Protestants account for over 13 percent. There is also a small Jewish population. A sizable number of people consider themselves nonreligious or atheist.

Demographics

Because of the geography of the area, the country has experienced a large degree of isolation and, as a result, is more ethnically homogeneous than most of South America. Of the 13 million people who live in Chile, some 95 percent are mestizo (of mixed European and Indian blood), 3 percent are Indian (mostly Araucanian), and less than 2 percent are solely of European descent.

f━━━━━━━━━━━━━━━**CULTURAL NOTE**

amily respect and loyalty are primary concerns in Chile, even taking precedence over business responsibilities. Extended families are often found living close together and tend to be very dependent upon one another. Machismo remains an important aspect of Chilean culture.

Cultural Orientation

Cognitive Styles: How Chileans Organize and Process Information

In Chile, information is readily accepted for the purpose of discussion, but negotiations may be extensive, with little movement from the initial position. Well-educated persons may process information conceptually and analytically, but most are associative in their thinking. They see each problem as having a particular solution rather than looking to a universal rule or law.

Negotiation Strategies: What Chileans Accept as Evidence

Facts are not nearly as important in negotiating a position as are feelings. Truth tends to be subjective and personal. However, faith in a strong Catholic or Protestant ideology may form the basis for truth.

Value Systems: The Basis for Behavior

This is not a culture of conquerors but of cosmopolitans who assimilated all European cultures into their social strata through marriage. The following three sections identify the Value Systems in the predominant culture—their methods of dividing right from wrong, good from evil, and so forth.

Locus of Decision Making

This is a semicollective culture in which the extended family is a dominating factor in the individual's decision-making process. Expertise is less important than the ability to be a member of the group. Thus, kinship and friendship play a major role in one's business associations. It is essential that one become friends with the participants in a problem-solving situation.

Sources of Anxiety Reduction

The extended family is the primary source of structure and stability. Kinship is the key to membership in any group. Marriage into the right family is essential, as family ties are a major determinant of success. Social structure is strong, and poverty or wealth is generally accepted as destiny. One can be reconciled to one's existing status.

Issues of Equality/Inequality

In general, people are equal because each one is unique, and no law needs to be passed to ensure this equality. There is a class-conscious tiny elite, and a larger middle class than in most other Latin American countries. The Mapuche Indians still suffer discrimination.

Business Practices

Appointments

━━━━━━━━━━━━━━━━━━━━━━━━ PUNCTUALITY

- ◆ Be punctual at meetings. Punctuality is appreciated and expected from North Americans. Do not be offended, however, if your counterpart is up to thirty minutes late.
- ◆ On the other hand, everyone (even foreigners) is expected to arrive at social functions late. Be about fifteen minutes late to a dinner, and thirty minutes late to a party.

- Remember that many Europeans and South Americans write the day first, then the month, then the year (e.g. December 3, 1999, is written 3.12.99). This is the case in Chile.
- Business hours are 9:00 A.M. to 5:00 P.M., Monday through Friday. A two-hour lunch is taken at 12:00.
- Government offices are open 9:00 A.M. to 4:30 P.M., Monday through Friday.
- The best times to make appointments are from 10:00 A.M. to 12:00 and 2:30 to 5:00 P.M. Following up a late morning appointment with a business lunch is also popular.
- Make appointments about two weeks in advance of your arrival, and reconfirm them when you get there.
- A popular time for vacations is January and February (summer holidays). This is not the time to try to do business in Chile.

 Negotiating

- Personal relationships are paramount in business relations in Chile. The initial visit should be by an upper-level executive, accompanied by mid-level executives. These mid-level executives are the ones who will make subsequent visits to conduct more detailed business negotiations. At a first meeting, spend most of the time establishing a rapport, then gradually steer the conversation toward introducing your firm.
- Attitudes toward trading with North America are positive.
- Conservative values in politics, economics, and social attitudes prevail. Honesty and integrity are highly valued. A sense of humor is appreciated, but generally serious, businesslike behavior is expected.
- There is a strong sense of personal honor on the part of Latin American business people. Therefore, do not criticize a person in public, pull rank, or do anything that will cause him or her embarrassment.

t━━━━━━━━━━━━━━━━━━ **CULTURAL NOTE**

he decision-making process is centralized, residing mostly with the upper-level *presidente* or *gerente general*. Next in importance comes the *gerente*, followed by mid- and low-level managers; all provide support to the upper levels. But all levels usually have input, so business transactions may take place at a slower pace than in North America or Europe. Be patient and expect delays. Several trips may be necessary to conclude a business transaction.

- Chileans are straightforward and take negotiating quite seriously. A hard-sell approach, however, will not work. Have your bottom line and other terms clearly drawn out. Also outline a strong financial package with options such as nontraditional financing terms.
- Businesswomen will be at a slight disadvantage because of the machismo ethic that continues to exist in Chile. However, many women are professionally advanced, and a woman will have better success here than in most other Latin American countries.
- Show commitment to the business relationship through a willingness to provide continued service to your client, despite the long distances involved. Remember that Chileans strive to overcome the isolation imposed on them by geography.
- Making a good impression includes staying at one of the finer international hotels while in Chile.
- South Americans generally converse in closer proximity than North Americans. Do not pull away from a person who is speaking quite close to you, even if you are uncomfortable. This may be interpreted as a personal affront.
- Have business cards printed with English on one side and Spanish on the other. Present cards to everyone in a meeting except secretaries.
- Third parties are very important for making contacts in Chile. Banks and consulting firms can make introductions.
- The business atmosphere tends to be more formal than in other South American and European countries. Correct etiquette and dress are expected.
- Chileans avoid behavior that may appear aggressive. Kindness and respect for others are valued.
- Learn a little about Chile's history, culture, economy, exports, and so forth, and be prepared to discuss them. This will impress and please your contacts.

CULTURAL NOTE

*C*hileans do not bargain in either stores or street markets. Note that it is illegal to sell something and not issue a receipt. When a receipt is not issued, this often means that the merchant is not declaring the sale on tax reports.

Business Entertaining

- Breakfast is usually eaten between 7:00 and 9:00 A.M. Lunch, the largest meal of the day, is eaten at noon. *Onces* is a light snack between 5:00 and 6:00 P.M. in preparation for dinner, which is served between 8:00 and 9:00 P.M. If you are invited for drinks at a home, you will probably be invited for dinner as well.
- It is not customary to send a thank you gift or note following an invitation to a Chilean home, but flowers or candy sent to the hostess in advance are appreciated. If you wish to convey your thanks, do so by telephone rather than by mail.
- Entertaining is often done in large hotels and restaurants. Make arrangements concerning the bill with the maitre d' in advance to avoid competition for paying. If you are a guest, reciprocate the hospitality at a later date.
- Proper table manners are very important in Chile. In general, follow Western standards. Pour wine with your right hand, and try to at least taste everything that is served to you.
- Good topics of conversation include family, Chilean history, cuisine, wines, and sights that they might recommend. Many Chileans are very interested in world travel, so mention other places you have visited. Skiing and fishing are very pop-

ular in Chile. Topics to avoid include local politics, human rights violations, and religion. Do not criticize Chile, even if your host is doing so.

Time
- Chile is four hours behind Greenwich Mean Time (G.M.T. - 3). This makes it one hour ahead of U.S. Eastern Standard Time (E.S.T. + 1). Chile goes on daylight saving time from mid-October through mid-March.

Protocol

 ### Greetings
- Men will shake hands when greeting someone. Women will often pat each other on the right forearm or shoulder instead of shaking hands. If they are close, women may hug or kiss each other on the cheek.
- At a party, greet and shake hands with each person individually. Do not ask a person his or her occupation directly, but wait for the information to be volunteered.

 ### Titles/Forms of Address
- Do not address a Chilean by his or her first name unless invited to do so. Generally, only children, family members, and close friends address each other by their first names.
- Persons who do not use professional titles should be addressed as Mr., Mrs., or Miss, plus their surname. In Spanish, these are
  - Mr. = *Señor*
  - Mrs. = *Señora*
  - Miss = *Señorita*
- Most Hispanics have two surnames: one from their father, which is listed first, followed by one from their mother. Only the father's surname is commonly used when addressing someone, e.g., Señor Juan Antonio Martinez García is addressed as Señor Martinez and Señorita Ana María Gutierrez Herrera is addressed as Señorita Gutierrez. When a woman marries, she usually adds her husband's surname and goes by that surname. If the two people in the above example married, she would be known as Señora Ana María Gutierrez Herrera de Martinez. Most people would refer to her as: Señora de Martinez or, less formally, Señora Martinez.
- Most Chileans do not use a professional title. Those who do, expect to be addressed with that title followed by their surname. Physicians always are called *Doctor*.

 ### Gestures
- The Chilean people converse at a closer distance than U.S. and Canadian citizens are used to—often with a hand on the other person's lapel or shoulder. Restrain yourself from trying to back away; a Chilean will probably step forward and close the distance.

- Maintaining eye contact is necessary to show interest and sincerity—something that North Americans may find difficult when speaking to a person at such close quarters.
- At a meal, keep your hands above the table at all times.
- Do not raise your right fist to head level, as this is a Communist sign.
- See the first Cultural Note for more gestures.

Gifts

- Gifts are not expected in business until the relationship is a close one.
- When visiting a Chilean home, send flowers in advance (avoid yellow roses, which signify contempt) or bring wine or liquor. Other popular gifts include leather appointment books, quality pens or cigarette lighters, perfume, and local crafts from home.
- If you receive a gift, open it promptly in the presence of the giver and extend thanks.
- Give gold jewelry to a girl on her fifteenth birthday. This birthday (called the *quinceanos;* the party is called a *quinceanera*) is a very important celebration in Chile; to be invited to one is a privilege.

Dress

- Business: Dress is generally more conservative than in the United States. Men may wear a dark blue or gray suit, a light shirt, and a conservative tie. Bright colors and flashy fashions are not suitable, nor is wearing anything on the lapel. Women should wear a suit and heels.
- Casual: When not doing business, pants or good jeans and a shirt are appropriate. Shorts will rarely be seen in public. Chile experiences temperature extremes from the beaches to the mountains. You will need warmer clothes at higher altitudes.

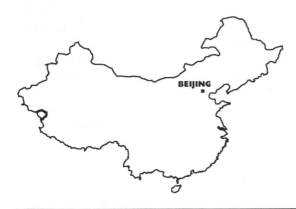

BEIJING

China

Country Background

History

The Chinese boast the world's oldest continuous civilization, with more than 4,000 years of recorded history. Beijing (old Peking) has been the capital of China for over 800 years and is the country's political, economic, and cultural hub.

China was ruled by strong dynasties for thousands of years. The first recorded dynasty, the Hsia, existed around 2200 B.C., and the last dynasty, the Ch'ing, ended in 1911. Some of the most important cultural achievements in history were produced during this time, i.e., papermaking, the compass, gunpowder, and movable-type printing.

After the fall of the last dynasty, Sun Yat-sen founded the Republic of China and was succeeded by Chiang Kai-shek in 1927.

Mao Tse-tung's Communist forces took control in 1949 and established the Communist government that still exists, although events—from the massacre in Tiananmen Square in June of 1989 on—have shown an increasing popular demand for democratic reform.

China has been divided into twenty two provinces, five autonomous regions, and three municipalities.

Type of Government

The People's Republic of China has a Communist government. There is a single legislative house, the National People's Congress; all members belong to the Communist party. The National People's Congress elects the Standing Committee, which holds executive power and is made up of the premier and leading ministers. The premier is the head of the government; the president is the chief of state. The position of secretary general of the Central Committee of the Chinese Communist party is also an office of great power; it is often held by the current president.

All aspects of life are controlled by the Communist regime, which is highly centralized and authoritarian.

Language

The official national language is standard Chinese, based on the Mandarin dialect. It is spoken by more than 70 percent of the population. Many Chinese speak the Cantonese, Wu, and Kejia dialects. Each of the fifty-five, officially recognized minorities speaks its own dialect or language. English is spoken by many business people.

a————————————**CULTURAL NOTE**

lthough spoken Chinese has many dialects (some of which are as different as English is from German) there is one common written language. Therefore, many Chinese movies have Chinese subtitles, so that Cantonese-speaking Chinese audiences can understand the Mandarin-speaking actors.

Religion

Although the government encourages atheism, the Chinese constitution guarantees religious freedom (within certain constraints). Buddhism, Islam, and Christianity are the three major formal religions practiced in China. However, even larger numbers of Chinese believe in traditional Chinese philosophies, notably Confucianism, and folk precepts such as Taoism.

Confucianism, although not a religion with a divine deity, has great influence on Chinese society. Confucius was a Chinese scholar and statesman who lived during feudal times over 2,000 years ago. He established a rigid ethical and moral system that governs all relationships.

Confucius taught that the basic unit of society is the family. In order to preserve harmony in the home, certain reciprocal responsibilities must be preserved in relationships. These relationships are between ruler and subjects, between husband and wife, between father and son, between elder brother and younger brother, and between friends. Since all but the last are hierarchal, rank and age are very important in all interactions. All actions of the individual reflect upon the family, and filial devotion is of utmost importance. The virtues of kindness, propriety righteousness, intelligence, and faithfulness are deeply revered.

Demographics

China has 1.17 billion inhabitants (1992 estimate), making it the most populous country in the world. One quarter of the earth's population lives there. Although there are many minority groups, over 91 percent of the population is ethnic (Han) Chinese. China has implemented a rigorous birth control program that limits couples to only one child.

Cultural Orientation

Cognitive Styles: How the Chinese Organize and Process Information

The Chinese are generally circumspect toward outside sources of information. They usually process information through a subjective perspective, derived from experience—unless they have been educated at a Western university. Universalistic behavior that follows the Communist party line is demanded under the Communist government. The favoritism shown to Communist party members is overtly particularistic.

Negotiation Strategies: What the Chinese Accept as Evidence

Faith in the Communist party line is the dominant source of truth in all negotiations. In general, truth is subjective, and one's feelings are a primary source of the truth. Facts are accepted, but not if they are in conflict with the other two sources.

Value Systems: The Basis for Behavior

China is a truly collectivistic culture dominated by the Communist party. The following three sections identify the Value Systems in the predominant culture-their methods of dividing right from wrong, good from evil, and so forth.

Locus of Decision Making

In a centrally controlled economy, responsibility rests with the government planners and the Communist party, but individuals are held responsible for their decisions within the system. Local decisions are made by the head of the collective, and members must behave accordingly. Collectives are insular, closed entities in which individual goals are subordinated to those of the collective. In the pockets of free enterprise, businesses are experimenting with freedom from party rule but not from the collectivist way of thinking.

Sources of Anxiety Reduction

The family, school, work unit, and local community are the basic social structures that give stability to one's life. There is a strong commitment to the extended family. The state, rather than religion, dictates the symbols of wisdom, morality, and the common good. One can feel secure in the hands of the state. However, there is a very high social consciousness of face. Strict obedience to parents and the Communist party are an absolute rule. Harmony must be maintained at all costs.

Issues of Equality/Inequality

Relative to the general population (over one billion), the number of people who are powerful members of the Communist party is small. There has always been some concern about inequality in a system in which equality is the purpose, but being a member of the party is the only avenue to a position of authority. Free enterprise is purported to breed inequality and uncertainty, but there are isolated pockets where it is allowed to flourish. Age is the only noticeable interpersonal indicator of inequality because it is still revered. Women are purported to be equal to men, but economic and social inequalities continue.

Business Practices

Appointments

PUNCTUALITY

♦ It is very important to be punctual in China, not only for buiness meetings, but for social occasions as well. Lateness or cancellation is a serious affront.

- Remember that written Chinese does not have tenses, but there are many words to indicate the passage of time—tomorrow, now, and so forth.
- It is important to establish contacts in China before you invest in a trip. The U.S. Department of Commerce/East Asia and Pacific Office can assist in arranging appointments with local Chinese business and government officials, and can identify importers, buyers, agents, distributors, and joint venture partners.
- The best times to schedule business trips are April to June and September to October.
- Business and government hours are 8:00 A.M. to 5:00 P.M., Monday through Saturday. However, a five-day workweek has been initiated in some large cities.
- Shop Hours: 9:00 A.M. to 7:00 P.M., daily. Most stores in Shanghai stay open until 10:00 P.M.
- Between noon and 2:00 P.M. everyone takes a break. Everything stops, including manually operated elevators and switchboards.
- Do not plan business trips during the Chinese New Year, since many businesses close for a week before and after the festival. The date of the New Year varies according to the lunar calendar.

 Negotiating

CULTURAL NOTE

*b*e prepared for the Chinese to supply an interpreter. If possible, bring your own interpreter as well to help you understand nuances in the discussion.

Avoid slang or jargon, especially figures of speech from sports. Use short, simple sentences, and pause often to make sure that your exact words are understood.

- Expect to make presentations to many different groups at different levels.
- Have at least twenty copies of your proposal available for distribution when you arrive. Photocopy facilities in China can be difficult to find.
- Use black and white for your collateral materials, since colors have great significance for the Chinese.
- U.S. executives have a reputation for impatience, and the Chinese will drag out negotiations well beyond your deadlines just to gain an advantage. They may try to renegotiate everything on the final day of your visit, and they will continue to try for a better deal even after the contract is signed.
- Never exaggerate your ability to deliver, because the Chinese believe humility is a virtue—and also because they will investigate your claims.

- Most Chinese will not make any important decisions without first consulting the stars for an auspicious day and hour.
- Be patient. Expect to make several trips to China before negotiations are final. The Chinese are very cautious in business matters, and will expect a strong relationship to be built before they close a deal.
- Weights and measures are mainly metric, but several old Chinese measures are still used.
- Bring business cards with a translation printed (in Mandarin Chinese) on the reverse side. Gold ink is the most prestigious color for the Chinese side. Never place a person's card in your wallet and then put it in your back pocket.
- When entering a business meeting, the highest ranking member of your group should lead the way.
- The Chinese expect the business conversation to be conducted by the senior officials of each side. If subordinates interrupt, the Chinese will be shocked.
- Familiarize yourself with all aspects of China before you arrive. The Chinese appreciate Western visitors who demonstrate an interest in their culture and history.
- Be patient, expect delays, show little emotion, and do not talk about your deadlines.
- At the end of a meeting, leave before the Chinese.

CULTURAL NOTE

*R*elocating management-level employees to Shanghai is extremely expensive, and keeping them there can easily run $300,000 a year. Be sure to thoroughly prepare not only your employee but his or her entire family for the cultural differences they will encounter before making such an investment.

Business Entertaining

- Business lunches have become more popular, but you will probably be treated to at least one evening banquet. You should always return the favor.
- Banquets at restaurants can be ordered in varying degrees of extravagance. Be sure to reciprocate at the same price per person as your Chinese host spent at your banquet—never surpass your host in the degree of banquet lavishness.
- Most banquets start between 6:30 and 7:00 P.M. and last for about two hours. You should arrive about thirty minutes before your guests—they will arrive on time.
- If you are the guest, always arrive promptly or even a little early.
- Business is not generally discussed during a meal.
- Never begin to eat or drink before your host does.

CULTURAL NOTE

*I*t is polite to sample every dish. The Chinese may even test your fortitude on purpose with exotic delicacies like marinated, deep-fried scorpions, completely intact with their stingers, on a bed of rice.

- When eating rice, it is customary to hold the bowl close to your mouth.
- At a meal, eat lightly in the beginning, since there could be up to twenty courses served. Expect your host to keep filling your bowl with food whenever you empty it. Finishing all of your food may be an insult to your host, since it can mean he did not provide enough food. Leaving a bowl completely full is also rude.
- The Chinese use chopsticks for eating and a porcelain spoon for soup. Your attempts at using chopsticks will be appreciated. When you are finished, set

your chopsticks on the table or on the chopstick-rest. Placing them parallel on top of your bowl is considered a sign of bad luck.

- Sticking your chopsticks straight up in your rice bowl is rude, since they will resemble the joss sticks used in religious ceremonies.
- Try not to drop your chopsticks; it is considered bad luck.
- Serving dishes are not passed around. Reach for food with your chopsticks, but do not use the end you put in your mouth! It is perfectly acceptable to reach in front of others to get to the serving dishes.
- Good topics of conversation include Chinese sights, art, calligraphy, and inquiries about the health of the other's family. Generally, conversation during a meal focuses on the meal itself and is full of compliments to the preparer.
- Bones and seeds are placed on the table or a dish—never back in the rice bowl.
- At a banquet, expect to be served rice in an individual bowl by a waiter. In a home, your hostess will serve the rice.
- Toasting is big in China. At banquets, the host offers the first toast, and the ceremony continues all evening. It is acceptable to toast with a soft drink, but wine and beer will be available.
- Never take the last bit of food from a serving dish; this can signify that you are still hungry.
- The serving of fruit signals the end of the meal.
- If you don't want refills of tea, leave some in your cup.
- If you smoke, offer your cigarettes to others in your group.
- Generally, women should not drink alcoholic beverages. Businesswomen should accept a drink if offered, take a sip, and leave it.

Time
- China is eight hours ahead of Greenwich Mean Time (G.M.T. + 8), or thirteen hours ahead of U.S. Eastern Standard Time (E.S.T. + 13). Despite the immense size of the country, it has only one time zone.

Protocol

Greetings
- The Chinese nod or bow slightly when greeting another person, although handshakes are common. Wait for the Chinese to extend a hand first.
- Visitors to factories, theaters, or schools may be greeted with applause as a sign of welcome. The usual response is to applaud back.
- Introductions tend to be formal, with courtesy rather than familiarity preferred.

Titles/Forms of Address
- The Chinese are very sensitive to status and titles, so you should use official titles such as General, Committee Member, or Bureau Chief when possible. Never call anyone "Comrade" unless you are a Communist also.
- Names are listed in a different order from Western names. Each person receives a family name, a generational name, and a given name at birth—in that order. Generational and given names can be separated by a space or a

hyphen, but are often written as one word. For example, President Li Teng Hui has the family name of Li, a generational name of Teng, and a given name of Hui. (His name could also be rendered Li Teng-Hui or Li Tenghui.)

- Most people you meet should be addressed with a title and their name. If a person does not have a professional title (President, Engineer, Doctor), simply use Mr. or Madam, Mrs., or Miss, plus the name.
- Chinese wives do not generally take their husband's surnames, but instead maintain their maiden names. Although Westerners commonly address a married woman as Mrs. plus her husband's family name, it is more appropriate to call her Madam plus her maiden family name. For example, Li Chu Chin (female) is married to Chang Wu Jiang (male). While westerners would probably call her Mrs. Chang, she is properly addressed as Madam Li.
- Thankfully, many Chinese adopt an English first name so that English speakers can have a familiar-sounding name to identify them. Thus, Chang Wu Jiang may call himself Mr. Walter Chang. Others use their initials (Mr. W.J. Chang).
- If many Chinese seem to have similar clan names, it is because there are only about 400 different surnames in China! However, when these surnames are transcribed into English, there are several possible variations. For example, Wong, Wang, and Huang are all English versions of the same Chinese clan name.

 Gestures

- Avoid making exaggerated gestures or using dramatic facial expressions. The Chinese do not use their hands when speaking, and become distracted by a speaker who does.
- The Chinese do not like to be touched by people they do not know. This is especially important to remember when dealing with older people or people in important positions.
- Members of the same sex may be seen publicly holding hands, but public affection between the opposite sexes is not condoned.
- Use an open hand rather than one finger to point.
- To beckon, turn the palm down and wave the fingers toward the body.
- Do not put your hands in your mouth (biting your nails, dislodging food from your teeth); this is considered disgusting.

 Gifts

- Gift giving is a sensitive issue in China. Technically, it is against the law, but the acceptance of gift giving is increasing.
- Avoid giving anything of value in front of others, as it could cause the recipient both embarrassment and trouble.
- A gift from your company to the Chinese organization or factory is acceptable. Make it clear that the gift is on behalf of the whole company you represent and is for the whole group on the receiving end. Be sure to present the gift to the acknowledged leader of the Chinese delegation. Gifts of this sort might include items from your region of the country, like local crafts, historical memorabilia, or an illustrated book.
- A banquet is considered an acceptable gift. Your Chinese hosts will certainly give you one, and you should reciprocate.
- High-quality pens are a luxury any Chinese appreciates. Other good gifts include kitchen gadgets and expensive liquors, like a good cognac.

- Stamps are also popular social gifts, as stamp collecting is a big hobby in China. Barrettes and combs, cigarette lighters, T-shirts of U.S. sports teams, and solar-powered calculators are also good.
- When giving or receiving a gift, use both hands. The gift is not opened in the presence of the giver.
- The Chinese traditionally decline a gift three times before accepting; this prevents them from appearing greedy. Continue to insist; once they accept the gift, say you are pleased that they have done so.
- Gifts of food are always appreciated by Chinese, but avoid bringing food gifts with you to a dinner or party (unless it has been agreed upon beforehand). To bring food may imply that your host cannot provide enough. Instead, send food as a thank-you gift afterwards. Candy and fruit baskets are good choices.
- The Chinese associate all of the following gifts and colors with funerals—avoid them:
  - Straw sandals,
  - clocks,
  - a stork or crane (although the Western association of storks with births is known to many young Chinese),
  - handkerchiefs (often given at funerals; they symbolize sadness and weeping), and
  - gifts (or wrapping paper) in which the predominant color is white, black, or blue.
- Do not wrap a gift before arriving in China, as it may be unwrapped in Customs.
- If possible, wrap gifts in red, a lucky color; pink and yellow, happy, prosperous colors, are also good choices. Do not use white, which is the color for funerals. Ask about appropriate paper at your hotel or at a store that wraps gifts.
- All business negotiations should be concluded before gifts are exchanged.
- At Chinese New Year, it is customary to give a gift of money in a red envelope to children and to the service personnel you deal with on a regular basis. This gift is called a *hong bao.* Give only new bills in even numbers and even amounts. Many employers give each employee a *hong bao* equivalent to one month's salary.

 Dress

- For business, men should wear conservative suits, shirts, and ties. Loud colors are not appropriate. Women should also wear conservative suits, with high-necked blouses, and low heels—their colors should be as neutral as possible.
- At formal occasions, no high heels or evening gowns are necessary for women unless the event is a formal reception given by a foreign diplomat. Men may wear suits and ties.
- Casual wear is still somewhat conservative. Revealing clothing may be offensive, but jeans are acceptable for both men and women. Shorts are appropriate when exercising.

CULTURAL NOTE

*I*n 1964, archaeological discoveries found evidence that humans were living and working along the Yellow River more than 600,000 years ago. There is also proof that China's "Peking Man" inhabited caves near Beijing more than 400,000 years ago.

BOGOTA

Colombia

CULTURAL NOTE

Colombians have distinctive methods for indicating height and length:

- To indicate the height of an animal, Colombians hold one hand horizontally at the appropriate height, as if they were resting their hand on top of the animal's head. However, to describe the height of a person, the hand is held *vertically* (palm out, thumb on top), as if it were resting on the *back* of the person's head. To describe a person's height using a horizontal hand is to dismiss him or her as an animal.
- North Americans often indicate length by holding both hands out with the index fingers extended. This means that the length is the distance between the two fingers. However, two pointing fingers is an obscene gesture in Colombia. Colombians indicate length by extending their right arm and placing their left hand at the point on the arm where the distance from the fingertips on the right hand to the point marked by the left hand is equal to the length being indicated.

Country Background

History

Colombia has been inhabited for thousands of years. At the time of Christopher Columbus' discovery of the New World, Colombia was home to several Amerindian peoples. None of these native peoples could overcome the Spanish conquistadores, who arrived in the early 1500s.

Colombia became part of the Spanish Viceroyalty of New Granada, which encompassed present-day Ecuador, Panama, Colombia, and Venezuela. Bogotá was designated the capital of the entire Viceroyalty in 1717.

Along with other colonies, Colombia sought independence from Spain at the beginning of the nineteenth century. Under its first president, Simón Bolívar, Colombia achieved independence from Spain in 1813. Bolívar also founded Colombia's Conservative Party; his rivals founded the Liberals. These two parties continue to this day, and have frequently alternated as the party in power.

An attempt to keep the Viceroyalty lands together as the Republic of Greater Colombia failed; Ecuador and Venezuela left the union in 1830. Panama remained a part of Colombia until 1903, when it broke away with the support of the United States of America. (Colombia had refused to yield the concessions the United States wanted in building the Panama Canal, so United States set Panama up as a client state.)

Political instability plagued Colombia throughout the nineteenth century. The struggle for power between the Conservatives and the Liberals often resulted in bloodshed. Fortunately, Colombia has been more stable in the twentieth century, and Colombians are proud of their democratic traditions.

The current constitution dates back to 1886, although there have been numerous amendments since then. There has been a peaceful transfer of power in Colombia since 1957.

Type of Government

The Republic of Colombia is a unitary, multiparty republic with two legislative houses: the 102-seat Senate and the 161-seat House of Representatives. The president is elected to a single four-year term and cannot succeed himself. The president is both chief of state and head of the government.

CULTURAL NOTE

Colombia is divided by three mountain ranges, and this has led to the development of strong regional movements. When these movements fail to find common ground with the government in Bogotá, guerrilla movements (usually left-wing) evolve. Some guerrilla movements accept government amnesty and become political parties, such as the *April 19 Movement Democratic Alliance* (a.k.a. *M-19*). Others continue to fight the government. The end of the cold war also ended foreign subsidies for Marxist guerrillas; therefore, some have increasingly turned to kidnapping and drug smuggling to earn funds. However, there is no mistaking the guerrillas for the drug cartels; the late Pablo Escobar failed to convince anyone that his Medellín drug cartel was a political organization.

Language

The official language is Spanish; some Amerindians speak only their native languages. Many business people understand English.

Religion

The vast majority (95 percent) of Colombians are Roman Catholic. The constitution guarantees freedom of religion.

Demographics

The population numbers around 33 million. Mestizos constitute the majority, some 58 percent of the population. Europeans account for 20 percent (Colombia's power elite come from this group). There are 4 percent of African descent (living on the north coastal areas), 14 percent mulatto, and 3 percent mixed African-Amerindian. Pure-blooded Amerindians now constitute only 1 percent of the population.

Cultural Orientation

Cognitive Styles: How Colombians Organize and Process Information

In Colombia one perceives an openness to discuss any topic, but do not expect attitudes to change based upon these discussions. Colombians process information primarily on a subjective, associative level unless they have extensive higher education. They tend not to abstract to higher principles, but rather treat each situation as a unique experience.

Negotiation Strategies: What Colombians Accept as Evidence

Feelings are the primary source of truth. Colombians' interpersonal reality is such that they will give you the "truth" as they think it should be or as you would like it to be. Thus, their use of facts is nebulous. There are no ideologies strong enough to make faith a source of the truth.

Value Systems: The Basis for Behavior

The drug cartels cut across all levels of Colombian society. The following three sections identify the Value Systems in the predominant culture—their methods of dividing right from wrong, good from evil, and so forth.

Locus of Decision Making

There are informal, yet very powerful decision-making groups called *roscas*. Individuals make their own decisions but are influenced by their need to satisfy their families or groups. Kinship plays a major role in one's business associations because traditional elements of trust and mutual dependence among relatives are very strong, no matter how distant the relationship.

Sources of Anxiety Reduction

It is one's role in the social structure and the presence of the extended family that gives a sense of stability to life. This also brings anxiety, as one must be a success in the eyes of both the extended family and society. There is a strong need for consensus in the group, but values differ with the situation, and the rules are learned only by experience.

Issues of Equality/Inequality

The economic and political elite are generally European in heritage. They handle most of the business, commerce, and industry. Society is very class-conscious and is stratified by skin color and class membership, with limited vertical mobility. Colombian women are among the most politically active in Latin America, in spite of cultural restrictions on their social and work behavior.

Business Practices

Appointments

PUNCTUALITY

- As a foreigner, you are expected to be punctual. Be on time for all business appointments.
- Colombians are not known for punctuality. They may arrive at a business meeting fifteen or twenty minutes late, yet feel they are on time. Do not expect them to apologize for being late.
- Even foreigners are expected to be late to social occasions. Arrive fifteen to thirty minutes late for a party; some Colombians will be a full hour late.

- Remember that many Europeans and South Americans write the day first, then the month, then the year (e.g. December 3, 1999, is written 3.12.99). This is the case in Colombia.
- Schedule appointments at least one week before your arrival in Colombia. Do not depend upon regular mail service to arrange appointments; use the phone, fax, telex, or registered mail.
- Unless you are traveling only to the coastal lowlands, it is best to arrive a day early so that you can adjust to the high altitude. This is especially true in the capital, Bogotá, which is 8,600 feet (2,600 meters) above sea level.
- Business hours are 9:00 A.M. to 5:00 P.M., Monday through Friday.

- Store hours vary, but are generally from 9:00 A.M. to 12:30 P.M. and then from 2:00 P.M. to 7:00 P.M., Monday through Saturday.

Negotiating

- Inland Colombians are among the most formal and traditional of Latin Americans. Only along the coast does a more relaxed attitude prevail.
- It will be difficult, if not impossible, to conduct business without hiring a local contact. This contact not only will introduce you to the Colombians you must deal with, but often will pick you up at the airport and reserve a room for you at a hotel.
- When dealing with the government, you will need to use Spanish or have an interpreter. However, many business people speak English.
- Never change the members of your negotiating team. Such a change could bring the negotiations to a halt. Colombians feel that they are negotiating with people, not a corporation.
- Expect delays. It will take you a week in Colombia to accomplish something that you could do in two days in the United States.
- Avoid discussing politics, terrorism, or illegal drugs in Colombia.
- Avoid any comparisons between the United States and Colombia.
- Colombians are very proud of their nation and its achievements. It is a good idea to be informed about Colombian culture, literature, and history, or, at least, to show curiosity about such things.
- Business cards printed with English on one side and the translation in Spanish on the other are most effective. These should be presented with the Spanish side facing your Colombian colleague.

Business Entertaining

- Lunch is the main meal of the day, and is a popular choice for a business meal.

*d*inner is normally eaten between 7:00 and 9:00 P.M., but a dinner party will begin and end later. Guests will not arrive until at least 8:00 P.M., and people will sit down to dinner any time from 10:00 P.M. to midnight. Many people eat something before going to a dinner party, so that they will not starve (or be drunk) by the time dinner begins. A dinner party will end soon after the meal, but a cocktail party (with dancing) may go on until 5:00 A.M. Expect formal dress for either event.

CULTURAL NOTE

- Colombians have a tradition of hospitality and frequently invite guests to their homes.
- Let the host be the first to make a toast; then you might wish to make one.
- Theoretically, the person who has initiated the invitation will pay for a meal in a restaurant. In practice, you may have to fight for the check even when you issued the invitation.
- Leave a small amount of food on your plate to demonstrate that you have had enough to eat.

Time

- Colombia is five hours behind Greenwich Mean Time (G.M.T. - 5), which is the same as U.S. Eastern Standard Time.

Protocol

Greetings

- The standard greeting is the handshake. It is also used when departing.
- Among close friends, women may clasp forearms or kiss each other on one cheek. Men embrace and slap each other's back; this manly hug is called the *abrazo*.
- Colombians often complain that North Americans and Europeans don't know how to greet someone. Colombians take a long time in greetings; they feel that this conveys respect for the other person. After the handshake (or hug), Colombians ask numerous polite questions. North Americans typically progress beyond the greeting phase after one or two questions. Expect inquiries as to your health, your trip, your relatives, and any friends or acquaintances you have in common. Don't rush! Rushing is interpreted as callousness or disrespect.

Titles/Forms of Address

- Do not address a Colombian by his or her first name unless invited to do so. In general, only children, family members, and close friends address each other by their first names.
- Persons who do not use professional titles should be addressed as Mr., Mrs., or Miss, plus their surname. In Spanish, these are:
  - Mr. = *Señor*
  - Mrs. = *Señora*
  - Miss = *Señorita*
- Most Hispanics have two surnames: one from their father, which is listed first, followed by one from their mother. Only the father's surname is commonly used when addressing someone; e.g., Señor Antonio Felipe Martinez García is addressed as Señor Martinez and Señorita Ana María Gutierrez Herrera is addressed as Señorita Gutierrez. When a woman marries, she usually adds her husband's surname and goes by that surname. If the two people in the above example married, she would be known as Señora Ana María Gutierrez Herrera de Martinez. Most people would refer to her as Señora de Martinez, or, less formally, Señora Martinez.
- The only professional title in common use is *Doctor* (*Doctora* for women). However, it is often applied to any accomplished or educated person, whether or not he or she has a Ph.D. Indeed, the poor often refer to any upper-class person as *Doctor*.

Gestures

- Colombians stand somewhat closer together when conversing than do North Americans. However, Colombians engage in less physical contact during conversations than some South Americans.
- The formality of inland Colombians extends to their mannerisms; they do not engage in expansive gestures and animation. Residents of the coastal regions tend to be more expressive and less formal.

- It is considered impolite to yawn in public.
- Colombians indicate that someone is stingy by tapping their fingers on their elbow.
- The North American "O.K." gesture (thumb and forefinger curled into a circle) has a different meaning in Colombia. A Colombian places the circle over his nose to indicate that someone is homosexual.
- Bare feet are acceptable only at the beach. Slippers or sandals should be worn at all other times, even when going to or from the bathroom.
- In a restaurant, some Colombians summon a waiter by raising their hands over their head and clapping. Others use a hissing sound. Neither method is considered courteous, and both should be avoided by foreigners.

 ## Gifts

- If you are given a gift, you should be very effusive in your thanks.
- When invited to a home for a meal, bring flowers, pastries, or chocolates. Avoid lilies and marigolds, which are used at funerals.
- You may give perfume to women.
- If you know you will meet a business associate's family, it is a good idea to bring a gift for the children.
- Although gifts are always appreciated, a wrapped gift is generally not opened in the presence of the giver, since Colombians feel that this would make them appear greedy. Indeed, the gift may never be mentioned again. You can be sure, though, that it was noted and appreciated.
- Other good gifts are fine wines and liquors. Do not bring foreign beer; Colombia brews fine local beers.

 ## Dress

- In general, formality increases as you move inland. The coastal resort areas are the most casual, and shorts may be worn in public there.
- On the coast, where it is hot, some men will wear a *guayabera* shirt to work, and women will wear sleeveless dresses. Foreigners, however, are expected to dress more formally for business meetings.
- Inland, it is important to adopt conservative business attire. Men should wear a jacket and tie even in hot weather. Suits in dark colors are preferred. Expect to wear the jacket and tie to social occasions as well.
- Women should dress conservatively and modestly. A suit or dress is appropriate for business, while a cocktail dress will be required for most social occasions.
- Although Colombia is an equatorial country, the high elevations of some cities result in cool weather. Wool sweaters or jackets are needed in Bogotá and sometimes in Medellín.

SAN JOSE

Costa Rica

*i*n 1987, Costa Rican President Oscar Arias Sánches won the Nobel Peace Prize for authoring the Central American Peace Plan.

Country Background

History

Costa Rica (meaning "rich coast") was discovered by Columbus in 1502 and colonized by Spain. Together with other Central American countries, it gained independence in 1821 through a nonviolent revolution. These countries formed the United Provinces of Central America, but when this state collapsed in 1838, Costa Rica became an independent republic.

Unlike other Central American nations, Costa Rica has developed and maintained a stable democratic government. Only three military coups have broken this pattern. Since the current constitution prohibits an army, peace is maintained by the Civilian and Rural Guard. Turbulent situations in neighboring Nicaragua and Panama, however, continually threaten peace.

Type of Government

The government is a unitary multiparty republic, composed of a president, a unicameral legislative assembly made up of fifty-seven deputies, and the Supreme Court of Justice. The president is both the chief of state and the head of the government. The president and his deputies may only hold one successive four-year term of office. Judges are elected to eight-year terms. A fourth branch of government, the Supreme Electoral Tribunal, oversees the electoral process.

The people of Costa Rica are politically active and proud of their government. Elections, with voting mandatory for anyone over eighteen years old, are likened to a party, with festivities and celebrations lasting many days. Governments swing from moderately conservative to moderately progressive, as the political parties traditionally alternate power with each election.

Language

The official language is Spanish. Creole is also spoken. English is widely understood, especially in urban centers and among the young.

Costa Rica's institutes of higher learning award degrees in many fields—including law. Costa Rica has a higher number of lawyers per capita than any other country in Central America.

Religion

Roman Catholicism is the official religion. However, various evangelical Protestant sects have been growing.

Demographics

The population of three million is 95 percent of European descent (including some 7 percent mestizo—mixed European and Indian blood), 3 percent black or mulatto, 1 percent East Asian (primarily Chinese), and 1 percent Amerindian.

About 51 percent of Costa Ricans live in urban centers.

Cultural Orientation

Cognitive Styles: How Costa Ricans Organize and Process Information

Costa Ricans love to use language and are open to discussions on any topic. However, they have very strong beliefs and are not easily persuaded to another's point of view. They are primarily associative in their thinking and look at each situation as a unique happening. They are intuitive and use rules only as guidelines.

Negotiation Strategies: What Costa Ricans Accept as Evidence

Facts are usually interpreted through subjective feelings, though Costa Ricans will sometimes use faith in a humanitarian ideology as a source of the truth. Frank criticism is rare because the use of tentative language is much more conducive to saving face. The truth is what is believed at the moment.

Value Systems: The Basis for Behavior

This is a very humanitarian, fiercely democratic culture with a belief in peace through negotiations. The following three sections identify the Value Systems in the predominant culture—their methods of dividing right from wrong, good from evil, and so forth.

Locus of Decision-Making

The individual is central to the culture. He or she is independent, but with a strong sense of responsibility to the family or group. Favored treatment is given to kin. Upward mobility often means using the group for one's own advancement. One trusts only those with whom one's uniqueness is appreciated. Costa Ricans have a strong self-image but loath arrogance and expect people in high places to act humble.

Sources of Anxiety Reduction

Family lineage is important to who you are; it determines your identification and status. Success is in the eyes of the extended family. There is a strong work ethic, but progress toward the goal of the project is not as important as working on the project. Costa Ricans prefer to think small, go slowly, and avoid risks, anxiety, or overwork. They generally try to avoid precise commitments, although they may make them vocally to avoid hurting your feelings.

Issues of Equality/Inequality

Costa Ricans believe strongly in the philosophy of the equality of all people because each one is a unique individual—more so than any other Latin American culture. Wealth and family lineage are the primary determinants of social position. There is a strong emphasis on the equality and dignity of work regardless of your social class. Machismo is very strong, with the double standard being accepted by both sexes. The husband is the center of the family; all concede to his wishes. However, women maintain their own identity apart from that of their husband in all legal and business matters.

Business Practices

Appointments

PUNCTUALITY

- ◆ Costa Ricans are by far the most punctual people in Central America.
- ◆ While punctuality is not as quite important as in the United States, North Americans are expected to be on time for appointments.
- ◆ Since Costa Ricans allow themselves only a limited time for their midday break, everyone is expected to be on time for a business lunch.

- Remember that many Europeans and South Americans write the day first, then the month, then the year (e.g. December 3, 1999, is written 3.12.99). This is the case in Costa Rica.
- Business hours are 8:00 A.M. to 5:00 P.M., Monday through Friday and 8:00 to 11:00 A.M., Saturday. Businesses close for lunch from 11:00 or 11:30 A.M. to 1:00 P.M., daily.
- Government offices are open from 8:00 A.M. to 4:00 P.M., Monday through Friday.
- Good times to do business in Costa Rica are February to March and September to November. The rainy season runs from May through November (with rain heaviest on the Caribbean coast), and popular vacation times are December and January and around the Christmas and Easter holidays.
- Make appointments in advance by mail or cable and reconfirm before arrival.
- In the public sector, the fiscal year is the same as the calendar year.

 Negotiating

- Decision makers are readily accessible and also frank and open in discussions. Business takes place on a personal basis in Costa Rica. It is important to establish a relationship with your Costa Rican counterpart before proceeding to business discussions.
- There is a strong sense of personal honor and social equality on the part of the Costa Rican businessperson. More so than anywhere else in Central America, every person is assumed to have value and dignity. Therefore, avoid any behavior that would demean another person, especially in public.

- Decisions are made by consensus of all involved, not just by top officials. This may slow the process down; avoid showing impatience. Impatience lowers your credibility and puts you at a disadvantage.
- Because persons at all levels of a company have input, remember to be polite to everyone you meet.
- Foreign investment is aggressively competitive in Costa Rica. Contacts are very important to doing business. Remember to treat your business counterparts with the same respect with which you would treat a valued client in the U.S.A.
- Time estimates and deadlines may not be strictly observed. Also, late payments are very frequent. Be prepared to travel to Costa Rica several times to finalize plans. Be tolerant of delays, and remain flexible by building these factors into your own plans.
- Women in business will meet with greater acceptance in Costa Rica than in other Latin American countries. Women have even been elected vice president of Costa Rica.
- Costa Ricans are much more formal and serious than other Latin Americans. Therefore, keep jackets on during business meetings.
- Have business cards, proposals, and other material printed in both English and Spanish. While most executives speak English well, many technical workers do not.

 Business Entertaining

- Do not visit homes unexpectedly unless you know the family very well.
- Good topics of conversation are children, families, and the beauty of Costa Rica.
- The Costa Rican people enjoy discussing politics, particularly with foreigners. Costa Rica's history of stable democracy provides a good topic for conversation. Foreigners should have some knowledge of the political history of Central America in order to speak intelligently on the subject.
- Most business entertaining takes place in the evening, since lunch is the main meal of the day. Spouses are welcome at business dinners.

Time
- Local time is six hours behind Greenwich Mean Time (G.M.T. - 6); this is one hour behind U.S. Eastern Standard Time (E.S.T. - 1).

Protocol

 Greetings

- Men will shake hands with other men in greeting. Women will often pat each other on the right forearm or shoulder instead of shaking hands.
- Women who are close friends may hug or kiss each other on the cheek. However, Costa Rican men do not usually hug other men. The hearty male *abrazo* (backslapping embrace) seen in other Latin American countries is rare in Costa Rica.
- In rural areas, some men will touch their hat and nod instead of shaking hands.

- Costa Ricans who are used to greeting North Americans may offer a firm handshake, but others' handshakes will tend to be limp with a loose grip. Adjust your grip to the other person's handshake.
- Do not refer to the people as *ricans*, since this word has a bad connotation. The people of Costa Rica are referred to as *ticos*.
- At parties, it is customary to be introduced to and shake hands with everyone in the room.

Titles/Forms of Address

- Most people you meet should be addressed with a title and their surname. Only children, family members, and close friends address each other by their first names.
- Persons who do not have professional titles should be addressed as Mr., Mrs., or Miss, plus their surname. In Spanish, these are:
  - Mr. = *Señor*
  - Mrs. = *Señora*
  - Miss = *Señorita*
- Most Hispanics have two surnames: one from their father, which is listed first, followed by one from their mother. Only the father's surname is commonly used when addressing someone; e.g., Señor Juan Antonio Martinez García is addressed as Señor Martinez and Señorita Ana María Gutierrez Herrera is addressed as Señorita Gutierrez. When a woman marries, she usually adds her husband's surname and goes by that surname. If the two people in the above example married, she would be known as Señora Ana María Gutierrez Herrera de Martinez. Most people would refer to her as Señora de Martinez or, less formally, Señora Martinez.
- When a person has a title, it is important to address him or her by that title. Usually the title alone is preferred; no surname is necessary. A Ph.D. or a physician is called *Doctor*. Teachers prefer the title *Profesor*, engineers go by *Ingeniero*, architects are *Arquitecto*, and lawyers are *Abogado*.

Gestures

- Making a fist with the thumb sticking out between the middle and index fingers is obscene. This gesture is known as the "fig."
- Most North American gestures will be understood in Costa Rica.
- Don't rest your feet on any furniture except items expressly designed for that purpose.

Gifts

- Costa Ricans will exchange gifts frequently for all kinds of special occasions.
- Because of the large number of U.S. citizens in Costa Rica and the lack of import restrictions, U.S. goods are freely available there. It will not be easy to find a U.S. product for a gift that can't be bought in Costa Rica.
- If you are invited to a home for dinner, bring flowers, chocolates, scotch, or wine. Do not bring calla lilies; they are associated with funerals.

Dress

- Business: Men should wear a conservative dark suit. In warmer climates, a jacket is optional. Women should wear a dress or skirt and blouse. Pants are never worn by women.
- Casual: Shorts are worn only on the beach. Revealing clothing for women is not acceptable. Bring a sweater or jacket to wear at night in the higher elevations.
- Bring multiple changes of clothes. Because of the heat, people in Costa Rica bathe frequently—often more than once a day.

PRAGUE
•

Czech Republic

t ───────────────── **CULTURAL NOTE**

he Czech Republic has undergone two radical but nonviolent changes in recent years: the "Velvet Revolution" that removed the U.S.S.R.-backed Communists from power and the peaceful separation of Czechoslovakia into two independent nations, the Czech and Slovak Republics. Even at their most angry moment, when protesters jammed Prague's Wenceslas Square demanding the removal of the Communists, the protesters admonished one another not to trample on the flower beds!

Country Background

History

The Czech Republic represents the westernmost migration of Slavic tribes into Europe. During the fifth century A.D., these tribes arrived in what would eventually become Czechoslovakia. Two distinct Slavic groups emerged: the Czechs, who settled in the west, and the Slovenes (or Slovaks), who took the east. By 900 A.D. the Slovak tribes were conquered by the Magyars (Hungarians), who formed the short-lived Great Moravian Empire. In the west, the city of Prague was developing into one of the most important cultural and political centers of the Holy Roman Empire. In the fifteenth century, Prague became a focal point for the Protestant Reformation. Protestant leader Jan Hus, burned at the stake in 1415, is still a national hero to the Czechs. But the Battle on the White Mountain in 1620 put an end to Czech resistance, and both Czechs and Slovaks came to be ruled by the Austrian Hapsburg dynasty until the twentieth century.

While all of Czechoslovakia spent centuries under the control of the Austro-Hungarian Empire, these two ethnic areas developed independently. The western Czech provinces (Bohemia and Moravia) were industrialized; they prospered under direct Austrian control. However, the eastern Slovenian lands were run by the Hungarians; Slovenia was deliberately kept agricultural and undeveloped.

After its defeat in World War I, the Austro-Hungarian Empire was broken up into smaller states in accordance with Woodrow Wilson's principles of self-determination. The Czechs and the Slovenes found themselves lumped together in the newly independent state of Czechoslovakia. The aggressive, educated, and more numerous Czechs quickly took charge, and the Slovenes felt excluded from their own government. The existence of other minorities within the Czechoslovakian borders, notably the ethnic Germans in the Sudetenland, also caused friction. Nevertheless, Czechoslovakia managed to remain a democracy until it was overrun by Nazi Germany in 1938-1939.

d ———————————————————————**CULTURAL NOTE**
uring World War II, the Czech areas were kept under direct German control, but the Slovene territory was allowed to become a pro-German Slovak Republic from 1939 to 1945. Its collaborationist president was the Catholic Monsignor Josef Tiso, and he attempted to run an anti-Semitic, theocratic "parish republic." The minor differences between the Czech and Slovak languages were emphasized, and Tiso presented himself as a defender of Slovak Catholicism against the secular decadence of the Czechs.

This heritage of distrust between Czechs and Slovaks is one of the greatest problems facing the new republics today. While the Protestant Jan Hus is a hero to Czechs but not to the Catholic Slovenes, the Slovaks still admire Msgr. Tiso, whom the Czechs feel was justly executed as a war criminal in 1947.

Liberated by the Red Army in 1945, Czechoslovakia became a Soviet satellite. Despite repressive measures, the Communist leadership in Prague was unable to keep protests from periodically erupting, notably in 1968 and 1977. The Warsaw Pact invasion that put down the 1968 "Prague Spring" embittered the Czechoslovaks against everything to do with the U.S.S.R., including the Russian language (the mandatory foreign language taught in schools). Finally, the tide of reform that washed over Eastern Europe in 1989 allowed the Czechoslovak people to elect a truly popular, non-Communist government. Czechoslovakia became a parliamentary democracy and remained so until 1992, when political and social events resulted initially in the establishment of a multiparty republic of two equal states, and eventually in two separate countries—the Czech and Slovak Republics.

As an independent state, the new Czech Republic came into being on January 1, 1993.

Type of Government
The new Czech Republic is a multiparty parliamentary democracy. The president is the chief of state—a largely ceremonial office. The prime minister is the head of the government. Parliamentary procedure is in a state of flux, but the parliament has been meeting as two separate houses, an upper Senate and a lower House.

Language
The official language is Czech, which is a West Slavic language related to Polish. Although the Czechs and the Slovaks have gone to great lengths to differentiate their languages, the Czech and Slovak languages are actually quite similar and are mutually intelligible.

Education
The populace is well-educated, with a 99 percent literacy rate. Emphasis has been placed on scientific research, and the educated elite is the equal of any in the world.

Religion
As religion was actively discouraged under the former Communist regime, the numbers of worshipers is now in flux. Roman Catholics and various forms of Protestants predominate, although a significant number of Czech are atheists.

Demographics

The ten million inhabitants of the Czech Republic are primarily Czech (94 percent), although there are some Slovaks (4 percent) and Gypsies (2 percent).

Cultural Orientation

Cognitive Styles: How Czechs Organize and Process Information

The Czechs have always been open to information on most issues. They tend to be more analytic than associative, but they value relationships more than obedience to abstract rules of behavior.

Negotiation Strategies: What Czechs Accept as Evidence

Czechs find truth through a mixture of subjective feelings and objective facts. Their faith in the ideologies of humanitarianism and democracy will influence the truth in nearly every situation.

Value Systems: The Basis for Behavior

The amicable separation of Czechoslovakia into the Czech and Slovak Republic is an example of the humanitarian value systems of both cultures. The following three sections identify the Value Systems in the predominant culture—their methods of dividing right from wrong, good from evil, and so forth.

Locus of Decision Making

The responsibility for decision making rests on the shoulders of the individual. Individualism has always been encouraged, and individual achievement is more important than family in determining status. Czechs feel that they have a right to a private life; their friends are few and specific to their needs. Czechs feel that the same values should apply to all members of their culture.

Sources of Anxiety Reduction

With the demise of Communist rule, the guarantee of full employment ended. This produces considerable day-to-day anxiety. Although the traditional role of the family as the basic educating and socializing unit has been weakened, the family unit is still recognized as a stabilizing force. The Church seems to be regaining its influence on family life and social structure, and with this comes more security for both the individual and the family.

Issues of Equality/Inequality

The homogeneity of the Czech culture has eliminated most of the ethnic bias that existed before the breakup of Czechoslovakia. There is keen competition for status, but when one is recognized for one's accomplishments, one gains prominence among equals. The desire for power may undercut the humanitarian need for equality. This drive for power can yield strong, hierarchical structures in government, business, and society.

The husband is the titular head of the home. However, since most women work outside the home, husbands take some responsibility for raising the children.

Women have complete legal, political, social, and economic equality with men.

Business Practices

Appointments

PUNCTUALITY

+ Punctuality is important; be on time for business and social engagements.

- Remember that many Europeans and South Americans write the day first, then the month, then the year (e.g. December 3, 1999, is written 3.12.99). This is the case in the Czech Republic.
- For many years, Russian was the foreign language most frequently studied in schools. Since the Velvet Revolution of 1989, Western languages like English and German have become the most popular. Expect to hire a translator; most people old enough to be in positions of business authority will not have studied English.
- Appointments should be made well in advance. Allow two weeks' notice for an appointment made by telephone or telex. Give a full month for appointments made by mail, as even air mail letters may take a week to be delivered.
- Business letters may be written in English, although your counterpart will be favorably impressed if you take the trouble to translate the letter into Czech.
- It is generally advisable to address letters to a business rather than to an individual executive.
- As the business day begins early and ends in mid-afternoon, expect to schedule your appointments between 9:00 A.M. and 12 noon or between 1:00 and 3:00 P.M.
- Most Czechs receive four weeks of vacation per year. The traditional vacation time runs from mid-July to mid-August, so do not expect to be able to conduct business during this period.
- Business hours are 8:00 or 8:30 A.M. to 4:00 or 5:15 P.M., Monday through Friday.
- Store hours are 8:00 or 9:00 A.M. to 5:00 or 6:00 P.M., Monday through Friday. Some establishments will be open on Saturdays until noon. Small shops may close for lunch from noon to 2:00 P.M.

 ## Negotiating

- Expect the decision-making process to operate at a slower pace than in the United States
- Many Czechs have adopted the German propensity for slow, methodical planning. Every aspect of the deal you propose will be pored over by many executives. Do not anticipate being able to speed up this process.
- Only a few entrepreneurs are ready to move more quickly. However, you should move cautiously with the ones who offer you a partnership, as you will be the one putting hard currency into the enterprise.
- The radical alteration of business laws has resulted in a tangle of regulation. Don't depend on your joint-venture partner to understand the law. Hire a Czech business lawyer.
- While Czechs are known for their hospitality, they may take a lot of time to establish a close business relationship. Keep in mind that their contact with foreigners was restricted until recently.

- Executives usually understand enough English to decipher a business card, so it is not necessary to have your card translated. However, it is preferable to have promotional materials and instruction manuals translated into Czech.
- Bring plenty of cards; quite a few Czechs may wish to exchange business cards with you.
- If your company has been around for many years, the date of its founding should be on your business card.
- Since education is highly respected, be sure to include any degree above the bachelor's level on your card.

- Do not get down to business too quickly. Czechs typically converse before talking business. Expect to be asked about your flight, your accommodations, where you are from in America, your impressions of the country, and so forth.
- Your counterparts may not mind asking or being asked personal questions. You will want to ask about an executive's family. Part of establishing a relationship is expressing an interest in each other's family, although it may be a long time before you actually meet any of them.
- While political discussions cannot be avoided, don't ask embarrassing political questions. Many of the people with enough money to conduct business are former Communists or black marketeers. Also do your best to avoid siding with Czechs against Slovaks, or vice versa.
- Czechs tend to be well informed about politics and to have firm political opinions. They are also honest, and may tell you their opinions. While they dislike what Communism has done to their country, they may not be as approving of the West as you might expect.
- Sports are a good topic for conversation; soccer, ice hockey, hiking, and cycling are popular sports. Music is a good topic as well.
- The Czechs also make some excellent beers. The pilsner style of beer was developed here. The town of Budweis (now renamed Ceské Budějovice), after which "Budweiser" was named is in the Czech Republic. A beer drinker will be happy to explain about Czech beer
- Coffee is usually served during business meetings. Taste it before you add sugar; it may already be sweetened. The coffee is Turkish, and will probably have grounds at the bottom.

Business Entertaining

- Historically, business meetings have been confined to offices. Business lunches were rare; the only meal one shared with a business associate was a celebratory dinner. However, this segregation was due in part to restrictive government regulations—fraternization with Westerners was actively discouraged. Czechs are becoming more accustomed to Western business practices, including business lunches.
- Breakfast meetings are uncommon in the Czech Republic. However, business lunches are becoming popular.
- At a business luncheon, be aware that business may be discussed before and (sometimes) after the meal, but rarely during the meal itself. If you are invited out to a luncheon, you may offer to pay, but expect your host to decline your offer. Insist on paying only when you have made the invitation.
- The few restaurants tend to be very busy. Always make a reservation. It may be easier to ask your counterpart to choose a restaurant; just make sure to explain that you intend to pay for the meal.

- Do not anticipate good service in all restaurants; many were recently Communist-run, and the staff got the same pay no matter how busy they were. Additional customers were simply an inconvenience. These attitudes take time to change.
- Because of the lack of good restaurants, you may be invited to eat lunch in the company cafeteria.
- Czechs do not often entertain business associates in their homes. If you are invited into a home, consider it a great honor. Do not be surprised if the living quarters are very crowded.
- A host will invite you to eat additional portions. It is traditional to turn down the first invitation.
- When eating, always use utensils; very few items are eaten with the hands. Place your utensils together on one side of the plate when you have finished eating. If you just wish to pause between courses, cross your utensils on the plate.

Time
- The Czech Republic is one hour ahead of Greenwich Mean Time (G.M.T. + 1), or six hours ahead of U.S. Eastern Standard Time (E.S.T. + 6).

Protocol

Greetings
- Always shake hands, firmly but briefly, when introduced. When introduced to a Czech woman or an elderly person, wait to see if he or she extends a hand before offering to shake.
- In formal social situations, older men may kiss the hand of a woman in greeting. However, foreigners are not expected to kiss hands.
- In both business and social situations, always shake hands upon arriving and upon departing from any meeting.
- When several people are being introduced, take turns shaking hands. It is impolite to reach over someone else's handshake.
- Never keep your left hand in your pocket while shaking hands with your right.
- In formal situations, it is better to be introduced by a third person than to introduce yourself. However, in informal situations, it is appropriate to introduce yourself.
- When you are the third person making an introduction between two parties, give the name of the younger (or lower-ranking) person first.

Titles/Forms of Address
- The order of names is the same as in the United States: The first name is followed by the surname.
- Traditionally, only family members and close friends address each other by their first names. While young people are using first names more frequently, most business people you meet will prefer to be called by their title or surname.
- The decision to address each other by first names is arrived at by mutual consent.

- When speaking to persons who do not have professional titles, use Mr., Mrs., or Miss and the surname:
  - Mr. = *Pan* (pronounced "Pahn")
  - Mrs. (or Ms.) = *Pani* ("PAH-nee")
  - Miss = *Slecna* ("SLEH-chnah")
- It is important to use professional titles. Attorneys, architects, engineers, and other professionals will expect you to address them as *Pan* or *Pani* plus title. This goes for anyone with a Ph.D. as well.

 Gestures

- To get someone's attention, raise your hand, palm facing out, with only the index finger extended. Avoid waving or beckoning.
- When sitting, cross one knee over the other, rather than resting your ankle on the other knee. Do not prop your feet up on anything other than a footstool.
- The eldest or highest-ranking person enters a room first. If their age and status are the same, men enter before women.
- When a man and a woman walk down a street, the man walks closest to the curb. On a path or a corridor, the man walks on the woman's left. When there are three people, a sole man walks between the women; a sole woman walks between the men. If two women are walking together, the younger woman should walk on the curb side (or on the left).
- Don't talk to someone with your hands in your pockets or while chewing gum.

 Gifts

- Under the Communist regime, the frequent shortages made gift giving simple: You gave whatever was in short supply in Czechoslovakia. Now that most consumer items are freely available (albeit expensive), gift giving is more of a problem.
- By and large, businessmen do not give or expect to receive expensive gifts. A gift should be of good quality, but not exorbitantly expensive.
- Appropriate gifts include good-quality pens, pocket calculators, cigarette lighters, and imported wine or liquor, especially scotch, bourbon or cognac.
- When invited to dinner at a Czech home, bring a bouquet of unwrapped flowers (if you can find some) for your hostess. The bouquet should have an uneven number of flowers, but not thirteen. Red roses are reserved for romantic situations, and calla lilies are for funerals.

 Dress

- Business dress tends to be conservative. Of course, under the former regime the selection of clothing was very limited. You may encounter business people who celebrate their newfound freedom by dressing in trendy European styles.
- Generally, businessmen wear dark suits, ties, and white shirts. Businesswomen also dress conservatively, in dark suits or dresses and white blouses.
- Follow the lead of your colleagues with regard to removing jackets or ties in hot weather. The more formal executives may remain fully dressed in sweltering heat.

- Business wear is also appropriate for most formal social events: parties, dinners, and the theater.
- Formal wear is expected for the opening night of an opera, concert, or play. Men are expected to wear their best dark suit or tuxedo, and women a long evening gown. Virtually every Czech institution, including business associations and libraries, hosts a formal ball sometime during February, and formal wear is required for them.
- Casual wear is essentially the same as in the United States. Jeans are ubiquitous, but they should not be worn, torn, or dirty.

COPENHAGEN

Denmark

CULTURAL NOTE

*d*anish children are often taught to greet people formally. Do not be surprised if a Danish child gives you a crisp handshake, maintains direct eye contact, and follows it with a bow.

Country Background

History

During the Middle Ages, the Viking raiders and conquerors were largely Danes. For a time the Danish realm included most of Scandinavia and England. The Danish kingdom was a major power in northern Europe until the seventeenth century, when it lost a large portion of land to what is now southern Sweden. As punishment for supporting Napoleon, the Congress of Vienna took Norway from Denmark in 1815.

Denmark has existed since around the year 750. The monarchy became constitutional in 1849.

Danish possessions include the Faeroe Islands and Greenland (the world's largest island). Iceland was a former Danish possession, but it declared its independence when Denmark was occupied by Nazi Germany in World War II.

CULTURAL NOTE

*u*nited States-Danish relations are friendly. There are approximately 225 American firms with branches in Copenhagen. Although there is no U.S. Chamber of Commerce in Denmark, there is an American Club.

Type of Government

The Kingdom of Denmark is today a constitutional monarchy. The symbolic chief of state is the queen or king. The only real power in that position lies in the ability to appoint the prime minister (who is the head of the government) and the cabinet ministers. These officials represent the true power in government.

There is one legislative body, the 179-seat *Folketing*.

Language

Danish is the official language. English is taught after the fifth grade; it is the predominant second language, and a majority of Danes speak it with a high level of competency. Most are eager to use their English with visitors from the English-speaking countries.

Religion
The official religion of Denmark is Evangelical Lutheran. The vast majority (around 97 percent) of Danes belong to this church.

Demographics
The population of Denmark is a little over 5.1 million. The two largest cities are Copenhagen (the capital) and Århus. Almost 99 percent of the Danes live in cities. Denmark continues to have an extremely homogeneous society, but the numbers of Eskimos and Faeroese are growing. Denmark's per capita GDP, at $20,000, is one of the highest in the world, and personal income is evenly distributed.

Cultural Orientation

Cognitive Styles: How Danes Organize and Process Information
The Danes are a proud people who tend to be satisfied with their own accomplishments and thus do not need (and are not open to) information or help from others. Their education is moving away from rote learning and toward the application of abstractive, conceptual thinking. They tend to follow universalistic rules of behavior rather than react to particular situations.

Negotiation Strategies: What Danes Accept as Evidence
Truth is centered in a faith in the ideology of social welfare, with objective facts used to prove a point. Subjective feelings do not play a part in negotiation processes.

Value Systems: The Basis for Behavior
Denmark is a social welfare state in which the quality of life and environmental issues are given top priority. The following three sections identify the Value Systems in the predominant culture-their methods of dividing right from wrong, good from evil, and so forth.

Locus of Decision Making
Danes have a strong belief in individual decisions within the social welfare system. There is a strong self-orientation, but with an obligation to help those who are not able to help themselves. There is an emphasis on individual initiative and achievement, with one's ability being more important than his or her station in life. The dignity and worth of the individual is emphasized, along with the right to a private life and opinions.

Sources of Anxiety Reduction
Life's uncertainties are accepted, and anxiety is reduced by a strong social welfare system—the government is there to serve the people. Though individualistic, Danes are resigned to a social welfare state in which there is little distinction available through individual accomplishment. Young people are encouraged to mature early and to take risks to develop a strong self-image.

Issues of Equality/Inequality
Denmark basically has a middle-class society, with family needs as the central issue of social policy and governmental intervention. Danes strive to minimize social differences, so there is very little evidence of poverty or wealth, although they exist. Nationalism transcends social differences, and a largely homogeneous

population minimizes ethnic differences. In this society, upper-class husbands and wives share the responsibilities of child care.

Business Practices

Appointments

————————————————————————PUNCTUALITY

- ◆ Punctuality is very important; be exactly on time for all business appointments.
- ◆ Danes expect punctuality for social engagements as well.

- Remember that many Europeans and South Americans write the day first, then the month, then the year (e.g., December 3, 1999, is written 3.12.99). This is the case in Denmark.
- As in the rest of Scandinavia, summer is a time of leisure. It is both difficult and inconsiderate to try to conduct serious business during July and August. Many firms close for extended periods during these two months to allow their employees to take summer vacations. Danes have five weeks of paid vacation per year.
- Business hours vary throughout Denmark. Opening times range from 8:00 to 9:00 A.M. and closing times from 4:30 to 5:30 P.M. Offices operate on a five-day schedule.

 ## Negotiating

- The Danes tend to get down to business right away, with a minimum of small talk.
- Danes are relatively informal. You can introduce yourself to the executive with whom you will meet, rather than expecting the secretary to introduce you.
- Be prepared to give detailed briefings, since Danes are rather meticulous.
- Danes are often quite frank in their manner of speaking. Statements are often direct but are not meant to be insulting in any way.
- Avoid making any comments that could be regarded as personal. Even complimenting someone on his or her clothes can be taken as too invasive!
- The Danish sense of humor, in general terms, is more reserved or dry than the United States citizen.
- Danes find the U.S. custom of striking up conversations with people we don't know very odd. Don't be surprised or insulted if a Dane with whom you attempt to make small talk is not responsive.
- Danes are very tolerant; it is not advisable to criticize other people or systems.

 ## Business Entertaining

- The main meal of the day is dinner.
- The smorgasbord, a cold buffet, is very popular.

- Toasts in Denmark can be quite formal. Never toast your host or anyone senior to you in rank or age until he or she has toasted you first. Never taste your drink until the host has said the traditional toasting word, *Skoal.*
- A traditional Danish drink, *aquavit* (literally, "water of life"), is quite potent. Be forewarned, as Danes often like to share this alcoholic beverage with their guests.

CULTURAL NOTE

- If you are invited to a Danish home for dinner, be prompt. There is usually no predinner cocktail, so you may be led straight to the dinner table.
- In a Danish home, assume very proper manners. For example, your host will suggest where you should sit. (At the table, the host and hostess usually sit at opposite ends, with the guest of honor next to the host.)
- Expect to be at the table for a long time. Danish dinners can stretch out over four or five hours. You should not rise from the table before your hostess does.
- It is impolite to leave a host's home too soon after dinner. Cocktails are taken after dinner, not before. These may be at the table or in the main room. It is not unusual for a dinner party to last until 1 A.M.
- Danes hold their fork in their left hand, while their knife remains in the right.
- To indicate that you have finished eating, place the knife and fork side by side on the plate, pointed away from you. Be sure the fork's tines are up; tines down means that you want more food.

Time

- Local time is one hour ahead of Greenwich Mean Time (G.M.T. + 1), or six hours ahead of U.S. Eastern Standard Time (E.S.T. + 6).

CULTURAL NOTE

*A*ll foreigners visiting Denmark must register with the local police within twenty four hours of their arrival. This is normally taken care of by hotels and other public accommodations, but if you are being privately housed, you must do it yourself. Forms can be obtained from the local police or at the post office.

Protocol

Greetings

- It is common to rise when being introduced to someone, and to shake hands with both men and women. Handshakes are firm but brief. When greeting a couple, it is customary to shake hands with the woman first.
- Your colleague will usually shake your hand when leaving as well.
- Danes say the traditional greeting *heij*, which sounds exactly like the American "Hi," when both greeting and departing.
- The common U.S. greeting "Hi, how are you?" will lead a Dane to think you really want to know how he or she is doing. A preferable greeting would be "Hi, I'm pleased to meet you."

Titles/Forms of Address

- The order of Danish names is the same as in the United States: first name followed by surname.
- It is appropriate to use a person's title until the use of first names is suggested.

i **CULTURAL NOTE**

*i*f you belong to an old firm, have the date your company was established printed on your business card. Danes respect tradition.

 Gestures

- The gesture North Americans use to indicate that someone is crazy (index finger circling while pointed at one's temple) is used to insult other drivers while on the road.
- The North American "O.K." gesture (thumb and forefinger forming a circle) can be taken as an insult in Denmark.
- Summon waiters by raising your index finger.
- When ascending a flight of stairs, men precede women. When descending, women precede men.
- At the theater, enter a row with your back to the stage (so that you face people seated in the row). It is considered insulting to squeeze past seated people with your backside facing them.

 Gifts

- Gifts are not required in a business relationship.
- It is quite acceptable to bring a bouquet of flowers or chocolates to a host's home. If you wish to give flowers to your hostess, it is best to have them sent ahead of time, so as not to burden her with taking care of them when you arrive.
- An illustrated book from your region of the United States makes an appropriate gift.

 Dress

- High-ranking Danish executives frequently host black-tie dinners. Male executives should consider bringing a tuxedo along; women will need an evening gown.
- Danish business practices are similar to American traditions. Conservative dress will always be appropriate.
- Danish casual attire is still conservative, although jeans that are clean and pressed will be seen. At the beach many women wear topless bathing suits.
- Red is a positive color in Denmark.

QUITO

Ecuador

Country Background

History

Archaeological evidence indicates that Ecuador has been continuously occupied for some 5,000 years. The powerful Inca Empire reached its height in this area just prior to Columbus' discovery of the New World.

The Spanish conquistadores' arrival came at a time when the Incas were weakened by a brutal civil war. The Spanish conquest of Ecuador was complete by 1534. Ecuador became part of the Spanish Viceroyalty of Peru. The colony got off to a poor start when the conquistadores began assassinating one another. This precedent for political change accompanied by violence has been repeated many times in Ecuador.

Along with other colonies, Ecuador sought independence from Spain at the beginning of the nineteenth century. Independence was declared in 1809, but was not secured until 1822. At first, Ecuador joined with Colombia, Panama and Venezuela to form the Republic of Greater Colombia. But this turbulent union soon fell apart, and Ecuador became an independent nation in 1830.

Ecuador suffered through both political unrest and border disputes with both Colombia and Peru. Revolts and dictatorships became common; rarely did one freely elected government succeed another.

Political instability continued throughout the twentieth century. Peru invaded in 1941, and the two countries still dispute their borders. Ecuador's turbulence is reflected in the leadership of José María Velasco Ibarra, who was elected president five times between 1944 and 1972, yet was allowed to complete only one full term in office!

Despite this instability, Ecuador often managed to be better off than its neighboring countries, both politically and economically.

The current constitution was adopted in 1979, and there has been a peaceful transfer of power since then.

Type of Government

Ecuador was ruled by civilian and military dictatorships from 1968 to 1979, when a peaceful transfer of power from the military junta to the democratic civilian government occurred. Political parties have historically had difficulties with disorganized platforms (or lack of platforms), charismatic leaders who do not follow specific programs, and small factions within the parties.

The Republic of Ecuador is a unitary multiparty republic. It has a single legislative house, the National Congress. The president is both the chief of state and the head of the government, and serves a single four-year term.

According to Ecuador's constitution, the president may not be reelected, and legislators must sit out a term before running again for a two-year term.

Voting is compulsory in Ecuador from age eighteen to sixty-five for all literate citizens.

e—————————————————————**CULTURAL NOTE**
cuador is South America's second-largest producer of oil. The drop in oil prices since 1982, plus an earthquake in 1987 that crippled the country's main oil line, forced Ecuador to temporarily suspend interest payments on its foreign debt. Recent administrations have achieved some notable economic improvements and reduced the fiscal deficit. Ecuador resigned from OPEC in 1992, stating that the cartel failed to benefit smaller oil producers.

Language

The official language is Spanish; however, some Indians speak only Quechua. Many business people understand English.

Religion

The vast majority (95 percent) of Ecuadorans are Roman Catholic. The constitution guarantees freedom of religion.

Demographics

The population numbers around 11 million (1991 estimate). About 25 percent of the population is Amerindian; another 65 percent is mestizo (mixed European and Indian blood). Along the north coast lives a small black minority. The populationis evenly split between urban and rural residents.

Cultural Orientation

Cognitive Styles: How Ecuadorans Organize and Process Information

In Ecuador the basic tendency is to accept information on any topic for discussion. However, Ecuadorans are not easily moved from their positions. Their beliefs are arrived at through association and experiential thinking. They look at each particular situation rather than using universal rules or laws to guide their behavior.

Negotiation Strategies: What Ecuadorans Accept as Evidence

One's feelings about a topic or situation are the primary source of the truth. Faith in an ideology of class structure may influence the truth. Facts are less important when arguing a point.

Value Systems: The Basis for Behavior

Rigid class distinctions are supported by a strong tradition of social distance between the upper class and the common people. The following three sections identify the Value Systems in the predominant culture—their methods of dividing right from wrong, good from evil, and so forth.

Locus of Decision Making

There is a preoccupation with the individual as opposed to the group. This lends itself to the belief in *personalismo*—an exaggerated attention to one's own personal relations and status. The individual is responsible for his or her decisions. Self-identity is based on the social system and the history of the extended family. Kinship and friendship play a major role in one's business associations.

Sources of Anxiety Reduction

One's role in the social structure and the presence of the extended family and kinship groups give a sense of stability to life. The Catholic church has a strong influence on personal and social behavior. There is a strong work ethic, but progress toward the goal of the project is less important than working on the project.

Issues of Equality/Inequality

The *Sierra* elite (conservative) consider themselves the upper class by birth and intermarriage, so there is a power struggle between the *Sierra* and *Costa* (liberal). There are extreme contrasts between rich and poor, and there is a concept that powerful people are entitled to special privileges that come with an important office. Machismo is the model for young men, and they continue to expect women to be subordinate. The man is the unquestioned head of the household; the woman is responsible for managing it.

Business Practices

Appointments

PUNCTUALITY

- ◆ As a foreigner, you are expected to be punctual to all business appointments.
- ◆ Be aware that Ecuadorans do not stress punctuality among themselves. If Ecuadorans arrive at a meeting fifteen or twenty minutes late, they still feel they are on time.

- Remember that many Europeans and South Americans write the day first, then the month, then the year (e.g. December 3, 1999, is written 3.12.99). This is the case in Ecuador.
- Make appointments about two weeks in advance.

- It is best to arrive in Quito a day before you begin work, because it takes time to adjust to the high altitude.
- Business hours are 9:00 A.M. to 1:00 P.M. and 3:00 to 6:00 P.M., Monday through Friday. (However, many executives arrive late, so do not schedule appointments for earlier than 10 A.M.)
- Stores are open from 8:00 A.M. to 2:30 P.M., although some stores vary their hours.

 Negotiating

- Ecuadorans are more relaxed and informal in business settings than some other Latin Americans.
- It will be difficult to conduct business without hiring a local contact, who can be either a business consultant or an Ecuadoran lawyer.
- When dealing with the government, you will need to use Spanish or have an interpreter. However, many private business people speak English.
- Business cards printed with English on one side and the translation in Spanish on the other are most effective. These should be presented with the Spanish side facing your Ecuadoran colleague.
- Never change the members of your negotiating team. Such a change could bring the negotiations to halt. Ecuadorans feel they are negotiating with people, not a corporation.
- Expect delays and many contract iterations.
- Avoid discussing politics, especially Ecuador's relations with Peru. (The two countries have had many disputes over borders.)
- Ecuadorans are sensitive to U.S. attitudes of superiority; be careful not to give the impression that you feel that the United States is superior.
- It is a good idea to be informed about local culture and history, or at least to show curiosity about Ecuador.

 Business Entertaining

- Lunch is the main meal of the day, and is the usual business meal.
- Ecuadorans are very hospitable and friendly.
- Let the host be the first to make a toast; then you might wish to make one.
- It is considered rude to suggest an ending time for a social gathering.
- It is acceptable to order a cocktail (such as scotch) before the meal.
- Wine may be served with the lunch. Keep in mind that Ecuadorans will be accustomed to a heavy meal with alcohol at midday.
- Ecuadorans are very friendly; if you establish a good relationship, you may be invited to your associate's home or farm. Consider this an honor.
- Women should note that while it is acceptable to drink wine, Ecuadorans are not accustomed to seeing a woman drink whiskey or other hard liquor.
- If a businesswoman wishes to pay for an Ecuadoran man's meal, she should make arrangements ahead of time. If the check is presented at the end of the meal, the man will probably refuse to let her pay.

Time
- Ecuador is five hours behind Greenwich Mean Time (G.M.T. - 5), which is the same as U.S. Eastern Standard Time.

Protocol

Greetings

- The standard greeting is the handshake, both for men and women and between the sexes.
- The handshake is also used when departing.
- Among close friends, women kiss each other on one cheek. Men embrace; generally, men only honor elders (of either sex) with a kiss on one cheek.

Titles/Forms of Address

- Do not address an Ecuadoran by his or her first name unless you are invited to do so. In general, only children, family members, and close friends address each other by their first names.
- Persons who do not use professional titles should be addressed as Mr., Mrs., or Miss, plus their surname. In Spanish, these are:
  - Mr. = *Señor*
  - Mrs. = *Señora*
  - Miss = *Señorita*
- Most Hispanics have two surnames: one from their father, which is listed first, followed by one from their mother. Only the father's surname is commonly used when addressing someone; e.g., Señor Juan Antonio Martinez García is addressed as Señor Martinez and Señorita Ana María Gutierrez Herrera is addressed as Señorita Gutierrez. When a woman marries, she usually adds her husband's surname and goes by that surname. If the two people in the above example married, she would be known as Señora Ana María Gutierrez Herrera de Martinez. Most people would refer to her as Señora de Martinez or, less formally, Señora Martinez.
- Be sure to use an Ecuadoran's professional title, if he or she has one.

Gestures

- Ecuadorans stand closer together when conversing than do North Americans. There is a good deal more contact, including touching on the arm, shoulder, and lapel. Try not to back away; an Ecuadoran is likely to move forward to restore what he or she feels is the proper distance.
- Instead of using head motions to indicate "yes" or "no," it is safest to indicate consent or disagreement verbally. Not all Ecuadorans may be able to interpret your physical signals.
- It is considered impolite to yawn in public or to point at others.
- Nervous, repetitive movements (toe tapping, knee jiggling, thumb twiddling, and so forth) should be minimized. Ecuadorans find them disturbing.
- In a restaurant, some Ecuadorans summon a waiter by raising their hands over their head and clapping. This is not considered courteous, and should be avoided by foreigners.

Gifts

- If you are given a gift, you should be very effusive in your thanks.
- When invited into a home for a meal, bring flowers, pastries, or chocolates. Avoid lilies and marigolds, which are used at funerals.
- Fine wines and liquors are also good gifts.
- You may give perfume and name-brand gifts to women.
- If you know you will meet a business associate's family, it is a good idea to bring gifts for the children.

Dress

- In general, formality increases as you move inland. The coastal resort areas are the most casual, and shorts may be worn in public there (although bikinis are rarely seen, even on the beach).
- On the coast, where it is hot, some men will wear a *guayabera* shirt to work, and women will wear sleeveless dresses. Foreigners, however, are expected to dress more formally for business meetings.
- Inland, it is important to adopt conservative business attire. Men should wear a jacket and tie even in hot weather. Suits in dark colors are preferred. Expect to wear the jacket and tie to social occasions as well.
- Women should dress conservatively and modestly. A suit or dress is appropriate for business, while a cocktail dress will be required for most social occasions.

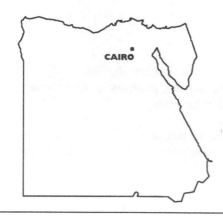

CAIRO

Egypt

Country Background

History

As reliable agriculture along the Nile requires dams and irrigation, Egypt was one of the first places on Earth to develop civilization and centralized government. Its recorded history dates back 7,000 years. Protected by deserts on both sides, ancient Egypt achieved unprecedented levels of wealth, architecture, and culture. Yet its wealth made it an irresistible target of powerful outside states. The Persians occupied Egypt in 525 B.C. Later occupying forces included Alexander the Great, then the Roman Empire, various Islamic rulers (including the Ottoman Empire), and finally Great Britain, which established a protectorate over Egypt. For over two thousand years, the rulers of Egypt were not Egyptians.

This came to an end with the 1952 revolution, which marks the beginning of the Republic of Egypt. Both the British and the Egyptian King Farouk (who was of a dynasty founded by an Albanian Muslim named Muhammad Ali) were thrown out of the country. Lt. Col. Gamal al-Nasir (known as Nasser in the West) emerged as Egypt's leader. The Egyptian people are intensely proud that their leaders are now native Egyptians. The ruling class that dominated the country's politics and economy before 1952 (a mixture of Europeans, Turks, and Levantines) is now much reduced in influence, but will still be encountered in business affairs.

Type of Government

The Arab Republic of Egypt is a democratic republic. The president is the chief of state. The prime minister is the head of the government. The main legislative body is the People's Assembly, which has 444 elected members and ten members appointed by the president. There is also a consultative council called the Shura; its function is mostly advisory. Under the current government, the judiciary has increased its independence. The legal system is derived from European models, primarily the French Napoleonic Code, but it is also highly influenced by Islamic law.

e—————————————————————**CULTURAL NOTE**

gypt's support for the Allied invasion of Kuwait in the Gulf War proved to be generally popular, although there were some protests. Egypt's economy suffered badly during the hostilities, between the unemployment of Egyptian workers who had previously been employed in Kuwait and the destruction of the tourist trade, which brings Egypt badly needed foreign currency. The temporary exile of many rich Kuwaitis and Kuwaiti businesses to Egypt did not make up for these losses. Egypt would like to maintain a strong role in the Gulf, including participation in an Arab peacekeeping force. Its position is weakened, however, by adamant Iranian opposition to any Egyptian participation and by the fact that Egypt itself is not a Gulf state. (Egypt's coasts are on the Mediterranean and Red seas, not the Persian Gulf.)

Terrorist violence occasionally breaks out in Egypt, but it does not usually affect non-Israeli foreigners. The speaker of the Egyptian Assembly was assassinated in October of 1990 by *Islamic Jihad*, the same group responsible for the death of President Anwar al-Sadat in 1981. A number of Israeli tourists were also killed. Recently, liberal Egyptian writers have been attacked.

In general, the Egyptian people are friendly and welcoming to foreigners. However, Egypt faces serious economic and population problems in the years ahead. As always, when Arab populations see no hope in political or economic solutions, Islamic Fundamentalism gains strength.

Language

Nearly all Egyptians speak Arabic. Most business people who deal with foreigners speak English, French, or both.

Religion

About 90 percent of Egyptians are Sunni Muslims, and most of the remaining 10 percent are Coptic Christians. (The Copts are the direct descendants of the ancient Egyptians.) Before 1952 there were some 80,000 Jews in Egypt, but as a result of Arab-Israeli tensions, only a few hundred remain.

Demographics

Some 95 percent of Egypt's 56 million people live within the Nile Valley, creating some of the highest population densities in the world. Unfortunately for Egypt's economy, the country also has one of the world's highest birth rates (41 percent per 1,000 compared to a world average of 27 percent; the U.S. rate is 17 percent).

Most Egyptians fall into the class known as *fellahin*, or peasants. The majority of *fellahin* are employed in farming or food-related industries. Only 3 percent of Egyptian land is suitable for agriculture. Nomadic Bedouins constitute less than 2 percent of the population.

Cultural Orientation

Cognitive Styles: How Egyptians Organize and Process Information

The Egyptians are open to information that does not conflict with Islamic values. They are more open to Western ideas than other Arabic cultures. Most Egyptians are trained to think associatively, so information is processed from a subjective, experiential perspective. Islamic law is adhered to in all situations, making the Egyptians universalistic. However, this same law says that one trusts brothers and cousins before outsiders because one must take care of one's own, and this is a particularistic (not universalistic) trait.

Negotiation Strategies: What Egyptians Accept as Evidence

Faith in the Islamic ideology is the primary source of truth. This truth is modified by the personal feelings one has about the problem or situation. The highly educated may use facts and reason objectively.

Value Systems: The Basis for Behavior

The Islamic religion is a critical component in Egyptian life, playing an important role in all aspects of social structure. Solutions to all problems are in the correct interpretation and application of Islamic law. The following three sections identify the Value Systems in the predominant culture—their methods of dividing right from wrong, good from evil, and so forth.

Locus of Decision Making

The male leader is the locus of decision making, but he makes decisions through the consensus of the group or collective. The individual is always subordinate to the family, tribe, or collective. Leadership and identity come from one's lineage and one's ability to protect the honor of the extended family. This is a kinship culture with little social identity outside the network of kin relationships.

Sources of Anxiety Reduction

The family is the cornerstone of the individual's social identity. Security is found in family loyalty and absolute submission to Islamic law. The most deeply held values—honor, dignity, and security—are available to an individual only as part of a larger kin group. There is a strong sense of fatalism, since one's destiny is in the hands of God. One can do nothing about this, so one tends to accept the status quo.

Issues of Equality/Inequality

Within Islam all believers are equal and united in the *ulmma*. There is cultural homogeneity among tribes. Most are Sunni Muslims adhering to *Wahabi* religious formulations. There is some ethnic bias against the Bedouin nomads and the Nubians. Egypt is under the social, political, and cultural dominance of a small elite, and there is great disparity between rich and poor. Education is the ticket to upward mobility. Men and women are not treated as equals.

Business Practices

Appointments

PUNCTUALITY

- Punctuality is not a traditional virtue in Egypt. Your client may be late for an appointment or not show up at all. You, however, should endeavor to be prompt.
- It is standard Arab practice to keep supplicants (including foreign business people) waiting. Until you get to know your clients, it is unwise to schedule more than one appointment per day.
- Don't forget that Cairo has some of the worst traffic jams in the world. Delays are frequently caused by traffic.

■ An appointment is rarely private among traditional Arab business people. Expect your visit to be interrupted by phone calls and visits from your client's friends and family. Westerners frequently find these distractions infuriating; try to maintain your equanimity.

- Friday is the Muslim holy day; no business is conducted on Fridays. Most people do not work on Thursdays, either. The workweek runs from Saturday through Wednesday.
- Working hours for businesses, banks, and government offices are truncated during the month of Ramadan. (See "Contacts and Holidays" in the appendix.)
- Government hours are 8:00 A.M. to 2:00 P.M. Government offices are closed on either Thursday and Friday or Friday and Saturday (the variation is designed to reduce traffic on congested Cairo streets).
- Business hours vary widely. In the winter, many businesses close for much of the afternoon and reopen for a few hours in late afternoon. A typical business schedule would be 8 A.M. to 2 P.M. in the summer; 9 A.M. to 1 P.M. and 5 P.M. to 7 P.M. in the winter.
- Remember that the Islamic calendar uses lunar months of 28 days, so an Islamic year of 12 months is only 354 days long. Holidays will thus be on different dates (by the Western calendar) every year. Any listed Muslim holiday dates are approximations since they depend upon actual lunar observations.
- Paperwork should carry two dates, the Gregorian (Western) date and the *Hijrah* (Arabic) date. Be aware that Christian Egyptians (Coptics) have yet another calendar, different from both of the above.

Negotiating

CULTURAL NOTE

gyptians often consider their country to be a bridge between the European West and the Arab East. Thus, business practices may resemble European or Arab practices or anything in between.

- The pace of business is much slower in Egypt than it is in the West. Be patient.
- Business meetings always start slowly, with long inquiries into one's health and journey.
- Decisions will take a long time to be made.
- Egyptians operate at their own pace. Trying to force them into making a decision will probably be futile, if not downright counter-productive.
- An Egyptian will not even consider doing business with you until he knows and likes you. Thus, the social aspects of a deal are just as vital as the business ones.
- Egyptians love language. Expect a lot of talking. There will also be a lot of exaggeration, poetics, flowery language, and emotion.
- You are required to have an Egyptian agent to do business in Egypt. If you are doing business in both Cairo and Alexandria, it is recommended that you have a separate agent for each city.
- Business cards should be printed in English on one side and in Arabic on the other.
- Egyptians speak at a much closer distance than North Americans are used to. Do not back up or shy away. There is also more physical contact, and conversations usually involve touching.
- Coffee is often served toward the end of a business meeting. This is a signal that the meeting will soon conclude. Incense may be lit at this time, as well.
- Arab men often walk hand-in-hand, although Westernized Egyptians rarely do this. If an Egyptian holds your hand, take it as a sign of friendship.

- Arabic is a language of hyperbole. When an Egyptian says "yes," it usually means "possibly." Be encouraged by this, but do not assume that the negotiating is over.
- Saving face and the avoidance of shame are vital to Egyptians. Always be aware of this. You may have to compromise on some issue to protect someone's dignity, not for any substantive reason.
- Do not bring up the subject of women unless your Egyptian counterpart does so first. Do not even inquire as to the health of an Egyptian's wife or daughter.
- The topic of Israel should similarly be avoided.
- Egyptian achievements, both ancient and modern, are good topics of conversation.
- Sports are a good topic of conversation. Soccer (football), basketball, and boxing (in which Egypt has won several Olympic medals) are the most popular sports. Horse racing, tennis, and all water-related sports (especially sailing and swimming) are also popular.
- Egyptians are fond of jokes and often make fun of themselves (Egyptian bureaucracy is a favorite target). However, no matter how self-deprecating their humor gets, you should not poke fun at Egypt or the Egyptians.

 Business Entertaining

- Hosting visitors is considered a virtue among Egyptians, so they will take care of much of the entertaining within their country.
- Be prepared to remove your shoes before entering a building. Follow the lead of your host.
- In Egypt, the male guest of honor is traditionally seated to the right of the host (rather than at the opposite end of the table).
- Remember that alcohol and pork are prohibited to strict Muslims. If you invite an Egyptian to a social event, make sure that there are nonalcoholic drinks available (unless you know that he or she drink alcohol).
- Hard liquor is available only in international hotels. Most Egyptian restaurants serve only beer and wine.
- Only in the more Westernized Egyptians' homes will you encounter eating utensils.
- Do not eat everything on your plate. Leaving a little food is a sign that you have had enough.
- When eating in an Egyptian home, it is insulting to add salt to your food.
- Realize that *baksheesh* (tipping) is expected for many types of services and courtesies.

Time
- Egypt is two hours ahead of Greenwich Mean Time (G.M.T. + 2), or seven hours ahead of U.S. Eastern Standard Time (E.S.T. + 7).

Protocol

 Greetings

- Since there are several styles of greetings in Egypt, it is safest to wait for your Egyptian counterpart to initiate the greeting, especially at a first meeting.
- Westernized Egyptian men shake hands with other men.
- Some Egyptian men will shake hands with Western women. Western business-women should wait for an Egyptian man to offer his hand.
- Women constitute about 10 percent of the Egyptian workforce. Most are employed in the service and professional sectors. There are many female secretaries and female physicians, but few female executives. When you encounter a woman decision maker in business, she will probably be very Western-oriented in her behavior. You can count on her to initiate a handshake, with either men or women.
- A traditional Arab male will not necessarily introduce his wife. Follow his lead; if he acts as if she isn't there, you should do the same.
- A more traditional Arab greeting between men involves each grasping the other's right hand, placing the left hand on the other's right shoulder, and exchanging kisses on each cheek. However, kisses are always between members of the same sex. Men may kiss men, women may kiss women, but men and women may not kiss in public.
- The verbal component of an Egyptian greeting is effusive. Tradition demands that an Egyptian welcome you several times at your first meeting.

 Titles/Forms of Address

- Westerners frequently find Arabic names confusing. The best solution is to request the names—written in English—of any Egyptians you will have to meet, speak to, or correspond with. Find out both their full names (for correspondence) and how they are to be addressed in person.
- Egyptian names are written in Arabic. In part because short vowels are not written in Arabic, translating from Arabic to other alphabets is not an exact science. Thus, Arabic names may be spelled several different ways in English (i.e., the leader of Libya's name is variously rendered Colonel Muammar al-Qaddafi, Mu'ammar al-Qadhafi, Qaddhafi, Qathafi, Gaddafi, and so forth).
- In general, Egyptian names are written in the same order as English names: title (if any), given name, sometimes a middle name (often a patronymic), and surname (family name). Thus, the former leader of Egypt was President Anwar al-Sadat; his title was president, his given name was Anwar, and al-Sadat was his family name.
- The term *al* literally means "from" in Arabic. A name like al-Barudi could mean "son of Barudi" or "from the town of Barudi." Do not mistake the term *al-* for the Western nickname Al (short for Alex or Albert).
- Most Egyptians should be addressed by title and surname (e.g., Doctor al-Nahhas), just as you would address a Westerner. Some Egyptians prefer title plus first name. In writing, use the full name. If an Egyptian does not have a title, just use Mr., Mrs., or Miss.

- Egyptians may address one another in different ways, depending upon the setting. An Egyptian you were on a first-name basis with at a party might address you by your title in a business meeting.

 Gestures

- The left hand is considered unclean in the Arab world. Always use the right hand in preference to the left (unless you are handling something that is considered unclean). Never eat with the left hand; eat only with your right hand. Avoid gesturing with the left hand.
- It is acceptable to use both hands when one is insufficient.
- While Egyptians constantly gesture with their hands while speaking, they do not point at another person. This would be considered impolite.
- As a general rule, keep both feet on the ground. Traditional Arabs do not cross their legs when sitting. Never show the bottom of your foot to an Arab; this is considered offensive. When one removes one's shoes (as when entering a mosque), the soles of the shoes are placed together, preventing the sole from being pointed at anyone.
- The "thumbs up" gesture is offensive throughout the Arab world.
- A gesture meaning "calm down" or "wait a minute" is accomplished in this way: With your palm facing you, touch all your fingers to your thumb, and bob your hand up and down (as if you were weighing something).

*N*ot only do Egyptians speak to each other at a closer distance than North Americans, they naturally gravitate toward others in public. In a nearly empty theater, an Egyptian will choose the seat next to you. On public transportation, when you are sitting alone on a long seat, an Egyptian will sit right next to you instead of at the other end. This does not necessarily mean that he or she wants to talk to you. ————CULTURAL NOTE

 Gifts

- If you are invited to an Egyptian home, bring a gift of baked goods or chocolates. Flowers are acceptable for very Westernized Egyptians, but they were traditionally used at funerals and weddings.
- Sometimes a beautifully made compass can be a good gift. A compass enables a devout Muslim to always know where Mecca is—even when traveling.
- Small electronic gadgets make popular gifts.
- Make sure you give or receive gifts with the right hand, not with the left (although using both hands is acceptable).

 Dress

- While foreigners are not exempt from Egyptian standards of modesty, do not adopt traditional native clothing. Egyptians may find it offensive to see foreigners dressed in their traditional clothes.
- Despite the Egyptian heat, most of the body must remain covered.
- Men should wear long trousers and a shirt, preferably long-sleeved. A jacket and tie are usually required for business meetings. Keep shirts buttoned up to the collarbone. Men should avoid wearing visible jewelry, especially around the neck.

- While few urban Egyptian women wear traditional clothing, all women—including foreigners—are expected to wear modest clothing in public. The neckline should be high, and the sleeves should come to at least the elbows. Hemlines should be well below the knee, if not ankle-length. The overall effect should be one of baggy concealment; a full-length outfit that is tight and revealing is not acceptable. Therefore, pants or pantsuits are not recommended. While a hat or scarf is not always required, it is wise to keep a scarf at hand. The suitability of your attire will be apparent as soon as you venture out; if Egyptian men stare lewdly at you, your dress is not sufficiently modest.

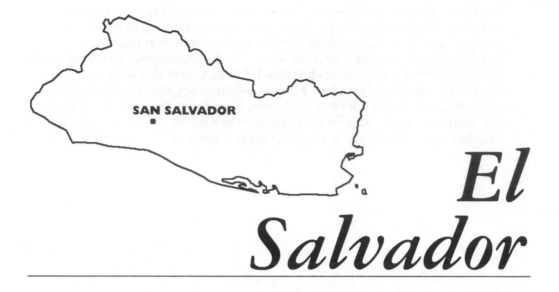

SAN SALVADOR

El Salvador

i──────────────────────**CULTURAL NOTE**

*I*t should be noted that many organizations that support the poor against the ruling elite of El Salvador have been subject to intimidation. Lutheran Bishop Medardo Gómez left El Salvador in 1989 after numerous death threats. The U.S. Peace Corps pulled its workers out in 1979. And among traditionally Catholic nations, El Salvador probably has the worst record for the murder of clergy. In addition to the well-known murders of Archbishop Romero in 1980 and six Jesuit priests in 1989, at least 600 other Catholic clergy or lay workers died or "disappeared" during the 1980s.

Country Background

History/Date of Origin

Although El Salvador was not a center of Indian civilization, it was populated by several Amerindian peoples. The first to fall before the Spanish were the Pipils, a tribe of the nomadic Nahua Indians (related to the Aztecs). The remaining tribes, the Pokoman (related to the Mayans) and Lenca Indians, were also soon defeated. By 1525 the Spanish had consolidated their rule, and the region came to be administered by the Audiencia de Guatemala.

In 1811, San Salvador became the first city in Central America to revolt against Spanish rule. El Salvador declared independence from both Spain and Guatemala in 1821, and a Mexican army was repulsed the following year. El Salvador was briefly part of the United Provinces of Central America. This federation dissolved in 1838, but El Salvador did not acknowledge its status as an independent republic until 1856.

Since that time, revolutions have characterized politics in the country. The government has usually been controlled by wealthy landowners, in conjunction with the military.

In 1969, El Salvador and Honduras fought the brief but violent Soccer War. Some 300,000 Salvadorans had left their overcrowded country to seek work—often illegally—in Honduras. Tensions over land and border disputes were brought to a head during a series of soccer matches between the two countries. After five days, a cease-fire was reached, and El Salvador withdrew from the 29 kilometers of Honduran territory it had occupied during the dispute. The borders have since been agreed upon, and a peace treaty was formally signed in 1980.

In 1979, guerrilla warfare broke out as a result of economic conditions and unpopular agrarian reforms. Brutal executions were carried out by vigilante rightist "death squads" to counter the growing leftist uprising. In 1980, moderate civilian leaders and reform-minded military officers joined to form a revolutionary junta. A provisional government was formed, headed by José Napoleón Duarte, until elections could be held in 1982. The newly elected assembly drafted a constitution and held presidential elections. In 1984, José Napoleón Duarte became the first freely elected president of El Salvador in over fifty years.

However, in spite of the initiation of moderate political and economic reforms, the uprisings did not stop. The war intensified during the 1984 election and again in 1989 during the presidential election of Alfredo Cristiani.

During the 1980s, the United States poured $4 billion into El Salvador in an effort to support the government and stop the Communist guerrillas. Not only did the rebels survive, but the gap between rich and poor Salvadorans widened. Relations with the United States were soured by the murders of six Jesuit priests, their housekeeper, and her daughter in 1989. Previously, in 1980, the widely respected Archbishop Oscar Arnulfo Romero had been assassinated.

Finally, after twelve years of fighting, a peace accord was signed between the government and the major leftist guerrillas (the *FMLN*, or *Farabundo Martí National Liberation Front*). Some 80,000 lives had been lost.

Type of Government

The Republic of El Salvador is a multiparty republic with a unicameral legislative house, the 84-seat Legislative Assembly. The president is the chief of state and the head of the government.

Language

The official language is Spanish, although many Indians speak Nahua and other native languages. English is understood in tourist centers and by much of the well-educated populace.

Religion

El Salvador has no official religion. Although the Salvadorans have traditionally been Roman Catholic, various Protestant sects have gained ground in recent years, and now constitute some 10 percent of the population.

CULTURAL NOTE

*b*eginning in the 1950s, some Roman Catholic clergy embraced what is called "liberation theology" and a "preferential option for the poor." In essence, this meant that the Catholic church could not endorse a government that kept the vast majority of Salvadorans living in poverty. Such elements of the church became, in the eyes of some Salvadorans, "enemies of the state." This led to the growing popularity of Evangelical Protestantism as an alternative faith, especially among the privileged classes. Many business people in El Salvador are now members of Neopentecostal groups, which equate wealth with God's favor (hence the poor are being punished by God for their lack of faith).

Demographics

The population of 5.5 million (1993 estimate) is composed of three ethnic groups: Mestizo (a mixture of European and Indian) 89 percent, Amerindian 10 percent, and European 1 percent.

Cultural Orientation

Cognitive Styles: How Salvadorans Organize and Process Information

In El Salvador there is great skepticism about information supplied by outsiders or those on the opposite side of an issue. They may discuss it but not act on it. Children are brought up to be subjective and associative. The elite are educated in the United States and so may be objective and abstractive. Even so, Salvadorans approach each issue from a personal perspective and seldom resort to universal rules or laws to solve problems.

Negotiation Strategies: What Salvadorans Accept as Evidence

Personal feelings about a situation or issue are the most important source of truth. Some Salvadorans may be influenced by faith in a religious or political ideology, but few will accept objective facts as valid evidence.

Value Systems: The Basis for Behavior

This is a culture dominated both politically and economically by a landed oligarchy backed by the military. The following three sections identify the Value Systems in the predominant culture—their methods of dividing right from wrong, good from evil, and so forth.

Locus of Decision Making

The oligarchy is the seat of decision making. Individuals are responsible for their decisions, but the best interests of the family, group, organization, or nation are dominating factors. Self-identity is based on the social system and the history of the extended family. Expertise is less important than the ability to be a member of the group.

Sources of Anxiety Reduction

It is one's role in the social structure and the presence of the extended family that give a sense of stability to life. Family lineage establishes social position. A fatalistic attitude keeps the people functioning. The Catholic church is not as strong in El Salvador as in other Central and South American countries, but its rituals give structure to society. Protestantism has grown very rapidly.

Issues of Equality/Inequality

There is a legacy of economic and social inequality and political authoritarianism. The middle class is very small and there are extreme contrasts between rich and poor. There are basic social, economic, and political inequalities. Changes in the system are often made by revolution or military coup. Machismo is very high. Women may be able to fight side by side with their men in the war, but when they return home, they lose any semblance of equality.

Business Practices

Appointments

PUNCTUALITY

◆ Punctuality, although not strictly practiced by Salvadorans, is appreciated in business circles and expected from foreigners.

- Remember that many Europeans and South Americans write the day first, then the month, then the year (e.g., December 3, 1999, is written 3.12.99). This is the case in El Salvador.
- Business hours are 8:30 A.M. to 12:30 P.M. and 2:00 to 6:00 P.M., Monday through Friday and 8:00 A.M. to noon on Saturday. Government offices are open 7:30 A.M. to 3:30 P.M., Monday through Friday.
- Make appointments a month in advance of your trip by telephone or by telex.
- The best time to visit El Salvador is February through June and September through November. Common vacation times are the two weeks before and after Christmas and Easter, and the month of August. The rainy season lasts from May to October.

 ## Negotiating

- Business is done only after a relationship has been established. Spend time forming a friendship before jumping into business discussions.
- Business tends to take place at a much slower pace than in North America or Europe. Be calm and patient with any delays. Several trips may be necessary to complete a transaction.
- Contacts are very important in establishing business relationships. Try to find contacts through embassies, banks, shipping corporations, and so forth.
- Be careful not to refer to U.S. citizens as Americans. Latin Americans are also Americans and are sensitive to this.
- Salvadorans tend to speak softly. Match your volume to that of your Salvadoran counterpart.
- Personal honor and saving face are very important to people in El Salvador. Therefore, never criticize a person, pull rank, or do anything that will embarrass someone in public.
- Although the situation is changing, it is still rare to find women in upper levels of business in El Salvador. A visiting businesswoman should act professionally and convey that she is representing her company, rather than speaking for herself personally.
- Business is discussed in an office or over a meal. It is not discussed in the home or around family. If you are invited to a Salvadoran home, this is a purely social function.

Business Entertaining

- If you are invited to a Salvadoran home, be sure to compliment the hostess (and her cooks) on the food and hospitality.
- Good topics of conversation are sports, family, work, and the natural beauty of El Salvador.
- Topics to avoid include political unrest, violence, religion, and intervention by the United States in Latin America. Remember that El Salvador has gone through twelve years of civil war, and emotions still run high.
- The main meal of the day is at noon. This will probably include black beans, tortillas or meat, and fruit and vegetables.
- In a home, each person serves himself or herself. It is rude to take food and leave it on your plate uneaten.

Time

- Local time is six hours behind Greenwich Mean Time (G.M.T. - 6); this is one hour behind U.S. Eastern Standard Time (E.S.T. - 1).

Protocol

Greetings

- Men shake hands with each other in greeting. Women will often pat each other on the right forearm or shoulder instead of shaking hands. Women who are close may hug or kiss each other on the cheek. Sometimes only a nod of the head is given.
- While Salvadoran men are willing to shake hands with women, the woman must first extend her hand. Foreign men should wait for a Salvadoran woman to extend her hand.
- Only Salvadorans familiar with North American habits will shake hands with a firm grip. Do not be surprised to receive a limp handshake; adjust your grip. Salvadoran handshakes may also last longer than normal U.S. handshakes.
- At parties and gatherings, it is customary to greet and shake hands with everyone in the room individually.
- Keep the vocal component of your greeting soft. Many Salvadorans dislike loud persons.

Titles/Forms of Address

- Most people you meet should be addressed by their title or by their surname. Only children, family members, and close friends address each other by their first names.
- Persons who do not have professional titles should be addressed as Mr., Mrs., or Miss, plus their surname. In Spanish, these are
    - Mr. = *Señor*
    - Mrs. = *Señora*
    - Miss = *Señorita*

- Most Hispanics have two surnames: one from their father, which is listed first, followed by one from their mother. Only the father's surname is commonly used when addressing someone, e.g., Señor Hernan Antonio Martinez García is addressed as Señor Martinez and Señorita María Elisa Gutierrez Herrera is addressed as Señorita Gutierrez. When a woman marries, she usually adds her husband's surname and goes by that surname. If the two people in the above example married, she would be known as Señora María Elisa Gutierrez Herrera de Martinez. Most people would refer to her as Señora de Martinez or, less formally, Señora Martinez.
- When a person has a title, it is important to address him or her by that title. Usually the title alone (without the surname) is preferred. A Ph.D. or a physician is called *Doctor*. Teachers prefer the title *Profesor*, while engineers go by *Ingeniero*, architects are *Arquitecto*, and lawyers are *Abogado*.

Gestures

- The Salvadoran people converse at a closer distance than U.S. citizens are used to—sometimes with a hand on the other person's lapel or shoulder. Restrain yourself from trying to back away; a Salvadoran will probably step forward and close up the distance.
- Do not point your fingers at anyone.
- To beckon someone over, extend the arm and wriggle the fingers with the palm down. Only summon close friends with this gesture.

Gifts

- If you are invited to a Salvadoran home, it is appropriate to bring a gift of candy or flowers.
- Avoid giving white flowers, they are associated with funerals.

Dress

- For business, men should wear a conservative, lightweight suit. Women should wear a blouse and skirt or dress.
- For casual situations, men should wear pants and a shirt in cities and a sweater in the cooler highlands. Women should wear a skirt and blouse. Short pants and jeans are not appropriate; women in pants or revealing clothing are very uncommon and may offend some people.

LONDON

England

<hr>

CULTURAL NOTE

george Bernard Shaw said it best: "America and Britain are two nations divided by a common language." Here are a few examples of the many English words that have completely different meanings in England and in the United States:

- To the English, to "table" a subject means to begin a discussion of it, while in the United States it means to postpone the discussion.
- The "ground floor" in England is our first floor, and the "first floor" is our second floor.
- "Whiskey" means scotch and only scotch. Ask for bourbon by its name.
- A "cigarette" is commonly called a "fag" in England.
- And of course, the British version of U.S. "french fries" are referred to as "chips."

Country Background

History

England was first brought into contact with the world when it was invaded by Rome in the first century B.C. Rome ruled much of England until its withdrawal in the fifth century A.D. Various tribes from Europe and Scandinavia—the Angles, Saxons, and Jutes—invaded England after the Romans departed.

In 1066, the Normans invaded from France. This event, the Battle of Hastings, was the last successful invasion of England. The Normans transformed England, making it a feudal kingdom.

England was frequently at war with continental powers over the next several centuries. As an island, England had a tremendous defensive advantage. England realized it needed a strong navy to protect itself, and this navy made the British Empire possible.

Great Britain was the strongest of the European powers in the nineteenth century, with many territories abroad. The Industrial Revolution first manifested itself on British soil. In 1926 the United Kingdom granted autonomy to New Zealand, Australia, and Canada; later in this century, it granted independence to India, Egypt, and its African colonies.

Type of Government

England is a constitutional monarchy. Its constitution is unwritten, and consists partly of statutes and partly of common law and practice. In the executive branch of government, the monarch is the chief of state, while the prime minister is the head of government. In practice, it is the cabinet (selected from Parliament by the prime minister) that has power, rather than the monarch. The prime minister is the leader of the majority party in the House of Commons. The Parliament consists of the House of Commons and the House of Lords, with the Commons having more real power. The Commons is elected by universal suffrage every five years, although the prime minister may ask the monarch to dissolve Parliament and call for new elections. Unlike the U.S. Supreme Court, the English judiciary cannot review the constitutionality of legislation.

After World War II, many sectors of the British economy were nationalized, but in the 1980s, privatization of industry was encouraged.

Education

England's educational system is quite good, and boasts some of the finest educational institutions in the world. A large part of tax revenues is spent on the educational system. Schooling is free and compulsory from age five to age sixteen. Literacy is 99 percent, and school attendance is almost 100 percent. There are over forty universities in the United Kingdom, and many professional schools.

Religion

England has an official religion, the Anglican church, or Church of England. Most English belong to this church, which was founded when England split from the Roman Catholic church during the reign of King Henry VIII. The church no longer has political power. Other religions represented in England are Roman Catholicism, Presbyterianism, Methodism, and Judaism. Religion is considered to be a very private subject.

Demographics

The population of the United Kingdom is 57 million. London, the capital, has about 6.7 million in its metropolitan area. England is an urbanized and suburbanized nation, and has one of the highest population densities in the world.

Cultural Orientation

Cognitive Styles: How the English Organize and Process Information

The English are generally closed to outside information on most issues. They will participate in debate but are not easily moved from their perspective. They are quite analytical and process information in an abstractive manner. They will appeal to laws or rules rather than looking at problems in a subjective manner. Company policy is followed regardless of who is doing the negotiating.

Negotiation Strategies: What the English Accept as Evidence

Objective facts are the only valid source of truth. Little credence is given to the feelings one has about an issue. Faith in few if any ideologies will influence decisions. They are the masters of understatement.

Value Systems: The Basis for Behavior

The usefulness of a monarchy is being questioned more seriously because of the expense of financing it. The following three sections identify the Value Systems in the predominant culture—their methods of dividing right from wrong, good from evil, and so forth.

Locus of Decision Making

The English are highly individualistic, taking responsibility for their decisions, but always within the framework of the family, group, or organization. Individual initiative and achievement are emphasized, resulting in strong individual leadership. They do not find it difficult to say "no." The individual has a right to his or her private life, and this should not be discussed in business negotiations. Friendships are few and specific.

Sources of Anxiety Reduction

There are established rules for everything, and this gives a sense of stability to life. Well-entrenched external structures (law, government, organizations) help to insulate them from life. They are very time-oriented, and anxiety is developed over deadlines and results. Emotions are not to be shown in public; the phrase "keep a stiff upper lip" is a good example of their demeanor.

Issues of Equality/Inequality

There is an inherent trust in the roles people play (but not necessarily in the people) within the social or business system, and a strong feeling of the interdependency of these roles. There are necessarily inequalities in these roles, but the people are supposed to be guaranteed equality under the law. There is some bias against ethnic groups. There is a high need for success, and decisions are made slowly and deliberately. Women have a great deal of equality in both pay and power.

Business Practices

Appointments

————————————————————— PUNCTUALITY

♦ Always be punctual. In London, traffic can make this difficult, so allow plenty of time to get to your appointments.

- Schedule your visits at least a few days ahead of time, then confirm your appointment upon your arrival in England.
- The workweek is 9:00 A.M. to 5:00 P.M., Monday through Friday, although government offices close from 1:00 to 2:00 P.M. and stay open until 5:30 P.M.
- Executives leave their offices by about 5:30 P.M.

Negotiating

- The best way to make contact with English business people is through a third party.
- It is not appropriate to have this same third party intervene later.
- If you do not have a contact, write to the company rather than to an individual or a department.
- The hierarchy in business is as follows: the managing director (CEO in the United States), the deputy (corporate vice president to U.S. executives), the divisional officers, the deputy directors, and, finally, the managers.
- Normally, a secretary will introduce you to the executive; otherwise, introduce yourself.
- The English are normally more interested in short-term results than in the long-term future.

- Change is not necessarily a good thing to the English.
- After a meeting, be sure to leave detailed data with your English partners.
- The English do not often reveal excitement or other emotions; try to keep yours restrained as well. They also traditionally underplay dangerous situations.
- Similarly, the English refrain from extravagant claims about products or plans.
- Some English stereotype U.S. business people as condescending; to be safe, make every effort to avoid this impression.
- Avoid the hard sell.
- Decision making is slower in England than in the United States.
- Don't rush the English toward a decision.
- Allow the English executive to suggest that the meeting has finished, then do not prolong your leave taking.
- While U.S. executives are known for being direct, the English are even more so. Don't be offended if there's no hedging about whether your suggestion is good or not.
- It is best for a company to send older executives to England, as they are more respected and usually more restrained in conduct.

a————————————————————**CULTURAL NOTE**

n oral agreement is considered binding, followed by written confirmation; only major agreements will require legal procedures.

Be discreet when you suggest contacting an attorney (called a solicitor in the United Kingdom).

- Exchanging business cards is not essential, but if your name is unusual, you should give out your card.

a————————————————————**CULTURAL NOTE**

lthough U.S. business people may consider everyone in the United Kingdom "British" or "English", the Scots, Welsh, and Irish are not called English. Use the terminology of the people you are with.

- The English do not consider themselves European. This is vital when discussing issues regarding the European Union.
- Don't ask the typical U.S. conversation starter "What do you do?" as the English feel it is too personal. Avoid other personal questions as well, even "What part of England are you from?"
- Avoid controversial topics such as politics or religion, and do not discuss the English work ethic.
- Speak in complete sentences. Many U.S. executives have a habit of starting a sentence and then allowing it to trail off without ever completing the thought. This can be annoying to the English.
- While the English are often self-critical, visitors should avoid criticizing the ways of the people; similarly, if they share their complaints with you, do not participate.
- The English apologize often, for even small inconveniences (as do many people in the United States).
- The English usually enjoy talking about animals.
- Do not make jokes about the royal family.
- It is not good form to discuss one's genealogy.

Business Entertaining

- Business breakfasts are not commonplace in England.
- Breakfasts in hotels are very large.
- Lunch is between noon and 2:00 P.M.
- A business lunch will often be conducted in a pub and will be a light meal.
- With senior executives, lunch will be taken in the best restaurants or in the executive dining room.
- Dinner is from 7:00 to 11:00 P.M. in most restaurants.
- When you go out after work, do not bring up the subject of work unless your English associates do, otherwise, you will be considered a bore.
- Most business entertaining is done in restaurants and pubs rather than at home.
- To call the waiter over, simply raise your hand.
- If you smoke, always offer the cigarettes around to others before taking one for yourself.
- It is not polite to toast those who are older or more senior than you.
- If you are the guest, you must initiate your departure, as your hosts will not indicate that they wish the evening to come to an end.
- Do not invite a business associate out until you know him or her fairly well.
- When inviting the English out, it is best to include people of the same background and professional level in the invitation.
- When you are the host, be sure to offer the seat of honor to the most senior person. He or she may decline, offering it to you as host; accept it graciously.
- While U.S. citizens hold the fork in the right hand, or switch from left to right, the English hold it in the left hand.
- When passing items around the table, always pass them to the left.
- Always keep your hands above the table (but no elbows on the table!).
- The knife above your plate is used for butter.
- When dining out, it is not considered polite to inquire about the food you see around you.
- Likewise, you should not ask to sample the dishes of others.
- In general, maintain very proper manners.
- The English still respect the tradition of men holding doors open for women and rising when women enter the room.
- The English are only beginning to be concerned about diet and health; don't press your views on this matter.

Time

- The English are on Greenwich Mean Time, which is five hours ahead of U.S. Eastern Standard Time (E.S.T. + 5).

Protocol

Greetings

- A handshake is standard for business occasions and when visiting a home.
- Women do not necessarily shake hands.
- A woman may extend her hand; men should wait for women to do so.

- When introduced, say "How do you do?" instead of "Nice to meet you." The question is rhetorical.

Titles/Forms of Address

- Business titles are not used in conversation.
- Find out the honorary titles of anyone you will be in contact with, and use them no matter how familiar you are with the person.
- Doctors, clergy, and so forth are addressed by title plus last name; however, surgeons are addressed as Mr., Mrs., or Miss.
- Rather than "sir," you should use the title of the person you are addressing (i.e., "Yes, Minister", and not "Yes, sir").
- The English are beginning to use first names as is done in the United States. However, you should do so only at the initiative of your hosts.
- Avoid repeating the other person's name during the conversation.

Gestures

- It is considered impolite to talk with one's hands in one's pockets.
- The British often do not look at the other person while they talk.
- In business, a light handshake is standard.
- When visiting a home, a handshake is proper; however, a handshake is not always correct at social occasions. Observe what others do.
- Don't point with your fingers, but instead indicate something with your head.
- Sitting with your ankle resting on your knee may be seen as impolite.
- If you give the "victory" sign (a "V" with two fingers), do so with the palm facing outward.
- Tapping your nose means confidentiality, or a secret.
- It is inappropriate to touch others in public; even backslapping or putting an arm around the shoulders of another can make the English uncomfortable.
- In addition, the English maintain a wide physical space between conversation partners.
- Avoid excessive hand gestures when speaking.
- Men give their seats to women on crowded public transportation.
- Stand to the right on escalators.

Gifts

- Gifts are not part of doing business in England.
- Rather than giving gifts, it is preferable to invite your hosts out for a meal or a show.
- When you are invited to a English home, you may bring flowers (not white lilies, which signify death), liquor or champagne, and chocolates. Send a brief, handwritten thank-you note promptly afterwards, preferably by messenger rather than by mail.
- When bringing flowers, consult with the florist about the appropriate type and number.
- Be cautious in making purchases, as there is usually no refund or exchange policy.

Dress

- Conservative dress is very important.
- Men should wear laced shoes, not loafers.
- Men's shirts should not have pockets; if they do, the pockets should be empty.
- Men should not wear striped ties; the British "regimentals" are striped, and yours may look like an imitation.
- Men's clothes should be of excellent quality, but they do not necessarily have to look new. Well-broken-in clothes are acceptable.
- Women should also dress conservatively.

HELSINKI

Finland

Country Background

History/Date of Origin

The Finnish people have maintained their separate cultural identity despite centuries of rule by foreigners. Sweden ruled the country for almost 500 years. By the eighteenth century, Sweden's military decline had led Finns to doubt whether Sweden could protect them. In 1808, a war between Sweden and Russia resulted in Sweden's defeat. Finland was ceded to Russia, an action most Finns did not object to, since the Russian czar, Alexander I, promised to respect the laws and institutions of Finland. But, like Poland, the Grand Duchy of Finland was eventually subjugated. Russian governors stamped out emerging Finnish nationalism, and by the time of the First World War, many Finns were ready for armed rebellion against Russia.

Finland declared independence from Russia in 1917, but independence was marred by a civil war between Finnish socialists (Reds) and conservatives (Whites).

The interwar years saw Finland subjected to increased pressure from Russia. By 1939, the then-Soviet Union was demanding territorial concessions from Finland. When the Finns refused, Soviet troops invaded on November 30, 1939.

Finland put up an unexpectedly strong resistance in the Winter War, and much of the world cheered as tiny Finland battled the Soviet Goliath. While Finland could not defeat the Soviets, its stubbornness—plus the world's disapproval—made the U.S.S.R. settle for dismembering Finland rather than absorbing it, which was the fate of nearby Lithuania, Latvia, and Estonia. Finland lost much land and 12 percent of its population, but remained independent.

Finland then turned to Nazi Germany for protection, and allowed German troops to be stationed in country. When Germany and the U.S.S.R. went to war against each other in 1941, Finland found itself drawn into the war on the Nazi side. However, the Finnish government remained in control, and the Nazis were not allowed to take action against the Finnish Jews.

At the end of World War II, Finland once again lost territory to the U.S.S.R. However, it was not occupied by the Red Army and did not become a member of the Warsaw Pact. Instead, Finland chose to remain neutral in the cold war, maintaining cordial relations with both the West and the Soviet Union.

t ————————————————————**CULTURAL NOTE**
he Finnish economy was once based on lumber, Finland's principal resource, but has since diversified and is now highly industrial. Exports account for one-fourth of the GDP of Finland, with the United States as one of the main markets. The United States also ranks sixth among exporters to Finland. Finland's social welfare system, which includes health and child care allowances, is highly developed.

Type of Government

Finland is a constitutional republic. In the executive branch, the president is the head of state and shares power with the prime minister, who is chief of government. The president is elected and serves for six years. The prime minister and other members of the cabinet, or Council of State, are appointed by the president. They are not necessarily affiliated with a certain party. The legislative branch is made up of a unicameral 200-seat body called the *Eduskunta*. There have been many coalition governments in this century; rarely does a single party have a majority.

Women are very much accepted in high levels of government and business. In 1906, Finland was the first European country that granted women the right to vote, and now forty percent of the seats in parliament are occupied by women. Finland also boasts Europe's only female defense minister.

f ————————————————————**CULTURAL NOTE**
inland was a member of the European Free Trade Association (EFTA) but not the European (EC) [now the European Union (EU)]. It was thought that membership in the EU would compromise Finnish neutrality. With the end of the cold war, Finland is now debating whether or not to become a member of the EU.

Language

Finland has two official languages: Finnish and Swedish.

English is the principal foreign language studied, and many Finns are multilingual. Business can be conducted in English. Older Finns usually speak German.

Religion

The principal religion of Finland is Lutheranism; 89 percent of the people belong to this group. Although freedom of religion has been in effect since 1923, the Evangelical Lutheran Church is still supported by state taxes.

Demographics

The population of Finland is almost 5 million. Helsinki, the capital, has about 485,000 people in its metropolitan area.

Cultural Orientation

Cognitive Styles: How Finns Organize and Process Information

In Finland, people feel that they have obtained what they need, and therefore they do not seek or accept information or help from others. Finnish higher education is becoming more conceptual, and information is being processed from an analytical perspective rather than a subjective, associative one. Finns follow universalistic laws and rules of behavior rather than considering each situation as a unique problem.

Negotiation Strategies: What Finns Accept as Evidence
Faith in the ideology of social welfare is the basis for Finns' search for truth. They tend to use objective facts rather than subjective feelings in making their case.

Value Systems: The Basis for Behavior
Finland is a social welfare state with strong humanitarian and environmental concerns. The following three sections identify the Value Systems in the predominant culture—their methods of dividing right from wrong, good from evil, and so forth.

Locus of Decision Making
The individual is given the responsibility for decision making within the boundaries of the social welfare ideology. One has the dual obligation of developing a strong self-orientation and at the same time helping those who are not able to help themselves. One's ability is more important than one's station in life. Finns cherish their right to a private life and personal opinions.

Sources of Anxiety Reduction
The social welfare state and a strong nuclear family give Finns stability and security. This reduces life's uncertainties and the anxiety that comes with them. Finns are highly nationalistic, with a liberal philosophy of tolerance for dissent and deviation. However, anxieties develop between the need to have a strong self-image and being a member of a social welfare state.

Issues of Equality/Inequality
Finland has an egalitarian society in which those at all power levels have an inherent trust in people. The population is homogeneous, which minimizes ethnic strife. Finland is basically a middle-class society where the government helps with family needs. The minimizing of social differences also minimize the evidence of poverty and wealth. In this society husbands and wives share the responsibilities of child care.

Business Practices

Appointments

 ———————————————————— **PUNCTUALITY**

- ◆ Always be punctual for business appointments.
- ◆ Punctuality is also expected at social occasions.

- Remember that many Europeans and South Americans write the day first, then the month, then the year (e.g., December 3, 1999, is written 3.12.99).This is the case in Finland.
- Make appointments several weeks in advance.
- The workweek is 8:00 A.M. to 4:30 P.M., Monday through Friday. During the winter (September to May), some businesses operate from 9:00 A.M. to 5:00 P.M.

- Government offices operate from 8:00 A.M. to 4:15 P.M. in the winter, and from 8:00 A.M. to 3:15 P.M. in the summer.
- Stores are open until 4:00 or 5:00 P.M., Monday through Friday. On Saturday they close somewhere between 1:00 and 3:00 P.M.
- Many businesses close the afternoon before a holiday.
- Finns take four or five weeks of vacation per year.
- Avoid business travel to Finland in July, August, and early September, when most people will be away on vacation.

 ## *Negotiating*

- You will find a mix of British English and American English spoken. Titles are British style, so the CEO is known as the managing director and the corporate vice president as deputy. Try to do your negotiating with the managing director, who will be the decision maker.
- The Finns often begin business right away, without small talk.
- Avoid any attitude of superiority.
- Finns can be very quiet. Do not be put off by long silences.
- Business cards are important in Finland. They may be presented as an introduction or during the course of the meeting.
- Look people directly in the eye when conversing.
- Finns tend to be fairly quiet and unemotional in public.
- The Finns enjoy discussing politics; there are many political views in this country with its multiparty system, so keep this in mind.
- Good topics of discussion are hobbies, travel, sports, and politics.
- Personal questions should be avoided.
- The Finns appreciate nature and are concerned about the environment.

 ## *Business Entertaining*

- For casual lunches, milk and coffee are the usual beverages. Finns love coffee, and cafes are everywhere.
- Finns tend to appreciate a knowledge of good wines.
- You may be taken out for dinner by a business associate. Spouses are generally invited to dinners.

CULTURAL NOTE

*Y*ou may be invited to take a sauna with your host. Indeed, the consummation of a business deal is often celebrated with an expansive meal followed by a sauna.

- The sauna is a quasi-religious experience to Finns; treat an invitation to a sauna as a great honor.
- Saunas are usually segregated by sex. Where only one sauna is available, the women use it first.
- Finns are usually nude in a sauna, except when they intend to go swimming in a public place immediately afterwards (for that they wear a bathing suit). However, they will not mind if you prefer to wear a swimsuit or a towel in a sauna.
- Saunas are usually followed by a snack of bread, sausage, and fish. Expect the fish to be salty; it is intended to replace body salt lost in the heat of the sauna.

- Always write a thank-you note the next day to your host.
- It is not appropriate to be "fashionably late" to a meal.
- When invited to a Finnish home for dinner, take flowers for the hostess.

- The Scandinavians are known to be heavy drinkers at mealtime so, if you drink, pace yourself. Drunk driving laws are very strict in Finland.
- A toast is usually proposed at the beginning of a meal.
- The fork is held in the left hand, and the knife remains in the right.
- The cold table (buffet) is known as *voileipapoyta.*

a————————**CULTURAL NOTE**
n evening's entertainment often ends in dancing. Surprisingly, the most popular dance among the somber, quiet Finns is the tango!

Time

- Finnish time is two hours ahead of Greenwich Mean Time (G.M.T. + 2) or seven hours ahead of U.S. Eastern Standard Time (E.S.T. + 7).

w————————**CULTURAL NOTE**
hen using a Finnish telephone book, remember that names beginning with those uniquely Scandinavian letters (they look like "a" and "o" but with diacritical marks) are alphabetized at the end of the book.

Protocol

Greetings

- A firm handshake is the standard greeting for men and women. Even children are encouraged to shake hands.
- When greeting a group, it is proper to shake hands with the women first.
- For introductions, people use both names, or a title and last name.
- Only close friends and family greet with hugs or kisses.

Titles/Forms of Address

- The order of Finnish names is the same as in the United States: first name followed by last name.

w————————**CULTURAL NOTE**
hen pronouncing Finnish names or words, pronounce double letters twice as slowly as single ones (e.g., "aa" is twice as long as "a"). The stress always falls on the first vowel in a word.

- Do not use first names unless you are invited to do so.
- Executives prefer to be addressed by their titles followed by their surnames. (This is especially important when writing.)
- Anyone without a title should be addressed as Mr., Mrs., Miss, or Ms. plus surname.

Gestures

- It is not appropriate to fold one's arms; this signifies arrogance.
- A toss of the head is a motion for "come here."
- Finns are not comfortable with physical contact such as backslapping.
- It is not polite to talk with one's hands in one's pockets.
- Sitting with the ankle resting on the knee is too casual.
- A warm smile is appreciated.
- A man should remove his hat when speaking with another person or when entering a building.

Gifts

- A bottle of wine is a good token of appreciation when you go to a Finnish home (along with the flowers for the hostess).
- Business gifts should not be too extravagant or too skimpy, and should not be given at a first meeting.
- A personalized gift, such as a book on a topic of interest to your client, is appreciated.
- Fiskars scissors (with the orange handles) are the most commonly imitated Finnish product. Avoid giving any type of gift that may compete with them.

Dress

- Although Finns are very stylish, business clothing remains fairly conservative.
- Finnish men wear suits constantly, both to business and to social events. You may remove your suit jacket in the summer if you see Finns doing likewise.
- Men may need a tuxedo for formal engagements.
- Businesswomen should wear a dress or suit. Bring a cocktail dress for social functions.
- In winter, women usually wear snow boots to work, then change into shoes once they get inside.

PARIS

France

f————————————————**CULTURAL NOTE**

rance has a civil-law system, rather than the common-law system of the United States. Commercial agreements are short because they refer to the legal code. Many business people have studied law and can draw up their own contracts. Parties to an international contract may choose which country's laws will govern it.

Country Background

History

The cultural roots of the French go back to the Celtic Gauls, who were conquered by Julius Caesar in 51 B.C. Five hundred years later, Clovis extended Frankish rule over much of Europe; and after Charlemagne's death in 814, France became one of the successor kingdoms. France developed into the strongest of the unified Continental monarchies (as opposed to Germany and Italy, which were unified later).

The French Revolution (1789-1793) overthrew the monarchy, and established the First Republic. Napoleon ruled over the First Empire (1804-1815), and successive governments led to the existing Fifth Republic (1958 to present).

Type of Government

France is a multiparty republic. The head of the government is the prime minister; the president is chief of state. The French people elect the president and the two houses of parliament. The president, who appoints the prime minister (but subject to the election results), serves for seven years. The president has a large share of the power, including the right to dissolve the lower house of parliament, the Assemblée Nationale, and call for new elections. According to the constitution, it is the government and not the president that decides on national policy.

Language

French is the official language. The French people are very proud of their language, which was the international language of diplomacy for centuries. If you do not speak French, it is advisable to apologize for this. However, many French business people speak English.

Religion

There is no official religion. France is principally a Catholic country (90 percent), although new immigrants represent other religions, such as Islam.

Demographics

The population of France is 56 million. Urbanization occurred after World War II, and now cities are home to 75 percent of the people. Paris has 8.7 million; the other important centers (Lyon, Marseille, and Lille) have under 1.5 million. Growing areas are Lyon, Grenoble (in the Alps), and the southern coast (Toulouse, Montpelier, Nice).

Cultural Orientation

Cognitive Styles: How the French Organize and Process Information

The French will readily accept information for the purpose of debate and may change their minds quickly, but strong ethnocentrism will not allow the acceptance of anything contrary to the cultural norm. Ideas are very important to them, and they approach knowledge from an analytical and critical perspective. They look at each situation as a unique problem and bring all their knowledge to bear on it.

Negotiation Strategies: What the French Accept as Evidence

Arguments tend to be made from an analytical, critical perspective with eloquent rhetorical wit and logic. There is a great love for debate, striving for effect rather than detail and image over facts. Feelings and faith in some ideology may become part of the rhetoric.

Value Systems: The Basis for Behavior

Pride in their heritage sometimes makes them appear egotistical in their behavior. The following three sections identify the Value Systems in the predominant culture—their methods of dividing right from wrong, good from evil, and so forth.

Locus of Decision Making

The French are strongly individualistic and have a centralized authority structure that makes quick decisions possible. The relationship between the participants becomes a major variable in the decision-making process. One's self-identity is based on his or her accomplishments in the social realm. Education is the primary variable in social standing. Individual privacy is necessary in all walks of life.

Sources of Anxiety Reduction

The French seem to be preoccupied with status, rank, and formality. Contacts are of utmost importance. Their attachment to a public figure gives them a sense of security. Yet, individuality is preferable to conformity. They are reluctant to take risks, so little long-range planning is done, as the future is uncertain. One is allowed to show both positive and negative emotions in public.

Issues of Equality/Inequality

There is a highly stratified class system, but most people are middle-class. However, there is much hostility between social groups. Superiors demand obedience from subordinates in all walks of life. Power is a basic fact of society, and leaders with the ability to unify the country or group are highly prized. Sex roles in society are fluid, and one's status is more important than one's sex.

Business Practices

Appointments

————————————————————————— PUNCTUALITY

♦ Always make appointments for both business and social occasions. Be as punctual as you would be in the United States, although in the south, the French are more relaxed about time.

■ Most French get four or five weeks of summer vacation, and take it in July and August. Indeed, except for the tourist industry, France virtually shuts down in August. Try to conduct business during other months.

■ Always present your business card. When receiving the cards of others, treat them very carefully.

■ It is best to have your business card printed in French upon arrival. One side can be in English, with the translation in French on the other side. On the French side, include any academic credentials, and your school if it is a prestigious one.

■ Business hours are from 8:30 or 9:00 A.M. to 6:30 or 7:00 P.M. Lunch may last for two hours or more. In Paris, lunch begins at 1:00 P.M.; in the provinces, at noon or 12:30 P.M. Executives often stay in the office until 7:00 or 8:00 P.M.

■ The best times to schedule meetings are around 11:00 A.M. or 3:30 P.M.

 Negotiating

————————————————————— CULTURAL NOTE

*M*ost English-speaking French have studied British-style English, which can lead to communication breakdowns with speakers of American-style English. For example, in the United States, a presentation that "bombs" has failed, but in England it has succeeded.

Words in French and English may have the same roots, but different meanings or connotations. If you don't speak French, don't be offended too easily. For example, a French person might "demand" something, because *demander* simply means "to ask." If you speak some French, don't assume that an English word will have the same connotation in French. For example, if you ask for the bathroom and use the translation *salle de bains*, it will not be understood that you are asking for *la toilette*.

■ Eye contact among the French is frequent and intense—so much so that North Americans may be intimidated.

■ Because of the strong "old-boy network" and lack of merit-based promotions, employees stick to their job descriptions. Know who does what. If you are in charge of a service-oriented company, make it a policy to promote your French nationals based on good service, because your French management may not do so. Be sure to effectively communicate your company's standards for service.

■ The French are known for their formal and reserved nature. A casual attitude during business transactions will alienate them.

■ During negotiations, the French may make you seem to be the demandeur (petitioner), thus putting you in the weaker position.

- Hierarchies are strict. Junior executives will give a problem to a superior. Try to cultivate high-level personal contacts. The top executive is known as the *PDG* (pronounced pay-day-ahjay), or *president-directeur-general.*
- Women should not mistake French gallantry for condescension.
- Don't start a conversation by asking personal questions.
- Don't mistake a high-pitched voice and excited gestures for anger; they usually just mean great interest in the subject.
- The French are very formal in their letter-writing style.

 Business Entertaining

- Business can be conducted during any meal, but lunch is best.
- Though the French are familiar with "le power breakfast," they are not enthusiastic about it.
- Lunch can last two hours. Dinner is late (8:00 or 9:00 P.M.).
- At a business lunch or dinner, show enthusiasm about the food before beginning a business discussion.
- The business drink should not be held in a cafe; they are too noisy. Try a quiet hotel bar.
- Whoever initiates the meal or drink is expected to pay.
- Reservations are necessary in most restaurants, except in brasseries and in hotels. In choosing a restaurant, stick to French rather than ethnic ones.
- The French have a great appreciation for good conversationalists.
- When eating, keep both hands on the table at all times. Food comes gradually, so don't fill up too soon. When finished, place your fork and knife parallel across your plate. Cheese is served at the end of the meal; do not put it directly on your bread, and do not serve yourself twice.
- Don't drink hard liquor before meals or smoke between courses. The French believe this deadens the taste buds.
- Wine is customary with meals. If you do not want any, turn your glass upside down before the meal.
- Respect privacy. The French close doors behind them; you should do the same. Knock and wait before entering.

Time

- France is one hour ahead of Greenwich Mean Time (G.M.T. +1). This makes it six hours ahead of U.S. Eastern Standard Time (E.S.T. + 6).

Protocol

 Greetings

- Always shake hands when being introduced or when meeting someone, as well as when leaving. In general, the woman offers her hand first. French handshakes are not as firm as in the United States.
- In social settings, with friends, expect to do *les bises*, or touching cheeks and kissing the air.

Titles/Forms of Address

- Find out the titles of older French people you meet, and address them in that way both during the introduction and in the course of conversation. Even simple titles like Madame should be used as you converse, whether in English or French.
- Use Madame for all women except young girls.
- Don't use first names until you are told to do so. Don't be put off by the use of last names; it doesn't mean that the French are unfriendly. If you speak French, use the *vous* form until you are told to use *tu*.
- The French sometimes say their last names first, so that Pierre Robert might introduce himself as "Robert, Pierre." Ask!

 Gestures

- The "thumbs up" sign means "O.K."; the U.S. "O.K." sign (forming a circle with thumb and forefinger) means "zero" in France.
- Slapping the open palm over a closed fist is vulgar.
- To call for the check, make a writing gesture.
- Don't chew gum in public!
- Men should stand up or make a move to stand up when a visitor or a superior enters the room.

 Gifts

- Don't give a business gift at your first encounter.
- Avoid the too-lavish and the too-skimpy. Avoid gifts with your company logo. Good taste is everything.
- Don't include your business card with a gift.
- Good gifts include books or music, as they show interest in the intellect. Bring American best-sellers, especially biographies. The thicker and more complex the book, the better; simplicity is not a virtue in France.
- Bring flowers (not roses or chrysanthemums) or fine chocolates or liqueur to the host, and present them before, not after, the party. Do not bring wine, as it has probably already been carefully selected for the occasion by the host.
- For thank-you's, send (at least) a note the next day, and flowers or a basket of fruit if you wish. Since not all orders can be paid for with a credit card over the phone, ask the hotel if it is possible to add the payment to your hotel bill.

 Dress

- The French are very aware of dress. Be conservative and invest in well-made clothes.
- In the north and in the winter, men should wear dark suits.
- North American men should be aware that French suits are cut differently.
- Let your colleagues make the first move toward a more relaxed look.

BERLIN

Germany

CULTURAL NOTE

*m*ost Germans feel a deep connection to the environment. The historical image of brave German tribesmen successfully resisting the Roman Empire, fighting amidst the vast, majestic forest, is as important to Germans as the conquest of the western frontier is to North Americans. Germany was one of the first countries in which a political party dominated by an environmental platform, the Greens, won seats in a national legislature.

Country Background

CULTURAL NOTE

*t*he recently reunified German nation has adopted the official name of the Federal Republic of Germany (F.R.G.), the name of what used to be West Germany. The former East German title, German Democratic Republic (G.D.R.), is no longer in use (to the pleasure of Germans and non-Germans alike; the old title made Communist East Germany sound more democratic than West Germany). What to call the former G.D.R. is somewhat problematic. The German *Bundeswehr* (federal army) refers to the W Zone and O Zone. The politicians, after struggling with various obtuse nomenclatures, are now calling it the BGTD, an acronym for *Beigetretene Teil Deutschlands* (newly adhered parts of Germany). Some newspapers are using the less unwieldy acronym FNL, meaning "five new lander" or *fünf neve Länder.* And any German using the historical term *Mitteldeutschland* is revealing something about his or her politics, since to call the former G.D.R. "middle Germany" implies that Prussian lands now occupied by Poland are still "east Germany." As part of the price for being allowed to reunite, Germany had to reaffirm the inviolability of the Oder-Neisse border between Poland and Germany that was imposed by the Allies after World War II.

History

While Germany has been populated for thousands of years, the German nation is only approximately 120 years old. German settlements have been dated back to 3500 B.C., and these tribes fought so fiercely that Germany marked the northern border of the Roman Empire. After the fall of Rome, some Germanic-speaking tribes came under Frankish rule. But Germany was soon to break up into dozens of small kingdoms and principalities. During the Middle Ages, most of these principalities were united in a loose confederation known as the Holy Roman Empire (the "First Reich"). The Holy Roman Empire lasted until it was conquered and dissolved by Napoleon in 1804.

The Protestant Reformation, starting with Martin Luther's ninety-five theses in 1517, ushered in years of warfare and internecine strife. As religion was inseparable from politics, the official religion of each German principality was used as a political tool. Protestant rulers fought Catholics with great ferocity, and Germany came to be divided almost equally between the two religions—something that is still true today. In general, the southern areas remained Catholic and the northern states tended toward Protestantism.

By the eighteenth century, two German-speaking kingdoms had come to dominate Central Europe: Prussia and Austria. Austria felt it was in its interest to keep the German principalities separate; Prussia wanted to unite (and rule) them. Austria's Metternich succeeded in replacing the Holy Roman Empire with a loose union called the German Confederation (the Bund). But Prussia eventually won out when Otto von Bismarck manipulated the German principalities into war, first against Denmark, Austria, and the Austrian-allied German kingdoms, then against France. As a result of Bismarck's efforts, the Prussian King William I was crowned Kaiser (emperor) of all Germany in 1871. The German nation dates its existence from this event. This "Second Reich" was to last until Germany's defeat in the First World War.

After the war, Germany became a republic. Burdened with enormous war reparations and the Great Depression, power fell into the hands of the "National Socialists," as they are known to Germans—the term Nazi was rarely used within Germany. The atrocities of Adolf Hitler's "Third Reich" present a moral dilemma that each new generation of Germans must face.

At the end of World War II, Germany was occupied by England, France, the United States, and the U.S.S.R. Having suffered the greatest number of casualties of the Allies, the Soviets were determined to keep their portion of Germany under their thumb. This resulted in the division of Germany into the successful, NATO-allied F.R.G. and the Communist, Warsaw Pact G.D.R. Only the changed priorities of Mikhail Gorbachev's Soviet Union allowed the two halves of Germany to reunite on October 3, 1990.

Type of Government

The reunited Federal Republic of Germany is a democratic federal multiparty republic. Voting is done by proportional representation. There are two legislative houses: the 68-seat Federal Council and the 662-seat Federal Diet. The president is the chief of state, and the chancellor is the head of the government.

The government's current preoccupation is with bringing the former East Germany up to the standards of the West. East Germany was in far worse shape than anyone realized, and despite massive aid there is high unemployment in the East.

L————————————————————————**CULTURAL NOTE**

ike most of the former Warsaw Pact nations, East Germany is badly polluted. These environmental problems are delaying investment, as few investors are willing to risk purchasing an industrial site that may turn out to be extensively polluted (and that they would be responsible for cleaning up).

Language

German is the official language. While 99 percent of the population speaks German, there are several dialects. The textbook German learned in school (both inside and outside of Germany) may be quite different from the local dialect.

Religion

The population is split almost evenly between Roman Catholics and Protestants (mostly of various Lutheran sects). There are small populations of Jews and Muslims.

Demographics

The reunited Germany has a population of about 79 million. While the population density is high, both East and West Germany have had negative population growth rates for years. The population is rapidly aging.

Cultural Orientation

Cognitive Styles: How Germans Organize and Process Information

The Germans are generally closed to outside information, and they do not freely share information among units of the same organization. The younger generations are becoming more open. Germans are analytic and conceptual in their information processing. They are strongly committed to the universals of their culture. Friendships are not developed quickly, but they are deep and highly selective.

Negotiation Strategies: What Germans Accept as Evidence

Objective facts form the basis for truth. Feelings are not accepted in negotiations. A strong faith in the social democratic ideology influences Germans' perceptions of the truth.

Value Systems: The Basis for Behavior

One may find some differences in the value systems between what was once East and West German. The following three sections identify the Value Systems in the predominant culture—their methods of dividing right from wrong, good from evil, and so forth.

Locus of Decision Making

Germans are strongly individualistic, but cultural history must be considered in the decision-making process. Decision making is slow and involved, as all peripheral concerns must be taken care of in the process. Once a decision is made, it is unchangeable. Individual privacy is necessary in all walks of life, and personal matters are not to be discussed in business negotiations. It is important to develop a personal friendship with your counterparts.

Sources of Anxiety Reduction

Universal rules and regulations combined with strong internal discipline give stability to life and reduce uncertainty. There is a high need for social and personal order, and a low tolerance for deviant behavior. There is very little show of emotion because of strong internal structures and control. Fear or skepticism about the future (economic, political, social) breeds anxiety and pessimism.

Issues of Equality/Inequality

Strong but subtle biases exist against foreign workers, refugees, Gypsies, and, perhaps, the East Germans, as they may be a threat in the job market and do not conform to national norms. Germany has a distinctly hierarchical society, with classes established to fill organizational roles and give structure and order. Equal rights for all are guaranteed by law but may not be practiced in the marketplace. Women still have a strong bias to overcome in both pay and power.

Business Practices

Appointments

PUNCTUALITY

+ Nowhere in the world is punctuality more important than in Germany. Be on time for every appointment, whether for business or social engagements.
+ Arriving just two or three minutes late can be insulting to a German executive, especially if you are in a subordinate position.

- Remember that many Europeans and South Americans write the day first, then the month, then the year (e.g., December 3, 1999, is written 3.12.99). This is the case in Germany.
- Although English is widely spoken in Germany, some German business persons may prefer to conduct discussions in German. Inquire about this in advance, so that you or your hosts will be prepared with a translator.
- Appointments should be made well in advance. Give at least one or two weeks' notice for an appointment made by telephone or telex; allow at least a month for appointments made by mail (it may take a week for air mail letters to be delivered). If you don't have that much lead time, a short preliminary meeting may sometimes be arranged on a few days notice.
- Business letters may be written in English. Keep your letters formal, businesslike, and grammatically correct. Address them to the firm ("Dear ladies and gentlemen:") rather than to an individual executive. Everyone in Germany takes at least four weeks of vacation per year, and if your letter is addressed to an executive who is on vacation, the response will be a long time in coming.

CULTURAL NOTE

*i*t is still a common practice for German firms to send a letter with a correspondence number, but without the author's name and title, typed beneath the signature. Obviously, this makes it difficult to know with whom one should continue the correspondence.

- Be aware that if two Germans sign a business letter, this indicates that both of them make decisions. Both must be in agreement before a decision is made.
- The preferred times for business appointments are between 11:00 A.M. and 1:00 P.M. or between 3:00 and 5:00 P.M. Late afternoon appointments are not unusual.
- Do not schedule appointments on Friday afternoons; some offices close by 2:00 or 3:00 P.M. on Fridays. Many people take long vacations during July,

August, and December, so check first to see if your counterpart will be available. Also be aware that little work gets done during regional festivals, such as the Oktoberfest or the three-day Carnival before Lent.

- In the former East Germany, businesses did not schedule appointments on Wednesdays. This has been changing since reunification.
- Business hours: 8:00 or 9:00 A.M. to 4:00 or 5:00 P.M., Monday through Friday.
- Store hours: 8:00 or 9:00 A.M. to 5:00 or 6:00 P.M., Monday through Friday. On Saturday, most shops close by 2:00 P.M., except for one Saturday per month, when they remain open into the evening.

CULTURAL NOTE

*t*he government-mandated lack of evening shopping hours poses considerable difficulties for working women, who do the bulk of family shopping in Germany.

Negotiating

- U.S. executives sometimes assume that, since Germany makes products that are as good as those made in the United States, German companies will do business like U.S. firms. But the pace of German corporate decision making is much slower than in the United States.
- The decision-making process in German firms can be a mystery to outsiders. In addition to the official chain of command, German companies often have a parallel "hidden" series of advisers and decision makers. The approval of this informal "kitchen cabinet" is mandatory.

CULTURAL NOTE

*g*ermans abhor hype and exaggeration. Be sure you can back up your claims with lots of data. Case studies and examples are highly regarded.

The preference for facts over emotion can be seen in German print advertisements. Where an advertisement in the United States might call a product glamorous or exciting, in Germany there will be much more ad copy attesting to the product's superiority.

Be prepared to supply reams of information at short notice. Some of the requests may seem trivial; be assured that they are important to the Germans.

- The German reputation for quality is based (in part) on slow, methodical planning. Every aspect of the deal you propose will be pored over by many executives. Do not anticipate being able to speed up this process. This slowness extends through all business affairs. Germans believe that it takes time to do a job properly.
- German punctuality does not extend to delivery dates. Products may be delivered late without either explanation or apology.
- Germans also take a lot of time to establish a close business relationship. Their apparent coldness at the beginning will vanish over time. Once they get to know you, Germans are quite gregarious.
- Since most German executives understand some English, it is not necessary to have your business card translated. However, all promotional materials and instruction manuals should be translated into German.
- Bring plenty of business cards; quite a few Germans may wish to exchange them with you.

- If your company has been around for many years, the date of its founding should be on your business card.
- Since education is highly respected in Germany, be sure to include any title above the bachelor's level on your card.
- Germans may or may not socialize before getting down to business. It is quite possible that you will walk into an office and start talking business immediately after introducing yourself.
- When Germans decide to chat before getting down to business, expect to be asked about your flight, your accommodations, where you are from in the United States, and so forth.
- Germans smile to indicate affection. They generally do not smile in the course of business, either at customers or at coworkers.
- Business is serious; Germans do not appreciate humor in a business context.
- Compliments tend to embarrass Germans; they expect to neither give nor receive them. They assume that everything is satisfactory unless they hear otherwise.
- When a problem arises, be prepared to explain it clearly, in detail, and unemotionally. You may have to do this in writing. Germans are not accustomed to informally "passing the word."
- Never follow the U.S. business habit of saying something positive before saying something negative. This compliment/complaint juxtaposition will sound contradictory to Germans, and they may reject your entire statement.
- Privacy is very important to Germans. Doors are kept closed, both at work and at home. Always knock on a closed door and wait to be admitted.
- Germans tend to stand further apart than North Americans when talking. The positioning of furniture reflects this; you may find yourself giving a sales pitch from a chair that seems uncomfortably far away. Do not move your chair closer; rearranging a German's office furniture is highly insulting.
- Avoid asking personal questions of a German executive. If an executive wants you to know if he or she is married or has children, he or she will find a way to communicate this to you. Family life is kept separate from work in Germany.
- Obviously, embarrassing political questions should be avoided. Do not ask about the Second World War or anti-semitism.
- Germans tend to be well informed about politics and to have firm political opinions. They are also honest, and may tell you their opinions about your country (or its actions), even if these opinions are negative.
- Sports are a good topic for conversation. Many Germans are passionate soccer (*Fussball*) fans; skiing, hiking, cycling, and tennis are also popular. However, the collapse of the state-run East German Olympic sports program may be an uncomfortable subject.
- Germany makes some of the finest beer in the world. A German beer drinker will be happy to explain about the local brews, especially the seasonal beers and the specialty brews like Berliner Weisse, a Berlin beer made from wheat.

Business Entertaining

- Breakfast meetings are unheard of in Germany. However, business lunches are common.
- At a business luncheon, be aware that business may be discussed before and (sometimes) after a meal, but never during the meal itself. If you are invited

out to a luncheon, you may offer to pay, but expect your host to decline your offer. Insist on paying only when you have made the invitation.

- Be on time to social events. Drinks are served before the meal, but usually with few appetizers. The meal itself will start soon after.
- Germans do not often entertain business associates in their homes. If you are invited to a home, consider it a great honor.
- When eating, always use utensils; very few items are eaten with the hands. Place your utensils vertically side by side on the plate when you are finished eating.
- If you smoke, always offer cigarettes before lighting up.

Time

- Germany is one hour ahead of Greenwich Mean Time (G.M.T. + 1), or six hours ahead of U.S. Eastern Standard Time (E.S.T. + 6).

i———————————————————**CULTURAL NOTE**
f you arrive late to an event, the doors will probably be closed, and you must wait until the intermission to gain access to the show.

Protocol

Greetings

- Always shake hands, firmly but briefly, when introduced to a German businessman. When introduced to a woman, wait to see if she extends her hand before offering to shake.
- In formal social situations, older German men may kiss the hand of a woman in greeting. However, this is rare, and foreigners are not expected to kiss hands.
- While customs vary in different regions of Germany, the general rule is to shake hands both upon meeting and upon departing.
- When several people are being introduced, take turns shaking hands. It is impolite to reach over someone else's handshake.
- Never keep your left hand in your pocket while shaking hands with your right.
- In accordance with German formality, it is better to be introduced by a third person than to introduce yourself. However, if no one is available, it is acceptable to introduce yourself. This applies to both business and social situations.
- When you are the third person making an introduction between two parties, give the name of the younger (or lower-ranking) person first.
- In most regions of Germany, men stand when women enter a room. Women need not rise. Indeed, as long as a woman remains standing, any man talking to her will probably remain standing as well (unless the man is elderly or of much higher social rank).

Titles/Forms of Address

- The order of names in Germany is the same as in the United States: the first name followed by the surname.

- Traditionally, only family members and close friends address each other by their first names. You may never establish a close enough relationship with your German colleague to get to a first-name basis.
- When speaking to persons who do not have professional titles, use Mr., Mrs., or Miss, plus the surname. In German, these titles are
  - Mr. = *Herr*
  - Mrs. (or Ms.) = *Frau*
  - Miss = *Fräulein*
- *Fräulein* is nowadays used only for very young women (under age eighteen). Any businesswoman you meet should be addressed as *Frau* (surname), whether she is married or not.
- It is very important to use professional titles. Attorneys, engineers, pastors, and other professionals will expect you to address them as *Herr* or *Frau* plus title. This goes for anyone with a Ph.D. as well, e.g., *Herr* (or *Frau*) *Doctor Professor*. However, make sure you know the correct professional title.
- When entering or leaving a shop, it is considered polite to say "hello" and "good-bye" to the sales clerk.

 Gestures

- While Germans are open and generous with close friends, they tend to be formal and reserved in public. You will not see many smiles or displays of affection on German streets.
- The avoidance of public spectacle is reflected in the way Germans will get quite close to each other before offering a greeting. Only the young and the impolite wave or shout at each other from a distance.
- To get someone's attention, raise your hand, palm facing out, with only the index finger extended. Don't wave or beckon.
- When sitting, cross one knee over the other, rather than resting your ankle over one knee. Do not prop your feet up on anything other than a footstool.
- The eldest or highest-ranking person enters a room first. If their age and status are the same, men enter before women.
- When a man and a woman walk down a street, the man walks closest to the curb. On a path or a corridor, the man walks on the woman's left. When there are three people, a sole man walks between the women; a sole woman walks between the men. If two women are walking together, the younger woman should walk on the curb side (or on the left).

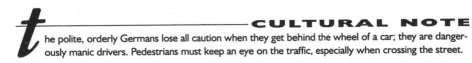

CULTURAL NOTE

*t*he polite, orderly Germans lose all caution when they get behind the wheel of a car; they are dangerously manic drivers. Pedestrians must keep an eye on the traffic, especially when crossing the street.

- Don't talk to someone with your hands in your pockets or while chewing gum.
- Expect to be hushed if you so much as cough while attending an opera, play, or concert. German audiences remain extraordinarily silent, rarely even shifting in their seats.

Gifts

- German businessmen do not give or expect to receive expensive gifts. A gift should be of good quality but not of exorbitant cost.
- Appropriate gifts include good quality pens, pocket calculators, or imported liquor.
- The only article of clothing considered an appropriate gift is a scarf. Other clothing, perfume, and soap are considered too personal.
- When invited to dinner at a German home, always bring a bouquet of unwrapped flowers for your hostess. The bouquet should not be ostentatiously large and should have an uneven number of flowers (but not thirteen). Red roses are reserved for courting, and calla lilies are for funerals. Heather should never be included in a bouquet in Northern Germany. Because of its hardy nature, heather is often planted on graves, and deemed bad luck to bring into a house.
- While an imported liquor is appropriate, a gift of a locally available wine can be interpreted as saying that your host's wine cellar is inadequate. However, a good wine brought from your home country (one not sold in Germany) or a top-quality imported red wine will be appreciated. Germans make some of the finest beers in the world, so it is unlikely that you could bring a foreign beer of interest to them.

CULTURAL NOTE

germans are often fans of odd facets of Americana; it is not unusual to run into a German aficionado of zydeco music or cowboy novels. If one of your business associates is in this category, a gift from the United States in his or her area of interest (i.e., a zydeco album or an Indian arrowhead) would be greatly appreciated.

Dress

- Business dress in Germany is very conservative. Virtually all businessmen wear dark suits, sedate ties, and white shirts. However, blue blazers and grey flannel pants are also considered formal. Khaki or seersucker suits are not acceptable! Women dress equally conservatively, in dark suits and white blouses.
- Follow the lead of your German colleague with regard to removing your jacket or tie in hot weather; do not be surprised if he or she remains fully dressed in sweltering heat.
- Business wear is also appropriate for most formal social events: parties, dinners, and the theater. Remember that one is obliged to check one's coat in German theaters; if you tend to be cold, bring a sweater. On the opening night of an opera, concert, or play, men are expected to wear their best dark suit or tuxedo, and women a long evening gown.
- Casual wear is essentially the same as in the United States. Jeans are ubiquitous, but they should not show signs of wear. Most German men wear sandals during the summer.

ATHENS

Greece

Country Background

History

The invention of democracy is credited to the ancient Greeks. However, the democratic era of Athens was relatively short-lived, and was followed by various forms of dictatorship. Democracy proved unable to cope with the pressures of war between Athens and other city-states. Modern Greek politics has inherited both these traditions: the history of democracy and a heritage of fractious regional (and ideological) violence.

Occupation and domination by outsiders—the Romans, the Turks, and (in this century) Nazi Germany—has made the Greek people ferociously nationalistic. Yet when there are no exterior threats, this ferocity is sometimes turned upon fellow Greeks.

During the Second World War, resistance to the German and Italian occupying armies was carried out by guerrilla bands, which fought each other almost as frequently as they fought the Nazis. With the end of World War II, Greece tried to form a democratic government, despite the presence of these competing guerrilla organizations. The Communist guerrillas, seeing their brethren in neighboring Eastern European states come to power, decided to revolt. The Communist rebellion in Greece lasted from 1946 to 1949, and was ended only when neighboring Yugoslavia left the Soviet orbit. The Yugoslavs closed their borders to the Soviet-backed Greek Communists. The United States took over the responsibility for Greek reconstruction from an impoverished Great Britain, and U.S. intelligence agencies worked frantically to deprive the Communists of any power in the new Greek government.

Greece was a constitutional monarchy at this time. Governments came and went in dizzying succession. Distressed by the inability of the parliament to maintain stability, King Constantine increasingly operated outside the confines of representative government. In late 1966 the king authorized the formation of an extra-parliamentary government to rule until new elections could be held the following year. This resulted in a military coup d'etat in 1967, first ruling "in the king's name" and then, when the king tried to stage his own coup, without the king.

The junta, ruled by Col. George Papadopoulos, gave Greece stability and a degree of economic prosperity at the cost of some human rights. By 1973, opposition to the authoritarian regime (among both students and some military officers) had grown strong enough that Papadopoulos decided to institute reforms. The monarchy was formally abolished, civil liberties were promised and free elections were scheduled. But the head of the Greek military police, General Ioannides, decided that Papadopoulos's reforms were too liberal; Ioannides staged a coup in late 1973 before the planned elections could be held.

Within a year this new coup had yielded to the demand for elections. The new Greek Republic was declared on December 9, 1974. A new constitution was adopted in 1975, and Greece has had peaceful transitions from one government to the next ever since.

Type of Government

Today, Greece is a presidential parliamentary republic. Its constitution dates from 1975. There is a president elected by the parliament and served by an advisory body, the Council of the Republic. The president is the chief of state. The real power is held by the prime minister, who is the official head of the government. The prime minister is the leader of the majority party of the unicameral parliament. There are 300 seats in the parliament, which is called the Greek Chamber of Deputies.

Language

Greek is the official language. It is written in the Greek alphabet, which was developed in about 1000 B.C.

Religion

The Greek Orthodox church is the official religion, with 98 percent of the population as members. Greek Orthodox principles are learned in school, and the state supports the church. However, freedom of religion is guaranteed. There is a small minority of Muslims, Roman and Greek Catholics, Protestants, and Jews.

Demographics

The population of Greece is a bit over ten million. Its capital, Athens, has four million. The population is almost entirely ethnic Greek. There are small numbers of Macedonians, Turks, and Albanians.

More than five million tourists visit Greece each year to explore the monuments of Greek civilization and the beautiful islands.

Cultural Orientation

Cognitive Styles: How Greeks Organize and Process Information

The Greeks are open to discussion of most topics but may find it difficult to change their position on issues. They process information more from a subjective, associative perspective than an objective, abstractive one. Interpersonal relationships are of major importance in the overall scheme of things. This leads them to consider the specifics of a situation rather than making decisions on the basis of universal rules or laws.

Negotiation Strategies: What Greeks Accept as Evidence

Subjective feelings are the basis for the truth, although faith in various ideologies (the church, ethnocentrism) may strongly influence the outcome. Objective facts will not be accepted if they contradict either of these.

Value Systems: The Basis for Behavior

Greece is the historical home of democracy, and, although it has toyed with other forms of government, it has always returned to a democratic form of government. The following three sections identify the Value Systems in the predominant culture—their methods of dividing right from wrong, good from evil, and so forth.

Locus of Decision-Making

The individual is responsible for all decisions, but he or she takes into consideration those that depend on him or her (family, group, and so forth). One's private life is influenced by family, friends, and organizations. Through this process one develops opinions. Friendships are deep and carry obligations. One must establish a relationship with one's counterpart before negotiations can be successful. Education is the primary vehicle for moving up the social ladder.

Sources of Anxiety Reduction

It is one's role in the social structure, the extended family, and deep friendships that give structure and security to the individual. There is a strong work ethic, but a laid-back approach to life promotes an image of much activity but little progress. There is a strong need for consensus in groups, but it is hard to see how this is accomplished. Failures are often attributed to external circumstances rather than one's own behavior.

Issues of Equality/Inequality

There is a definite social hierarchy, with some bias against classes, ethnic groups, and religions. Greeks have an inherent trust in people because of the social interrelationships between extended families and friends. There are extreme contrasts between rich and poor, but Greeks are people-oriented, with quality of life and the environment being important considerations. Machismo is very strong.

Business Practices

Appointments

PUNCTUALITY

✦ Always be punctual, although you will note that punctuality is not stressed by your Greek counterparts.

- Scheduling an appointment is not always necessary, but it is courteous.
- It is not considered necessary to set a limited time for a business appointment.
- From May to October, the workweek is Monday through Friday, generally 8:00 A.M. to 1:30 P.M. and from 4:00 P.M. to 7:30 P.M. From October to May, hours are from 8:00 A.M. to 1:00 P.M. and from 4:30 to 7:30 P.M.
- Stores are usually open from 8:00 A.M. to 2:30 P.M., although some may vary.

 ## Negotiating

- The senior members of a group are always shown great respect. All authority rests with them.
- To do business in Greece, one must be patient, yet use quick judgment. Greeks are excellent bargainers.
- It is advisable to have one side of your business card printed in English and the other in Greek. Present it with the Greek side up.
- A topic to avoid in conversation is international politics affecting Greece, such as the situation in Cyprus.
- Avoid making judgments about the Greek style of describing things. Many Greeks may seem to brag or exaggerate a bit when telling stories, but this is not unusual.

 ## Business Entertaining

- Business is usually done over a cup of coffee and often in a coffee house or *taverna*.
- Lunch is the main meal of the day. It is eaten between noon and 2:00 P.M.
- The elderly are always served first.
- Dinner is a small meal and is eaten at around 8:00 or 9:00 P.M.
- Often, many dishes are ordered and shared by all at the table.
- In restaurants, customers sometimes decide what to order by going into the kitchen and looking into the pots.
- When dining in a Greek home, you will probably be offered seconds and thirds in an insistent way. Accepting more food is a compliment to your host.

 CULTURAL NOTE

*b*e ready to dance at social occasions; you will probably be invited to join in.

Time
- Greece is two hours ahead of Greenwich Mean Time (G.M.T. + 2), making it seven hours ahead of U.S. Eastern Standard Time (E.S.T. + 7).

Protocol

 Greetings
- In first business encounters, a handshake is typical.
- The greeting can take many forms in Greece; a handshake, an embrace, or a kiss can all be encountered at first meetings or among friends and acquaintances.

 Titles/Forms of Address
- Older people are greatly respected in Greece, and therefore are always addressed formally (using titles, and so forth).
- The order of Greek names is the same as in the U.S.: given name first, followed by surname.

 Gestures
- To indicate "no," use an upward nod of the head (similar to the U.S. gesture for "yes," although less pronounced).
- To indicate "yes," tilt your head to either side.
- Recently Greeks have begun to use North American gestures for "yes" and "no"; this can be confusing.
- Anger is sometimes shown by a smile.
- After giving or receiving a compliment, Greeks sometimes make a puff of breath through the lips to ward off the "evil eye".

 Gifts
- The Greeks are very generous; if you compliment an object too enthusiastically, it may be given to you.
- For business associates, do not give a gift on the first encounter.
- Avoid the too lavish and the too skimpy, and gifts that are only a means of showing your company logo.
- If you are invited to a home, compliment the children of the household and give them a small gift; flowers or a cake is also appropriate for the hostess.

 Dress
- Conservative business clothing is best.
- Women should wear dresses or suits in subtle colors.

GUATEMALA

Guatemala

CULTURAL NOTE

guatemala was the center of the Mayan civilization, considered by many to be the most advanced pre-Columbian culture in the Americas. The Mayans built monumental cities, developed sophisticated writing and mathematical systems, and dominated Mesoamerica for over 1,000 years. Although Mayan civilization peaked in the ninth century, it was still a formidable presence six hundred years later when the Europeans arrived. If the Mayan Empire had possessed a single leader, it might have fared better against the Spanish conquistadores. But the Mayan civilization was akin to classical Greece, with warring city-states and shifting alliances. The conquistadores turned one Mayan city against another. Defeated by division and disease, the Mayans saw thirteen centuries of rule end in less than a decade.

Country Background

History

Guatemala was home to the Mayan people, who developed a highly advanced civilization. Overrun in the Spanish conquest of 1523-1524, the country was placed under Spanish colonial rule. Independence was declared in 1821; several other Central American countries also broke with Spain at this time. Guatemala was briefly part of the Mexican Empire; later it joined the United Provinces of Central American Federation. When the federation broke up in 1838, Guatemala passed through a period of several military dictatorships.

In 1944, the incumbent dictator was overthrown and a civilian government took power. Between 1945 and 1954, several attempts were made to modernize the society and bring about social reform. However, a military-backed group took control in 1954, and the military continued to dominate Guatemalan politics until 1985.

After 1960, guerrilla movements began to grow in force, finally erupting into full-scale terrorist activities concentrated in Guatemala City. Many leading political figures, including the U.S. ambassador, were killed. A state of siege continued through several elections and changes in power.

In 1982, Brig. General Efraín José Ríos Montt led a military junta that canceled the constitution, dissolved Congress, and suspended political parties. A state of siege was again declared, severely restricting civil liberties, and a special system of courts was established. These courts were independent of the regular court system and were to assist in the return to democracy. Ríos Montt was himself deposed by the army in 1983.

Oscar Humberto Mejía Victores then became head of state. He called for Constituent Assembly elections to begin drafting a new constitution. On January 14, 1986, the new constitution went into effect. Civilian governments have led Guatemala ever since, although both the military and the rebels continue to pose threats to political stability.

Terrorist activities have been increasing since 1990.

Type of Government

Guatemala has had a difficult political history since its independence from Spain in 1821. It has seen dictators, revolutions, and violent transfers of power. Since 1986, however, the country has been under civilian rule.

The Republic of Guatemala has a unicameral legislative house, called the Congress of the Republic. The president is both chief of state and head of the government.

Voting is compulsory for all literate persons over the age of eighteen.

Language

Spanish is the official language. Over 40 percent of the population speaks one of the twenty-three Indian dialects used in the interior of the country. English is understood in places frequented by tourists.

Religion

Guatemala has no official religion. Until the 1950s the vast majority of the people were Roman Catholic. Today, it is in Guatemala that Evangelical Protestantism has made the greatest number of converts among a traditionally Catholic population. At least a quarter of Guatemalans are now Protestants. Since Catholic Guatemalans rarely attend Mass, the Protestants make up the largest number of churchgoers in the country. Evangelical Protestants have even been elected president of Guatemala. Myriad Evangelical Pentecostal and Neopentecostal sects are active in Guatemala; most are associated with a church in the United States. Televangelists have also become popular.

CULTURAL NOTE

*a*s elements of the Catholic church became associated with the betterment of the poor, Catholicism lost popularity among the wealthy. (Indeed, those Catholics whose "liberation theology" allied them with guerrillas came to be considered enemies of the state.) Much of the Guatemalan ruling elite has come to embrace the "prosperity theology" of some Neopentecostal sects. These sects preach that God wants people to be wealthy, and that peasants are impoverished because they lack faith. Expect to encounter such beliefs among Guatemalan business people.

Demographics

With almost 10 million inhabitants, Guatemala is the most populous country in Central America (excluding Mexico, which is usually considered part of North America). The estimated population is 45 percent Ladino (mestizo, which is Indian and European mixed), 45 percent Indian, 5 percent white, 2 percent black; the remaining 3 percent includes a substantial Chinese population.

P——————————————————**CULTURAL NOTE**

> recise population figures are impossible to determine, and reports of the proportion of Indians are often politically motivated. Guatemalan officials state that the proportion of Indians has been getting smaller, and that Indians now constitute less than half the population. On the other hand, supporters of Indian movements estimate that as many as 70 percent of Guatemalans are Indians.
>
> It is clear that the Indians are demanding a greater voice in decision making. The issues in dispute include land reform and more cultural recognition on behalf of the Indians. There is no unanimity among Indian leaders on what to call themselves; many accept the traditional terms *indio* (Indian) or *indígena* (indigenous person). Others prefer the term Maya, despite the fact that Guatemala was home to many Indian tribes; the Mayans were simply the best-known Indian people.

The economy is primarily agricultural. The main crops (which are also exported) are sugarcane, corn, bananas, coffee, beans, and livestock.

Cultural Orientation

Cognitive Styles: How Guatemalans Organize and Process Information

Guatemalans love to talk and discuss. In a discussion, foreigners can easily perceive Guatemalan acceptance of information where no such acceptance exists. Guatemalans process information subjectively and associatively rather than objectively or abstractly. They will look at the particulars of each situation, rather than appeal to a rule or law to solve their problems.

Negotiation Strategies: What Guatemalans Accept as Evidence

Subjective feelings are much more important than objective facts in determining the truth. There is some faith in the ideology of the church (Protestant and Catholic) in providing the truth, but Guatemalans are more apt to trust in the ideology of their ethnic heritage.

Value Systems: The Basis for Behavior

The value systems of the indigenous Indians are very different from those of the ruling class.

Locus of Decision Making

The individual is responsible for his or her decisions, but these must be viewed in the context of the needs of the family, group, and organization. In Guatemala, "friends do things for friends"—thus it is necessary to develop friendships with those you are doing business with. In the workplace, your ability to get along with colleagues is more important than your expertise. Remember that 1 percent of the ruling class control most of the business sector.

Sources of Anxiety Reduction

Wealth and family ties give the individual status and security. Trust and loyalty are centered on close kin. The Catholic church has little influence in the government, but its precepts permeate the population and give structure to life. Often, it seems more important to make a pronouncement than to actually carry out the action. Progress in any endeavor takes a long time, which protects those who are threatened by change.

Issues of Equality/Inequality

Deep-seated social, economic, and political inequity exists, particularly between the mestizos and the Mayans. These ethnic relations have been changing and are dynamic, ranging from cordial and tolerant to open hostility and violence. Changes in the political system are often made by revolution or military coups. Guatemalan machismo is often displayed by being antireligious, avoiding manual work, and showing wealth through conspicuous consumption. Women are still considered subordinate.

Business Practices

Appointments

PUNCTUALITY

- ♦ Punctuality, although not strictly adhered to in daily living, is expected from foreigners and in business circles.
- ♦ There are many Asian-owned manufacturing companies in Guatemala. A business run along Asian management lines will consider punctuality very important.

- Remember that many Europeans and South Americans write the day first, then the month, then the year (e.g., December 3, 1999, is written 3.12.99). This is the case in Guatemala.
- Business hours are 8:00 A.M. to noon and 2:00 to 6:00 P.M., Monday through Friday. Government offices are open 8:00 A.M. to 4:30 P.M. or 9:00 A.M. to 3:30 P.M., Monday through Friday and do not close for lunch.
- Make appointments one month in advance by telephone or telex.
- The best times to visit Guatemala are February through July and September through November. Common vacation times are the two weeks before and after Christmas and Easter, Independence Day (September 15), and the month of August.

 Negotiating

- Business is done among Guatemalans only after a relationship has been established. Spend time forming a friendship before jumping into business discussions.
- Business tends to take place at a much slower pace than in North America or Europe. Be calm and patient with delays. Several trips may be necessary to accomplish a transaction.
- There is a strong sense of personal honor on the part of the Guatemalan business person. Therefore, do not criticize a person in public, pull rank, or do anything that will cause him or her embarrassment.
- The majority of Guatemalan *maquiladoras* (manufacturing plants) are Asian-owned (primarily owned and managed by South Koreans). Among Asians (as among Guatemalans), it is important to avoid causing a loss of face.
- Business is discussed in an office or over a meal. It is not discussed in a home or around family.

- Guatemalans find loud voices annoying. Speak in soft, well-modulated tones (especially in public).
- Contacts are very important in establishing business relationships. Try to find contacts through embassies, banks, or shipping corporations.
- It is still rare to find women in upper levels of business in Guatemala. Visiting businesswomen should act extremely professional and convey that they are representing their company, rather than speaking for themselves personally.

Business Entertaining

- Business breakfasts or lunches are preferred to dinners.
- An invitation to a Guatemalan home is offered for the purpose of getting to know you personally. This is not the time to discuss business. Spouses are usually invited to such gatherings.
- Good topics of conversation are Guatemalan tourist sites, your family, your job, and so forth. Topics to avoid include the political unrest and violence.

> *t*he Cold War is not over in Latin America. Do not be surprised if some Guatemalans still see a clear and present Communist threat. It is also not unusual to claim that the military is defending Guatemala's "territorial integrity" against incursion from neighboring Central American nations. It is true, however, that Guatemala has Latin America's longest-running guerrilla opposition. None of the above makes good dinner conversation.
>
> **CULTURAL NOTE**

- If you speak to a married couple, the man will be the one who will converse or answer your questions.
- The main meal of the day is taken at noon. This will probably include black beans, tortillas or meat, and fruit and vegetables.
- Meals are usually taken "family style" with each person serving herself or himself. It is rude to take food and leave it on your plate uneaten.

Time

- Local time is six hours behind Greenwich Mean Time (G.M.T. - 6); Guatemala is in the same time zone as U.S. Central Standard Time (E.S.T. - 1).

Protocol

Greetings

- Men always shake hands when greeting. Women sometimes shake hands with men; this is done at the woman's discretion.
- The handshake is usually accompanies by a verbal greeting, such as *¡Buenos dias!* (good morning/day), *¡Buenas tardes!* (good afternoon), or *¡Buenas noches!* (good evening).
- Expect to receive fairly limp handshakes; give the same in return.

- Close male friends may hug or pat each other on the back in greeting. Women will often pat your right forearm or shoulder instead of shaking hands. If they are close friends, they may hug or kiss each other on the cheek.
- At parties or business gatherings, it is customary to greet and shake hands with everyone in the room individually.

 Titles/Forms of Address

- Most people you meet should be addressed by their title alone, without their surname. Only children, family members, and close friends address each other by their first names.
- Persons who do not have professional titles should be addressed as Mr., Mrs., or Miss, plus their surname. In Spanish, these are
  - Mr. = *Señor*
  - Mrs. = *Señora*
  - Miss = *Señorita*
- Most Hispanics have two surnames: one from their father, which is listed first, followed by one from their mother. Only the father's surname is commonly used when addressing someone; e.g., Señor Juan Antonio Martinez García is addressed as Señor Martinez and Señorita Ana María Gutierrez Herrera is addressed as Señorita Gutierrez. When a woman marries, she usually adds her husband's surname and goes by that surname. If the two people in the above example married, she would be known as Señora Ana María Gutierrez Herrera de Martinez. Most people would refer to her as Señora de Martinez or, less formally, Señora Martinez.

 Gestures

- Guatemalans wave good-bye using a gesture that looks like someone fanning themselves: hand raised, palm toward the body, and a wave of the fingers back and forth, with the fingers together as if encased in a mitten.
- To beckon someone, extend your arm (palm down) and make a slight scooping motion toward your body (more with the fingers than the wrist).
- The "fig" gesture (thumb-tip protruding from between the fingers of a closed fist) is considered obscene in Guatemala. (However, in some parts of South America it is considered a "good luck" gesture!)
- The "O.K." sign (thumb and forefinger forming a circle) as used in the United States is considered obscene.
- Make eye contact while speaking with someone in Guatemala.

 Gifts

- If invited to a home, it is appropriate to bring a small gift of flowers or candy.
- Do not bring white flowers as a gift; they are reserved for funerals.
- Gifts are given in the business setting, although not necessarily on an initial visit. If you will be returning to Guatemala, you may ask your counterpart if there is something you can bring from the United States.

*r*emember that Guatemala is in a tectonically active zone, with frequent earthquakes and occasional volcanoes. Easily breakable gifts may not be the best choice.

Dress

- For business, a lightweight suit is appropriate for men; women should wear a dress or skirt and blouse.
- When dressing casually, men should wear pants and a shirt in cities and a sweater in the cooler highlands; women should wear a skirt and blouse. Short pants and jeans are not appropriate for cities and more rural areas. Women in pants are very uncommon and may offend some people.
- Military clothing is illegal; it can neither be worn nor brought into the country.

TEGUCIGALPA
•

Honduras

Country Background

*d*uring the 1980s, anti-Communist Honduras was seen by the United States as a pivotal outpost of stability in Central America. Consequently, Honduras was the recipient of massive financial and military aid from the United States. Since 1990, Honduras has tried to reduce its dependence on the United States by encouraging investment from other nations. A large number of foreign-owned manufacturing plants (*maquiladoras*) have been built, with owners in Hong Kong, Singapore, Taiwan, and especially South Korea. These industries were attracted by tax advantages and Honduras' low wages.

————————————————CULTURAL NOTE

History

The Mayan Indians achieved an advanced level of civilization in Honduras. But the Mayan Empire had passed its peak before the arrival of Europeans. By the time Christopher Columbus reached Honduras on his final trans-Atlantic voyage in 1502, the Mayans had already abandoned many of their cities. Spain succeeded in conquering the Honduran Indians in the 1530s and established colonial rule. The province of Honduras was ruled out of neighboring Guatemala.

————————————————CULTURAL NOTE

*t*he Indian leader Chief Lempira led his Lenca tribe in a valiant but futile resistance against the Spanish conquistadores. The Hondurans have honored the memory of his bravery by naming their currency the *lempira*.

In 1821, Honduras (together with the other Central American provinces) declared independence from Spain. Honduras briefly joined the United Provinces of Central America but attained full independence in 1838 when this federation collapsed. However, Honduras had to continue resisting domination by Guatemala.

Like its Central American neighbors, Honduras periodically experienced both instability and dictatorship. This continued into the twentieth century.

In 1956, a military coup placed a junta in charge of Honduras. This junta allowed the formation in 1957 of a national legislature, which appointed the Liberal Party candidate Dr. Ramón Villeda Morales as president.

During Villeda's term, great strides were made in liberal constitutional reforms. But during the 1963 elections, conservative military officers overthrew Villeda in a bloody coup, then exiled the Liberal Party and turned the national police into special security forces.

The military's National Party continued to control the country through the several successive presidencies.

Under President Jimmy Carter, the United States encouraged Honduran leaders to turn the country back to civilian rule. The United States even negotiated a settlement of a border dispute between Honduras and El Salvador. A Honduran constitutional assembly was elected in 1980, and general elections were held in 1982. President Roberto Suazo Córdova of the Liberal Party came to power. Through extensive aid and cooperative efforts, Honduras joined with the United States to combat economic recession and the political instability of its Central American neighbors. Peaceful elections have continued since that time.

Type of Government

The Republic of Honduras is run by a president (who is both chief of state and head of the government), a Council of Ministers, and a unicameral National Congress with 128 seats.

Voting is compulsory for anyone over the age of eighteen.

CULTURAL NOTE

*C*olonial Honduras was rather neglected by Spain. As a result, a local oligarchy did not evolve to dominate Honduras (at least, not to the extent that oligarchies dominate other Central American nations). Although economic disparity between rich and poor exists in Honduras, it is not as severe as elsewhere.

Since independence from Spain in 1821, Honduras has experienced great political instability. There have been nearly 300 civil wars, rebellions, and changes of government—almost half of them during this century. In the last decade, however, the political situation has been relatively stable, in comparison to the turbulence of its Central American neighbors.

Language

Spanish is the official language, although several Indian dialects are also spoken in more remote areas. Many Hondurans have a basic understanding of English and it is widely understood in urban and tourist centers.

Religion

The Roman Catholic church has a strong cultural influence in Honduras, with 85 percent of the population following its teachings. Various Protestant sects account for another 10 percent.

Demographics

The population of Honduras is about 5 million. The ethnic makeup is 90 percent mestizo (a mixture of Indian and European heritage), 7 percent Indian, 2 percent black, and 1 percent white. There is a small population of Arabs and Lebanese, who are disproportionately represented in Honduran business.

*h*onduras is one of the poorest and least developed countries in Central America. However, the people are warm and hospitable, despite their humble circumstances. They are proud of their heritage and value the traditions and ties of the family. It is common to find an extended family of grandparents, uncles, aunts, and children all living in one house. Among working Hondurans, 62 percent are engaged in agriculture.

Cultural Orientation

Cognitive Styles: How Hondurans Organize and Process Information

In Honduras one will find a relatively open society that readily accepts change. Negotiations may take a long time to complete. Since education is by rote, information processing is subjective and associative. Hondurans become personally involved with all problems, seldom using universal rules or laws to make decisions.

Negotiation Strategies: What Hondurans Accept as Evidence

Subjective feelings are the primary source of truth, ameliorated by faith in the church or the cultural heritage. Objective facts are seldom seen as a useful basis for the truth.

Value Systems: The Basis for Behavior

The pluralistic atmosphere of Honduran social and political life stems from a more homogeneous mestizo society, which developed without extensive, institutionalized slavery.

Locus of Decision Making

Since one gains one's identity from family lineage and one's role in society, the individual's ability to make decisions is compromised by his or her need to satisfy family and social groups. One's ability to maintain a harmonious group is more important than one's expertise. A small elite group, mostly foreigners, control all economic resources. They are relatively weak politically, as they have not formed a cohesive group.

Sources of Anxiety Reduction

The Catholic church gives social structure to life through its precepts and holidays, though it is not a strong political force. One's role in the social structure and the presence of a strong extended family give one a sense of security. Hondurans are always busy, but progress is not a major goal. This laid-back behavior helps to reduce anxiety.

Issues of Equality/Inequality

Honduras is the poorest country in Latin America. The homogeneity of the mestizo society only makes for a large, poor middle class, with the few rich above and the poorer Miskito Indians in the east at the bottom of the social ladder. Yet Hondurans feel they are all equal because each individual is unique, and there is an inherent trust in people because of the social interrelationships of extended families and friends. Machismo is strong, and there are clear and classic role differences between the sexes.

Business Practices

Appointments

—————————————————————— **PUNCTUALITY**

- ◆ Scheduled appointments may be delayed, and punctuality is not strictly adhered to in daily life. However, punctuality is expected from foreigners.
- ◆ For social events (such as parties), arrive about thirty minutes late.

- Remember that many Europeans and South Americans write the day first, then the month, then the year (e.g., December 3, 1999, is written 3.12.99). This is the case in Honduras.
- Business hours are 7:30 A.M. to 4:30 P.M., Monday through Friday. Government offices are open from 8:00 A.M. to 3:30 P.M.
- Personal relationships are exceedingly important. Be sure to make contacts through appropriate intermediaries.
- The best time to visit Honduras is between February and June. The rainy season lasts from May to November, and December and August are popular vacation times.
- Meetings may take place at breakfast, lunch, or dinner. Let your counterpart suggest the time.

Negotiating

- Business tends to take place at a much slower pace than in North America or Europe. Be calm and patient with delays. Several trips may be necessary to conclude a business transaction.
- Personal friendships are vital to business in Honduras. Hondurans are looking for a long-term relationship based on mutual trust and reliability. It is important to spend time building a relationship before jumping into business discussions. Plan to make repeated visits and have contact after your trips. Try to have the same person involved in the contact, since much of the business relationship will be based on this personal friendship.
- Latin Americans respect the value of individual dignity and honor, regardless of social status or wealth. Therefore, do not pull rank, publicly criticize, or do anything that would cause a person to lose face.
- In their desire to please, Hondurans are likely to give you the answer they think you want to hear. Be careful how you phrase your questions. For example, a question such as "Does the market open at 8:00?" will probably be answered "yes," whether this is the truth or not, since this is the answer they think you want to hear. Instead, phrase questions so that they require more detailed answers, such as "What time does this market open?"
- Remember to avoid saying "no" in public while in Honduras; always avoid embarrassing anyone. "Maybe" or "we will see" generally means no.
- Because of the desire to tell people what they want to hear, get all agreements in writing. A verbal "yes" may have been given out of politeness and may not be considered binding.

- When negotiating, emphasize the trust and mutual compatibility of the two companies. Stress the benefits to the person and his or her family and pride. This emotional approach will be more effective than the logical bottom line of a proposal. If there is a disagreement, do not expect a compromise, since this is seen as showing weakness.
- Decisions are not made quickly. Indeed, snap decisions are suspect; take time before announcing a final decision, even if your mind is already made up.
- Include a margin for bargaining in your beginning price, but do not over-inflate proposals. This will cause suspicion. Using graphs and other visuals in making a presentation will make a positive impression.
- Although the situation is rapidly changing, it is still rare to find women in upper levels of management. A woman may face some initial lack of respect in Honduras. Since titles and position are valued, a businesswoman should emphasize that she is representing her company rather than speaking for herself.
- Hondurans are status-conscious. At least one member of the negotiating team should be from higher-level management. Mention university degrees that you may hold, stay in good hotels, and eat at good restaurants.
- Hondurans are proud of their heritage and their individuality. Therefore, be careful of sensitivities in referring to citizens of the United States as "Americans," since this term applies to all North and Latin Americans.
- Do not be offended if another is served before you in a line. Preference is given to the elderly and those with higher positions and social status.
- Do not overly admire another's belongings. The owner may feel obligated to give them to you.
- Have business cards and other material printed in Spanish as well as English. Not everyone at all business levels speaks English well enough to read without difficulty. Even those fluent in English will appreciate the effort. Present your card to a Honduran Spanish side up.

 Business Entertaining

- Good topics of conversation are Honduran tourist sites, your family and job at home, and sports (especially soccer, the national sport). Topics to avoid are local politics and the unrest in Central America.
- The best times for business meetings are breakfast and lunch, the main meal of the day. If you are invited to a local home or invited to a meal where spouses are also included, do not expect to discuss business. Instead, socialize and get to know the family. Dinner is taken between 8:30 and 9:00 P.M. Arrive about thirty minutes late.
- Foreign businesswomen should never invite their male counterparts to a business dinner unless spouses also attend. For business lunches, eat at your hotel and have the bill added to your tab; otherwise the man will never let you pay.

Time
- Honduras is six hours behind Greenwich Mean Time (G.M.T. - 6), which is the same as Central Standard Time in the United States (E.S.T. - 1).

Protocol

Greetings

- Men shake hands in greeting. Women often pat each other on the right arm or shoulder instead of shaking hands. If they are close friends, they may hug or kiss each other on the cheek.
- Do not be surprised to receive a limp handshake; give the same in return.
- At parties it is customary to greet and shake hands with everyone in the room.

Titles/Forms of Address

- Note that only children, family members, and close friends address each other by their first names.
- Titles are very important in Honduras. People with professional titles should be addressed by their title alone, without their surname.
- Persons who do not have professional titles should be addressed as Mr., Mrs., or Miss, plus their surname. In Spanish, these are:
  - Mr. = *Señor*
  - Mrs. = *Señora*
  - Miss = *Señorita*
- Most Hispanics have two surnames: one from their father, which is listed first, followed by one from their mother. Only the father's surname is commonly used when addressing someone; e.g., Señor Juan Antonio Martinez García is addressed as Señor Martinez and Señorita Ana María Gutierrez Herrera is addressed Señorita Gutierrez. When a woman marries, she usually adds her husband's surname and goes by that surname. If the two people in the above example married, she would be known as Señora Ana María Gutierrez Herrera de Martinez. Most people would refer to her as: Señora de Martinez, or, less formally, Señora Martinez.

Gestures

- Several gestures are unique to this area. Placing a finger below the eye indicates caution. A hand below the elbow means that a person is stingy. "No" is indicated by waving the index finger. Joining one's hands together shows strong approval.
- Conversations take place at a much closer distance than may be considered comfortable in the United States. Pulling away from your counterpart may be interpreted as rejection.
- Honduran men are warm and friendly and make a lot of physical contact. They often touch shoulders, or hold another's arm. To withdraw from such a contact is considered insulting.

Dress

- Business: Men should wear a conservative business suit. Women should wear a skirt and blouse or a dress. Honduran businessmen commonly wear a *guayabera*, which is a decorative shirt, rather than a shirt and tie.
- Casual: A light shirt and pants for men and a skirt and blouse for women may be worn in urban areas. Revealing clothing for women and shorts for either sex are not appropriate. Pants for women are rarely seen and may offend some locals.

VICTORIA

Hong Kong

CULTURAL NOTE

*t*he vast majority of Hong Kong residents are Chinese. Hong Kong Chinese who do business with Westerners usually choose for themselves a name (or a nickname) that Westerners can pronounce and remember. They expect a similar courtesy from you: Your surname should be transliterated into Chinese. This is not an actual translation; Chinese sounds will be selected that are similar to the sounds of your surname. (You may not think your transliteration sounds very much like your surname. What is important is that it sounds similar to Cantonese ears.) Since Chinese is a monosyllabic language, each syllable of your surname will be represented by a different Chinese character. Make sure to have a native speaker of Chinese help you, since it is easy to select a good sound with an unfortunate meaning. Don't repeat the mistake Coca-Cola made in the 1920s: its Chinese transliteration sounded like the words "Coca-Cola"—but it meant "bite the wax tadpole!"

Country Background

History

In 1699 the British East India Trading Company started using Hong Kong Harbor to trade with China. It continued to monopolize trade until 1834, when the monopoly was abolished.

The Opium War (1839-1842) started when the Chinese tried to prevent opium shipments to China, and culminated with a treaty that ceded Hong Kong Island to the United Kingdom and opened five Chinese ports to the British traders. The Kowloon Peninsula, Stonecutters Island, and the New Territories were later added to the colony. Hong Kong was declared a duty-free port in 1841.

Type of Government

Hong Kong is a British Crown Colony. The British monarch is the chief of state. The head of the government is the governor, who is appointed by the British government.

Hong Kong's governor directs the colony's government along with two councils. The Executive Council is an advisory body and traditionally includes Chinese and Portuguese members. The Legislative Council enacts legislation and approves

the budget. There is also an independent judiciary. The current governor is expected to serve until 1997.

Because the ninety-nine year lease for the New Territories will expire in 1997,
the British and Chinese governments began discussions in 1982 to determine Hong
Kong's future. The agreement they reached will make Hong Kong a special administrative region of China in 1997. It will also provide for the continuation of Hong
Kong's unique economic, legal, and social systems for fifty years after 1997. Under
an agreement in 1985, Britain and China concluded that Hong Kong would be permitted to keep its capitalist system for fifty years after 1997.

Unfortunately, international confidence in the smooth transition of Hong Kong
from the British to the Chinese has been eroded by events such as the Tiananmen
Massacre in June of 1989.

Language

Hong Kong's two official languages are Chinese and English. The most com-
mon Chinese dialect is Cantonese, which is a loudly expressed tonal language.
However, since mainland China uses the Mandarin dialect of Modern Standard
Chinese as its official language, Mandarin is being taught in Hong Kong's schools.

Religion

There is no official religion. There are about one-half million Christians in Hong
Kong, divided equally between Protestants and Roman Catholics. There are also
small numbers of Muslims and Hindus.

Many Chinese follow the teachings of a variety of religions at the same time.
Strong elements of Confucianism and Taoism (which originated in China) along
with Buddhism (from India) influence many aspects of Chinese life.

t   **CULTURAL NOTE**

raditional Chinese philosophy is founded on the concepts of order and harmony. This is reflected
in many traditions of conformity and the Chinese business person's awareness of his or her position in relation to ancestry, social position, and the family or business unit. Ancient beliefs and religious
practices that support this "universal order" can be observed in the Chinese reliance on the lunar calendar, various rituals in the home and at work, and the use of "diviners" to determine auspicious times and
dates for important occasions.

Demographics

Hong Kong's estimated population in 1992 was 5.9 million. The population density is at least five times greater than that of Tokyo, Japan.

Less than 2 percent of the population is European. The Chinese make up over
90 percent of the labor force, and stem from five major groups in Southern China:

- The Cantonese—the largest percentage of the population, from Kwan tung
  province
- The Fukkien
- Hainan
- The Chui Chow
- The Hakka—from the New Territories

Cultural Orientation

Cognitive Styles: How Hong Kong Citizens Organize and Process Information

In Hong Kong, the Chinese process information associatively unless they have had an extensive Western education, in which case they will be more abstractive. As a collective culture they hold group loyalty above personal feelings, but they also feel that particular relationships are more important than personal values.

Negotiation Strategies: What Hong Kong Citizens Accept as Evidence

The Hong Kong Chinese are basically feeling-oriented, but faith in the ideology of the group may be a more relevant source of the truth. Those with higher education may accept objective facts over personal feelings. They stress wholeness over fragmentation.

Value Systems: The Basis for Behavior

As in China, the Hong Kong Chinese consider it imperative to save face. A person's actions reflect on his or her family, plus any other groups of which he or she is a member. The following three sections identify the Value Systems in the predominant culture—their methods of dividing right from wrong, good from evil, and so forth.

Locus of Decision Making

Decisions are made through consensus of the group, where group members defer to persons with the highest ethos. The Hong Kong Chinese will use polite vagaries rather than say "no." The self is down played. One's face is maintained by adherence to the ethical norms of society in all human dealings, and one must never cause another embarrassment. There is a strong authoritative structure demanding impartiality and obedience.

Sources of Anxiety Reduction

The Hong Kong Chinese's feelings of ethnic pride are juxtaposed against the uncertainty of the political situation, and this induces anxiety. The family is the most important unit of social organization. Life is an organization of obligations to relationships. Emotional restraint is prized, and aggressive behavior is frowned upon. One must maintain intragroup harmony and avoid overt conflict in interpersonal relations.

Issues of Equality/Inequality

Age is revered. Respect and deference are directed from the young to the old, and authority and responsibility from the old to the young. There is an inherent trust in people because of the homogeneity of the populace and social pressure. Although no one feels like Hong Kong is home, there is a natural bias against foreigners. There are clearly differentiated sex roles in society, but Western-style equality is creeping in. Men still dominate in public situations.

Business Practices

Appointments

────────────────────────────── PUNCTUALITY

* Punctuality is considered a virtue among Chinese business people. Make every effort to be on time, which is not easy given Hong Kong's congested streets. Punctuality demonstrates respect.
* In Chinese tradition, no one is exempt from apologizing. Be sure to apologize profusely if you are late, even if it was not your fault.
* Do not show offense if your Hong Kong counterpart is a half-hour late. You immediately put yourself at a disadvantage if you appear to be under a time constraint.

- Appointments should be made as far in advance as possible. It is not unusual to schedule appointments two months before your arrival in Hong Kong.
- Many Hong Kong residents go on vacation during the summer and the weeks surrounding Christmas, Easter, and the Chinese New Year. Try to schedule business trips in October, November, and March through June.
- Some Chinese businesses close for the entire week of Chinese New Year.
- Offices may close from 12:00 noon to 2:00 P.M., and many executives may take a longer lunch. In China, many people nap at this time, although this is not common in Hong Kong.
- Much of Hong Kong follows a six-day workweek. Hours start about 9:00 A.M. and finish at 5:00 P.M., Monday through Friday. Saturdays from 9:00 A.M. to 1:00 P.M. is normal; longer hours are common.
- Never refuse an invitation to lunch or dinner if at all possible. If you cannot make it, immediately suggest an alternative time. Your success in business depends upon establishing social relationships.
- Greet everyone when you arrive, beginning with the most senior or elderly.

Negotiating

────────────────────────────── CULTURAL NOTE

*h*ave business cards prepared with Chinese on one side and English on the other. Take a large supply of them with you, since exchanging cards is almost a ritual. Examine all cards presented to you with respect and interest.

- Age is respected by the Chinese. If your Hong Kong clients are Chinese, your chief representative should not be young. A person aged 50 or older will command respect.
- Present all materials and ideas in a modest and patient manner. Aggression is out of place, and if someone loses face during negotiations, the contract may be lost.
- The Chinese are exceptional diplomats when it comes to conversation. They will go to great lengths to ensure that no potentially insulting or embarrassing statements are made.
- Never confront a Chinese person with an unpleasant fact in public; discuss it in private. Appearances are extremely important.

- The word "yes" does not necessarily mean "I agree with you." A closer meaning would be "I heard you."
- "It would be difficult" may be the closest a traditional Chinese businessperson ever gets to saying "no."
- Always prepare many alternatives in order to give the Chinese negotiator room to negate several options with dignity.
- Be conscious of the positions and status of the Chinese players. It is not appropriate to direct all information to the senior negotiator. His or her presence may be ceremonial, and the more junior staff may be expected to relay the material to the group leader.
- Keep the same negotiating team throughout the process.
- Negotiations can seem exceedingly slow, with extensive attention to detail. This is a normal process. Toward the end, the Chinese negotiating team may request a large discount—which they may refer to as a "compromise."
- The Chinese custom of consulting a *fengshui* man (a diviner or geomancer) to determine auspicious dates and arrangements for opening new offices, moving, and so forth, should be observed. There are many issues that can be resolved in a efficient manner by respecting your Chinese counterparts' belief in the *fengshui's* prophecies.

CULTURAL NOTE

*N*egotiation occurs over cups of tea. Always accept an offer of tea, whether you want it or not. When you are served, wait for the host to drink first.

Chinese negotiators commonly use the teacups as visual aids. One cup may be used to represent your company, another cup to represent the Hong Kong company, and the position of the cups will be changed to indicate how far apart the companies are on the terms of an agreement.

Business Entertaining

- Entertain at prestigious restaurants and banquet halls. First-class hotels usually can provide facilities.

CULTURAL NOTE

*S*eating etiquette is important. The guest of honor traditionally sits opposite the host. The next most important guest sits to the left of the guest of honor; the third-ranking person is placed to the right of the guest of honor. This continues all the way around the table. Surprisingly to Westerners, this results in the least important people being seated next to the host!

Chinese tables are traditionally round, with a maximum of twelve seats. Since there is no "head" of the table (as there is at a rectangular table), the seat of honor is the one furthest from the entrance. The host sits opposite, in the seat closest to the door.

Placing the host closest to the entrance has advantages. This puts him or her in a better position to oversee the wait staff. Furthermore, the host is expected to escort honored guests out to their car.

- Banquets are a large part of Hong Kong's Chinese culture. Celebrating a productive business meeting or a new alliance usually occurs over eight to twelve courses of a well-prepared banquet.
- A banquet is a very acceptable gift for a Chinese client, and must definitely be reciprocated if offered to you.

- Pace yourself at a Chinese banquet! Eat sparingly of each course. The best dishes tend to be served in the middle courses.
- Using chopsticks will enhance your reputation. Remember, one end of the chopsticks is used for eating, the other end for serving. Do not stick chopsticks straight up in the rice bowl; this makes them look very similar to the joss incense sticks used in religious ceremonies.
- Rice is seen as a filler, so do not eat extensive amounts of it. Leave most rice untouched during the last course; doing otherwise will imply that there was not enough food.
- Entertaining business clients over lunch or dinner often takes place at a restaurant in a private club.
- A very traditional Chinese restaurant might not provide napkins. You are expected to wipe your hands on the tablecloth. At such a restaurant, leaving a messy tablecloth indicates that you have eaten well and enjoyed the food.
- Banquets are long, so everyone leaves soon after the final course.
- It is rare for spouses to be included in an invitation for a business dinner.

Time
- Hong Kong is eight hours ahead of Greenwich Mean Time (G.M.T. + 8), or thirteen hours ahead of U.S. Eastern Standard Time (E.S.T. + 13).

Protocol

 Greetings

- The traditional Chinese greeting is a bow. When bowing to a superior, you should bow more deeply and allow him or her to rise first.
- Either traditional English or Chinese greetings are appropriate. Men and women shake hands, and sincere compliments are given. The Chinese appreciate compliments, although their self-effacing nature will not allow them to accept them. It would be poor manners to agree.
- Traditional Chinese greetings often refer to food. "Have you eaten rice yet?" is a common greeting. The question is rhetorical, so always answer, "yes," whether you have eaten recently or not.
- Always recognize and greet the most senior or elderly person in a group first, and politely inquire about their health.
- Courtesy and formality in behavior and in dress are an integral part of Chinese manners. Do not offer opinions too freely, and avoid inquiring about an individual's plans or where he or she is going. The Chinese find the disclosure of excessive amounts of information vulgar.
- Avoid any behavior that could be construed as aggressive or loud. Decorum is important in both Chinese and British traditions.
- If you only speak English, understand that you may have difficulty interpreting the emotional content of a conversation in Chinese. A simple Chinese conversation (especially in Cantonese) may sound like a heated argument to Western ears.

Titles/Forms of Address

- Most people you meet should be addressed with a title and their surname. If a person does not have a professional title (President, Engineer, Doctor), simply use Mr., Madam, Mrs., or Miss, plus their surname.
- Chinese names generally consist of a family name followed by two (sometimes one) personal names. In the name Chang Wu Jiang, Chang is the surname (or clan name). He would be addressed with his title plus Chang (Mr. Chang, Dr. Chang).
- When writing in English, Hong Kong Chinese tend to hyphenate their personal names. Thus, Chang Wu Jiang is likely to write his name as Chang Wu-Jiang. Mainland Chinese sometimes dispense with the hyphen and write the two personal names as one: Chang Wujiang.
- Chinese wives do not generally take their husband's surnames, but instead maintain their maiden names. Although Westerners commonly address a married woman as Mrs. plus her husband's family name, it is more appropriate to call her Madam plus her maiden family name. As an example, Li Chu-Chin (female) is married to Chang Wu-Jiang (male) Westerners would probably call her Mrs. Chang. She is properly addressed as Madam Li.
- Thankfully, many Chinese adopt an English first name so that English speakers can have a familiar-sounding name to identify them by. Thus, Chang Wu-Jiang may call himself Mr. Wally Chang. Others use their initials (Mr. W.J. Chang).
- If many Chinese seem to have similar clan names, it is because there are only about 400 different surnames in China! However, when these surnames are transcribed into English, there are several possible variations. For example, Wong, Wang, and Huang are all English versions of the same Chinese clan name.

Gestures

- Members of the same sex may hold hands to signify friendship, but members of the opposite sex may not.
- Although women may cross their legs, men should keep their feet on the floor. Place your hands in your lap while sitting.
- The Chinese may communicate in closer proximity than is common in the United States.
- Do not pat people on the shoulder or initiate any physical contact. It is not appreciated.
- "Come here" is signified by turning the palm face down and waving the fingers.

Gifts

- Gift giving is an intricate and important custom in Hong Kong. The best-intentioned businessperson can offend counterparts by giving
    - Clocks (they connote death)
    - Books (they represent a "Curse to Lose" for gamblers)
    - Blankets (they stifle the recipient's prosperity)
    - Unwrapped gifts (this is rude)
    - Gifts wrapped in blue (the color of mourning)
    - Green hats (they suggest that you are a cuckold or your sister is a prostitute)

- Do not open a gift in the presence of the giver.
- Accept and give gifts with both hands.
- Gifts from the Chinese may seem extremely generous, even somewhat extravagant. This is generally just their way of communicating their feelings of respect and friendship.
- Timing the presentation of a gift is vital.
- Bring items from your home with you as gifts (i.e.: handicrafts, jazz CDs, Western items like belt buckles, and so forth).
- Hosting a banquet is a very acceptable gift for Chinese clients, and is required if they have hosted one for you.
- If you are invited to a home, take candy, fruit, scotch, and so forth. Do not excessively admire anything—your host may feel obligated to give it to you.

g————————————**CULTURAL NOTE**

ifts are often exchanged between business associates during Christmas and the Chinese New Year. It is customary to give a gift of money in a red envelope to children and to the (nongovernmental) service personnel you deal with on a regular basis. This gift is called a *hong bao*. Give only new bills in even numbers and even amounts. Many employers give each employee a *hong bao* equivalent to one month's salary at the Chinese New Year.

 Dress

- Business suits in dark colors for men and muted colors for women are appropriate. Washable, lightweight fabrics are used.
- Do not wear blue or white at social functions, as these colors are associated with death and mourning.

Hungary

Country Background

Hungary is a landlocked Central European nation approximately the size of the state of Indiana.

Location

Hungary is bordered by the Slovak Republic to the north; Austria to the west; the former Yugoslavian Republics of Slovenia, Croatia, and Serbia to the south (all of which were once part of the Austro-Hungarian Empire); and Romania and Ukraine to the east. Since the breakup of the U.S.S.R., Hungary no longer has a common border with Russia. The Danube River, which passes through the capital, Budapest, affords limited shipping to Hungary.

History

An amazingly fertile country, Hungary was intentionally kept agricultural while it was part of the Austro-Hungarian Empire. After World War II, however, the U.S.S.R. instituted massive industrialization projects. Industry now provides 40 percent of the Hungarian GNP. Besides the soil's fertility, Hungarian resources include coal, natural gas, and bauxite.

The liberalism that swept Eastern Europe in the late 1980s fostered changes in Hungary. Long-time Communist leader János Kádár was forced to resign in 1988. The Communists became just another political party, and were roundly defeated in the elections of 1990.

Type of Government

The Republic of Hungary is now a multiparty republic. There is a single legislative body, the National Assembly, with 394 seats.

The prime minister is the head of the government. The state president of Hungary is commmander-in-chief of the armed forces, in addition to being head of state; this gives the position more importance than in most European countries.

Formerly one of the most prosperous members of the Warsaw Pact, Hungary is undergoing a relatively smooth transition from a one-party Communist state to a democracy.

Language

Although Hungary has a significant minority population (primarily German, Slovak, Romanian and Gypsy), 98 percent of the people speak Magyar (Hungarian).

M——————————————————**CULTURAL NOTE**
agyar is not a simple language for English speakers to learn, as it is unrelated to the majority of European languages. Magyar is part of the Finno-Ugric group of the Uralic family of languages; its closest European relatives are Finnish and Estonian.

Religion

About 68 percent of Hungarians are Roman Catholic; 28 percent belong to Protestant denominations. Jews and Orthodox are also present.

Demographics

The population of Hungary is 10.6 million (1991 estimates). Some 62 percent of Hungarians live in urban areas.

Cultural Orientation

Cognitive Styles: How Hungarians Organize and Process Information

The new found freedom in Hungary gives it an atmosphere of openness. However, the training of most business people was under the closed thinking of Communism. Hungarians' basic education causes them to process information associatively, but the more highly educated will think more abstractively. They have a natural tendency to value particular relationships more than stringent adherence to regulations.

Negotiation Strategies: What Hungarians Accept as Evidence

The cataclysmic demise of the Communist party as the ideological focus for all arguments has opened the door to other forms of reasoning. The more exposed to outside influences the participants are, the more they may use objective facts in their reasoning rather than subjective feelings or faith in the ideology of party or group. Intentions, feelings, and opinions are openly expressed, since it is better to be direct than devious, and spontaneity of action is favored.

Value Systems: The Basis for Behavior

With the fall of Communism, Hungary is now open to explore the values of other systems and is subject to all the internal turmoil this brings. The following three sections identify the Value Systems in the predominant culture—their methods of dividing right from wrong, good from evil, and so forth.

Locus of Decision Making

As the movement toward freedom and privatization advances, it is putting the responsibility for decision making on the shoulders of the individual. In many instances the individual may transfer this responsibility to the group as a whole or to a consensus of privileged individuals. It is not clear yet whether the model to be followed will be that of capitalist or socialist democracy.

Sources of Anxiety Reduction

Formerly, the party structure, power, and full employment were the primary stabilizing forces in the lives of the people. Now there is a great deal of day-to-day anxiety over job and family security. The family unit is still recognized as a stabilizing force in society, but the church, which has always been an influence in family life, will now take a more active role.

Issues of Equality/Inequality

The removal of Communist Party control has allowed perceived feelings of inequality to surface. Ethnic disputes have become visible, along with humanitarian needs for equality and the establishment of strong, hierarchically structured systems in government, business, and society.

The dominance of the male head of the family has diminished, since many women are now working outside the home.

Business Practices

Appointments

PUNCTUALITY

- Punctuality is expected in all matters related to business: appointments, deliveries, payments, and so forth.

- Establish a relationship with a Hungarian representative prior to your visit. This individual can initiate contacts for you and accompany you to your appointments. Select this contact person carefully, since your new Hungarian clients will expect you not to change representatives.
- Request appointments in writing two weeks in advance. Business letters may be written in English.
- While all businesses can translate letters from English, not all of them have staff members who can speak it. Consider hiring an interpreter.
- Business hours are 8:30 A.M. to 5:00 P.M., Monday through Friday, and 8:30 A.M. to 1:30 P.M., Saturday.
- Appointments are never made on Saturdays.
- Avoid making business trips to Hungary during July and August, and from mid-December to mid-January. These are holiday and vacation periods.

 Negotiating

- It is difficult to predict how long it will take to negotiate a business deal. Under the former regime, contracts would take months.

 CULTURAL NOTE

*I*t took six months for Sweden's Electrolux Co. to acquire Hungary's Lehel Appliance Works (following two years of background work). If the government is involved, expect negotiations to proceed slowly.

On the other hand, some of Hungary's new entrepreneurs are anxious to move quickly. With small enterprises, this is sometimes possible.

- Whether fast or slow, deals in Hungary cannot be finalized without a lot of eating, drinking, and entertainment.
- Bring plenty of business cards, and give them out to everyone you meet.
- It is not necessary to have your business card translated into Hungarian. Indeed, Hungarian has many foreign loanwords, so your title in English may be similar to what it would be in Hungarian.
- Hungary's relations with its neighbors (especially those it ruled during the days of the Austro-Hungarian Empire) have not always been cordial. Do not bring up your background if you are of Romanian, Slovak, Polish, or Gypsy descent.
- Hungarian food, wine, horses, and sightseeing are good topics to discuss.

Business Entertaining

- Hungarian hospitality is legendary. You will have to fight with your Hungarian counterparts to pay a bill.
- Meals are primarily social occasions. Very little can be accomplished during a lunch, and nothing related to business should be brought up at dinner.
- Expect dinners to last a long time; restaurants usually have musicians or entertainers in the evening.
- If your schedule will not permit a full night's entertainment, suggest a business lunch instead.
- Ice water is not served in Hungarian restaurants.
- Once you have signed or completed a contract, throw a cocktail party at a prestigious hotel.

Time
- Hungary is one hour ahead of Greenwich Mean Time (G.M.T. + 1) and six hours ahead of U.S. Eastern Standard Time, (E.S.T. + 6). There is a daylight saving system in the summer; the clocks are turned one hour ahead from April to September.

Protocol

Greetings

- A handshake is customary not only when being introduced, but also when leaving or departing. A man waits for a woman to extend her hand before shaking it. Old fashioned Hungarian men will sometimes bow to a woman while shaking her hand.
- Only close friends will greet each other with an embrace. For men, the sequence goes as follows: shake hands, embrace, make cheek-to-cheek contact on the left cheek, then on the right cheek. Close female friends do the same but omit the handshake.

Titles/Forms of Address
- Relatives and close adult friends address each other on a first name basis; they will also call children by their first names. Young people typically use each

other's first names. It is safest to address all adults by their titles and surnames unless invited to do otherwise.

CULTURAL NOTE

*I*n Hungary, the surname is listed before the given (first) name. Thus, the Hungarian musicians Béla Bartók and Franz Liszt are known in their homeland as Bartók Béla and Liszt Franz (or, more precisely, Liszt *Ferenc*, since *Ferenc* is the Hungarian equivalent of Franz). Foreign names, however, are listed in the order that is customary in their country of origin.

- Always use professional titles (Doctor, Director, Minister, and so forth) when addressing someone. Either use title and surname (Professor Szabo) or add Mr., Mrs., or Miss to the title (Mrs. Architect).
- The Hungarian words for Mr./Mrs./Miss come after the surname.
  - Mr. = *ur*: Mr. Architect = *Epitesz ur*; Mr. Smith = Smith *ur*
  - Miss = *kisasszony*: Miss Doctor = *Orvosno kisasszony*
  - Mrs. has two forms in Hungarian. The most common form is the suffix *-ne* added to the husband's surname: Mrs. Smith = Smith*ne*; Mrs. Janos = Janos*ne*
  - There is also a rarely used form of Mrs. that is usually reserved for foreign married women of distinction. Like the words for Mr. and Miss, this term, *asszony*, follows the surname but is not attached to it: Mrs. Hillary Clinton = Hillary Clinton *asszony*.

Gifts

- When visiting a company, it is not necessary to bring gifts. However, if you do, bring many small gifts and give them out freely.
- Because of a housing shortage, you may not be invited into a Hungarian home. This is especially true in Budapest, where some 20 percent of the total Hungarian population resides. If you are asked to visit, Western liquor (not wine, as Hungarians are proud of the wines they produce) and wrapped flowers (but not red roses or chrysanthemums) are recommended gifts.

Dress

- Dress tends to be conservative, especially among business people.
- Appropriate business dress for men is a dark suit, a white shirt, and a tie. Women should wear suits or dresses.
- Jeans are standard casual wear. Shorts are uncommon in the city, and are best reserved for the beach or the countryside.
- Standard business wear is appropriate for formal social occasions, restaurants, and the theater. For the opera, men should wear a dark suit or a tuxedo; women are expected to wear formal gowns.

CULTURAL NOTE

*h*ungarians consider themselves a "nation of horsemen," and invitations to foreigners for horseback riding are not uncommon. It may be prudent to bring riding clothes.

NEW DELHI

India

Country Background

History

The Indian subcontinent has been home to advanced civilizations since before recorded history. It has also known its share of invaders. The Aryans (predecessors of the Hindus) conquered most of the subcontinent before 1500 B.C. The Muslim Moghuls ruled much of India until the advent of the European invaders. The Portuguese first arrived in 1489. French, Dutch, and English traders followed. The British East India Company became ascendant, essentially ruling India from 1760 to 1858, when India was formally transferred to the British Crown.

After long years of struggle against British rule, India became an independent country on August 15, 1947.

When the British left in 1947, British India was partitioned into primarily Hindu India and mostly Muslim Pakistan. The centuries-old antagonism between Hindus and Muslims has erupted into open warfare between India and Pakistan three times since independence.

Type of Government

The Republic of India is a multiparty federal republic. The head of government is the prime minister, while the president is the chief of state. There are two multiparty legislative houses. The Council of States has a maximum of 250 seats; the House of the People has 545.

In the 1920s, Mahatma Gandhi made the Indian National Congress into India's leading political force. Its successor, the Congress Party, has ruled India for most of the years since independence.

India's first Prime Minister was Mahatma Gandhi's compatriot Jawaharlal Nehru. Power remained with the Congress Party until 1977, when Prime Minister

Indira Gandhi (Nehru's daughter) was voted out of office. Janata Party leader Morarji Desai became prime minister, but his Janata coalition broke up in 1979. An interim government called new elections, and Indira Gandhi returned to power in 1980. She was assassinated by her own Sikh bodyguards in 1984, and was succeeded by her son, Rajiv Gandhi. He attempted to steer the country toward a more market-oriented economy, but was defeated in the 1989 elections by another Janata coalition, and Vishwanath Pratap Singh became prime minister.

V. P. Singh's minority government's most serious crisis resulted from its determination to reserve some 49 percent of government jobs for lower castes (which make up 54 percent of India's 890 million people). Insurgencies in Punjab, Kashmi, and Assam further weakened the government. The Singh government fell in November 1990.

Rajiv Ghandi was assassinated during the elections of May 1991.

t ————————————————————**CULTURAL NOTE**

he current leadership of India is implementing sweeping changes to encourage international business in India, from privatization to the liberalization of trade.

Language
More than fourteen major and three hundred minor languages are spoken in India. English is widely used, especially by businessmen, industrialists, politicians, and educators. The official languages of India are English and Hindi.

Religion
Religion plays a major role in the daily lives of most Indians, and two of the world's great religions—Buddhism and Hinduism—were born here. Although 83 percent of the people are Hindu, India also has one of the world's largest Muslim populations. Other major religions include Christianity, Sikhism, and Jainism. The Republic of India has no official religion.

The origins of the caste system are unclear, but it has existed in India for thousands of years. Even though discrimination on the basis of caste has been outlawed by the government, caste still plays a significant role in the politics and business of the country. Although there are only four traditional castes, these are broken down into thousands of subcastes.

Demographics
India's population is some 890 million people. One-sixth of the world's population calls India home. India is primarily rural, with 80 percent of the people living in more than 550,000 villages.

Cultural Orientation

Cognitive Styles: How Indians Organize and Process Information
In India information is accepted openly as long as it does not challenge religious and social structures. Because of rote learning and tradition, most thinking is associative. However, better-educated Indians are more abstractive and analytical. Although universal rules of behavior exist within the social structure, immediate situations and people are of major concern, but always within the constructs of the caste system.

Negotiation Strategies: What Indians Accept as Evidence

Personal feelings form the basis for the truth, but a strong faith in religious ideologies is always present. The use of objective facts is less persuasive than a combination of feelings and faith.

Value Systems: The Basis for Behavior

India has a very strong attachment to the caste system, with all of its social structure and liabilities. The following three sections identify the Value Systems in the predominant culture—their mode of dividing right from wrong, good from evil, and so forth.

Locus of Decision Making

India is a moderately collectivistic culture in which an individual's decisions must be in harmony with the family, group, and social structure. Success and failure are often attributed to environmental factors. Friendships and kinships are more important than expertise, although diplomas and certificates are coveted. One must build a relationship with other participants in the negotiation process by discussing friends and family. Indians are generally too polite to say "no."

Sources of Anxiety Reduction

With such a strong social structure, there is little anxiety about life because one knows and accepts one's place in the society or organization. Behaviors contrary to religious traditions are not tolerated. There is a strong sense of what Westerners call fatalism, so time is not a major source of anxiety, and passivity is a virtue. Emotions can be shown, and assertiveness is expected.

Issues of Equality/Inequality

There is a very rigid structure of inequality, even though there is equality under the law (seldom enforced). The belief that there are qualitative differences between the castes is ingrained. Traditional male chauvinism is strong, and women have few privileges. The abundant sexual symbols in society do not translate into an acceptance of public intimacy.

Business Practices

Appointments

——————————————————————— **PUNCTUALITY**

♦ Indians appreciate punctuality but don't always practice it themselves. Keep your schedule loose enough for last-minute rescheduling of meetings.

- Request appointments by letter about two months before arriving in India. Mail to and from India can be very slow, and many Indian companies do not have telexes. The notoriously unreliable Indian phone service makes fax service problematical.
- When making business contacts, go straight to the top of the company, as all decisions are made at this level. Be prepared to establish a close personal relationship based on mutual respect and confidence.

- Although they usually do not make decisions, middle managers do have input. A middle manager on your side can forward your proposal. Often they are more accessible, and they are willing to meet at any time of the day.
- Indian executives prefer late morning or early afternoon appointments, between 11:00 A.M. and 4:00 P.M.
- Business hours: 9:30 A.M. to 5:00 P.M., Monday through Friday (lunch is usually from 1:00 to 2:00 P.M.).
- Government office hours: 10:00 A.M. to 5:00 P.M., Monday through Saturday (closed for lunch from 1:00 to 2:00 P.M.). Note that government offices are closed the second Saturday of each month.
- The best time of year to visit India is between October and March, bypassing the seasons of extreme heat and monsoons.
- Business is not conducted during religious holidays, which are numerous. Different holidays are observed throughout the many regions and states of India. As dates for these holidays change from year to year, check with the Indian Tourist Office, Consulate, or Embassy before scheduling your visit. (See "Contacts and Holidays.")

 Negotiating

- Indians have a less hurried attitude toward time than North Americans. The concept "time is money" is alien to most Indians.
- While you should get sound legal and tax advice before negotiating any agreement, it is important to be flexible and not appear too legalistic during negotiations.
- Be prepared to offer competitive technology packages with close technical follow-up. The technical assistance you can provide and how well you can train your client's employees will be critical factors in the decision.
- Expect delays; they are inevitable. The Indian government moves at its own pace, and communication within India is often difficult. Be patient, and make a realistic assessment of the steps and time involved in finalizing any agreements.
- Always present your business card. It is not necessary to have it translated into an Indian language.
- Business in India is highly personal. It is also conducted at a much more leisurely pace than in the United States. A great amount of hospitality is associated with doing business. Tea and small talk are preludes to most business discussions.
- When refreshments are offered, it is customary to refuse the first offer, but to accept the second or third. To refuse any refreshment is an insult. Drink slowly if you wish to limit your intake of the sugary, milky Indian tea.
- The word "no" has harsh implications in India. Evasive refusals are more common, and are considered more polite. Never directly refuse an invitation, just be vague and avoid a time commitment. "I'll try" is an acceptable refusal.

CULTURAL NOTE

*i*n a monetary transaction, your change is simply placed in your hand, without explanation of the amount. Very often, if you remain standing with your hand outstretched, you will receive more change.

Keep lots of small change on hand, as street merchants and taxi drivers often claim they do not have change.

Business Entertaining

- Business lunches are preferred to dinners.
- Remember that Hindus do not eat beef and Muslims do not eat pork.
- Businesswomen may entertain Indian businessmen at a meal without causing awkwardness or embarrassment to the men, although the men may try to pay for the meal.
- If you are invited to dinner, be a few minutes late unless it is an official function. If the dinner is in a home, you may arrive fifteen to thirty minutes late.
- Eat only with the right hand, as the left hand is used for hygienic purposes and is considered unclean. (However, it is permissible to pass dishes with the left hand.)
- Touching a communal dish with your hands may cause fellow diners to avoid it.
- Never offer another person (even a spouse) food from your plate, as it is considered "polluted" as soon as it is placed on your plate.
- Washing your hands both before and after a meal is important. In Hindu homes, you are expected to rinse your mouth out as well.
- Do not thank your hosts at the end of a meal. Saying "thank you" for a meal is insulting because the thanks are considered a form of payment. Returning the meal by inviting your hosts to dinner shows that you value the relationship.

t————————————————**CULTURAL NOTE**

ipping in India is more than just a reward for good service; it is often the way to ensure that things get done. The term *baksheesh* encompasses both these meanings. Judicious (and discreet) use of *baksheesh* will often open closed doors, such as getting a seat on a "sold out" train.

Time

- India is five and one-half hours ahead of Greenwich Mean Time (G.M.T. + 5 1/2), or ten and one-half hours ahead of Eastern Standard Time (E.S.T. + 10 1/2 hours).

g————————————————**CULTURAL NOTE**

iving money to a beggar will result in your being besieged by dozens of them. Avoid even making eye contact.

When walking past an Indian temple, keep your hands in your pockets. If your hand is free, a stranger may offer to shake your hand. They are often street merchants who quickly slap a temple bracelet on your outstretched arm. Then you are expected to pay for the bracelet.

Protocol

Greetings

- In large cities, men and very Westernized Indian women will offer to shake hands with foreign men and sometimes with foreign women. Western women should not initiate handshaking with Indian men.
- There are numerous ethnic, linguistic, and religious groups in India, each with its own traditions.

- The majority of Indians are Hindu. Most Hindus avoid public contact between men and women. Men may shake hands with men, and women with women, but only Westernized Hindus will shake hands with the opposite sex.
- A minority of Indians are Muslim. Traditionally, there is no physical contact between Muslim men and women. Indeed, if a religious Muslim male is touched by a woman, he must ritually cleanse himself before he prays again. Because of this, women should not offer to shake hands with Muslim men (nor should men offer to shake hands with Muslim women). Of course, if a Westernized Indian offers to shake hands, do so.
- Other Indian religious groups, such as Sikhs and Christians, also avoid public contact between the sexes.
- The traditional Indian greeting is the *namaste*. To perform the *namaste*, hold the palms of your hands together (as if praying) below the chin, nod or bow slightly, and say *namaste* (nah-mas-tay). This greeting is useful for foreigners in any situation where a handshake might not be acceptable. It is a good alternative to a handshake when a Western businesswoman greets an Indian man.
- Indians of all ethnic groups disapprove of public displays of affection between people of the opposite sex. Do not touch (except in handshaking), hug, or kiss in greeting.

 Titles/Forms of Address

- Titles are highly valued by Indians. Always use professional titles, such as Professor and Doctor. Don't address someone by his or her first name unless you are asked to or you are close friends; use Mr., Mrs., or Miss.
- Status is determined by age, university degrees, caste, and profession. Occupationally, government service is far more prestigious than private business.
- Traditionally, Hindus did not have family surnames. A Hindu Indian male used the initial of his father's name first, followed by his own personal name. For example, V. Thiruselvan is "Thiruselvan, son of 'V.'" For legal purposes, both names would be written out with an "s/o" (for "son of") between the names: Thiruselvan s/o Vijay. In either case, he would be known as Mr. Thiruselvan. However, long Indian names are often shortened. He may prefer to be called either Mr. Thiru or Mr. Selvan.
- Hindu female names follow the same pattern: father's initial plus personal name. When fully written out, "d/o" (for "daughter of") is used instead of "s/o." When an Indian woman marries, she usually ceases to use her father's initial; instead, she follows her personal name with her husband's name. For instance, when S. Kamala (female) marries V. Thiru (male), she will go by Mrs. Kamala Thiru.
- Some Indians will use Western-style surnames. Christian Indians may have Biblical surnames like Abraham or Jacob. Indians from the former Portuguese colony of Goa may have surnames of Portuguese origin, such as Rozario or DeSilva. Such a person could be addressed as Dr. Jacob or Mr. DeSilva.
- Muslim names are usually derived from Arabic. Generally, a Muslim is known by a given name plus *bin* ("son of") plus their father's name. For example, Osman bin Ali is "Osman, son of Ali." He would properly be called Mr. Osman, not Mr. Ali—Mr. Ali would be Osman's father.
- A Muslim woman is known by her given name plus *binti* ("daughter of") plus her father's name. For example, Khadijah binti Fauzi is "Khadijah, daughter of Fauzi." She would be known as Miss Khadijah or, if married, as Mrs. Khadijah. For business purposes, some Indian women attach their husband's name.

Thus, if Khadijah was married to Osman, she might choose to be known as Mrs. Khadijah Osman. Note that in English, *binti* may also be spelled *binte*.

- Some Westernized Indians drop the *bin* or *binti* from their name.
- A Muslim male who has completed his pilgrimage to Mecca is addressed as *Haji*. A woman who has done so would be addressed as *Hajjah*. Note that these titles are not automatically conferred on spouses; they must be individually earned by making the pilgrimage. However, when in doubt, err on the side of generosity. It is better to give a superfluous title than to omit one.
- Indian Sikhs have a given name followed by either *Singh* (for men) or *Kaur* (for women). Always address them by a title and first name. To refer to a Sikh male as Mr. Singh is as meaningless as saying Mr. Man in English.

Gestures

- The head is considered the seat of the soul by many Indians. Never touch someone else's head, not even to pat the hair of a child.
- As in much of the world, to beckon someone, you hold your hand out, palm downward, and make a scooping motion with the fingers. Beckoning someone with the palm up and wagging one finger, as in the United States, can be construed as an insult.
- Standing tall with your hands on your hips—the "arms akimbo" position— will be interpreted as an angry, aggressive posture.
- The comfortable standing distance between two people in India varies with the culture. In general, Hindu Indians tend to stand about 3 or 3 1/2 feet apart.
- Pointing with a finger is rude; Indians point with the chin.
- Whistling under any circumstances is considered impolite.
- Winking may be misinterpreted as either an insult or a sexual proposition.
- The grasping of one's ears by an Indian designates sincerity or repentance. Ears are considered sacred appendages; to pull or box someone's ears is a great insult.
- Never point your feet at a person. Feet are considered unclean. If your shoes or feet touch another person, apologize.

Gifts

- Gifts are not opened in the presence of the giver. If you receive a wrapped gift, set it aside until the giver leaves.
- If you are invited to an Indian's home for dinner, bring a small gift of chocolates or flowers. Don't give frangipani blossoms, however, as they are associated with funerals.
- Don't wrap gifts in black or white, which are considered unlucky colors; green, red, and yellow are lucky colors.
- If you know that your Indian counterpart drinks alcohol, bring imported whiskey. The 27 percent tax can be avoided by purchasing the liquor on the airline or at the duty-free shop before arriving.
- Muslims consider dogs unclean. Do not give toy dogs or gifts with pictures of dogs to Indian Muslims.
- Should you give money to an Indian, make sure it is an odd number. Usually this is done by adding a single dollar; for example, give $11 instead of $10.

CULTURAL NOTE

bservant Hindus do not eat beef or use products made from cattle. This eliminates most leather products as gifts.

Dress

- For business dress, men should wear a suit and tie, although the jacket may be removed in the summer. Businesswomen should wear conservative dresses or pantsuits.
- For casual wear, short-sleeved shirts and long trousers are preferred for men; shorts are acceptable only while jogging. Women must keep their upper arms, chest, back, and legs covered at all times. Women who jog should wear long pants.
- Note that wearing leather (including belts, handbags, or purses) may be considered offensive, especially in temples. Hindus revere cows, and do not use leather products.

JAKARTA

Indonesia

t————————————————**CULTURAL NOTE**
hree calendars are in common use in Indonesia. The Western (or Gregorian) calendar is the official calendar. Islamic holidays are dated by the Arabic calendar, which loses about eleven days each year against the Western calendar. Finally, there is a Hindu-influenced Javanese calendar.

Certain days when different calendars coincide are considered lucky. For example, when the fifth day of the Western week falls on the fifth day of the Javanese week (which is only five days long), the occasion is considered auspicious.

Country Background

History

The Indonesian archipelago has been populated for thousands of years. Thanks to its central location, Indonesia has been a trading outpost for many centuries. Chinese trading settlements in Indonesia were established as early as the third century B.C. However, it was Indian traders who eventually had the greatest influence upon early Indonesia. By the second century A.D., several small states had organized on Indian models and flourished on Sumatra, Java, and Borneo.

Many Indian influences are to be seen in modern Indonesia. Although Hinduism was superseded by Islam on most islands, it is still the main religion on Bali. The native language of Java is written in a variant of the Indian Devanagari alphabet.

Various kingdoms rose and fell throughout Indonesia. The Majapahit Empire spread from Java to encompass much of modern-day Indonesia between the tenth and sixteenth centuries A.D. The history of the Majapahit Empire is considered a unifying cultural heritage in modern Indonesia, and the Majapahit kings are commemorated by naming streets after them.

Contact with Europe began in the sixteenth century. Beginning in 1511, the Portuguese dominated the region from their base in Malacca, in neighboring Malaysia. The Dutch arrived in 1596; they eventually reduced the Portuguese holdings in Indonesia to the eastern half of the island of Timor. Indonesia was ruled by the Dutch East India Company from 1602 to 1798, when the Dutch government took direct control. Only the wealthy island of Java received much attention from the Dutch until the end of the nineteenth century.

Nationalist sentiments grew during the early twentieth century, but Indonesia remained a Dutch colony until World War II. The Japanese occupied Indonesia from 1942 to 1945. During this occupation, native Indonesians were finally placed in positions of power and allowed by the Japanese to run the nation. One such leader, Sukarno, declared Indonesia an independent republic on August 17, 1945. The Dutch fought to regain control of Indonesia, but they finally relinquished all claims to their former colony in 1949.

Since independence, the Indonesian leadership has succeeded in turning the country into an industrialized nation.

CULTURAL NOTE

Since achieving independence after World War II, Indonesia has gone from a subsistence economy to one of the "young dragons" of the Pacific Rim. Its abundant natural resources and pro-development government has made Indonesia a focus of foreign investment. Lying athwart the oceanic trade routes between China and India, Indonesia has had centuries of experience in trade. For 250 years Indonesia was a colony of the Netherlands. Despite the distances involved, the Dutch found Indonesia a profitable investment. Fertile plantations yielded great profit in spices, coffee, and sugar. Later, Indonesia was found to possess great mineral wealth: tin, coal, bauxite, and—above all—oil.

Type of Government

The Republic of Indonesia declared its independence in 1945. Fighting against the Dutch continued until 1949. Indonesian politics since independence can be seen as the story of two presidents. The first president, Sukarno, was little more than a figurehead in the early 1950s, yet he skillfully accrued more and more power. When the Western powers refused to support him against the remaining Dutch presence in the area, Sukarno launched campaigns against "neocolonialism." He became hostile toward the West and received military assistance first from the U.S.S.R. and then from Communist China. Most Indonesian political parties were restricted in order to allow the Communist Party of Indonesia (PKI) to become the dominant political force. With Sukarno in ill health, the PKI decided to take power in a coup on September 30, 1965. The coup failed, and for the next six months Indonesia writhed in civil disorder. As many as a half million Indonesians, most of them suspected Communists, were slain. Ethnic Chinese were also slaughtered, on the excuse that they were in league with Communist China. In 1966, President Sukarno was forced out of power and General Suharto became president.

Although Indonesia was officially a nonaligned nation, Suharto pursued friendlier relations with the West. Since Suharto's accession in 1966, Indonesia has pursued a pro-business, pro-investment policy that has brought increased prosperity and development.

Indonesia is a unitary multiparty republic. The president is both head of state and head of the government. The Republic of Indonesia has two legislative houses. The House of People's Representatives has 500 seats; the People's Consultative Assembly has 1,000 members (500 of whom are also members of the other house).

As a diverse nation, separated by geography, language, ethnicity, and religion, Indonesia must constantly struggle against separatism and secession. Two areas of Indonesia threatened by separatist movements are Irian Jaya and East Timor, some 2,000 people were killed by government troops during a funeral march on East Timor in 1992.

Despite its human rights record, Indonesia presents excellent investment opportunities for international business people. Indeed, Indonesia is at a stage in its development analogous to that of South Korea or Singapore twenty years ago.

Language

The Republic of Indonesia has designated Bahasa Indonesia as the official language. Written in the Roman alphabet, Bahasa Indonesia evolved out of the "market Malay" trade language used throughout the region during the colonial era. The selection of Bahasa Indonesia as the official tongue was a conscious effort to unify all Indonesians; as a trade language, it did not have the literary history or prestige of other Indonesian tongues (notably Javanese). All advertising, media, and official communications are required to be in Bahasa Indonesia, and it is taught in all elementary schools.

b———————————————**CULTURAL NOTE**
ahasa Indonesia is similar to the national language of neighboring Malaysia, which is called Bahasa Malaysia. However, Malaysia was a British colony, so Bahasa Malaysia was influenced by English. As a colony of the Netherlands, the Dutch language influenced Bahasa Indonesia.

Religion

The early traders and settlers had brought Hinduism and Buddhism to Indonesia (the Majapahit Empire merged the two into a single state religion). Islam arrived in the sixteenth century, and eventually became Indonesia's major religion. As with earlier religions, the Indonesians adapted Islam to suit their needs, especially on the island of Java. Indonesia is the world's most populous Islamic nation, its population of 185 million is more than double Pakistan's 90 million. However, Islam in Indonesia is fragmented into numerous sects, many of which are antagonistic toward other Islamic sects, both inside and outside of Indonesia.

Demographics

t———————————————**CULTURAL NOTE**
he 1991 breakup of the U.S.S.R. caused extensive revision of world maps and demographic statistics. One result was a change in the list of the world's most populous nations. Indonesia has now moved into fourth place, behind China, India and the United States.

Indonesia, with 184,796,000 citizens in 1992, has a larger population than Russia, Japan, or Germany.

As a geographically divided archipelago with many diverse ethnic and religious groups, Indonesia struggles to maintain unity among its 185 million inhabitants. These ethnic groups include Javanese (45 percent of Indonesia's population), Sundanese (14 percent), Madurese, Chinese, Buginese, Batak, Dayak, Balinese, Minangkabau, and many others. Indonesia has a young population; about 65 percent of Indonesians are below the age of thirty, and 37 percent are under fifteen years old.

Cultural Orientation

Cognitive Styles: How Indonesians Organize and Process Information

Indonesians have a history of assimilating new ways of doing things into their indigenous systems. They are open to information. Independent thinking is discouraged in their education, so they tend to process information associatively. Those educated abroad may be more abstractive. Their focus is on the immediate situation and the people involved rather than on rules or laws that might govern behavior in similar situations.

Negotiation Strategies: What Indonesians Accept as Evidence

Most people will rely on the truth of their subjective feelings. However, this truth may be modified by a faith in the ideology of their religion. The most powerful influence is the desire for harmony. Those with higher education may rely on objective facts for their truth.

Value Systems: The Basis for Behavior

One should be aware of the value system of the Chinese, who conduct much of the business in Indonesia. The Indonesians have blended Hinduism, Buddhism, Islam, and Christianity into their mysticism. The following three sections identify the Value Systems in the predominant culture—their methods of dividing right from wrong, good from evil, and so forth.

Locus of Decision Making

Decision making traditionally goes through deliberation and consensus. All interested parties are welcome to participate. They strive for balance; conciliation without resentments or grudges is a trait of the Indonesian culture. Many government officials and entrepreneurs adhere to a mystical form of spirituality called *Kebatinan*, a metaphysical search for inner harmony and guidance in decision making. They do not subjugate the will of the individual to the will of the group.

Sources of Anxiety Reduction

There is a strong belief in the supernatural for protection and security. This faith goes beyond any one religion, although most Indonesians are at least nominally Muslims. The nuclear and extended family are basic to security and economic support, with marriage being used to reinforce economic and social alliances. The *adat* (common law) has become one of the major stabilizing factors maintaining the traditional rural societies. The military is the main arbiter of power in the government.

Issues of Equality/Inequality

In most organizations there is a strong authoritarian hierarchical system that demands obedience of subordinates. Although there are strong ethnic identities, there is also a strong national identity that is taught to all children in the primary school years. The Chinese and Arabs are sometimes the targets of ethnic antagonism, but the need for harmony is an overriding factor. Although the husband is considered the head of the household, the wife is not inferior in status, and both are expected to cooperate in maintaining their household and family. Equal rights for women have always been upheld in the community.

Business Practices

Appointments

PUNCTUALITY

♦ As a foreign business person, you are expected to be on time for all business appointments. This is especially true when you are meeting someone with a higher social standing than yourself.

- Everyone has a social ranking in Indonesia. It is the prerogative of the person of higher rank to make a person of lower standing wait.
- In general, the higher the status of an Indonesian, the more he or she is likely to appreciate punctuality. Many Indonesian laborers consider themselves punctual if they arrive within a few hours of an appointment. Executives and government officials will understand promptness—but they still have the right to make a subordinate wait.
- A majority of Indonesian business people are Chinese. Their culture is very work-oriented, and they are likely to be prompt. Other business people and the majority of government officials are ethnic Malays. Their culture is very different from that of the Chinese, and they have a looser concept of time. Promptness has never been a virtue in the Malay culture of Indonesia.
- Social events in Indonesia involve different rules. In general, Indonesians arrive at social events a half-hour late.
- Status is also important at social events. When invited to a social event, Indonesians try to ascertain who is the most important guest. They will then attempt to arrive later than lesser personages but earlier than more important ones. Invitations where an important guest is expected may state a time, then add "please arrive fifteen minutes early" (to ensure that no one arrives after the important guest).

t──────────────────────────**CULTURAL NOTE**

he Indonesian term *jam karet* (rubber time) refers to the indigenous casual attitude toward time. Only a true emergency, such as a death or serious illness, will impel most Indonesians (ethnic Malays) to haste or punctuality.

- The casual Indonesian attitude toward time allows you to schedule appointments on short notice. Only large corporations require you to schedule appointments more than a week in advance.
- Indonesian executives tend to be more accessible than executives in many countries. Even an Indonesian CEO is likely to meet with foreign business people.
- English is the language of many business transactions and much business correspondence in Indonesia. However, attempts to use Bahasa Indonesia are appreciated.
- Bahasa Indonesia is the official language of Indonesia. Although many government officials will speak some English, they may prefer to hold meetings in their native tongue. Fortunately, an English-speaking translator is usually close at hand.
- All official correspondence with government officials must be in Bahasa Indonesia. Use of the language is also mandated for many advertisements and publications.
- Indonesia is a former colony of the Netherlands. However, only older Indonesians have any familiarity with the Dutch language.
- Although the majority of Indonesians are Muslim, Indonesia does not follow the traditional Islamic workweek pattern (Friday is the Islamic holy day, so the traditional Muslim "weekend" is Thursday and Friday). Instead, the workweek runs for four full days, Monday through Thursday, then two half days on Friday and Saturday.
- Business hours are generally from 8:00 A.M. to 4:00 P.M., Monday through Thursday, with additional hours on Friday and Saturday mornings. Some businesses have a full workday on Fridays, although Muslim employees will take at least one hour off on Friday to pray. Saturday hours generally end by 1:00 P.M.
- The traditional lunchtime is from 12 noon or 12:30 P.M. to 1:30 P.M.; lunch is often the largest meal of the day.
- Most government offices keep an 8:00 A.M. to 4:00 P.M. schedule, with a half day on Friday and Saturday.

- Shop hours vary. Most shops will be open five or six days a week and will open at 9:00 or 10:00 A.M. and close at 6:00 or 7:00 P.M.
- The holidays in Indonesia represent an attempt to accommodate the celebrations of Islam, Hinduism, and Christianity.
- Observant Muslims fast from dawn to sundown during the month of Ramadan. Expect this to have a negative effect on business dealings. Also, do not eat or drink in front of fasting Indonesians.

Negotiating

- Indonesians do business only with persons they know and like. Establishing this personal relationship will take time, but it is vital for success.
- The pace of business negotiations in Indonesia is far slower than that of the United States. Be patient and do not rush.
- It would be unusual to complete a complicated business deal in only one trip. Expect to take several trips over a period of months. Indeed, little will happen at the first meeting except getting acquainted.
- Politeness is one of the most important attributes for successful relationships in Indonesia. This politeness in no way hinders the determination of Indonesian business people to get their own way.
- Standards of polite behavior vary widely between cultures. Many Indonesians will ask you highly personal questions (such as "Why aren't you married?" or "How much do you earn?") without realizing that Westerners find such questions intrusive. If you do not wish to answer, smile and explain that such topics are not discussed openly in your culture.
- Everyone has status in Indonesia, and everyone has a ranking on the "totem pole" of importance. In Bahasa Indonesia, you cannot successfully converse with a person until you know whether he or she is your superior, inferior, or equal. Even when the conversation is in English, Indonesians will not feel comfortable until they know your ranking. This is one reason why Indonesians will ask you very personal questions about your job, your education, and your salary.
- Indonesians show great deference to a superior. It is considered discourteous to show annoyance at a superior who is late. It is very bad form to openly disagree with a superior. Superiors are told what they want to hear; the truth is conveyed in private, up the grapevine—often by a friend of the superior. In their culture, Indonesians are showing honor to their superior by shielding him or her from receiving bad news in public.
- Since it is impolite to disagree with someone, Indonesians rarely say "no." You are expected to be perceptive enough to differentiate a polite "Yes (but I really mean no)" from an actual "yes." This is rarely a problem when speaking in Bahasa Indonesia, since the language has at least twelve ways to say "No" and many ways to say, "I'm saying 'yes' but I mean 'no'." This subtlety is lost in English. Westerners often interpret this as deceit, but Indonesians are simply being polite by their own cultural standards.
- This "no" is clear even in English: Any time an Indonesian says "yes, but . . .," it means "no."
- When there are any qualifications attached (such as, "It might be difficult"), this means "no".
- A clear way to indicate "no" is to suck in air through the teeth. This sound always indicates a problem.

- Evading is indicative of a "no," even if the person has said neither "yes" nor "no." He or she may even pretend the question was never asked.
- A deal is never complete until all the paperwork is signed. Since Indonesians (especially the Chinese) often consult astrologers, the signing may be delayed until a "lucky" day arrives.
- People in Indonesia may smile or laugh in situations that Westerners consider inappropriate. Smiles may hide embarrassment, shyness, bitterness, discord, and/or loss of face. Indonesian businessmen may laugh at the most serious part of a business meeting; this may be an expression of anxiety, not frivolity. An Indonesian nurse may giggle while tending to a seriously ill male patient; this could be from embarrassment at having to touch a man, not callousness. Learning to interpret smiles and laughter may take a foreigner years.
- In Indonesia, one who expresses anger in public has shamefully lost face. A person who loses his or her temper is considered unable to control himself or herself. Such a person will not be trusted or respected.
- Being embarrassed publicly (losing face) is known as *malu*.
- One result of "*malu* mentality" is that Indonesians may allow a person to pro- ceed incorrectly rather than risk embarrassing him or her by correcting him or her in public. In effect, an Indonesian can "honor" someone's authority while allowing him or her to make a disastrous error.
- It is considered polite among Indonesian Chinese to offer both the positive and negative options in virtually every decision. Even when speaking in English, they are likely to add a "yes/no" pattern to a question. Rather than asking, "Would you like to have dinner?" they are likely to ask, "You want dinner or not?" The phrases involved ("want or not want," "good or not," "can or can- not") are direct translations of Chinese phrases into English. They often sound unduly aggressive to Western ears.

i CULTURAL NOTE

t can be very difficult for a foreign manager to get accurate reports from Indonesian employees, since the employees are likely to say whatever they think will please their boss. This Indonesian trait, called *asal bapak senang* (broadly translated as "keeping father happy") is instilled in Indonesians since childhood. Foreign executives cannot circumvent this by being "one of the boys"—the boss is the father of his company. Foreigners must establish a network through which they can be told the truth in private. Indonesians trained and educated in the West can also help, since they may realize that their boss genuinely wants the truth.

- Be cautious in asking an Indonesian Chinese a question. English speakers would give a negative answer to the question "Isn't my order ready yet?" by responding, "No" (meaning, "No, it's not ready"). The Chinese pattern is the opposite: "Yes" (meaning, "Yes, it is not ready").
- Indonesians of all ethnic groups are comfortable with silence, in both business and social settings. A silent pause allows time for thought; it does not necessar- ily signal either acceptance or rejection. Westerners often find such pauses uncomfortable.
- In Indonesia, individuals are rarely singled out in public, either for praise or for condemnation. Individuals are expected to be part of a group, and it is the group that is addressed. If you must reprimand an individual employee, do it calmly and in private.
- Always be aware of social hierarchy. If you are part of a delegation, line up so that the most important persons will be introduced first. If you are introducing

two people, state the name of the most important person first (e.g., "President Suhardjono, this is Engineer Wong").

- Speak in quiet, gentle tones. Always remain calm. Leave plenty of time for someone to respond to a statement you make; people in Indonesia do not jump on the end of someone else's sentences. Politeness demands that they leave a respectful pause (as long as ten to fifteen seconds) before responding. Westerners often assume that they have agreement and resume talking before a Indonesian has the chance to respond.
- Topics to avoid in conversation include any criticism of Indonesian ways, religion, bureaucracy, human rights record, or politics. Also avoid any discussion of sex or the roles of the sexes. (However, do not be surprised to hear graphic discussions of birth control methods. The Indonesian government supports major population control programs.)
- Good topics for discussion include tourism, travel, plans for the future, organizational success (talking about personal success is considered impolite boasting), and food (while remaining complimentary to the local cuisine). Stories about your attempts to learn Bahasa Indonesia also make good conversation.
- Understand that there is little conversation while eating. Do not be upset by a silent meal.

Business Entertaining

- Many Indonesians have negative images of foreigners. Indonesia was exploited by foreigners for some 300 years. Social encounters are the best way for you to dispel that preconceived image.
- Take advantage of any invitations to social events. Establishing a successful business relationship hinges on establishing a social relationship as well.
- Invitations to social events may not come immediately. Be patient and let the Indonesians make the first invitation. You cannot successfully host a social event until you have been a guest at a Indonesian event.
- Respond to written invitations in writing. Among the Chinese, white and blue are colors associated with sadness; do not print invitations on paper of these colors. Red or pink paper is a good choice for invitations.
- Generally, spouses may be invited to dinner but not to lunch. However, no business will be discussed at an event where spouses are present.

CULTURAL NOTE

*h*osting a party for Indonesians can be complex. Send out written invitations (addressed to husband and wife) a week in advance, but do not expect many responses in writing, even if your invitations say R.S.V.P. Indonesians are somewhat cagey about committing themselves to a social event. Find excuses to follow up (either by phone or in person) to remind your guests of the affair. Be prepared to explain (1) what event the party is celebrating, (2) the entire guest list, and (3) who the guest of honor is. Be sure to invite many Indonesians of the same ethnic group. While the business executive husband probably speaks English, his wife probably does not. Hold the party early, from 7 to 9 P.M. (In the tropics, people arise early in the cool of dawn; they also go to bed early.) The guests will probably be gone by 9:30 P.M. Indonesians find buffets more comfortable than sit-down dinners with assigned places. Be sure the food is sophisticated; if you depend on Indonesian servants to plan the meal, they are likely to select working-class fare (tasty but unprestigious). Remember that observant Muslims do not drink alcohol. Finally, show great respect toward your guest of honor. He (or she) is the last to arrive and the first to go through the buffet line. Go with the guest of honor, explaining what each dish is. Guests will begin to excuse themselves around 9 P.M.; you should escort your guest of honor to his or her car.

Time

- Indonesia spans three time zones. Java and Bali are on West Indonesia Standard Time, which is seven hours ahead of Greenwich Mean Time (G.M.T. + 7). Central Indonesia Standard Time is eight hours ahead of Greenwich Mean Time (G.M.T. + 8); Lombok and Nusatenggara are on Central Time. The East Indonesia Standard Time Zone, which includes Maluku and Irian Jaya, is nine hours ahead of Greenwich Mean Time (G.M.T. + 9).

Protocol

 Greetings

- Indonesia has more than 300 ethnic groups, each with its own traditions. These range from isolated Stone Age tribes in the jungles of Irian Jaya to the cosmopolitan denizens of Jakarta.
- Expect to shake hands only upon initial introductions and before and after a long separation. Most Indonesian handshakes are more like handclasps; they are rather limp and last for some ten or twelve seconds. (By contrast, most North American handshakes last for only three or four seconds.) For special emphasis, the handshake can be intensified by placing one's hand over one's heart.
- Most ethnic Indonesians are Muslim; the majority of the others are Hindu. Traditionally, there is no physical contact between men and women in these cultures. (Indeed, if a religious Muslim male is touched by a woman, he must ritually cleanse himself before he prays again.) Because of this, women should not offer to shake hands with Indonesian men (nor should men offer to shake hands with Indonesian women). Of course, if a Westernized Indonesian offers to shake hands, do so.
- Upon greeting, the traditional Muslim Indonesian salutation is the word *selamat*, which means "peace."
- Among Indonesian Chinese, the traditional greeting was a bow. However, most now shake hands or combine a bow with a handshake. Chinese men are more likely than other Indonesian ethnic groups to be comfortable shaking hands with a woman.
- Above all else, greetings in Indonesia are stately and formal. Do not rush. Take your time; hurried introductions show a lack of respect. This applies to all Indonesians, from executives to laborers.
- The traditional Hindu greeting involves a slight bow with the palms of the hands together (as if praying). This greeting, called the *namaste*, will generally be used only by older, traditional Hindus. However, it is also an acceptable alternative to a handshake when a Western businesswoman greets a Hindu Indonesian man.
- Among all ethnic groups, kissing in public (even a quick peck on a cheek) is considered unacceptable. Only the most fashionable and cosmopolitan of Indonesians will give even a quick kiss in greeting.

*j*ust as the British greeting "How do you do?" is rhetorical, Indonesians have many rhetorical greetings. Chinese greetings often involve food. "Have you eaten?" and "Have you taken food?" are rhetorical greetings; answer "Yes," even if you are hungry. Similarly, a typical Indonesian greeting when meeting on the street is "Where are you going?" This is also rhetorical; "For a walk" or "Nowhere of importance" is a perfectly acceptable answer ("I'm eating the wind!" is a local idiomatic response). You are not expected to reveal your itinerary.

- Business cards should be printed (preferably embossed) in English. Since ethnic Chinese constitute the majority of Indonesian business people, you may wish to have the reverse side of some of your cards printed in Chinese (gold ink is the most prestigious for Chinese characters).
- Your business card should contain as much information as possible, including your business title and your qualifications. Indonesians include all of this data on their card, as well as any titles of nobility.
- Indonesia was a colony of the Netherlands, and usually uses Dutch academic titles. These include:
  - Drs = *Doktorandus*, a graduate in any field except engineering or law (male)
  - Dra = *Doktoranda*, the above degree when awarded to a woman
  - Ir = *Insinjur*, a graduate with an engineering degree (male or female)
  - S H = *Sarjana Hukum*, a graduate with a law degree (male or female)
- Westerners should use their usual academic titles, rather than translate them into the Indonesian equivalent.
- The exchange of business cards can be quite stately in Indonesia. After introductions are made, the visiting business person should offer his or her card. Make sure you give a card to each person present. Present your card with both hands. (The most deferential method is to present your card in your right hand, with your left hand lightly supporting your right wrist.) Give your card to the recipient with the print facing him or her (so he or she can read it). The recipient will receive the card with both hands, then study the card for a few moments before carefully putting it away in a pocket. You should do the same when a card is presented to you.
- Never put a business card in your back pocket, where many men carry their wallets. While it is useful to write information such as the pronunciation of a name on someone's business card, do not let the person see you writing on his or her card. Either of these actions may be interpreted as "defiling" a business card.

Titles/Forms of Address

- Every variation of personal naming patterns can be found among Indonesia's myriad ethnic groups. People may have one name or two, short names or long; given name followed by a family name or vice versa, or one name and one initial.
- Westerners often experience difficulty dealing with Indonesian names. Always take your time over an introduction. Repeat the title and name of the person and ask if you are pronouncing them correctly. If possible, write the name down phonetically.
- No matter how difficult or unusual-sounding a name, do not laugh at it. Names are considered sacred by most Indonesians. Indeed, among some Javanese, a person who has a string of misfortunes will change his or her name to one considered luckier.
- Most business people you meet should be addressed with at least a title and their name. If a person does not have a professional title (such as Engineer,

Doctor, or Teacher), a Westerner may use Mr. or Madam, Mrs., or Miss, plus their name. However, be aware that you may be omitting other titles, important both to the person and your understanding of that person.

- The traditional Indonesian forms of Mr. and Madam, Mrs., or Miss are
  - *Bapak* = Mr. (this term precedes any other titles)
  - *Ibu* = Madam, Mrs., or Miss (any woman, married or unmarried)

These are used in front of an individual's name (e.g., Mr. Wowungan would be properly addressed as *Bapak* Wowungan.) Note that *Bapak* literally means "father," and *Ibu* is "mother."

- In a formal introduction, the preferred sequence is
  - 1. *Bapak* or *Ibu*
  - 2. Academic title, if any (alternatively, an academic title may be stated at the end of this list)
  - 3. Honorific, if any (a title of nobility)
  - 4. The individual's given and family name
  - 5. Business or political title

Thus, a formal introduction for a male executive named Juanda (given name) Kusumaatmaja (family name) could be as long as *Bapak Doctor His Excellency* Juanda Kusumaatmaja, *Chief Accountant*. Fortunately, most Indonesians will accept good-natured, sincere attempts by Westerners to express native names and titles.

- As a general rule, among ethnic Indonesians, the average citizen will have only one name while the middle class will tend to have two. Usually, the higher the social standing, the longer the names. Long names are often shortened for everyday use. An individual with two names often uses one name plus the initial of the other name.
- A Muslim male who has completed his pilgrimage to Mecca is entitled to the honorific *Haji*. A woman who has done so has the title *Hajjah*. Note that these titles are not automatically conferred on spouses; they must be individually earned by making the pilgrimage. However, when in doubt, err on the side of generosity. It is better to give a superfluous title than to omit one.
- Chinese names generally consist of a family name followed by two (sometimes one) personal names. In the name Chang Wu Jiang, "Chang" is the surname (or clan name). He would be addressed with his title plus Chang (Mr. Chang, Dr. Chang).
- Chinese wives do not generally take their husband's surnames, but instead maintain their maiden names. Although Westerners commonly address a married woman as Mrs. plus her husband's family name, it is more appropriate to call her Madam plus her maiden family name. As an example, Li Chu Chin (female) is married to Chang Wu Jiang (male). Westerners would probably call her Mrs. Chang. She is properly addressed as Madam Li.
- To accommodate Westerners, many Chinese adopt an English first name so that English speakers can have a familiar-sounding name to identify them by. Thus, Chang Wu Jiang may call himself Mr. Wally Chang. Others use their initials (Mr. W. J. Chang).
- As you inquire of an Indonesian how you should address him or her, be forward in explaining what he or she should call you. Indonesians may be equally unsure as to which of your names is your surname. Follow their lead as to the degree of formality. Don't tell an Indonesian to "just call me Bob" when you are calling him Dr. Armizal.

Gestures

- Aside from handshakes, there is no public contact between the sexes in Indonesia. Do not kiss or hug a person of the opposite sex in public—even if you are husband and wife. On the other hand, contact between people of the same sex is permitted. Men may hold hands with men or even walk with their arms around each other; this is interpreted as nothing except friendship.
- Among both Muslims and Hindus, the left hand is considered unclean. Eat with your right hand only. Where possible, do not touch anything or anyone with your left hand if you can use your right hand instead. Accept gifts and hold cash in the right hand. (Obviously, when both hands are needed, use them both.)
- The foot is also considered unclean. Do not move anything with your feet, do not point with your feet, and do not touch anything with your feet. Feet should not be rested on tables or desks.
- Do not show the soles of your feet or shoes. This restriction determines how one sits: you can cross your legs at the knee but not with one ankle on your knee.
- Pounding one fist into the palm of your other hand is an obscene gesture among some Indonesians.
- The head is considered the seat of the soul by many Indonesians. Never touch someone's head, not even to pat the hair of a child.
- As in much of the world, to beckon someone, you hold your hand out, palm downward, and make a scooping motion with the fingers. Beckoning someone with the palm up and wagging one finger, as in the United States, can be construed as an insult.
- It is impolite to point with your forefinger. Point with your right thumb and a closed fist (like a hitchhiker). This gesture is also used to mean "you go first."
- Standing tall with your hands on your hips—the "arms akimbo" position—is always interpreted as an angry, aggressive posture. Indeed, this position is used as a ritualized symbol of anger in the Indonesian *wayang* (shadow puppet) theater.

 Gifts

- Gift giving is a traditional part of Indonesian culture. Although gifts may be small, they are given often.
- You will give gifts to celebrate an occasion, when you return from a trip, when you are invited to an Indonesian home, when a visitor comes to tour your office or workplace, and in return for services rendered.
- It is not the custom to unwrap a gift in the presence of the giver. To do so would suggest that the recipient is greedy and impatient. Worse, if the gift is somehow inappropriate or disappointing, loss of face would result. Expect the recipient to thank you briefly, then put the still-wrapped gift aside until you have left.
- Food makes a good gift for most occasions. When one visits an area of Indonesia where a delicacy is available, one is expected to bring some back for one's friends.
- Since pork and alcohol are prohibited to observing Muslims, do not give them as gifts to Indonesians. Other foods make good gifts, although meat products must be halal (the Muslim equivalent of kosher). The prohibition against pork and alcohol also precludes pigskin products and perfumes containing alcohol.
- Muslim Indonesians consider dogs unclean. Do not give toy dogs or gifts with pictures of dogs.

- Pets that are prized by Indonesians include cats and birds, especially songbirds. Cassette tapes of the songs of champion songbirds are distributed; such a tape makes a good gift for an Indonesian bird fancier.
- Remember that personal gifts from a man to a woman can be misinterpreted as romantic offerings. When a foreign businessman gives a personal gift (such as perfume or clothing) to an Indonesian woman, he must let everyone know that he is simply delivering a gift from his wife.
- The Chinese traditionally decline a gift three times before accepting; this prevents them from appearing greedy. Continue to insist; once they accept the gift, say that you are pleased that they have done so.
- Gifts of food are always appreciated by Chinese, but avoid bringing food gifts with you to a dinner or party (unless it has been agreed upon beforehand). To bring food may imply that your host cannot provide enough. Instead, send food as a thank-you gift afterwards. Candy or fruit baskets are good choices.
- The Chinese associate all of the following with funerals—do not give them as gifts:
  - Straw sandals,
  - clocks,
  - a stork or crane (although the Western association of storks with births is known to many young Chinese),
  - handkerchiefs (often given at funerals; they symbolize sadness and weeping), and
  - gifts (or wrapping paper) where the predominant color is white, black, or blue.
- Also avoid any gifts of knives, scissors, or cutting tools; to the Chinese, they suggest the severing of a friendship.
- Although the Chinese traditionally brought flowers only to the sick and to funerals, Western advertising has popularized flowers as gifts. Make sure you give an even number of flowers; an odd number would be very unlucky.
- At Chinese New Year, it is customary to give a gift of money in a red envelope to children and to the (nongovernmental) service personnel you deal with on a regular basis. This gift is called a *hong bao*. Give only new bills in even numbers and even amounts. Many employers give each employee a *hong bao* equivalent to one month's salary.
- Observant Hindus do not eat beef or use cattle products. This eliminates most leather products as possible gifts.

 ## Dress

- Indonesia straddles the Equator, and thus is hot and humid all year long. Most of the lowlands have a daytime temperature range of 75 to 95°F, and humidity around 75 percent.
- Lower temperatures occur only in the mountainous areas, where business people rarely venture (except for tourism).
- The rainy season runs from September through February, but sudden showers occur all year long. Many people carry an umbrella every day.
- Because of the heat and humidity, business dress in Indonesia is often casual. Standard formal office wear for men is dark trousers and a light-colored long-sleeved shirt and tie, without a jacket. Many businessmen wear a short-sleeved shirt with no tie.
- If an invitation specifies a "lounge suit" for men, that means that men should wear a standard Western business suit.

- Businesswomen wear long-sleeved blouses and skirts. Stockings and business suits are reserved for more formal offices. The colors should by dark and muted; bright, vivid colors are not appropriate for a businesswoman.
- As a foreigner, you should dress more conservatively until you are sure what degree of formality is expected. Men should expect to wear a suit jacket and tie, and remove them if it seems appropriate. Whatever you wear, try to stay clean and well groomed; bathe several times a day if necessary.
- Many Indonesian men wear an open-necked batik shirt to work. This is also popular for casual wear. Jeans are good for casual wear, but shorts should be avoided.
- In deference to Muslim and Hindu sensibilities, women should always wear blouses that cover at least their upper arms. Skirts should be knee-length or longer.

JERUSALEM

Israel

*u*ntil the founding of the state of Israel, Hebrew was primarily used for religious purposes, as Latin was used among Roman Catholics. Hebrew was not the daily language of any Jewish population. It has now been revived and serves as a unifying force among Jews.

Country Background

History

Israel (including the West Bank) was the historical homeland of the Jews in Biblical times. In 66 A.D. the Jews staged their Great Revolt against the Roman Empire, temporarily throwing off the Roman yoke. But the Roman armies returned, capturing Jerusalem and destroying the Temple in 70 A.D. The Diaspora (dispersion) of the Jews began; the Jewish people were scattered all over the ancient world. Some Jews remained in Israel, but they constituted a small minority.

In the late nineteenth century, some European Jewish thinkers decided that the Jewish people would never be safe until they had a country of their own. Led by a Viennese journalist named Theodor Herzl, the Zionist movement was born. Jews began moving back into Palestine (as the area was known), which was then part of the Ottoman Empire.

The United Kingdom promised to support the Zionists in return for Jewish support in World War I. However, in part because of the opposition of the local Arab peoples, Israel did not become a reality until after World War II. The modern state of Israel was created in 1948; the neighboring Arab states immediately declared war.

Two portions of the Occupied Territories—the Gaza Strip and the city of Jericho—are being handed over to Palestinian administration. Palestinians hope that this limited self-rule will one day evolve into an independent Palestinean state.

Type of Government

Israel is a parliamentary multiparty democracy. There is one legislative house, called the Knesset; it has 120 seats. The chief of state is the president, who is allowed to serve for no more than two five-year terms. The head of government is the prime minister, who is also the head of the Cabinet.

Most of the Palestinians in the Occupied Territories are not Israeli citizens. They have had no vote, and they were tried not in the Israeli criminal courts but in special military courts. The planned limited self-rule will offer them a chance to elect leaders and police themselves.

Language

The official languages of Israel are Arabic and Hebrew. Other languages frequently heard in Israel are English, French, Yiddish, and Russian.

Religion

Although Israel was established as the Jewish homeland, the state of Israel has no official religion. Except for the failed Soviet experiment of the "Jewish Autonomous Oblast" near the Russian-Chinese border, Israel is the only Jewish homeland in existence.

" — CULTURAL NOTE

*W*hat is a Jew?" is a question that is constantly debated in Israel. While Israeli law allows any Jew to immigrate to Israel, Israeli authorities must constantly decide who is Jewish and who is not. At times, persons who professed to be Christians but who were born of Jewish parents have been denied Israeli citizenship. On the other hand, many Soviets who claimed Jewish ancestry have been accepted, even though they had never worshipped as Jews. Religion classes are offered to Russian immigrants who know next to nothing about the Jewish faith.

A large segment of Israeli Jews are secularists, who rarely observe the forms of the Jewish faith.

Ethnic Jews now make up slightly more than 82 percent of the population. The rest are primarily Arabs, mostly Palestinian. The majority of Palestinians are Sunni Muslims, but there are Christian Palestinians as well. There are also small numbers of a bewildering array of ethnic and religious groups. The largest of these are the Druze (1.6 percent), an obscure Arab people who keep their religious beliefs a secret. They are known to venerate the Biblical figure Jethro, the father-in-law of Moses, whose tomb is in northern Israel.

Demographics

The current population of Israel is about 4.7 million. This is rapidly increasing as Soviet Jews pour into the country. Russian Jewish immigration fluctuates according to conditions in the former U.S.S.R.; as many as one million of them are expected.

Cultural Orientation

Cognitive Styles: How Israelis Organize and Process Information

The Israelis are open to information that advances the state, but their positive pragmatism and determination will not allow the acceptance of information that is contrary to the culture's goals. Information is processed analytically and abstractively. The personal aspects of a situation are more important than obeying universal rules or laws, but these aspects may involve the principles of Judaism and the needs of the state.

Negotiation Strategies: What Israelis Accept as Evidence

Subjective feelings tend to be the basis for the truth. However, faith in the ideologies of Judaism, including the fact that the state must succeed, problems have to be solved, and security has to be maintained, may modify the truth as one sees it. Objective facts are used to supplement feelings and faith.

Value Systems: The Basis for Behavior

Israel's need to survive as a state permeates all value systems. The following three sections identify the Value Systems in the predominant culture—their methods of dividing right from wrong, good from evil, and so forth.

Locus of Decision Making

Although there are still some collectives, there is an emphasis on individual initiative and achievement and a strong belief in individual decisions within the social and business context. Decisions are made with an effort to blend idealism with reality, emotion with firmness, physical labor with respect for the intellectual and spiritual realms, and a strong military posture with a sincere desire for peace. The dignity and worth of the individual is always emphasized, along with the right to a private life and opinions.

Sources of Anxiety Reduction

A strong nuclear family is the basis for socialization and gives its members a sense of social identity. It also serves as a focal point for emotional and physical security. The revival of Hebrew and its successful adaptation as a modern language bonds the society together with a linguistic identity. A deep consciousness of Jewish history and tradition produces a bond that gives structure and stability to everyday life and also sensitizes people to the anti-Jewish sentiment in the Arab countries that surround them.

Issues of Equality/Inequality

Israel is a democratic and egalitarian culture built on competition. The leveling and educational influences of general military service help to develop a sense of equality. Although there are inequalities in roles, equal rights are guaranteed to all. Strong negative biases exist against the Palestinians and other Arabs, as do some biases against Jews from different countries. The emphasis on the equality of women and men can be seen in all spheres of national life, for example, both are subject to compulsory army training.

Business Practices

Appointments

PUNCTUALITY

- Punctuality is not a traditional virtue in most Middle Eastern cultures. If your clients are Sephardim or Palestinians, they may be late for an appointment or not show up at all. However, they may have adopted a more Western attitude toward punctuality. Unless you know the individuals, there is no way to tell in advance.
- Most—but not all—Ashkenazim tend to be more prompt in business dealings.
- It is standard Middle Eastern practice to keep supplicants (including foreign business people) waiting. Until you get to know your clients, it is unwise to schedule more than two appointments per day.

- The population of Israel comes from all over the world (only 60 percent of Israeli Jews are native-born), so many different cultural traditions are represented. As a result, business practices may be North American, Russian, European, or anything in between.

- An appointment is rarely private among traditional Arab business people. Expect your visit to be interrupted by phone calls and visits from your client's friends and family. Westerners frequently find these distractions infuriating; try to maintain your equanimity.
- The Jewish holy day, the Shabbes, begins at sunset on Friday and ends at sunset on Saturday. In deference to the religious Jewish community, no business is conducted on the Shabbes. The workweek runs from Sunday through Thursday.
- Business hours vary widely. Even the days businesses are open depends upon the religion of the owner. Most Jewish businesses close on Fridays (especially in the afternoon) and Saturdays. Islamic-owned establishments will be closed all day on Fridays; Christian-owned ones will be closed Sundays. (Remember that Palestinians may be either Muslim or Christian.)
- A typical schedule for a Jewish-owned business would be 8 A.M. to 4 P.M,. Sunday through Thursday, and 8 A.M. to 1 P.M. on Fridays.
- Both Judaism and Islam use lunar calendars that are different from the Gregorian (Western) calendar. However, for official business purposes and when dealing with foreigners, most Israelis will use the Gregorian calendar.
- The Jewish and Islamic lunar calendars use lunar months of 28 days, so a lunar year of 12 months is only 354 days long. Holidays will thus be on different dates (by the Western calendar) every year.
- Note that when a schedule is agreed upon in terms of months (e.g., delivery in two months), an Israeli may be thinking in terms of twenty eight-day months while a Westerner may be assuming thirty-day months.

 Negotiating

- It often takes a long time for decisions to be made.
- Most Israelis have a very confrontational negotiating style, which may become very emotional. Don't hesitate to respond in kind.

P————————————————**CULTURAL NOTE**

erhaps as a result of being surrounded by hostile Arab countries that have frequently sought to destroy Israel, the Israeli people exhibit a strong strain of fatalism. When one assumes that one may be dead in a year, long-term plans are not given a high priority. Successful business deals in Israel must promise an immediate return. Long-term guarantees and warranties are rarely selling points.

Similarly, an Israeli's vigorous opposition to a plan may suddenly vanish without warning. There is an attitude of "Life is too short to keep arguing; let's make a deal and be done with it."

- Unlike most Israeli Jews, an Israeli Arab will not even consider doing business with you until he knows and likes you. Thus, the social aspects of a deal are just as vital as the business ones.
- In general, the pace of business is slower in Israel than it is in the West. Be patient.
- Middle Eastern business meetings traditionally start slowly, with long inquiries into one's health and journey.
- Business cards are important. Although most Israeli business people speak English, many foreigners have cards printed in English on one side and in Hebrew on the other.
- Engraved business cards are considered the most prestigious in Israel.

CULTURAL NOTE

*b*ecause strictly observant Orthodox Jews consider a menstruating woman to be "unclean," they avoid the touch of any woman. To avoid even an accidental touch, women are not supposed to hand anything directly to Orthodox men. Instead, the woman places the object on a table within easy reach of the man, who then picks it up. This technique must be used by foreign businesswomen, even when they are presenting their business cards.

- English is read from left to right; Hebrew is read from right to left. The front cover of an Israeli magazine is where English-speakers would expect the back cover to be. While most Israeli business people read English, so that sales material does not need to be translated into Hebrew, they may instinctively look first at the back cover of English promotional literature. Keep in mind that the first impression an Israeli has of your literature may be the back cover.
- Most Israelis speak at a much closer distance than North Americans are used to. Do not back up or shy away. There is also more physical contact, and conversations often involve touching. However, foreign businesswomen should avoid initiating physical contact.
- Coffee is often served toward the end of a traditional Middle Eastern business meeting. This is a signal that the meeting will soon conclude. Arabs may light incense at this time as well.
- Arab men often walk hand in hand, although Westernized Israeli Arabs rarely do this. If an Israeli holds your hand, take it as a sign of friendship.
- Arabic is a language of hyperbole. When an Israeli Arab says "yes," it usually means "possibly." Be encouraged by this, but do not assume that the negotiating is over.
- English-speaking Jews are often surprised to find themselves referred to as "Anglo-Saxons" by Israeli Jews. It is not meant as an insult.
- Israelis love to argue and are rarely at a loss for an opinion. You need not agree with all of their positions.
- Sports are always a good topic of conversation. Swimming, soccer, and basketball are among the most popular Israeli sports.

 Business Entertaining

- Hosting visitors is considered a virtue in the Middle East, so most Israelis will take care of the entertaining within their country.
- Be prepared to remove your shoes before entering an Arab building. Follow the lead of your host.
- Remember that religious Israelis have strict dietary laws. Pork is prohibited to observing Jews; strict Muslims do not consume either alcohol or pork. If you decide to host a gathering, know the dietary restrictions of your guests.
- The left hand is considered unclean in the Arab world. Among Arabs, always eat with the right hand only. Even if you are left-handed, eat with your right hand.
- Do not eat everything on your plate. Leaving a little food is a sign that you have had enough.
- Realize that tipping (*baksheesh*) is expected for many types of services and courtesies.

Time

- Israel is two hours ahead of Greenwich Mean Time (G.M.T + 2), or seven hours ahead of Eastern Standard Time (E.S.T. + 7).

Protocol

 ## Greetings

- While different cultural groups in Israel may have different styles of greetings, most Israelis who do business in foreign environments shake hands upon introduction.

CULTURAL NOTE

*b*ecause of the Orthodox prohibition against touching women, a foreign businesswoman should not offer to shake hands with an Israeli. Wait until they offer to shake hands, then follow their lead. Over 50 percent of Israeli Jews are considered "secular"—they do not observe the traditional Jewish rituals. The majority of business people dealing on an international basis belong to this group. Expect them to shake hands. Orthodox Jewish men traditionally wear a skullcap (yarmulke) or hat and black clothing.

- A traditional Arab or Orthodox Jewish male will not necessarily introduce his wife. Follow his lead; if he acts as if she isn't there, you should do the same.
- A traditional Arab greeting between men involves each grasping the other's right hand, placing the left hand on the other's right shoulder, and exchanging kisses on each cheek. However, Arabs used to dealing with foreigners will probably confine themselves to shaking hands on a first meeting.

 ## Titles/Forms of Address

- Israeli Jews come from all over the world, and their names usually reflect the tradition of their previous country. For example, Russian Jews will have a given name, followed by a patronymic ("son of . . .") and a surname.
- In general, an Israeli Jew's given name will come first and the surname will come last. Address them by their title, or Mr., Mrs., or Miss, and their surname, unless they indicate otherwise.
- Israeli Arabs have traditional Arabic names, which Westerners frequently find confusing. The best solution is to request the names—written in English—of any Arabs you will have to meet, speak to, or correspond with. Find out both their full names (for correspondence) and how they are to be addressed in person.
- Israeli Arabs write their names in Arabic. In part because short vowels are not written in Arabic, translating from Arabic to other alphabets is not an exact science. Thus, Arabic names may be spelled several different ways in English. (For example, the leader of Libya's name is variously rendered as Colonel Muammar al-Qaddafi, Mu'ammar al-Qadhafi, Qaddhafi, Qathafi, Gaddafi, and so forth.)
- In general, Arabic names are written in the same order as English names: title (if any), given name, sometimes a middle name (often a patronymic), and surname (family name). Thus, the previous leader of Egypt was President Anwar al-Sadat; his title was President, his given name was Anwar, and al-Sadat was his family name.
- The term *al* literally means "from" in Arabic. A name like al-Barudi could mean "son of Barudi" or "from the town of Barudi." Do not mistake the term *al-* for the Western nickname Al (short for Alex or Albert).
- The term *abu* means "father of" in Arabic. Israeli Arabs frequently refer to revered elders as Abu.

- Most Arabs should be addressed by title and surname (e.g., Doctor al-Nahhas), just as you would address a Westerner. In writing, use their full name. If they do not have a title, just use Mr., Mrs., or Miss.

 Gestures

- The left hand is considered unclean in the Arab world. In the Middle East, always use the right hand in preference to the left (unless you are handling something that is considered unclean). Never eat with the left hand; eat only with your right hand. Avoid gesturing with the left hand.
- It is acceptable to use both hands when one is insufficient.
- While Israelis constantly gesture with their hands when speaking, they avoid pointing at another person. This would be considered impolite, especially among Arabs.
- As a general rule, keep both feet on the ground. Traditional Arabs do not cross their legs when sitting. Never show the bottom of your foot to an Arab; this is considered offensive. When one removes one's shoes (as when entering a mosque), the soles of the shoes are placed together, preventing the sole from being pointed at anyone.
- Any gesture that displays an extended thumb—including the "thumbs up" gesture or a hitchhiker's gesture—is offensive throughout the Middle East.

 Gifts

- Avoid giving a gift until you know something about the person you are giving it to. Especially with Orthodox Jews and Arabs, a gift must not violate one of the restrictions of their belief system.
- If you are invited to an Israeli home, bring a gift of flowers or candy. Be sure a gift of food is kosher if it is going to an Orthodox person.
- Make sure you give or receive gifts with the right hand, not with the left (although using both hands is acceptable).

 Dress

- While foreigners are not exempt from Israeli standards of modesty, do not adopt traditional native clothing. Non-Jews should not wear yarmulkes (except when inside a synagogue), and non-Arabs should not wear turbans or other Arab headgear.
- Since Israeli law is mostly secular, there are few laws regarding clothing. But "immodest" dress will result in vocal disapproval from both Orthodox Jews and traditional Muslims.
- Despite Israel's heat, conservative tradition dictates that most of the body remain covered.
- Men should wear long trousers and a shirt, preferably long-sleeved. A jacket and tie are usually required for business meetings. Keep shirts buttoned up to the collarbone.

CULTURAL NOTE

*a*ll women—including foreigners—are expected to wear modest clothing in public, especially among traditional areas. The neckline should be high and the sleeves should come at least to the elbows. Hemlines should be well below the knee, if not ankle-length. The overall effect should be one of baggy concealment; a full-length outfit which is tight and revealing is not acceptable. Therefore, pants or pant suits are not recommended. While a hat or scarf is not always required, it is wise to keep a scarf at hand.

- Israeli social events almost never require tuxedos; the only regular black-tie affairs are those hosted by foreign embassies.
- Remember that Israeli summers tend to be hot and humid, while the winters are often chilly enough to require overcoats. Indoor heating is often poor, so sweaters or shawls are useful. Away from the coast, winters can be cold enough to require hats and gloves, especially at higher elevations.

ROME

Italy

Country Background

History

Italy has been the name of this region for over 3,000 years. Evidence of early Latin/Italic tribes dates from 2000 B.C. The Etruscans arrived around 1200 B.C. bringing their own culture and laws, and conquered vast central areas of the peninsula.

Greek civilization dominated southern Italy around 600 B.C., and much of Greek culture was subsequently adopted by the Romans. The Roman Empire had tremendous impact on Italian social, legal, political, artistic, and military culture.

With 3,000 miles of coastline, Italy proved a logical prey for invaders. After the fall of the Roman Empire, there were repeated invasions from many countries, including France, Austria, Spain, and Germany. Italy became a country of sharply diverse city-states.

By 1870 Italy had become a politically unified monarchy. The final monarch abdicated in 1946.

The most notorious political figure from Italy's recent past is Mussolini, the fascist dictator known as *Il Duce*. Mussolini controlled Italy's government from 1922 to 1943. He supported Hitler during World War II, until Italian supporters of the Allies assassinated him and overthrew the Fascists.

Italy did not become a politically unified constitutional republic until the 1946 national elections. Corruption scandals in the early 1990's tainted most major political parties, resulting in the 1994 election of reform candidates led by Prime Minister Silvio Berlusconi.

Type of Government
The Italian Republic is a multiparty parliamentary republic. There are two legislative bodies, a 325-seat Senate and a 630-seat Chamber of Deputies. The president is the chief of state, while the prime minister is the head of the government.

Language
Italian is the official language. There are many diverse dialects. English is spoken by many business people.

CULTURAL NOTE

*e*urope's oldest university was founded in Bologna in the twelfth century.

Religion
There is no official religion, although the population is predominantly Roman Catholic.

Demographics
The current population of Italy is 57 million (1991 estimates). The populace is overwhelmingly ethnic Italian; less than 2 percent are foreign-born.

Cultural Orientation

Cognitive Styles: How Italians Organize and Process Information
In Italy information is readily accepted and great discussions occur, but little movement is seen in the opinions of the participants. Information tends to be processed subjectively and associatively. Italians will look at the particulars of each situation rather than appeal to a law or rule to solve a problem.

Negotiation Strategies: What Italians Accept as Evidence
Subjective feelings are more important than faith in an ideology or objective facts when deciding what is true. However, the ideologies of the church do permeate nearly all transactions. Italians who have a higher education tend to use facts to back their arguments.

Value Systems: The Basis for Behavior
The ideologies of the Roman Catholic church exert the most influence. The following three sections identify the Value Systems in the predominant culture—their methods of dividing right from wrong, good from evil, and so forth.

Locus of Decision-Making
The individual is responsible for his or her decisions but is often expected to defer to the interests of the family or organizational unit. There is an admiration for urban life and an enduring loyalty to region and family.

Sources of Anxiety Reduction

The extended family is getting smaller but is still the major source of security and stability. Anxiety, as well as security, is produced by seeking success in the eyes of the extended family and society. There are strong Catholic and Communist segments that can work in opposition, but are not completely incompatible. The church gives a sense of structure to the majority. Italians are remarkably diverse, but they also have a strong capacity for social and cultural resilience and continuity.

Issues of Equality/Inequality

There are extreme contrasts between rich and poor. The population is stratified by income. Patron-client relationships provide a strong social and political base. Even though there is a large German-speaking group in the north, and many mutually unintelligible dialects, there is one standard language that binds the country together. Women have made slow progress toward equality.

Business Practices

Appointments

———————————————————— PUNCTUALITY

- ◆ Be on time, especially in the industrial north, where business is often conducted with "American-style" pressure and efficiency.

- Italian business people prefer to deal with people they know, even if that acquaintance has been a perfunctory handshake at a trade fair. Before you invest in travel to Italy, be sure to engage a strong contact representative who can make appropriate introductions and appointments for you.
- Write first for an appointment, in Italian if you want an immediate reply.
- Follow up your letter by telex, fax, or telephone call.
- Be very aware of summer vacation periods. Most firms are closed in August. If you write for an appointment in mid-July, you may not get a satisfactory reply until September.
- Italians like to get acquainted and engage in small talk before getting down to business. They are hospitably attentive. Expect to answer questions about your family.
- Plan appointments between 10:00 and 11:00 A.M., and after 3:00 P.M.
- Northern business hours are usually 8:30 A.M. to 12:45 P.M. and 3:00 to 6:30 P.M., Monday through Friday. Many businesses are open Saturday mornings.
- In central and southern Italy, business hours are from 8:30 A.M. to 12:45 P.M. then 4:30 or 5:00 to 7:30 or 8:00 P.M., Monday through Friday, and 8:30 A.M. to 12:45 P.M. Saturday. The southern business pace is more relaxed.
- There may be fewer public holidays in Italy than in many Latin countries, but business people must be aware that practically every Italian city celebrates the feast of its patron saint as a legal holiday and much of the city literally shuts down.

Negotiating

- It is important to understand corporate hierarchy. Titles may not coincide with the U.S. conception of responsibility, and authority goes with the individual, not necessarily the title.

CULTURAL NOTE

*C*orporations often have a horizontal chain of authority. Italians call it a *cordata* (which actually means a team of mountain climbers on the same rope). This parallel channel is based on levels of personal, reciprocal concern.

The *cordata* concept is very difficult to fully explain to outsiders. But it exists and, to facilitate business, one should have a reliable contact who has full knowledge of a company's inside structure.

- The pace of negotiations is usually slower than in the United States. The more important the contract, the more study is going on behind the scenes. Any obvious sense of urgency is thought to weaken one's bargaining position.
- A dramatic change in demands at the last minute is often a technique to unsettle the other side. Be patient and calm; just when it appears impossible, the contract may come together.
- One does not exchange business cards at social occasions; but it is normal at business functions— especially since an Italian would feel it impolite to ask a foreigner to spell out her or his name.
- Italian cards are often plain white with black print. Usually, the more important the person, the less information is on the card.
- Conversational subjects that are highly appreciated are Italian culture, art, food, wine, sports such as bicycling and especially soccer, family, Italian scenery, and films.
- Your host may be negative about something in his or her country or its politics, but don't agree too strongly and never offer criticisms of your own.
- Avoid talking about religion, politics, and World War II.
- Italians do not usually tell off-color jokes, and are uncomfortable when acquaintances do.
- Never ask someone you have just met at a social gathering about his or her profession. To do so is considered gauche, even insulting.

Business Entertaining

- Italian hospitality plays an important role in business life, and most often means dining in a restaurant. No matter how you feel, refusing an invitation will offend.

CULTURAL NOTE

*W*hen dining, Italians keep both hands above the table, not one resting on the lap. There may be three plates: a small one on top for antipasto, under it a deep dish for pasta or soup, and a large plate on the bottom for the main course.

Use your knife (not your fingers) to pick up cheese, and don't eat any fruit except grapes or cherries with your hand.

Italians consider wine as a food to be sipped, not as a means of relaxation. Therefore, to drink too much is considered very offensive.

- Business dinners involve only a small, important group. If you are the host, consult with your Italian contact before extending invitations. You cannot be aware of all the "inside" personalities and ranks, so ask for help.
- Ask your Italian client's secretary to suggest a favorite restaurant.
- Dining is a serious business, and real prestige can be gained or lost at the table. At the propitious moment one may bring up business.
- Paying may equate to prestige, and Italians may even slip the waiter a generous tip before dinner to make sure you do not get the bill.
- The check will not be brought until you ask for it. Get a waiter's attention by saying *senta*, an idiom meaning "hear me" or "come here." You may also raise your hand slightly and say *camariere* or *signorina*.
- Women executives will find it extremely difficult to pay.
- Keep the receipt for the restaurant bill. Sometimes "tax police" check restaurant bills outside for adherence to tax laws.
- In a restaurant you will have to ask for ice, since Italians usually do not serve drinks cold (they think ice-cold things are unhealthy).

CULTURAL NOTE

- Breakfast (*la prima colazione*) is normally at 8:00 A.M. and consists of rolls, bread, butter, perhaps some jam, and strong coffee or chocolate.
- "Lunch" (*la colazione*) is the full-course, main meal of the day, and serving starts at 1:00 P.M.
- "Dinner" (*la cena*) is again a light meal. Service starts around 7:00 P.M. and may be served in some areas until 10:00 P.M.

Time
- Italy is one hour ahead of Greenwich Mean Time (G.M.T. + 1), or six hours ahead of U.S. Eastern Standard Time (E.S.T. + 6).

Protocol

 ### Greetings
- As a guest, you will be introduced first. The most senior or eldest person present should always be given special deference.
- Shake hands with everyone present when arriving and leaving. At a large gathering, if no one is giving formal introductions, it is proper to shake hands and introduce yourself.
- Handshakes may include grasping the arm with the other hand.
- Women may "kiss" good friends on either cheek (it is rather more like pressing the sides of each face together).
- Close friends and male relatives often embrace and slap each other on the back.

 ### Titles/Forms of Address
- Do not use first names unless you are invited to—formality is still appreciated. Executives and subordinates in offices generally do not address one another by their first names.

- Educators, professors, and doctors are highly esteemed; use the title *Dottore* for a man and *Dottoressa* for a woman. It is better to use a title (even if you are unsure); always err on the side of caution. It will be accepted as an understanding of "status earned" even if not academically achieved.
- Personal titles are used in all forms of address, spoken and written. Like *Dottore* they can be used with or without the surname. Attorney Green is *Avvocato Verdi*, *Signorina Avvocata* is Miss Attorney, and so forth. Find out these details before the meeting if possible.

 Gestures

- Latins "talk with their hands," and most gestures are usually both expressive and innocuous.
- You may see a disgruntled man quickly stroke his finger tips under his chin and thrust them forward. This is a sign of defiance and/or derision, somewhat like thumbing your nose in the United States.
- Another gesture has two versions: Holding your hand palm down with the index and little fingers straight out, and the others curved inward, symbolized the devil's horns, and the message is to ward off evil. If the same gesture is done with the fingers pointing upward, it is an obscene message.

 Gifts

- Business gifts are sometimes given at a senior managerial level. They should be small and not obviously expensive, but made by craftsmen of prestige. Consumables like liquors or delicacies, or crafts from the visitor's country, may be appropriate.
- Do not give gifts that are obviously a vehicle for your company's logo.
- Note that some Italian firms have privately published glossy, top-quality illustrated books suitable for coffee-table display.
- A small gift may be given to any staff member who has been particularly helpful. Travel alarm clocks, pens, silver key chains, executive diaries, or calculators are good gifts as long as they are name brands. Flowers (see next paragraph) or chocolates are acceptable for a secretary.
- If you are invited to someone's home, bring gift-wrapped chocolates, pastries, or flowers. Never give an even number of flowers. Do not give chrysanthemums; they are used for funerals. Do not give a brooch, handkerchiefs, or knives, all of which connote sadness.
- If you give wine, be certain it is of excellent vintage—many Italians are wine connoisseurs.

 Dress

- In the business world, good clothes are a badge of success. Women dress in quiet, expensive elegance; men's ties and suits should also be fashionable and well-cut.
- Keep in mind Italy is a major center of European fashion. Even casual clothes are smart and chic.
- Women wear pants in cities, but shorts are a rarity. You may be stopped if you try to go into a church while wearing shorts or a sleeveless top.

TOKYO

Japan

Country Background

History

Japan has been occupied for thousands of years. The current emperor's dynasty is said to have been founded in 660 B.C.

Historically, Japan resisted outside influences, and frequently closed itself to foreigners. The United States forcibly opened Japan to foreign markets in 1853 when Commodore Perry sailed his fleet into Tokyo Bay.

What Westerners consider World War II was only part of an long-running Asiatic war in which Japan invaded neighboring nations. Korea was annexed in 1910, Manchuria was annexed in 1931, and China proper was invaded in 1937. Japan surrendered to the Allies in 1945, and was occupied until 1952.

The United States, wishing to demilitarize and democratize Japan, instituted many reforms after World War II. These efforts included a decrease in the power of the emperor and decentralization of the government. However, the Japanese have recentralized their government in the past forty years.

Type of Government

Japan is a parliamentary democracy under a constitutional monarch. The chief of state is the emperor; Emperor Akihito was crowned in 1990 after the death of his father, Emperor Hirohito. The head of the government is the prime minister.

Power within the government resides mainly in the prime minister, who is the leader of the majority party of the Diet, or parliament. The prime minister dissolves the House of Representatives every two or three years. The prime minister also appoints the Supreme Court and leads the Cabinet.

The Diet is made up of two houses, the House of Representatives and the House of Councilors. Both are elected, with the House of Representatives having more authority. Finally, the Cabinet is responsible to the Diet. In the Cabinet, it is the Ministry of Finance (MOF) and the Ministry of International Trade and Industry (MITI) that are the most important.

MITI, through involvement in business and industry following World War II, helped Japan gain its strength. Today MITI does not have the same authority it once did, both because it is not as needed as much as before and because of pressure from other governments (such as the United States). The idea that the government controls industry to such an extent that the country can be called Japan, Inc. is a myth. The government ministries instead serve as intermediaries and as think tanks.

Language

Japanese is the official language of Japan. It is a complex and subtle language, and is spoken nowhere else in the world as a primary tongue. Most sentences in Japanese can be expressed on at least four different levels of politeness. Japanese women almost always use one of the more deferential forms. Communication in Japan is often marked by great subtlety; information is left unspoken yet is perfectly understood.

Education

Literacy is close to 100 percent, and 95 percent of the population has a high school education. The Japanese educational system is similar to that of the United States, except that students must pass many qualifying exams. The pressure to study and to get good grades is very intense. Once a student has passed the entrance exam for college, however, exams are over. Students accepted to the top colleges are almost guaranteed top jobs. Classes in English begin at age twelve. The goal for students of English is to have passing exam grades rather than verbal communication skills.

Religion

The Shinto religion is unique to Japan; the institution of the emperor is supported by Shintoism. However, the Japanese are very tolerant of religious differences, and may even practice both Buddhism and Shinto concurrently. Many people are married in a Shinto ceremony but select a Buddhist funeral.

Christianity (about 4 percent) and other religions (18 percent) are also present in Japan. There is no official religion. The Japanese tend to adapt their religion to modern life; for example, they will have new businesses blessed.

Demographics

Japan's population approaches 125 million. This dense population is cited as the prevailing factor explaining the Japanese "group mentality." The following statistics are useful for understanding just how crowded Japan is: Its land represents only 0.3 percent of the world's land mass, yet its people represent 3 percent of the world's population. In these conditions, conformity and group activity have proved to be the best way to avoid conflict. Over 99 percent of the population consists of native-born Japanese. The largest minority (less than 1 percent) are Koreans. Although farmers have a disproportionate amount of political influence, they represent less than 7 percent of the labor force. Some 33 percent work of Japanese in manufacturing or construction. Most of the remaining 60 percent are in trade or services.

Cultural Orientation

Cognitive Styles: How Japanese Organize and Process Information

The Japanese generally close all doors to outside influences but are open to ideas within their group. They are subjective and experiential in their thinking, holding fast to traditional values. Strong loyalty to their groups makes them look to the particular and specific rather than the universal and abstract. They pride themselves on anticipating others' needs.

Negotiation Strategies: What Japanese Accept as Evidence

Since they tend to be more subjective than objective, the Japanese rely more on their feelings than on facts. However, because they insist on consensus within their groups, others may interpret this behavior as being grounded in faith in an ideology that says that they are superior to others. Their controlled communicative behavior exacerbates this situation with unknowing foreigners.

Value Systems: The Basis for Behavior

Traditional value systems are only recently being eroded in the younger generation. The following three sections identify the Value Systems in the predominant culture—their methods of dividing right from wrong, good from evil, and so forth.

Locus of Decision Making

Decisions are made within the group with little or no personal recognition. A person's actions reflect on the group, particularly his or her family. Outsiders must be accepted into the group before they can participate in decision making. The Japanese are only moderately collective.

Sources of Anxiety Reduction

The Japanese have very high anxiety about life because of the need to save face. There are constant pressures to conform. A very strong work ethic and strong group relationships give structure and stability to life. Emotional restraints are developed in childhood, and all behaviors are situation-bound. This makes it extremely difficult for a foreigner to understand the culture.

Issues of Equality/Inequality

Age is revered. There is a great deal of competitiveness among equals, but also an inherent trust in people. Ethnocentrism is very strong. Male dominance is strong in all public situations. Sex roles in society are clearly differentiated, but Western-style equality is strong in the youth.

Business Practices

Appointments

 ———————————————— **PUNCTUALITY**

◆ Be punctual at all times.

- The workweek is forty-eight hours without overtime pay, done in five and one-half working days. Recently large firms have begun to institute the five-day week. Few executives take their work home with them.
- Office hours are 9:00 A.M. to 5:00 or 5:30 P.M. (Many people go to dinner, then return to the office until 9:00 or 10:00 P.M.)
- During holidays, banks and offices close, while stores remain open.
- During three weeks of the year (New Year's holidays, December 28 to January 3; Golden Week, April 29 to May 5; and Obon, in mid-August), many people visit the graves of their ancestors. Conducting business and traveling are difficult during these periods.

Negotiating

- A Japanese response "I'll consider it" may actually mean "no."
- Negatively phrased questions will get a "yes" if the Japanese speaker agrees. A question such as "Doesn't Company A want us?" will be answered "yes" if the Japanese thinks that Company A indeed does not want you. In English, we would answer, "No, they do not want you."
- Incorporate the words "I'm sorry" into your vocabulary when you go to Japan. However, don't be ingratiating out of fear of offending; just be polite.
- Negotiations are begun at the executive level and continued at the middle level (working level).
- "Connections" are very helpful in Japan. However, choose your intermediaries carefully, because the Japanese will feel obliged to be loyal to them. Do not choose someone of lower rank than the person with whom he or she will have dealings. Intermediaries should not be part of either company involved in the deal.
- If you don't have a connection, a personal call is better than a letter. A letter might not even be answered.
- Use an intermediary, such as the one who introduced you to the company, to discuss bad news.
- Using a Japanese lawyer rather than a Western one indicates a cooperative spirit.
- The Japanese usually use the initial meetings to get to know you, while at the same time asking to hear about your proposal. Agreements of confidentiality are vague.
- Contracts are not perceived as final agreements. You or they may renegotiate.
- Because age equals rank, show the greatest respect to the oldest members of the Japanese group with whom you are in contact.
- You will not be complimented on good work, because the group and not the individual is rewarded. It is a bad idea to single out Japanese workers.
- The Japanese will not explain exactly what is expected of you.
- Most Japanese go through job rotation, in which they change jobs within the same company every few years. In this way, the employees get to know the company and its employees well.
- A quality circle is made up of people doing the same work who will discuss ways to improve their work.
- Suggestion boxes, so often ignored in the United States, are useful in Japan, simply because Japanese employees stuff them full of suggestions.
- Don't make accusations or refuse anything directly; be indirect. Also, don't ask questions that your interlocutor may be unable to answer.

- On the job, the Japanese are very serious and do not try to "lighten things up" with humor.
- When working with Japanese who know English, or when using an interpreter, be patient. Speak slowly, pause often, and avoid colloquialisms. Your interpreter may seem to be taking more time with the translation than you did with your statement; this is because she or he is using lengthy forms of respect.
- Do not be surprised if your interpreter translates Japanese into English almost simultaneously, but waits until English speakers are finished before translating into Japanese. Unlike English, Japanese is a very predictable language. By the time a Japanese business person is halfway through a sentence, the translator probably knows how the sentence will end. Indeed, it would be very impolite of a Japanese to end a sentence with an unexpected choice of words.
- At times you may need to pretend you are sure that your Japanese colleague or friend has understood you, even if you know this is not the case. This is important for maintaining a good relationship.

 ## Business Entertaining

- Business entertaining usually occurs after business hours, and very rarely in the home. You will be entertained often, sometimes on short notice. While the first evenings will probably be spent going from bar to restaurant to "hostess bar" (not a good idea for businesswomen), you may suggest alternatives later. These may include Sumo wrestling or *karaoke* ("empty orchestra") bars, where you sing along with a tape.
- When you are taken out, your host will treat.
- Allow your host to order for you (this will be easier, too, since the menus are in Japanese). Be enthusiastic while eating, and show great thanks afterwards.
- While business entertaining is primarily for building friendships rather than for doing deals, you may discuss business during the evening.
- If you are invited to a Japanese home, keep in mind that this is a great honor, and you should show great appreciation.
- For social occasions, it is appropriate to be fashionably late.
- When entering a Japanese home, take off your shoes at the door. You will wear one pair of slippers from the door to the living room, where you will remove them. You will put them on again to make your way to the bathroom, where you will exchange them for "toilet slippers." Don't forget to change back again.
- In a home, you will sit cross-legged, or with your legs to the side, around a low table with the family. You may be offered a backrest.
- Meals are long, but the evening usually ends at about 11 P.M.
- Never point your chopsticks at another person. When you are not using them, you should line them up on the chopstick rest.
- Use both hands to hold a bowl or a cup that you wish to be refilled.
- Eventually, you will wish to invite your hosts out. Be insistent, even if they claim that a foreigner should not pay for anything. It is best to choose a Western-style restaurant for this occasion.

Time
- Japan is nine hours ahead of Greenwich Mean Time (G.M.T. + 9), or 14 hours ahead of Eastern Standard Time (E.S.T. + 14).

Protocol

 Greetings

- The Japanese are very aware of Western habits, and will often greet you with a handshake. Their handshakes will often be weak; this gives no indication of their assertiveness of character.
- The bow is their traditional greeting.
- If someone bows to greet you, observe carefully. Bow to the same depth as you have been bowed to, because the depth of the bow indicates the status relationship between you.
- As you bow, lower your eyes. Keep your palms flat against your thighs.

t——————————————————————**CULTURAL NOTE**

he business card is extremely important for establishing credentials. Have it prepared in advance by JAL (the airline) or by a Japanese representative. It is best to have one side in English, with extra information such as membership in professional associations; and the reverse side in Japanese. If your status changes, have new cards printed immediately, and distribute them again.

- Cards are presented after the bow or handshake. Present your card with the Japanese side facing your colleague, in such a manner that it can be read immediately.
- Read the card presented to you, memorizing all the information. Ask for help in pronunciation and in comprehension of the title; if you understand without help, make a relevant comment.
- Handle cards very carefully. Do not put them in your pocket, or in your wallet if you plan to put it in your back pocket. Never write on a person's business card (especially not in his or her presence).

 Titles/Forms of Address

- Use last names plus *san*, meaning Mr. or Ms. Do not suggest that the Japanese call you by your first name.

 Gestures

- Japan is a high-context culture; even the smallest gesture carries great meaning. Therefore, avoid expansive arm and hand movements, unusual facial expressions, or dramatic gestures of any kind.
- The American "O.K." sign (thumb and forefinger curled in an "O") means "money" to the Japanese.
- Some Western gestures convey nothing to the Japanese. These include the shrug of the shoulders and the wink between friends.
- Pointing is considered impolite. Instead, wave your hand, palm up, toward the object being indicated, as the Japanese do.
- Beckoning "come here" is done with the palm down.
- Moving the open hand, with the palm facing left, in a fanning motion in front of the face indicates a negative response.
- Sniffing, snorting, and spitting in public are acceptable, but nose blowing is not. When you must blow your nose, use a disposable tissue and then throw it out. The Japanese find the idea of preserving mucus in a neatly folded handkerchief to be grotesque.

- To get through a crowd, the Japanese may push others. There is also a gesture meaning "excuse me," which involves repeating a bow and a karate chop in the air.
- The Japanese do not approve of male-female touching in public.
- Men do not engage in backslapping or other forms of touching.
- In conversation, the Japanese remain farther apart than do North Americans.
- Direct eye contact is not the norm.
- A smile can mean pleasure; but it can also be a means of self-control, as when it is used to hide displeasure.
- Keep a smile, even when you are upset.
- Laughter can mean embarrassment, confusion, or shock, rather than mirth.
- Silence is not uncomfortable for the Japanese as it is for North Americans; rather, it is considered useful.

Gifts

- Gift giving is very common in Japan. Business gifts absolutely must be given at midyear (July 15) and at year end (January 1). They are often given at first business meetings.
- For the Japanese, the ceremony of gift giving is more important than the objects exchanged. Don't be surprised by either modest or extravagant gifts.
- Take your clues from the Japanese with whom you are working. Allow them to present gifts first, and make your gift of the same quality as theirs.
- The Japanese do not usually open gifts directly upon receiving them. If they do, they will be restrained in their appreciation. This does not mean that they do not like what you have given. Again, follow their lead.
- Good gifts are imported scotch, cognac, or frozen steaks; electronic toys for children of associates; or items made by well-known manufacturers. Foreign name brands are always best.
- Always wrap your gifts in Japan or have them wrapped by hotel or store services. It is best to buy the paper there, so as not to choose a paper that is considered tasteful in the United States but unattractive in Japan (for example, black and white paper is unacceptable). Rice paper is ideal.
- If you are invited to a Japanese home, bring flowers, cakes, or candy. The flowers should not be white, as these are associated with death.
- Avoid giving gifts with even numbers of components, such as an even number of flowers in a bouquet. Four is an especially inauspicious number; never give four of anything.

Dress

- Men should wear conservative suits, and never appear casual.
- Slip-on shoes are best, as you will remove them frequently.
- Women should dress conservatively, keeping jewelry, perfume, and makeup to a minimum. Pants are not appropriate. High heels are to be avoided if you risk towering over your Japanese counterparts.
- In summer it is very hot in Japan, so bring cotton clothes. Be sure to have enough changes of clothes, because the Japanese are very concerned with neatness.
- If you wear a kimono, wrap it left over right! Only corpses wear them wrapped right over left.

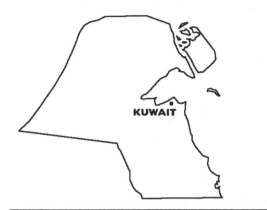

KUWAIT

Kuwait

Country Background

History

This corner of the Middle East has been occupied for thousands of years. There is archaeological evidence of settlements on Kuwait's Failaka Island dating back to around 1000 B.C. In medieval times, Kuwait was under the nominal rule of the Ottoman Empire. But control was difficult; the sultan in Istanbul ruled through his representative in Baghdad, who in turn ruled through the local governor in Basra. In practice, the Kuwaitis have always maintained autonomy by playing one ruler off against another. During that era, they usually pitted the Ottomans against the Persians (modern Iran).

In the sixteenth century, a new power entered Gulf politics. The Portuguese established forts to protect their shipping trade routes. Two centuries later, the British supplanted the Portuguese as the dominant European power in the Gulf. Again the Kuwaitis sought alliances, and they decided that they would have the most freedom under the British flag. The first treaties between Britain and Kuwait were signed in 1899.

Kuwait was at this time a small emirate with an economy dependent upon pearl diving. A political system had evolved in which the emir exercised all political authority but was dependent for revenue upon the powerful merchant families. The common people worked the pearl boats, in perpetual debt to the merchant families. At all levels, Kuwaiti society was based upon the family, and in bad times whole families moved away. This gave the merchant families indirect political power: If they moved out of Kuwait, they would take their fleets of pearl boats with them, and there would be no revenue for the emir. The influence of the merchant families remains to this day, although the advent of oil exports after World War II freed the Emir from the need to collect revenue from the merchants.

Despite its ancient history, Kuwait has been recognized as a fully independent nation only since 1961, when British rule ended.

Kuwait's massive oil reserves were not discovered until the 1930s, and development of the oilfields was delayed by World War II. Only in the 1950s did oil wealth remake Kuwait. The wealth transformed Kuwait's economy without making any basic changes in the political structure.

Following Kuwait's independence in 1961, Iraq made territorial claims on the country. These claims, which also formed the basis of Saddam Hussein's 1990 claims, are defensible only if one considers Iraq to be the legitimate successor state to the Ottoman Empire—a patently absurd notion, as Turkey is the logical successor to the Ottomans. In point of fact, it is Kuwait that could make territorial claims on Iraq. During the 1920s, Britain was called upon to delineate the borders of the region. To placate the powerful states of Iraq and Saudi Arabia, Kuwaiti land was allocated to each of these countries. Threatened intervention by Britain kept the Iraqis from invading in the 1960s. (Of course, by 1990 Britain was no longer the dominant military power in the Gulf, and Saddam Hussein convinced himself that the United States would not intervene militarily.) Despite their defeat at the hands of the coalition, Iraq continues to threaten Kuwait. The Iraqi media refer to Kuwait as "Iraq's nineteenth province."

The Allied military intervention of early 1991 restored the Al-Sabah family to power in Kuwait. They have been the ruling power in Kuwait since 1756.

Type of Government

The emir now rules Kuwait as a constitutional monarchy, although both the constitution and the National Assembly have been suspended since before the invasion.

Migration throughout the area continued into this century, which affects the status of Kuwaitis to this day. Only those families who can trace their residency in Kuwait to before the year 1920 are allowed the full benefits of citizenship. This leaves more than half of the 700,000 Kuwaiti nationals as second-class citizens in their own land. Furthermore, some 70,000 Kuwaiti Bedouins have been denied Kuwaiti citizenship of any sort. They remain stateless persons, unwanted by any country.

Traditionally, the emir of Kuwait—always a member of the al-Sabah family—exercised total authority. However, the emir was always careful to allow the powerful Kuwaiti merchant families to prosper. In effect, the merchants yielded their political power in return for economic power.

By and large, the al-Sabah emirs ruled adroitly. They managed to maintain Kuwait's identity despite being surrounded by powerful neighbors. Oil wealth brought changes. Health and educational services were transformed, and the populace (now educated and familiar with Western political ideas) agitated for a voice in government. By 1962 a constitution had been written for Kuwait, establishing a fifty-seat National Assembly patterned after an Assembly that had evolved back in the 1930s. Despite being an essentially conservative body, this modern Assembly did not support the emir on all issues. Friction between the Assembly and the emir increased until, in 1976, the Assembly was dissolved and the constitution was suspended. The Assembly remained suspended at the time of Iraq's 1990 invasion, although an advisory body, the seventy five-man National Council, was in existence. While in exile, the emir promised that the Assembly would be reconvened. Since the war, a new National Assembly has been elected and is helping to guide domestic policy.

Only educated males who can trace their Kuwaiti citizenship back before 1920 may vote. This represents about 65,000 people in a nation of some 700,000 citizens—to say nothing of the over one million foreign residents.

The emir is both head of state and head of government. There is an appointed prime minister. While there is currently no independent legislature, an independent judiciary does exist.

Language

Arabic is the national language, but English is widely spoken among the business classes.

CULTURAL NOTE

*b*usiness people traveling to Kuwait should remember that the Kuwaiti merchant classes have been traders since before the United States of America came into existence. Kuwaiti business people are very shrewd negotiators; they have had centuries of experience as traders and should not be underestimated.

Religion

Kuwait is an Islamic country. The majority—including the Kuwaitis in positions of power—are Sunni Muslims. Friction exists between the Sunnis and the Shiite minority (about 20 percent), which escalated into terrorist violence in the 1980s. Kuwait's version of Sunni Islam is quite conservative, and is highly influenced by the fundamentalist Wahabism of Saudi Arabia. Women are not accorded equal rights with men, although they are not forced to wear traditional clothing. Indeed, despite their lowly status, women make up over 10 percent of the Kuwaiti workforce.

Demographics

Nationality is a vital issue in Kuwait. Before the 1990 invasion, Kuwait had the highest per capita income in the world. Foreigners who worked in Kuwait outnumbered native Kuwaitis, but did not share in the country's benefits and are not permitted to become citizens. The largest group of foreigners (about 38 percent of the total) were non-Kuwaiti Arabs. This included over 300,000 Palestinians, most of whom have now fled Kuwait. Many Asians (Pakistanis, Indians, and Filipinos) have also left the country. From a pre-war population of slightly over 2 million, (including both citizens and foreigners), the Kuwaiti population is now well below 2 million. The Kuwaiti government wants to replace as many foreign workers as possible with native Kuwaitis, but to do so, it will have to instill a work ethic in its people that is essentially alien to its culture.

Cultural Orientation

Cognitive Styles: How Kuwaitis Organize and Process Information

In Kuwait one will find people's minds closed to all information that does not reflect Islamic values. Most university education is in the United States, which brings with it a degree of abstractive thinking. However, Kuwaitis are taught from youth to think associatively. They approach all problems subjectively according to the tenets of Islamic law.

Negotiation Strategies: What Kuwaitis Accept as Evidence

Truth is found in Islamic law, so faith in its ideologies permeates all discussions. Subjective feelings are the only way of knowing the truth of any situation. Thus, objective facts may have little use in negotiations.

Value Systems: The Basis for Behavior

The Moslem religion is the state religion and the main source of legislation. All behavior is judged by Islamic principles. The following three sections identify the Value Systems in the predominant culture—their methods of dividing right from wrong, good from evil, and so forth.

Locus of Decision Making

The male leader is the locus of decision making, but he respects the consensus of the group or collective. The individual is always subordinate to the family, tribe, or collective. Solutions to all problems lie in the correct interpretation and application of divine law. Leadership and identity come from one's lineage and one's ability to protect the honor of the extended family.

Sources of Anxiety Reduction

Security is found in family loyalty and absolute submission to Islamic law. Tribal loyalty will influence hiring and employment even among foreign companies. Loyalty to the ruling clan, not nationality, brings a feeling of national security. Tribal membership remains the cornerstone of the individual's social identity.

Issues of Equality/Inequality

Within Islam all believers are equal and united in the ulema. However, some tribes feel superior to others. Traditional respect for literacy and aversion to manual labor has created a need for large numbers of foreign workers, with varying degrees of acceptance. Men and women are considered to be qualitatively different in emotion and intellect. Public life has been the exclusive domain of men, although educated women are gaining more freedom.

Business Practices

Appointments

———————————————————————— PUNCTUALITY

- Punctuality was not traditionally considered a virtue in Kuwait. Your client may be late for an appointment or not show up at all. You, however, should endeavor to be prompt.
- It is standard practice to keep supplicants (including foreign business people) waiting. Do not expect to be able to keep more than one appointment per day.
- Some Western-educated Kuwaitis will be very prompt, and they will expect equal promptness from you.

- An appointment is rarely private. Expect your visit to be interrupted by phone calls and visits from your client's friends and family. Westerners frequently find these distractions infuriating; try to maintain your equanimity.
- Kuwaiti officials are prohibited by tradition from working more than six hours per day. Mornings are usually best for appointments.
- Understand that government employment of Kuwaitis is an aspect of the welfare system rather than a method of running an industrialized state. Kuwaiti officials may show up to work or not, as they please. The day-to-day work is done by foreigners, mainly non-Kuwaiti Arabs.
- Of the several people present at Kuwaiti business meetings, the person who asks you the most questions is likely to be the least important (this is often a

non-Kuwaiti professional). The real decision maker is probably a silent, elderly Kuwaiti who watches everything but never speaks to you directly.

- Since people wander in and out of meetings, you may be asked to repeat the entire presentation several times. Do so gracefully. Do not become angry, even if you are asked to repeat the presentation for an obviously unqualified, uncomprehending family member.
- Bring plenty of copies of promotional materials, so that each person can have one.

CULTURAL NOTE

Some foreign businessmen recommend holding business meetings in the lobby of an international hotel, rather than in a Kuwaiti's office. This has several advantages. There will be fewer people wandering in and out of the meeting. Their willingness to come to you demonstrates that the Kuwaitis are truly interested. Finally, you will have access to refreshments that may be more to your taste. (The local tea and coffee served by Kuwaitis is quite strong; in a hotel you can get Western-style drinks.)

- Friday is the Muslim holy day, and no business is conducted. Most people do not work on Thursdays, either. The workweek runs from Saturday through Wednesday.
- Government hours are 7:30 A.M. to 2:30 P.M., Saturday through Wednesday.
- Business hours vary widely, but most businesses close for much of the afternoon and reopen for a few hours in late afternoon.
- Paperwork should carry two dates, the Gregorian (Western) date and the Hijrah (Arabic) date.

 Negotiating

- The pace of business is much, much slower in Kuwait than it is in the West. Be patient.
- Since they are in no hurry, Kuwaitis have no fear of silence. Do not feel obligated to speak during every period of silence.
- Business meetings always start slowly, with long inquiries into one's health and journey. You may have two or three preliminary meetings (consisting entirely of small talk) before you ever get to make your presentation. The Kuwaitis will let you know when they are ready to talk about business.
- Business cards should be printed in English on one side and in Arabic on the other. Hand your card to a Kuwaiti with your right hand, with the Arabic side facing him.
- Kuwaitis speak at a much closer distance than North Americans are used to. Do not back up or shy away. There is also more physical contact. Conversations usually involve touching.
- Coffee is often served toward the end of a business meeting. This is a signal that it the meeting will soon conclude. Incense is often lit at this time, as well.
- Kuwaiti men often walk hand in hand. If a Kuwaiti holds your hand, take it as a sign of friendship.
- Arabic is a language of hyperbole. When a Kuwaiti says "yes," it usually means "possibly." Be encouraged by this, but do not assume that the negotiating is over.
- It is possible that you will never meet the true decision maker. It is also possible that the decision maker was silently observing you while you made your presentation.

- A clever Kuwaiti adviser will sound out the opinions of various decision makers before you meet with them. He will then put you in contact only with the ones most likely to favor your proposal. Do not rush your contact into introducing you. To do so is to risk having your proposal turned down because you met with the wrong persons.
- When business partners in Kuwait cannot come to an agreement, the case may be taken to court. Unlike Western courts, which hand down a decision, Kuwaiti courts are intended to be arbitrators, recommending an out-of-court settlement. A Westerner is usually well advised to accept such a compromise, even in a case where the Westerner feels he should win a judgment. Never allow a dispute between you and your Kuwaiti sponsor to be settled by a judge, unless you plan on terminating your Kuwaiti operations. If the judge rules against your sponsor, you will have caused your sponsor to lose face, and he will probably obstruct all future dealings you have in the country.
- Saving face and avoiding shame are vital to Kuwaitis. Always be aware of this. You may have to compromise on some issue not for any practical reason but to protect someone's ego.
- When a contract is finally drawn up, keep it as brief as possible. Arab contracts are traditionally only a few pages long.
- The legal, binding contract must be in Arabic, even if there is an English-language one as well.

Business Entertaining

- Hosting visitors is considered a virtue among Kuwaitis, so they will take care of all of the entertaining within their country.
- Be prepared to remove your shoes before entering a building. Follow the lead of your host.
- Remember that alcohol and pork are illegal, and that eating is done with the right hand only. Even if you are left-handed, eat with your right hand.
- Expect to encounter eating utensils only in the most Westernized of Kuwaiti homes.
- Consider it a compliment if you encounter a bloody sheep carcass at the entrance to a Kuwaiti home. This means that your host has slaughtered a sheep in your honor.
- Do not bring up the subject of women unless your Kuwaiti counterpart does so first. Do not even inquire about the health of a Kuwaiti's wife or daughter.
- The topic of Israel should similarly be avoided.
- Sports are a good topic of conversation. Soccer (football), horse and camel racing (with betting prohibited), hunting, and falconry are the most popular Kuwaiti sports.

Time

- Kuwait is three hours ahead of Greenwich Mean Time (G.M.T. + 3), or eight hours ahead of U.S. Eastern Standard Time (E.S.T. + 8).

Protocol

Greetings

- As several styles of greetings are currently in use in Kuwait, it is safest to wait for your Kuwaiti counterpart to initiate the greeting, especially at a first meeting.

- Westernized Kuwaiti men shake hands with other men.
- Some Kuwaiti men will shake hands with Western women. Western business-women should wait for a Kuwaiti man to offer his hand.
- Before the war, Kuwaiti women made up little more than 10 percent of the workforce, and few were in positions where they met with foreigners. Since the war, the Kuwaiti government has been deporting "unreliable" foreigners; many of these jobs have been taken over by Kuwaiti women. Wait for a Kuwaiti businesswoman to offer her hand.
- When a veiled Kuwaiti woman is with a Kuwaiti man, it is not traditional to introduce her.
- A more traditional Kuwaiti greeting between men involves grasping each other's right hand, placing the left hand on the other's right shoulder, and exchanging kisses on each cheek.

Titles/Forms of Address

- Westerners frequently find Arabic names confusing. The best solution is to request the names—written in English—of any Kuwaitis you will have to meet, speak to, or correspond with. Find out both their full names (for correspondence) and how they are to be addressed in person.
- Kuwaiti names are written in Arabic. In part because short vowels are not written in Arabic, translating from Arabic to other alphabets is not an exact science. Arabic names may be spelled several different ways in English. (For example, the leader of Libya's name is variously rendered as Colonel Muammar al-Qaddafi, Mu'ammar al-Qadhafi, and so forth.)
- In general, Kuwaiti names are written in the same order as English names: title, given name, middle name (often a patronymic), and surname (family name). Thus, the current ruler (emir) of Kuwait is Sheikh Jaber al-Ahmed al-Sabah; his title is Sheikh, his given name is Jaber (also spelt Jabir), al-Ahmed (or al-Ahmad) is a patronymic meaning "son of Ahmed," and al-Sabah is the family name.
- The terms *al* and *bin* (sometimes spelled *ibn*) both literally mean "from" in Arabic, so it is not immediately apparent whether a name like "bin Mubarak" indicates "son of Mubarak" or "from the town of Mubarak." Most Kuwaitis prefer *al* and use it in patronymics. However, both *al* and *bin* may be used in the same name.
- If an Arab's grandfather is (or was) a famous person, he sometimes adds his grandfather's name. Thus, Dr. Mahmoud bin Sultan bin Hamad al-Muqrin is "Dr. Mahmoud, son of Sultan, grandson of Hamad, of the house (family) of Muqrin."
- Westerners frequently mistake *bin* for the name Ben, short for Benjamin. Obviously, *bin* has no meaning by itself, and one cannot address a Kuwaiti as "bin." Kuwaitis do not use the name Benjamin.
- The female version of *bin* is *bint*. Thus, Princess Fatima bint Ibrahim al-Saud is "Princess Fatima, daughter of Ibrahim, of the house of Saud."
- Most Kuwaitis should be addressed by title and given name (e.g., Sheikh Khalil), just as you would address a member of the British aristocracy (e.g., Sir John). They can also be addressed as "Your Excellency." In writing, use the full name.
- In Kuwait, the title *Sheikh* (pronounced "shake," as in "shake and bake") designates membership in the Kuwaiti royal family.

Gestures

- The left hand is considered unclean in the Arab world. Always use the right hand in preference to the left (unless you are handling something considered unclean). Never eat with the left hand; eat only with your right hand. Avoid gesturing with the left hand.
- While Arabs constantly gesture with their hands while speaking, they do not point at another person. This would be considered impolite.
- As a general rule, keep both feet on the ground. Arabs do not cross their legs when sitting. Never show the bottom of your foot to an Arab; this is considered offensive.
- The "thumbs up" gesture is offensive throughout the Arab world.

Gifts

- Kuwaiti hospitality is legendary. You are not required to bring a gift when invited to a Kuwaiti home. However, flowers or candy will be appreciated.
- Appropriate gifts include crafts or picture books from your home. Avoid images or pictures of people or dogs; Islam proscribes images of the human body, and dogs are considered unclean.
- Good gifts for business people include gold pens, pencils, finely made compasses (so that they will always know where Mecca is), business-card cases, and cigarette lighters. Have the items engraved, when possible.
- Traditionally, every Kuwaiti who must broker or approve a business deal takes a percentage. Be careful that you do not run afoul of the U.S. Foreign Corrupt Practices Act.
- Avoid admiring an item too effusively; a Kuwaiti will feel obligated to give it to you.
- When offered a gift by a Kuwaiti, it is impolite to refuse.

Dress

- While foreigners are not exempt from the Kuwaiti standards of modesty, do not adopt native clothing [for men, a *ghotra* (headdress) and *thobe* (flowing white robe); for women, a veil and an *abaya* (black head-to-foot robe)]. Kuwaitis may find it offensive to see foreigners dressed in their traditional clothes.
- Foreigners should wear Western clothes that approach the modesty of Kuwaiti dress. Despite the heat of the desert, most of the body must remain covered.
- Men should wear long trousers and a shirt, preferably long-sleeved. A jacket and tie are usually required for business meetings. Keep shirts buttoned up to the collarbone. Men should avoid wearing visible jewelry, especially around the neck.
- While not all Kuwaiti women wear traditional clothing, all women—including foreigners—must wear modest clothing in public. The neckline should be high, and the sleeves should come to at least the elbows. Hemlines should be well below the knee, if not ankle-length. The overall effect should be one of baggy concealment; a full-length outfit that is tight and revealing is not acceptable. Therefore, pants or pant suits are not recommended. While a hat or scarf is not always required, it is wise to keep a scarf at hand. The suitability of your attire will be apparent as soon as you venture out; if Kuwaiti men stare lewdly at you, your dress is not sufficiently modest.

KUALA
LUMPUR

Malaysia

CULTURAL NOTE

*P*eople in Malaysia may smile or laugh In situations where Westerners consider this inappropriate. Smiles may hide embarrassment, shyness, bitterness, discord, and/or loss of face. Malaysian businessmen may laugh at the most serious part of a business meeting; this may be an expression of anxiety, not frivolity. Learning to interpret smiles and laughter may take a foreigner years.

Country Background

History

The proto-Malay people reached Malaysia several thousand years ago. Some of their modern-day descendants still live in the jungles of Borneo, their traditional cultures scarcely changed by the outside world. There are also some 100,000 non-Malay aboriginal people; the Semang and Pangan peoples are not Malay but are part of the Negrito ethnolinguistic group.

CULTURAL NOTE

*t*he word Malay has several related meanings. It can refer to the Malay linguistic group; Malaysia's official language, Bahasa Malaysia, is a standardized form of Malay (similar but not identical to Bahasa Indonesia). Malay can also refer to the dominant ethnic group of Malaysia. Finally, Malay has a geographic meaning; the peninsula shared by Thailand and West Malaysia is called the Malay Peninsula.

Geopolitically, several variants were used by the British during the colonial and post-colonial era: first Malaya, then the Malayan Union, and later the Federation of Malaya. Finally, the current nation was formed on September 16, 1963, taking the name the Federation of Malaysia. (Be sure to refer to the country by its current spelling: Malay plus "sia.") The citizens of Malaysia are *Malaysians*, while the *Malays* are dominant ethnic group in Malaysia.

Malaysia has long been a center of international trade. The country lies directly on the sea routes between China and India. For centuries, small kingdoms and sultanates in what is now Malaysia profited from this trade, either by assisting it or by preying upon it. In the sixteenth century, Europeans began trading in Asia. Trade bases were established, and the Malay "pirate kingdoms" were gradually conquered. Malaysia became a British colony.

The British were temporarily driven out by the Japanese during World War II. In 1946, faced with the nationalist aspirations of the Malay peoples, the British consolidated the patchwork of sultanates and states on the Malay Peninsula into a Crown Colony called the Malayan Union. The sultans were deprived of power, and all citizens were given equal rights.

Many ethnic Malays were dissatisfied with the Malayan Union. Some wished to restore the powers of their Islamic sultans. Furthermore, the Chinese minority had always been the most wealthy and educated ethnic group on the Malay Peninsula. The ethnic Malays, despite their numerical majority, feared that the aggressive Chinese would take over the new Crown Colony. (The Chinese-dominated Malayan Communist Party did conduct a guerilla war against British and Malay forces from 1948 until 1960.)

As a result, the Malayan Union was replaced in 1948 with the Malayan Federation. The sultans were restored to power, and the ethnic Malays were guaranteed favorable treatment. In effect, a balance was established between the Malays and the Chinese: The Malays would run the government, and the Chinese would run the businesses. This division is essentially still in effect today. (The Indian population at that time consisted mostly of poor agricultural laborers. They were not considered in the settlement.) The Federation of Malaya became independent from the United Kingdom in 1957. A new, expanded nation was now proposed, uniting the Malay Peninsula, the island Crown Colony of Singapore, and the three British-controlled territories on the island of Borneo: Sarawak, Brunei, and North Borneo (later renamed Sabah). The Sultan of Brunei, wealthy with oil revenues, declined to join. (Brunei remained a British protectorate until becoming an independent country in 1984.) The other Borneo territories, Sarawak and Sabah, joined the new federation, as did Singapore.

The new Federation of Malaysia (note the difference in spelling) came into being in 1963. Since 1963, the only change in the makeup of the Federation of Malaysia has been the secession of Singapore in 1965. (The overwhelmingly Chinese Singapore never fit in with the Malay-led federation.)

Type of Government

Malaysia is a federal parliamentary democracy with a constitutional monarch, and a member of the British Commonwealth. The monarchy is rather unique: the nine hereditary sultans elect from among themselves a "paramount ruler" for a five-year term. The paramount ruler—essentially a king with a five-year reign—is the chief of state of Malaysia. "Paramount ruler" is the English term; the actual Malay title is *Yang di-Pertuan Agong*.

The head of government of Malaysia is the prime minister. The United Malays National Organization (UMNO) is the most powerful political party. There are two legislative houses: a 69-member Senate and a 180-member House of Representatives.

t   **CULTURAL NOTE**

he UMNO leadership has big plans for Malaysia. They are taking their successful New Economic Policy one step further with their New Development Policy, which will require that 30 percent of Malaysia's wealth be in the hands of ethnic Malays (the *bumiputra*)—a direct challenge to Chinese economic domination. They are also challenging the power of the sultans. Despite the preferential treatment given to ethnic Malays, Malaysia remains a land of opportunity for international business executives. Malaysia's "Vision 2020" plan calls for Malaysia to be a fully developed nation by the year 2020. That goal can be met only by continuing to attract foreign trade.

Language

As a result of British colonialism, the English language is widely understood in Malaysia, and there are many English loan words in Bahasa Malaysia. (This is one of the factors that separates Bahasa Malaysia from Bahasa Indonesia—Indonesia was a colony of the Netherlands, so Bahasa Indonesia's loan words come from Dutch.) Although English has had a unifying effect on the diverse Malaysian population, the Malaysian authorities have made Bahasa Malaysia the official language of government and education. At home, a Malay family might speak one of several Malay dialects, just as a Chinese family might speak Mandarin or Hakka or Cantonese, or an Indian family speak Tamil or Hindi or Gujarati. This linguistic diversity has hampered the development of a national literature of Malaysia, since each group prefers to read authors in its own language. Some writers compromise by writing in English.

Religion

Malaysia's diversity is also reflected in its religions. Malaysia is officially an Islamic state; most Malays and some Indians are Muslim. But nearly half the population identifies itself as non-Muslim. Buddhists alone constitute some 17 percent, and there are many Hindus, Buddhists, Taoists, Christians, and others.

Demographics

Ethnic Malays make up just over 60 percent of the Malaysian population. Ethnic Chinese constitute almost 30 percent, and ethnic Indians number over 9 percent. Thus, Malaysia's population of 18.6 million is divided not only by geography but by race and language as well.

Cultural Orientation

Cognitive Styles: How Ethnic Malays Organize and Process Information

Although the ethnic Malays have assimilated many indigenous religious rituals into their Islamic religion, they adhere to the closed thinking of Islam when it comes to accepting outside information into their everyday lives. Information is processed subjectively and associatively, and this leads to personal involvement in problems rather than abstracting to the point where rules and laws can be used to solve these problems.

Negotiation Strategies: What Ethnic Malays Accept as Evidence

The subjective feelings of the moment form the basis for truth, with faith in the ideologies of Islam having a very strong influence on this truth. Only the most Westernized and secular of ethnic Malays will use objective facts as a source of the truth.

Value Systems: The Basis for Behavior

Much of the business in Malaysia is conducted by the Chinese and Indians, who have a very different system of values from the ethnic Malays. The following three sections identify the Value Systems in the predominant culture—their methods of dividing right from wrong, good from evil, and so forth.

Locus of Decision Making

The individual ethnic Malay makes his or her decisions taking into consideration the immediate situation and the relationships among those involved. These decisions are always in agreement with the Islamic code. Ethnic Malays are quick to organize and have the support of the group behind their decisions. They are not good at confrontations and try to communicate in such a way as to alleviate conflict. They seldom use a categorical "no." It is important for foreign business executives to develop a personal relationship with their Malaysian counterparts.

Sources of Anxiety Reduction

Solid religious beliefs among ethnic Malays give structure and stability to life. The norm is a nuclear household with strong ties to both the husband's and wife's extended families. The extended family is expected to help in time of need. There is little friction between common law and Islamic law, as they are often combined into a single pronouncement. Respect for authority, unbreakable family ties, and the performance of proper social behavior provide strength in times of stress.

Issues of Equality/Inequality

Most states have sultans, and the division between royalty and commoners is rarely bridged. Royalty is treated with great deference, which includes elaborate ritual and special terms of address. The ethnic Malays hold the power, but the politically dominant Malays and the economically dominant Chinese feed off of each other. Ethnocentrism and stereotypes abound, but virulent racism is largely absent. Malaysians practice the strong masculine hierarchy of a secular Muslim state.

Business Practices

Appointments

PUNCTUALITY

- ◆ It is important to be on time for all business appointments. Making a Malaysian executive wait can result in a loss of face.
- ◆ The majority of Malaysian business people are Chinese; they are likely to be prompt. The majority of government officials are ethnic Malays. Their culture is very different from that of the Chinese, and they have a looser concept of time. Although foreigners are expected to be on time, an ethnic Malay may or may not be prompt.
- ◆ The Indian minority has a conception of time that is closer to the Malay than to the Chinese. However, the only Indians a foreign business person is likely to come in contact with are professionals: lawyers, reporters, physicians, and so forth. They will expect punctuality.
- ◆ Social events in Malaysia involving different cultural groups have different rules. In general, when invited to a social event, most Malaysians arrive on time or slightly late. Never be more than half an hour late.
- ◆ A social event hosted by observant Muslims will be without alcohol. There will be no predinner "cocktail hour" and (probably) no appetizers, so the meal may be served close to the time given on the invitation.
- ◆ Once a close friendship has been established, guests may arrive a few minutes early to a social occasion. If you are the host and your guests are close friends, it is important to be ready early.

- Try to schedule appointments at least two weeks in advance. (If you have not yet arrived in Malaysia, you may want to schedule them a month ahead.) Malaysian executives are quite busy. Many travel frequently, especially to conferences in their area of specialization.
- English is the language of many business transactions and much business correspondence in Malaysia. However, the English spoken often has native inflections, syntax, and grammar, which can easily lead to misunderstandings.

- Bahasa Malaysia is the official language of Malaysia. Although most government officials will speak some English, they may prefer to hold meetings in their native tongue. Fortunately, an English-speaking translator is usually close at hand.
- All official correspondence with government officials must be in Bahasa Malaysia. You may accompany this correspondence with an English translation, if you wish.
- Unlike in nearby Singapore (which has mandated Mandarin Chinese as the official Chinese dialect), Malaysian Chinese often speak mutually unintelligible dialects of Chinese. As a result, the only spoken language a Cantonese-speaking Chinese may have in common with a Hakka-speaking Chinese is English. Similarly, the different linguistic groups within the Indian community often speak English between themselves. English is seen as a unifying force in Malaysia.
- Although most Malays are Muslim, not all of Malaysia follows the traditional Islamic workweek pattern (Friday is the Islamic holy day, so the traditional Muslim "weekend" is Thursday and Friday). Only the following five of the thirteen Malaysian states follow the Islamic workweek (Saturday through Wednesday): Perlis, Kedah, Kelantan, Terengganu, and Johore. All of these are in West (Peninsular) Malaysia. The Malaysian capital city, Kuala Lumpur, is in the state of Selangor, where the workweek is Monday through Friday.
- Business hours are generally from 8:00 A.M. to 5:00 P.M. Monday through Friday, (Saturday through Wednesday in those states that follow the Islamic workweek.) Some offices will be open for a half day on Saturday (Thursday in Islamic states), generally in the morning.
- The traditional lunchtime was from 12:00 noon (or 12:15 P.M.) to 2:00 P.M., but this generally has been reduced to a single hour, beginning at noon or 1:00 P.M. Nevertheless, many people will take longer than an hour for lunch. In those areas where Friday is a workday, Muslims will take a two-hour break to attend a mosque.
- Most government offices keep an 8:30 A.M. to 4:45 P.M. schedule, with a half day from 8:30 A.M. to noon on Saturday (on Thursday in the five aforementioned states).
- Shop hours vary. Most shops will open at 9:00 or 10:00 A.M., and will close at 6:00 or 7:00 P.M., five or six days a week.
- Executives will often work far longer days than their subordinates. The Chinese, especially, have reputations as workaholics.
- Holidays in Malaysia vary from state to state. The heavily Muslim states do not celebrate any non-Islamic holidays (including Easter, Christmas, and Western New Year's Day).

 Negotiating

- Malaysians do business only with persons they know and like. Establishing this personal relationship will take time, but it is vital for success.
- The pace of business negotiations in Malaysia is far slower than that in the United States. Be patient; it would be unusual to complete a complicated business deal in only one trip to Malaysia. Expect to take several trips over a period of months. Indeed, little will happen at the first meeting except getting acquainted.
- Politeness is the single most important attribute for successful relationships in Malaysia. This politeness in no way hinders the determination of Malaysian business people to get their own way.

- Standards of polite behavior vary widely between cultures. Many Malaysians will ask you highly personal questions (such as "Why aren't you married?" or "How much do you earn?") without realizing that Westerners find such questions intrusive. Simply smile and explain that such topics are not discussed openly in your culture—and be aware that you, too, will unknowingly violate local standards of polite behavior.
- Since politeness demands that a Malaysian not disagree openly, the word "no" is rarely heard. A polite but insincere "yes" is simply a technique to avoid giving offense. In Malaysia, "yes" can mean anything from "I agree" to "maybe" to "I hope you can tell from my lack of enthusiasm that I really mean 'no'."
- "Yes" really means "no" when there are any qualifications attached. "Yes, but..." probably means "no." "It might be difficult" is a clear "no."
- A clear way to indicate "no" is to suck in air through the teeth. This sound always indicates a problem.
- When it comes to making a decision, a "yes" often comes more quickly than a "no." This is because a way must be found to deliver the "no" politely, without loss of face. The "no" may even be delivered through a third party.
- Since Malaysians (especially the Chinese) often consult astrologers, signing a contract may be delayed until a "lucky" day arrives.
- In Malaysia, one who expresses anger in public has shamefully lost face. A person who loses his or her temper is considered unable to control himself or herself. Such a person will not be trusted or respected.
- It is considered polite among Malaysian Chinese to offer both the positive and negative options in virtually every decision. Even when speaking in English, they are likely to add a "yes/no" pattern to a question. Rather than asking, "Would you like to have dinner?" they are likely to ask, "You want dinner or not?" The phrases involved ("want or not want," "good or not," "can or cannot") are direct translations of Chinese phrases into English. They often sound unduly aggressive to Western ears.
- Be cautious in asking Malaysian Chinese a question. English speakers would give a negative answer to the question "Isn't my order ready yet?" by responding "no" (meaning, "No, it's not ready"). The Chinese pattern is the opposite: "yes" (meaning, "Yes, it is not ready.").

M————————————————**CULTURAL NOTE**
alaysians of all ethnic groups are comfortable with silence. A silent pause allows time for thought; it does not necessarily signal either acceptance or rejection. Westerners often find such pauses uncomfortable.

- Age and seniority are highly respected. If you are part of a delegation, line up so that the most important persons will be introduced first. If you are introducing two people, state the name of the most important person first (e.g., "President Smith, this is Engineer Wong").
- Speak in quiet, gentle tones. Always remain calm. Leave plenty of time for someone to respond to a statement you make; people in Malaysia do not jump on the end of someone else's sentences. Politeness demands that they leave a respectful pause (as long as ten to fifteen seconds) before responding. Westerners often assume that they have agreement and resume talking before a Malaysian has the chance to respond.
- Business cards should be printed (preferably embossed) in English. Since the majority of Malaysian business people are ethnic Chinese, you may wish to have

the reverse side of some of your cards translated into Chinese (gold ink is the most prestigious color for Chinese characters).

- Your business card should contain as much information as possible, including your business title and your qualifications. Malaysians include all of this data on their card, as well as any titles of nobility.
- The exchange of business cards is a formal ceremony in Malaysia. After introductions are made, the visiting businessperson should offer his or her card. Make sure you give a card to each person present. Present your card either with both hands or with your right hand (with the left hand lightly supporting your right). Give your card to the recipient with the print facing him or her (so the recipient can read it). He or she will receive the card with both hands, then study the card for a few moments before carefully putting it away in a pocket. You should do the same when a card is presented to you. Never put a card in your back pocket (where many men carry their wallets). Do not write on someone's business card.
- Topics to avoid in conversation include any criticism of Malaysian ways, religion, bureaucracy, or politics. Also avoid any discussion of sex or the roles of the sexes.
- Good topics for discussion include tourism, travel, plans for the future, organizational success (talking about personal success is considered impolite boasting), and food (while remaining complimentary to the local cuisine).

 Business Entertaining

- Take advantage of any invitations to social events. Establishing a successful business relationship hinges on establishing a social relationship as well.
- Food is vitally important in Malaysian culture. Social occasions always involve food. Indeed, the standard Chinese greeting literally means "Have you eaten?"
- Invitations to social events may not come immediately. Be patient and let the Malaysians make the first invitation. You cannot successfully host a social event until you have been a guest at a Malaysian event.
- Respond to written invitations in writing. Among the Chinese, white and blue are colors associated with sadness; do not print invitations on papers of these colors. Red or pink paper is a good choice for invitations.
- Generally, spouses may be invited to dinners but not to lunch. However, no business will be discussed at an event where spouses are present.

Time
- Malaysia is eight hours ahead of Greenwich Mean Time (G.M.T. + 8), making it thirteen hours ahead of U.S. Eastern Standard Time (E.S.T. + 13).

Protocol

 Greetings

- Malaysia has three major ethnic groups, each with its own traditions: Malay, Chinese, and Indian.
- With younger or foreign-educated Malaysians, a handshake is the most common form of greeting. The standard Malaysian handshake is more of a hand-

clasp; it is rather limp and lasts for some ten or twelve seconds. (By contrast, most North American handshakes last for only three or four seconds.) Often, both hands will be used.

- In Malaysia, Westernized women may shake hands with both men and women. Malaysian businessmen usually wait for a woman to offer her hand. It is perfectly acceptable for a woman to simply nod upon an introduction rather than offering her hand. Women should offer their hands only upon greetings; too-frequent handshaking is easily misinterpreted as an amorous advance. (Among themselves, men tend to shake hands both on greeting and on departure.)

- Ethnic Malays are generally Muslim. Traditionally, there is no physical contact between Muslim men and women. (Indeed, if a religious Muslim male is touched by a woman, he must ritually cleanse himself before he prays again.) Because of this, women should not offer to shake hands with Malay men, nor should men offer to shake hands with Malay women. Of course, if a Westernized Malay offers to shake hands, do so.

- The traditional Malay greeting is the *salaam*, which is akin to a handshake without the grip. Both parties stretch out one or both hands, touch each other's hand(s) lightly, then bring their hand(s) back to rest over their heart. This greeting is done only between people of the same sex: from man to man or from woman to woman. However, if cloth (such as a scarf or shawl) prevents actual skin-to-skin contact, then a Malay man and woman may engage in the *salaam*.

- Among Malaysian Chinese, the traditional greeting was a bow. However, most now shake hands or combine a bow with a handshake. Chinese men are likely to be comfortable shaking hands with a woman—more so than men from other ethnic groups of Malaysia.

- Many but not all Malay Indians are Hindu. Most Hindus avoid public contact between men and women, although not as vehemently as many Muslims. Men may shake hands with men and women with women, but only Westernized Hindus will shake hands with the opposite sex. Malaysian Indians may also be Sikhs or Christians or Muslims; all avoid public contact between the sexes.

- The traditional Indian greeting involves a slight bow with the palms of the hands together (as if praying). This greeting, called the *namaste*, will generally be used only by older, traditional Hindus. However, it is also an acceptable alternative to a handshake when a Western businesswoman greets an Indian man.

- Among all ethnic groups, kissing in public (even a quick peck on a cheek) is considered unacceptable. Only the most fashionable and cosmopolitan of Malaysians will give even a quick kiss in greeting.

- Just as the British greeting "How do you do?" is rhetorical, Malaysians have many rhetorical greetings. Chinese greetings often involve food. "Have you eaten?" or "Have you taken food?" are rhetorical greetings; answer "Yes," even if you are hungry. Similarly, a typical Malaysian greeting when meeting on the street is "Where are you going?" This is also rhetorical; "For a walk" or "Nowhere of importance" are perfectly acceptable answers —indeed, the latter is the English equivalent of the traditional Malay response. You are not expected to reveal your itinerary.

Titles/Forms of Address

- Addressing Malaysians properly is a complex affair, especially for Westerners unfamiliar with the naming patterns of Malaysian ethnic groups. Take your time over an introduction, which will probably involve business cards. Repeat the title and name of the person and ask if you are pronouncing them correctly. This often invites an explanation of the history or origin of titles or names, providing you with personal information that may be useful.

- Malaysia is a constitutional monarchy with nine royal houses. With so many royals, foreigners are likely to encounter one sooner or later. Titles and means of address vary; ask a native how a particular royal should be addressed.

- Most business people you meet should be addressed with a title and their name. If a person does not have a professional title (such as Engineer, Doctor, or Teacher), a Westerner may use Mr. or Madam/Mrs./Miss plus the name. However, be aware that you may be omitting other titles that are important both to the person and to your understanding of that person.

- The traditional Malay forms of Mr., Mrs., or Miss are
  - *Encik* = Mr.
  - *Puan* = Mrs. (a married woman)
  - *Cik* = Miss (an unmarried woman)

  These are used in front of an individual's name (e.g., Mr. Ahmadi would be properly addressed as Encik Ahmadi.) Although there is no Malay equivalent for "Ms.," the current trend is to use *Puan* ("Mrs.") for any adult female.

- Each of the three major ethnic groups in Malaysia has different naming patterns.

- Ethnic Malays did not traditionally have family names. Most Malays are Muslim, and Muslim names are usually derived from Arabic. Each Muslim is known by a given name plus *bin* (son of) plus their father's name. For example, Osman bin Ali is "Osman, son of Ali." He would properly be called Mr. Osman, not Mr. Ali—Mr. Ali would be Osman's father.

- A Muslim woman is known by her given name plus *binti* (daughter of) plus her father's name. For example, Khadijah binti Fauzi is "Khadijah, daughter of Fauzi." She would be known as Miss Khadijah or, if married, as Mrs. Khadijah. For business purposes, some Malay women attach their husband's name. Thus, if Khadijah was married to Osman, she might choose to be known as Mrs. Khadijah Osman. Note that, in English, *binti* may also be spelled *binte*.

- Some Westernized Malays drop the *bin* or *binti* from their name.

- A Muslim male who has completed his pilgrimage to Mecca is addressed as *Tuan Haji*. A woman who has done so would be addressed as *Hajjah* or *Puan Hajjah*. Note that these titles are not automatically conferred on spouses; they must be individually earned by making the pilgrimage. However, when in doubt, err on the side of generosity. It is better to give a superfluous title than to omit one.

- Chinese names generally consist of a family name, followed by two (sometimes one) personal names. In the name Chang Wu Jiang, "Chang" is the surname (or clan name). He would be addressed with his title plus Chang (Mr. Chang, Dr. Chang).

- Chinese wives do not generally take their husband's surnames, but instead maintain their maiden names. Although Westerners commonly address a married woman as Mrs. plus her husband's family name, it is more appropriate to call her Madam plus her maiden family name. As an example, Li Chu Chin (female) is married to Chang Wu Jiang (male). Westerners would probably call her Mrs. Chang. She is properly addressed as Madam Li.

- To accommodate Westerners, many Chinese adopt an English first name so that English speakers can have a familiar-sounding name to identify them by. Thus, Chang Wu Jiang may call himself Mr. Wally Chang. Others use their initials (Mr. W. J. Chang).

- If many Chinese seem to have similar clan names, it is because there are only about 400 different surnames in China! However, when these surnames are transcribed into English, there are several possible variations. For example, Wong, Wang, and Huang are all English versions of the same Chinese clan name.

- Indians in Malaysia may follow several different traditions. While they did not traditionally have surnames, some have now adopted a family name that all members of their family use, generation after generation.

- Traditional Indians have no family surname. An Indian male will use the initial of his father's name first, followed by his own personal name. For example, V. Thiruselvan is "Thiruselvan, son of V." For legal purposes, both names would be written out with an "a/l" (for *anak lelaki*, meaning "son of") between the names Thiruselvan a/l Vijay. In either case, he would be known as Mr. Thiruselvan. However, long Indian names are often shortened. He may prefer to be called either Mr. Thiru or Mr. Selvan.

- Indian female names follow the same pattern: father's initial plus personal name. When written fully out, "a/p" (*anak perempuan*, or "daughter of") is used instead of "a/l." When an Indian woman marries, she usually ceases to use her father's initial; instead, she follows her personal name with her husband's name. For instance: When S. Kamala (female) marries V. Thiru (male), she will go by Mrs. Kamala Thiru.

- Some Malaysian Indians will use Western-style surnames. Some Malaysian Indians are Christians (in which case they may have Biblical surnames like Abraham or Jacob). Or they may come from a former Portuguese colony (such as Goa or Malacca), in which case their surnames will be of Portuguese origin, such as Rozario or DeSilva. Such a person could be addressed as Dr. Jacob or Mr. DeSilva.

- Indian Sikhs have a given name followed by either *Singh* (for men) or *Kaur* (for women). Always address them by a title and first name. To refer to a Sikh male as Mr. Singh is as meaningless as saying Mr. Man in English.

- Muslim Indians will have names similar to those of Muslim Malays. Such names follow the same patterns.

- As you inquire of a Malaysian as to what you should call him or her, be forward in explaining what they should call you. They may be equally unsure as to which of your names is your surname. Follow their lead as to the degree of formality. Don't tell a Malaysian to "just call me Bob" when you are calling him Dr. Gupta.

Gestures

- Aside from handshakes, there is no public contact between the sexes in Malaysia. Do not kiss or hug a person of the opposite sex in public—even if you are husband and wife. On the other hand, contact between people of the same sex is permitted. Men may hold hands with men or even walk with their arms around each other; this is interpreted as nothing except friendship.

- Among both Muslims and Hindus, the left hand is considered unclean. Eat with your right hand only. Where possible, do not touch anything or anyone with your left hand if you can use your right hand instead. Accept gifts and hold cash in the right hand. (Obviously, when both hands are needed, use them both.)

- The foot is also considered unclean. Do not move anything with your feet, and do not touch anything with your feet.

- Do not show the soles of your feet (or shoes). This restriction determines how one sits: You can cross your legs at the knee, but not place one ankle on your knee. However, any form of leg crossing is ostentatiously casual in Malaysia; never cross your legs in the presence of Malaysian royalty.

- Do not prop your feet up on anything not intended for feet, such as a desk.
- It is impolite to point at anyone with the forefinger. Malays use a forefinger only to point at animals. Even pointing with two fingers is impolite among many Indians. When you must indicate something or someone, use the entire right hand (palm out). You can also point with your right thumb, as long as all four fingers are curled down. (Make sure all your fingers are curled—older Malays would interpret a fist with the thumb and little finger extended as an insult.)
- Pounding one fist into the palm of the other hand is another gesture that Malays consider obscene and that should be avoided.
- The head is considered the seat of the soul by many Indians and Malays. Never touch someone's head, not even to pat the hair of a child.
- Among Indians, a side-to-side toss of one's head indicates agreement, although Westerners may interpret it as a nod meaning "no." Watch carefully; the Indian head toss is not quite the same as the Western negative nod (which leads with the jaw).
- As in much of the world, to beckon someone, you hold your hand out, palm downward, and make a scooping motion with the fingers. Beckoning someone with the palm up and wagging one finger, as in the United States, can be construed as an insult.
- Standing tall with your hands on your hips—the "arms akimbo" position—is always interpreted as an angry, aggressive posture.
- The comfortable standing distance between two people in Malaysia varies with each culture. In general, stand as far apart as you would if you were about to shake hands (about two to three feet). Indians tend to stand a bit further apart (three or three and a half feet).

 Gifts

- The Malaysian Anti-Corruption Agency has strict laws against bribery. Avoid giving gifts that could be interpreted as bribes.
- Gifts are given between friends. Do not give a gift to anyone before you have established a personal relationship with them. Otherwise, the gift may have the appearance of a bribe.
- It is not the custom to unwrap a gift in the presence of the giver. To do so would suggest that the recipient is greedy and impatient. Worse, if the gift is somehow inappropriate or disappointing, loss of face would result. Expect the recipient to thank you briefly, then put the still-wrapped gift aside until you have left.
- Since pork and alcohol are prohibited to observing Muslims, do not give them as gifts to Malays. Other foods make good gifts, although meat products must be *halal* (the Muslim equivalent of kosher). The prohibition against pork and alcohol also precludes pigskin products and perfumes containing alcohol.
- Muslim Malays consider dogs unclean. Do not give toy dogs or gifts with pictures of dogs.
- Remember that personal gifts from a man to a woman can be misinterpreted as romantic offerings. When a foreign businessman gives a personal gift (such as perfume or clothing) to a Malaysian woman, he must let everyone know that he is simply delivering a gift from his wife.
- Don't wrap gifts to ethnic Malays in white paper; white is associated with funerals.
- The Chinese traditionally decline a gift three times before accepting; this prevents them from appearing greedy. Continue to insist; once they accept the gift, say that you are pleased that they have done so.

- Gifts of food are always appreciated by Chinese, but avoid bringing food gifts with you to a dinner or party (unless it has been agreed upon beforehand). To bring food may imply that your host cannot provide enough. Instead, send food as a thank-you gift afterwards. Candy or fruit baskets are good choices.
- The Chinese associate all of the following with funerals—do not give them as gifts:
  - Straw sandals,
  - clocks,
  - a stork or crane (although the Western association of storks with births is known to many young Chinese),
  - handkerchiefs (often given at funerals; they symbolize sadness and weeping), and
  - gifts (or wrapping paper) where the predominant color is white, black, or blue.
- Also avoid any gifts of knives, scissors, or cutting tools; to the Chinese, they suggest the severing of a friendship.
- Although the Chinese traditionally brought flowers only to the sick and to funerals, Western advertising has popularized flowers as gifts. Make sure you give an even number of flowers; an odd number would be very unlucky.
- At Chinese New Year, it is customary to give a gift of money in a red envelope to children and to the (nongovernmental) service personnel you deal with on a regular basis. This gift is called a *hong bao*. Give only new bills in even numbers and even amounts. Many employers give each employee a *hong bao* equivalent to one month's salary.
- Among Indians, the frangipani flower (used by Hawaiians to make leis) is used only for funeral wreaths.
- Should you give money to an Indian, make sure it is an odd number (just the opposite of Chinese tradition). Usually this is done by adding a single dollar; for example, give $11 instead of $10.
- Observant Hindus do not eat beef or use products made from cattle. This eliminates most leather products as gifts.

 ## Dress

- Just north of the Equator, Malaysia is hot and humid all year long. Most of the lowlands have a daytime temperature range of 75-95°F and humidity between 60 and 70 percent.
- Lower temperatures occur only in the mountainous areas, where business people rarely venture (except for tourism). Mountain temperatures can actually dip below freezing at night.
- The monsoon season runs from September through December, but sudden showers occur all year long. Many people carry an umbrella every day.
- Because of the heat and humidity, business dress in Malaysia is often casual. Standard formal office wear for men is dark trousers and light-colored long-sleeved shirt and tie, without a jacket. Many businessmen wear a short-sleeved shirt with no tie.
- Businesswomen wear light-colored long-sleeved blouses and skirts. Stockings and business suits are reserved for more formal offices. Fashions for businesswomen tend to be more frilly and decorative than those worn by U.S. businesswomen.

- As a foreigner, you should dress conservatively until you are sure what degree of formality is expected. Men should expect to wear a suit jacket and tie, and remove them if it seems appropriate. Whatever you wear, try to stay clean and well groomed; bathe several times a day if necessary.
- Many Malaysian men wear an open-necked batik shirt to work. This is also popular for casual wear. Jeans are acceptable for casual wear, but shorts should be avoided.
- In deference to Muslim and Hindu sensibilities, women should always wear blouses that cover at least their upper arms. Skirts should be knee-length or longer.

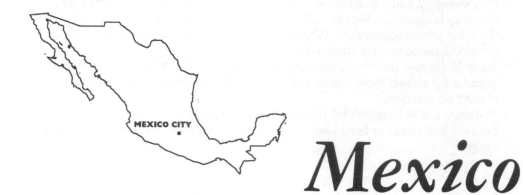

MEXICO CITY

Mexico

CULTURAL NOTE

m any Mexicans consider themselves *Guadalupeños*, a nickname for those who believe in the miracle of the Virgin of Guadalupe, the Virgin Mary as she appeared three times to a poor Aztec, Juan Diego, in 1513. She told him to build a church in Tepeyac, where the Aztec goddess Tonantín was worshipped. Today the basilica is visited by more than 1 million pilgrims annually, and images of the Virgin of Guadalupe are everywhere, a symbol of unity between the Aztec and Spanish cultures and of Mexican nationality.

Cultural Overview

Mexico is a Central American country almost three times the size of the state of Texas. (Note that Mexico is not a South American country; when the Americas are divided into North and South, Central America is categorized as part of North America.) Mexico borders the United States to the north and Guatemala and Belize to the south, having coasts on both the Gulf of Mexico and the Pacific Ocean.

CULTURAL NOTE

m exicans are proud of their heritage and their independence from the United States. Therefore, be careful of sensitivities in referring to U.S. citizens as "Americans," since this term applies to all North, Central, and South Americans.

Be aware that the official name of Mexico translates to "The United States of Mexico." Curiously, the polite Mexican term for a citizen of the United States is *norteamericano*, although Mexico itself is technically part of North America. Canadians are called *canadienses* to differentiate them from *nortemericanos*. A familiarity with Mexican history, culture, and art will help you make a favorable impression.

History

The origins of Mexican culture date back to the Mayan and Aztec Indians. These were among the most advanced pre-Colombian societies in the Americas, as evidenced by their expertise in astronomy (which yielded calendars of great accuracy), architecture, crop irrigation, and crafts. Their empires were destroyed by the Spanish conquistadores (as much by European diseases as by military action), and Mexico came under colonial rule in 1521. Independence was finally attained in 1810.

Type of Government

Today Mexico is a federal republic. The head of the government is the president, who is elected to a six-year term and cannot be reelected. The *Partido Revolucionario Institucional* (PRI) party has been in control for many years, enabling presidents to generally hand-pick their successors. There is a bicameral legislature and a judicial Supreme Court.

Language

Spanish is the official language of Mexico, although over 100 Indian languages are also spoken. English is widely understood by educated people and in urban centers.

Religion

There is no official religion, but almost 90 percent of Mexicans are Roman Catholic. Protestants account for around 5 percent, and their percentage is growing—notably among the Evangelical sects.

Demographics

The population of Mexico is almost 88 million. The ethnic composition of the country is 60 percent mestizo (a mixture of Indian and European), 30 percent Amerindian, 9 percent white, and 1 percent other. Catholicism has a significant influence on Mexican culture.

Mexico is one of the United States' most important trade partners. It is the third largest exporter to the United States, and its international trade products include oil exports, tourism, and the products of its many assembly plants (called *maquiladoras*). About 26 percent of the labor force is employed in the agricultural sector.

Cultural Orientation

Cognitive Styles: How Mexicans Organize and Process Information

In Mexico information is readily accepted for purposes of discussion, but little movement in attitude is seen. Mexicans process information subjectively and associatively, since most of their education is by rote. They become personally involved in each situation and look at the particulars rather than using a rule or law to solve problems.

Negotiation Strategies: What Mexicans Accept as Evidence

Subjective feelings form the basis for the truth, and this leads to the truth changing depending on what one is perceived to want. Faith in the ideologies of the Catholic church, though pervasive, does not greatly affect their perceptions of the truth. Objective facts are used by those with a higher education.

Value Systems: The Basis for Behavior

The closeness of Mexico to the United States of America, and a history of "bad deals" makes them suspicious of its intent. The following three sections identify the Value System in the predominant culture—their methods of dividing right from wrong, good from evil, and so forth.

Locus of Decision Making

The individual is responsible for his or her decisions, but the best interest of the family or group is a dominating factor. One must know a person before doing business with him or her, and the only way to know a person in Mexico is to know the family. Expertise is less important than how one fits into the group, so it is extremely important to cultivate personal relations with the right people in the right places.

Sources of Anxiety Reduction

It is one's role in the social structure and the presence of the extended family that give a sense of stability to life. However, families exert pressure on the behavior of their members. Group members are bound by intense friendship and personal relations, and commit themselves to assisting one another in case of need. This network of relatives, friends, and memberships is crucial to class affiliation and social mobility. All of these expect mutual support—a lifelong commitment.

Issues of Equality/Inequality

There are extreme contrasts between rich and poor, but Mexico has the largest upper class of all Latin American countries—all interrelated in one way or another. Machismo is very strong, and there is a general belief that if there is an opportunity for sex to occur, it will. For women, femininity is stressed in dress, makeup, and behavior.

Business Practices

Appointments

PUNCTUALITY

- Punctuality, although admired, is not strictly adhered to in daily life. Since it is expected from foreigners and in business circles, be on time for appointments, but bring some work in case your counterpart is late.
- Punctuality is not expected for parties, dinner invitations, and so forth. Be at least thirty minutes late when invited to a party at a Mexican home. In Mexico City, be at least one hour late.

- Make appointments two to four weeks prior to your arrival in Mexico by mail or telex, then reconfirm a week before. Establish your contacts as high up in the organization as possible. Use a local *persona bien colocada* (well-connected person) to make introductions and contacts for you.
- Meetings may take place at breakfast, lunch, or dinner. Let your counterpart select which time.
- Business hours are 9:00 A.M. to 6:00 P.M., with lunch between 1:00 and 3:00 P.M., Monday through Friday.

 Negotiating

- The business atmosphere is friendly, gracious, and easy-going.
- The pace will tend to be slower than that of the United States or Europe. Decisions are made at top levels, with consultation at lower levels. This may take time. Be calm and patient with delays and build them into your time expectations.
- Personal friendships are vital to business in Mexico. Mexicans are looking for long-term relationships based on mutual trust and reliability, or *personalismo*. It is important to spend time building these relationships, since your friendship will

mean more to your prospects than the big-name company you represent. Plan to make repeated visits and maintain contact after your trips.

- Be warm and personal, yet retain your dignity, courtesy, and diplomacy. Your Mexican counterparts may initially seem vague, suspicious, and indirect. Overcome that with mutual trust and goodwill.
- Mexicans highly value the individual dignity of a person, regardless of social standing or material wealth. Therefore, do not pull rank, publicly criticize anyone, or do anything that will embarrass anyone.
- Mexicans avoid saying "no." "Maybe" or "We will see" may actually mean "no." Do the same yourself. Get all agreements in writing, since the "yes" may have been said out of politeness and the agreement later reversed.
- When negotiating, emphasize the trust and mutual compatibility of the two companies. Stress the benefits to the person and his or her family and pride. This emotional approach may be more effective than the logical bottom line of a proposal.
- If there is a disagreement, do not overcompromise, since this would show weakness.
- Leave yourself a reasonable margin for negotiating in your prices.
- Use high-end, sharp visuals in your presentations.
- Although the situation is rapidly changing, it is still rare to find women in upper levels of management. A woman may face some initial lack of respect in Mexico.
- Mexicans are status-conscious. At least one member of the negotiating team should be from higher-level management. Mention university degrees that you may hold, stay in good hotels, and eat at good restaurants.
- One major barrier in negotiations is the issue of financing the cost of foreign goods and services. Be prepared with some creative financing solutions.

 Business Entertaining

- The best times for business meetings are either breakfast or lunch, the main meal of the day.
- If you are invited to a Mexican home, do not expect to discuss business. Instead, use this time for socializing and meeting the family. Dinner is eaten between 8:30 and 9:30 P.M. Arrive about thirty minutes late.
- Good topics of conversation include Mexican sights and your family and job at home. Topics to stay away from include historically sensitive issues such as the Mexican-American war and illegal aliens.
- It is customary for one person to pay the check for a group meal. This is often the oldest person in the group. It is good manners to haggle over paying the bill. Reciprocate by inviting the person out for another meal, insisting ahead of time that this will be your treat.
- You may be invited to a girl's fifteenth birthday party. This is called a *quinceanera*, and is an important occasion, resembling a coming-out party in the United States.
- There is a difference in altitude that will take time to adjust to. Minimize heavy eating, drinking, and smoking.
- It is not wise for foreign businesswomen to invite their counterparts to a business dinner unless other associates or spouses also attend. For business lunches, eat at your hotel and have the bill added to your tab. Otherwise men will resist having you pay.

Time

- Mexico is six hours behind Greenwich Mean Time (G.M.T. - 6), or one hour behind U.S. Eastern Standard Time (E.S.T. - 1).

Protocol

Greetings

- Men will shake hands in greeting. Women will often pat each other on the right forearm or shoulder instead of shaking hands. If they are close, they may hug or kiss each other on the cheek. Men may wait for women to initiate a handshake.
- Be prepared for a hug on the second or third meeting.
- At a party, give a slight bow to everyone as you enter the room. It is customary to greet and shake hands with each individual. Usually your host will introduce you. You are also expected to shake hands with each person when you leave.

Titles/Forms of Address

- Titles are very important in Mexico. Address a person directly by using his or her title only, such as *Profesor* or *Doctor*. First names are used only by people on familiar terms. Wait for your counterpart to initiate this switch to first names.
- Persons who do not have professional titles should be addressed as Mr., Mrs., or Miss, plus their surnames. In Spanish these are
  - Mr. = *Señor*
  - Mrs. = *Señora*
  - Miss = *Señorita*
- Most Hispanics have two surnames: one from their father, which is listed first, followed by one from their mother. Only the father's surname is commonly used when addressing someone; e.g., Señor Juan Antonio Martínez García is addressed as Señor Martínez and Señorita Ana María Gutiérrez Herrera is addressed as Señorita Gutiérrez. When a woman marries, she usually adds her husband's surname and goes by that surname. If the two people in the above example married, she would be known as Señora Ana María Gutiérrez Herrera de Martínez. Most people would refer to her as Señora de Martínez or, less formally, Señora Martínez.

Gestures

- Conversations take place at a much closer physical distance than what may be considered comfortable in the United States. Pulling away from your counterpart may be regarded as unfriendly—or a Mexican may simply step forward and close the distance up again.
- Mexican men are warm and friendly and make a lot of physical contact. They often touch shoulders or hold another's arm. To withdraw from such a gesture is considered insulting.

- Mexicans catch another's attention in public with a "psst-psst" sound. This is not considered rude.
- Men should avoid putting their hands in their pockets. Hands on your hips indicates that you are making a challenge.
- When indicating height, always use the index finger. Only the height of an animal is shown by using the whole hand.
- In a store, pay for purchases by placing the money in the cashier's hand, rather than on the counter.

Gifts

- Giving gifts to executives in a business context is not required. However, small gifts, such as items with a company logo (for an initial visit) or a bottle of wine or scotch (on subsequent trips), are appreciated. If a gift of greater value is called for, desk clocks, finely made pens, or gold cigarette lighters are good choices.
- Secretaries do expect gifts. A government secretary who performs any service for you is given a token gift. For secretaries in the private sector, a more valuable gift (such as perfume or a scarf) should be given on a return visit. A businessman giving such a gift to a female secretary should say that the gift was sent by his wife.
- Gifts are not required from a dinner guest. An extension of thanks and a reciprocal invitation are considered sufficient. However, a gift will be happily accepted if offered. Good choices are candy, flowers (if sent ahead, impress upon the florist that the delivery must arrive early or on time), or local crafts from home.
- When giving flowers, be aware that Mexican folklore maintains that yellow flowers represent death, red flowers cast spells, and white flowers lift spells.
- Avoid giving gifts made of silver; silver is associated with trinkets sold to tourists in Mexico.
- Gifts of knives should be avoided in Latin America, as they can symbolize the severing of a friendship.

Dress

- For business, men should wear a conservative dark suit and tie; women should wear a dress or skirt and blouse.
- Pants and a light shirt are casual wear for men; women may wear a skirt or nice pants. Jeans are not considered appropriate unless they are tailored and well pressed. Revealing clothing for women and shorts for either sex are inappropriate except at a resort. Men may wish to wear the traditional guayabera, a light shirt worn not tucked in.

AMSTERDAM

Netherlands

*t*he Kingdom of the Netherlands is often incorrectly called Holland. Holland refers only to a specific area in the Netherlands, encompassing the major cities of Amsterdam, Rotterdam, and The Hague. It is no more correct to call all of the Netherlands "Holland" than it would be to call all of Germany "Bavaria."

CULTURAL NOTE

Country Background

History

Julius Caesar's troops fought Germanic tribes in what is now the Netherlands. The strongest of these tribes were not subdued until 13 B.C. The Romans were neither the first nor the last to invade the Netherlands. Its fertile soil and useful rivers made it an attractive prize, and the flat lowlands provided little in the way of natural defenses.

The tribe known as the Frisians allied themselves with Rome and profited by trade along the Rhine and the North Sea coast. Ever since, the Netherlands has remained a center of trade; this mercantile tradition is now some 2,000 years old! The Frisians were later joined by the Saxons (from the east) and the Franks (from the south). These three tribes are the ancestors of the Dutch. Following the collapse of the Roman Empire, Charlemagne incorporated the Netherlands into his Kingdom of the Franks. The Low Countries, as the Netherlands and Belgium were then known, were subsequently claimed by one ruler after another, from the French Duke of Burgundy to the Austrian House of Hapsburg. All of these rulers were absentee landlords; they controlled blocks of land in scattered locations throughout Europe. Lacking any political power, the Dutch put their energies into trade and industry.

When Charles I of Spain came of age in 1516 A.D., he inherited title to the Netherlands. But a nation as distant as Spain was bound to have difficulty ruling the increasingly self-sufficient Dutch. The Protestant Reformation increased Dutch opposition; many Dutch became Calvinists and resisted Catholic Spain on religious grounds.

The Dutch revolution spanned eighty years, from 1568 to 1648. Although Spain was then the most powerful nation in Europe, it was unable to subdue the Dutch rebels. Under the Protestant Prince William of Orange, the Dutch rendered the Spanish position untenable. (The Dutch also benefited from Spain's error in widening the war; the Spanish Armada was destroyed while attacking England in 1588.) The northern districts of the Low Countries formally united in 1579 under the Union of Utrecht; this is often used as the date of origin of the Netherlands. An equally valid date is 1609, when the Spanish agreed to a twelve-year truce with the Dutch. But Spain did not recognize the Dutch Republic as an independent nation until the Peace of Munster in 1648. The southern Low Countries (Belgium) remained under Spanish control.

t———————————————**CULTURAL NOTE**

here were many revolts of commoners against monarchies during the seventeenth century. The Dutch Revolt is unique in that it was the only one to ultimately succeed: The "low-born" Dutch traders broke from the Spanish king and founded their own nation. This predated the American War of Independence by more than a century.

The Netherlands survived and prospered. They experimented with several forms of government, with and without kings. The current Kingdom of the Netherlands dates to the ascension of Prince William I as king in 1813. The people of the Low Countries remained divisive, and the Dutch monarchy has been seen as a unifying force. The southern portions of the Low Countries eventually became the independent states of Belgium and Luxembourg. (The end of the Napoleonic Wars left Belgium under Dutch control, but the Belgians were soon waging their own fight for independence. The Kingdom of Belgium became independent in 1830.)

Beginning in the seventeenth-century, the Netherlands enjoyed a "golden era" of economic supremacy as its trade spanned the world. Dutch colonies were founded in Asia and the Caribbean. However, the tiny size and small population of the Netherlands made it inevitable that Dutch economic supremacy would be eclipsed by Britain, France, and Germany.

The Netherlands remained neutral in World War I. However, in World War II, Nazi Germany invaded and occupied the Netherlands. The Netherlands' last major colony, Indonesia, was occupied by the Japanese. The Dutch never truly regained control of Indonesia after the war, and Indonesia became independent in 1949. The Dutch still retain control of the Netherlands Antilles and Aruba in the Caribbean.

Type of Government

The Kingdom of the Netherlands is a constitutional monarchy. There is a bicameral parliament, with a 75-seat First Chamber and a 150-seat Second Chamber. The monarch is the chief of state; the prime minister is the head of the government.

The Netherlands is a member of both NATO and the European Community.

Although the Dutch are known for frugality in their personal lives, they have a very generous social welfare system. The government is seeking ways to reduce this system, which is seen as a burden on the economy.

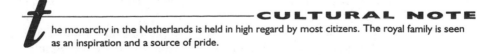

t———————————————**CULTURAL NOTE**

he monarchy in the Netherlands is held in high regard by most citizens. The royal family is seen as an inspiration and a source of pride.

Language
Dutch is the official language. A small percentage of the population speak Frisian, Turkish, and Arabic. The Dutch are among the most accomplished linguists in Europe. A majority of the Dutch speak at least one additional language. English is widely understood.

Education
With virtually 100 percent literacy, the Netherlands has one of the best educational records in Europe. Some 20 percent of adults continue their education beyond the secondary level. The educational system is also quite good at teaching foreign languages.

Religion
Although the Netherlands is thought of as a Protestant nation, Roman Catholics have a slight majority. The Dutch Reformed Church and Calvinists are the significant Protestant denominations. The largest group consists of persons professing no religion at all: 37 percent.

Demographics
The Netherlands has a population of a little over fifteen million. About 95 percent of the populace is Dutch or Frisian. The remainder consists mostly of Turkish and Moroccan immigrants.

Cultural Orientation

Cognitive Styles: How the Dutch Organize and Process Information
The Dutch are generally circumspect toward outside information. They are abstractive and process information objectively and analytically. There is an obligation to the universal rules of behavior, rather than to the individual. Friendships develop slowly and are very selective.

Negotiation Strategies: What the Dutch Accept as Evidence
Truth lies in the accumulation of objective facts, influenced by a strong faith in a social democratic ideology. No credence is given to subjective feelings. The Dutch tend to offer as little information as possible, and moderation is the rule. Subjective, emotional arguments are not accepted.

Value Systems: The Basis for Behavior
Planning is a way of life in the Netherlands. Planning, regulating and organizing are of major importance to the Dutch. The following three sections identify the Value Systems in the predominant culture—their methods of dividing right from wrong, good from evil, and so forth.

Locus of Decision Making
The Dutch are strongly individualistic, but cultural history must be considered in the decision-making process. Individual privacy is considered a necessity in all walks of life.

Decision-making is slow and involved, since all peripheral concerns must be taken care of in the process. Once the decision is made it is unchangeable. Planning is a way of life in the Netherlands. The Dutch are obsessed with planning, regulating, and organizing. Even though universal values are adhered to, it is important to develop the friendship of the participants.

Sources of Anxiety Reduction

Universal rules and regulations combined with strong internal discipline give stability to life and reduce uncertainty.

There is a high need for social and personal order and a low tolerance for deviant behavior. Everything is organized, including leisure time. The Dutch rarely show emotions, because of strong internal structure and control. But the Dutch have great faith in the ability of scientific method to solve human problems.

Issues of Equality/Inequality

The Netherlands is a distinctly hierarchical society, with classes established to fill organizational roles and give structure and order. Protest in the Netherlands is a crucial part of the democratic process, because the densely populated and overly structured country breeds dissent.

Equal rights for all are guaranteed by law, but may not be practiced in the marketplace. There is some racism (although its presence is denied).

Although there is still a strong paternal nuclear family orientation (including well-defined roles for males and females), this structure is beginning to erode as more females enter the workforce. The Dutch women's movement is among the least advanced in Europe.

Business Practices

CULTURAL NOTE

*I*n the United States, all business people regardless of their personal religious beliefs, have been affected by the "Protestant work ethic." Similarly, Calvinist ethics have influenced all Dutch business people. These are most evident in the Dutch virtues of frugality, honesty, and humility. The Dutch find ostentation, deviousness, and self-aggrandizement to be abhorrent.

Appointments

PUNCTUALITY

◆ Punctuality is very important in the Netherlands. Be certain to be on time for both business and social engagements.

◆ The Dutch place great importance on planning and efficient use of time. Arriving even a few minutes late to a business meeting may cause the Dutch to doubt your ability to utilize time well. In the Netherlands, a person who is late is suspected of being either incompetent or untrustworthy—or both!

◆ Another important aspect of punctuality in the Netherlands involves response time. Any company that cannot promptly deliver price quotes upon request will fail to win Dutch customers. It is also important to deliver products and services quickly.

■ Remember that many Europeans and South Americans write the day first, then the month, then the year. (e.g., December 3, 1999, is written as 3.12.1999).

■ A very high percentage of Dutch business people are fluent in English. In almost every situation, someone who can translate from English to Dutch will be close at hand.

■ The Dutch pride themselves on the efficient use of time. This requires advance planning. Appointments will be carefully scheduled; do not assume that they can be changed on short notice. Spontaneity is not considered a virtue in the Netherlands.

- Give at least one or two weeks' notice for an appointment made by telephone, fax, or telex; if possible, allow a full month for appointments made by mail (it may take a week for air mail letters to be delivered).
- Always acknowledge the receipt of important communications (contracts, price quotes, letters of intent, and so forth).
- Business letters may be written in English. Keep your letters formal, businesslike, and grammatically correct. When addressing individuals in writing, be sure to use their full and correct title, even if you are on a first-name basis.
- Many Dutch executives take long vacations during June, July, August, and late December, so confirm that your counterpart will be available.
- Large Dutch businesses often have a reception area with an attendant who may offer waiting business executives coffee or tobacco. It is traditional to tip this attendant when you exit.
- Business hours: 8:30 to 5:30 P.M., Monday through Friday.
- Banking hours: 9:00 A.M. to 4:00 P.M., Monday through Friday. Some banks have Thursday night hours as well.
- Store hours: 8:30 or 9:00 A.M. to 5:30 or 6:00 P.M., Monday through Friday. Some shops will have extended evening hours on Thursday or Friday. Note that most shops will be closed for a half day each week.

Negotiating

- Dutch executives are often straightforward and efficient. However, the pace of corporate decision making is slower in the Netherlands than in the United States.
- The decision-making process in Dutch firms is based upon consensus. Every employee who may be affected will be consulted. All opinions will be listened to, regardless of the status or seniority of the person. The process can take a good deal of time.
- Dutch society values diversity. Everyone has his or her say, and they do not have to agree. An effort will be made to accommodate all divergent opinions. This will include an attempt to make dissenters change their minds.
- Once a positive decision has been reached, Dutch firms will move swiftly. Everyone will be committed to the project. Be prepared to act quickly.
- A negative decision may be slower in coming. The one area in which many Dutch are not blunt is in saying "no." They may prevaricate or predict insurmountable complications instead of giving a direct "no."
- The Dutch admire modesty and abhor exaggeration or ostentation. Be sure you can back up your claims with lots of data. Keep your presentation simple and straightforward.
- Keep every promise you make, no matter how minor. A person who cannot be trusted to be punctual or to deliver price quotes on time will not be considered responsible enough to fulfill a contract.
- Most executives in the Netherlands understand English, so it is not necessary to have your business cards translated. However, all promotional materials and instruction manuals should be translated into Dutch.
- History is very important in the Netherlands. If your company has been around for many years, the date of its founding should be on your business card.
- Education is well respected in the Netherlands; include any degree above the bachelor's level on your card.

- The Dutch often do not spend a lot of time socializing before getting down to business. It is quite possible that you will walk into an office and start talking business immediately after introducing yourself. In a country with hundreds of years' experience in commerce, Dutch executives believe that they can quickly judge whether or not they wish to do business with someone.
- On the other hand, it is also possible that a Dutch executive will have background research done on prospective clients. This gives the executives hard data to back up his or her impressions, while maintaining a reputation for being a "canny judge of human character."
- When the Dutch decide to chat before getting down to business, expect to be asked about your flight, your accommodations, where you are from in the United States, and so forth. Contacts are vital to doing business in the Netherlands, so know the name of every possible person who could give you or your company a good reference. Be aware of recent political events, both in your own country and in the Netherlands; the Dutch frequently discuss politics.

a **CULTURAL NOTE**
void conveying information that you want kept confidential. The Dutch prefer to keep their operations open to suggestions from all employees in a company, so all employees are given access to information. Furthermore, the Dutch are generally uncomfortable with secrets.

- The Dutch respect honesty and forthrightness. It is better to be blunt than to appear devious or evasive.
- The Dutch do not usually give compliments to individuals. Everything is considered a team effort, and accolades are awarded to the group, not to individuals. Conversely, individuals are not usually singled out for blame. When something goes wrong, it is considered the fault of a system that failed to exercise proper oversight.
- When an individual must be either complimented or chastised, the Dutch always do so in private.
- Always avoid giving an impression of superiority. Egalitarianism is a central tenet of Dutch society. Everyone in a Dutch company, from the boss to menial laborers, is considered valuable and worthy of respect.
- Privacy is very important in the Netherlands. Doors are kept closed, both at work and at home. Always knock on a closed door and wait to be admitted.
- Keep personal questions superficial; if your counterpart wants you to know any detail about his or her family, he or she will tell you. Avoid talking about sex, including the fact that prostitution is legal in the Netherlands.
- The Dutch tend to stand somewhat further apart than North Americans when talking. The positioning of furniture reflects this, and you may find yourself giving a sales pitch from a chair that seems uncomfortably far away. Do not move your chair closer; it is not your place to rearrange the furniture.
- Dutch family life is kept separate from business dealings. However, executives do take work home with them and may be phoned at home about business matters.

a **CULTURAL NOTE**
lthough business is considered a serious matter, the Dutch occasionally enjoy humor in formal business presentations and official speeches. The Dutch sense of humor tends to be good-natured and earthy; wit, sarcasm, and verbal legerdemain are not prized.

Business Entertaining

- Although the Netherlands is not known for its cuisine, food constitutes an important part of Dutch entertainment.
- In addition to three meals a day, the Dutch often break for a snack at 10:00 A.M. and 4:00 P.M. Coffee is taken at the morning break; the afternoon drink is usually tea.
- The Dutch enjoy hosting foreign business people at lunches and dinners. These are usually held in restaurants rather than in Dutch homes.

CULTURAL NOTE

*a*s an alternative to a formal dinner, the Dutch often invite guests to come to their home after dinner. The guests are offered numerous hors d'oeuvres, plus alcohol and coffee. The amount of food and drink at these events can rival a full meal, but the setting is more relaxed and informal.

- All social events will be carefully scheduled and planned. The Dutch do not appreciate spontaneity, and they do not "do lunch" on a moment's notice.
- Remember to be on time to social events.
- Fine coffee is prized in the Netherlands; expect to drink a lot of it.
- When eating, always use utensils; very few items are eaten with the hands. Many Dutch even eat bread with a knife and fork!
- At the dinner table, do not rest your hands in your lap. Keep both hands above the table, with your wrists resting on the tabletop.

Time

- The Netherlands is one hour ahead of Greenwich Mean Time (G.M.T. + 1), or six hours ahead of U.S. Eastern Standard Time (E.S.T. + 6).

Protocol

Greetings

- Virtually everyone shakes hands in the Netherlands, both upon greeting and upon departure. Men shake hands, firmly but briefly, with other men, with most women, and even when being introduced to a child.
- Upon introduction, repeat your last name while you are shaking hands. It is not traditional to utter any greeting phrase (such as "How do you do?"), although many Dutch business people will do so to make a foreigner feel at ease.
- When you have not been formally introduced to everyone at a business or social gathering, it is your job to introduce yourself. Go around the room and shake hands with everyone, repeating your last name. Failure to do so may give a bad impression.
- Avoid standing with your hands in your pockets, and never leave your left hand in your pocket while shaking hands with your right.
- Aside from handshakes, there is very little public contact in the Netherlands. Close friends or relatives may hug briefly.

Titles/Forms of Address

- The order of names among the Dutch is the same as in the United States: the first name is followed by the surname.
- Traditionally, only family members and close friends address each other by their first names. It may take a long time to establish a close enough relationship with a Dutch colleague to get to a first-name basis.
- On the other hand, many Dutch executives are experts at dealing with foreign business people. Your Dutch counterpart may quickly suggest going to a first-name basis. Understand that he or she is trying to make you feel comfortable.
- When speaking to persons who do not have professional titles, use Mr., Mrs., or Miss, plus the surname:
  - Mr. = *Mijnheer* (also spelt *Mineer*)
  - Mrs. (or Ms.) = *Mevrouw*
  - Miss = *Juffrouw*
- Professional titles are not always used when speaking. Usually, an attorney, engineer, or doctor who wishes you to use a title will introduce himself or herself to you that way.
- On the other hand, written communication in the Netherlands is very formal. Know the recipient's correct professional title and be sure to use it in the letter.
- When entering a shop, it is considered polite to say "good day" to everyone present, customers and employees alike. However, do not interrupt—Dutch clerks will wait on only one person at a time.

CULTURAL NOTE

*Y*ou will find it advantageous to be polite to all service personnel. Dutch egalitarianism can manifest itself in what U.S. citizens would consider poor customer service. To North Americans, Dutch shop clerks sometimes act as if they are doing you a favor by waiting on you. But Dutch society emphasizes that everyone is equal, and no citizen needs to be another person's servant. Never adopt a superior attitude toward a Dutch clerk (or any Dutch citizen).

Gestures

- The Dutch are rather formal and reserved in public. They avoid any type of public spectacle. For example, when you notice an acquaintance in the distance, it is considered ill-mannered to shout a greeting. (You may wave to attract his or her attention, though.)
- When a man and a woman walk down a street, the man walks closest to the curb.
- A bent-arm gesture that involves tapping the underside of the elbow is a way of accusing someone of being unreliable—a serious accusation among Dutch business people.
- Sucking one's thumb is a way of saying "I don't believe you."
- To indicate that someone is miserly or cheap, glide the forefinger down the bridge of your nose a few times.
- The Dutch have several gestures to indicate that someone is deranged. This can be done by tapping the forefinger against the forehead or by brushing away imaginary insects flying in front of one's face.

- On the other hand, the North American gesture for "crazy" (making circles with the forefinger near the temple) is almost identical with the Dutch gesture for "you have a phone call" (the Dutch rotate their forefinger over the ear rather than over the temple).
- Offering a tiny applause by tapping the thumbnails together is a snide gesture best translated as "We are not amused."
- Don't talk to someone while chewing gum.

 Gifts

- Any gift to a Dutch executive should be of good quality but not of exorbitant cost.
- Appropriate gifts to business people include imported liquor, good-quality pens, pocket calculators, or any new gadget. Wine collecting is common, so do not give a gift of wine unless you can make an appropriate selection for that person.
- If you are invited to dinner at a Dutch home, bring a bouquet of unwrapped flowers for your hostess; or, you may send a bouquet or a plant the following day.
- Avoid bringing wine as a gift to dinner, since you don't want to imply that your host's wine cellar is inadequate.
- Chocolate or candy is also a good gift when you are invited to a Dutch home, especially if there are children in the house.

 Dress

- Business dress in the Netherlands is fairly conservative, but it varies with the industry. In the financial industries, most businessmen wear dark suits, sedate ties, and white shirts; women dress in dark suits and white blouses. Expect to wear the same clothes when invited to dinner.
- On the other hand, some industries allow very informal dress. Quite a few executives save their ties and jackets for outside the office.
- Surprisingly, the higher a person's rank, the more informally he or she can dress (in some industries). You may find the sales clerks in suits and the boss in jeans and a sweater.

t ————————————————CULTURAL NOTE

he Netherlands is not the place to "dress for success." The wealthier and more successful a Dutch executive has become, the harder he or she must work at appearing ordinary. Wealthy Dutch citizens do not wear fancy clothes, drive exotic cars, or live in expensive mansions. In a crowd, a Dutch CEO often cannot be distinguished from a low-ranking executive.

- As in many countries, Dutch men remove their jackets when working. Follow their lead.
- When the occasion calls for it, the Dutch enjoy dressing up. A tuxedo for men and an evening gown for women may be required for formal social events. These include formal parties, dinners, and opening night at the theater.
- Casual wear is essentially the same as in the United States. However, shorts are worn only when jogging or hiking.

WELLINGTON

New Zealand

*n*ew Zealand was initially administered by the British as part of the Australian colony of New South Wales. Even after New Zealand became a separate nation, most of its contact with Europe was secondhand, through Australia. New Zealanders came to resent this domination. Today, although New Zealand and Australia are military allies and trade partners, a considerable rivalry exists between the two countries. Never mistake a New Zealander for an Australian.

Country Background

*t*hree islands make up the bulk of New Zealand's land area. The North Island has fertile agricultural land with forests, a dairy region, and a volcanic plateau. About 75 percent of New Zealand's population lives on the North Island. The South Island contains a mountainous strip with glaciers, surrounded by plains, fjords, a heavily forested strip, and beaches. The South Island offers many opportunities for sports, including skiing in the mountains. Stewart Island is a small island to the south with fewer than 600 inhabitants. The other islands are even smaller, and are virtually uninhabited.

History

The earliest known inhabitants of New Zealand were the Maori tribespeople, who came across the sea from Polynesia around 900 A.D. The first European explorers were the Dutch, who arrived in 1642 and continued to visit while on whaling and trading expeditions. British exploration began in 1769 with Captain James Cook, who visited New Zealand on all three of his Pacific voyages. Cook thought highly of the islands and the natives; his journal, published in 1777, encouraged Europeans to trade with and colonize New Zealand.

Unlike nearby Australia, New Zealand never became a major penal colony for the United Kingdom. Most arrivals in New Zealand wanted to be there, although some were Australian convicts or impressed sailors seeking refuge. Increased colonization and missionary activity prompted the British to annex New Zealand in 1838.

The Maoris accepted English sovereignty in 1840 in return for legal protection and land ownership, although much of this land was taken away after the Anglo-Maori wars of the 1860s.

England granted the colony internal self-government in 1852, and New Zealand became an independent dominion within the British Commonwealth in 1907.

Along with Australia, New Zealand fought with the Allies in both the First and Second World Wars. During World War II, the early defeat of Britain's Pacific forces by the Japanese was a shock to New Zealanders. With Britain unable to defend it, New Zealand accepted military help from the United States. New Zealand troops fought under U.S. command, and U.S. troops were stationed in New Zealand.

Type of Government

New Zealand is a constitutional monarchy. Although independent from Great Britain, it acknowledges the British monarch as its chief of state. The monarch is represented in New Zealand by a governor general.

The present government is a parliamentary system without a written constitution. The unicameral House of Representatives has 97 members, elected to a three-year term. There is an independent court system. The executive branch is headed by a prime minister and a 20 member cabinet. The prime minister is the head of the government.

New Zealand is active in the United Nations. Relations with the industrial democratic nations of Asia are considered a priority. New Zealand also assists the underdeveloped countries of the Pacific region through economic and technical programs.

Relations with the United States, while cordial, are often strained. Since Great Britain was unable to defend them in World War II, New Zealand and Australia accepted military aid from the U.S. In 1951, Australia, New Zealand, and the U.S. signed the ANZUS mutual defense treaty. This treaty has been suspended, however, because of disagreement arising from nuclear arms control. The New Zealand government has proclaimed its territory to be a "nuclear free zone," prohibiting ships which carry nuclear arms to use its ports. Since the U.S. government will not disclose which of its ships carry nuclear weapons and which do not, all U.S. military ships are presently banned. Both the Labour and the National Parties have pledged to keep this ban in effect. Economic problems, however, are the major concern of most New Zealanders.

Language

English is the official language. While efforts are being made to preserve the Maori language, most Maoris speak English. A very distinct accent and slang has developed in New Zealand.

CULTURAL NOTE

remember that New Zealanders refer to themselves as "Kiwis." If someone says you are their "mate" or a "hard case," consider it a compliment, for they mean "friend" or a "funny person." Some Maori words are commonly used, including Kai ("food") and pakeha ("non-Maori").

Religion

Most residents are Christian. Anglicans are the most numerous, constituting about 22 percent of the population. Roman Catholics, Presbyterians, and Methodists are also present. Almost 20 percent of New Zealanders describe themselves as nonreligious.

Demographics

The population of New Zealand is about 3.5 million, divided between two primary ethnic groups. About 88 percent come from a European background, primarily British. The Maoris, the native people of New Zealand (of Polynesian background), make up 9 percent of the population. The Maoris still proudly protect and retain much of their traditional heritage, but are becoming more thoroughly integrated into New Zealand society. Although protected by law, the Maoris contend that they are not given the same rights and privileges as the rest of the population. The remaining 3 percent come mostly from other Pacific islands. About 84 percent of the population live in cities.

Cultural Orientation

Cognitive Styles: How New Zealanders Organize and Process Information

The prevailing culture of New Zealand is generally closed to outside information. It is a culture that has high regard for practical experience but processes information abstractively and conceptually. The New Zealander's humanitarianism keeps the welfare of the person as a top priority, but New Zealanders tend to solve problems by looking to universal rules or impersonal laws.

Negotiation Strategies: What New Zealanders Accept as Evidence

The accumulation of objective facts forms the basis for truth. Faith in the ideologies of nationalism may have some influence on this truth, but subjective feelings are given very little credence.

Value Systems: The Basis for Behavior

The culture of New Zealand has a deep humanitarian orientation where humanistic progress is as important as materialistic progress. The following three sections identify the Value Systems in the predominant culture—their methods of dividing right from wrong, good from evil, and so forth.

Locus of Decision Making

There is very high individualism in decision making, but the individual will follow the company policy; so one executive can be exchanged for another without disrupting business negotiations. New Zealanders have high self and other orientation, emphasizing individual initiative and achievement. They do not find it difficult to say "no." They do not expect others to assist them, but they do expect everyone to be subject to the same value system. Friendships are few and specific to needs.

Sources of Anxiety Reduction

There are enough external organizations and structures to insulate New Zealanders from everyday pressures and to provide a feeling of security.

n ───────────────── **CULTURAL NOTE**

ew Zealand is known for its advanced social legislation. It was the first member of the British Commonwealth to create, in 1898, old-age pensions. Other early innovations include voting rights for women in 1893, labor arbitration in 1894, and widow's pensions in 1911.

Anxiety occurs over deadlines and performance, but emotions are not shown in public. One's greatest reward is to be recognized for one's accomplishments.

There are established rules for almost everything, but these rules can be changed if need be. Experts are relied upon at all levels.

Issues of Equality/Inequality

All ethnic groups have been integrated into a truly multiracial society, although some bias against the Maoris continues. There are structured social inequalities that give one an opportunity to work one's way up the social ladder. While inequalities do exist, New Zealanders believe that equal rights should be guaranteed to all. Traditional sex roles are changing, but women are still fighting for equality in pay and power.

Business Practices

Appointments

PUNCTUALITY

- ◆ Always be on time or a little early for appointments. Tardiness is seen as a bad business practice.
- ◆ Social events tend to start on time.

- Business hours are 8:30 A.M. to 5:00 P.M., Monday through Friday, and 9:00 A.M. to 12:30 P.M. on Saturday.
- Shops are open from 9:00 A.M. to 5:30 P.M. (until 9:00 P.M. on Fridays).
- The best times to visit New Zealand for business are February through May, and October and November. December and January are summer months, and many people are on vacation.
- The New Zealand fiscal year runs April 1 through March 31.
- If possible, arrange meetings by telex or telephone three weeks prior to your arrival.

 Negotiating

- New Zealanders value their egalitarian society and are very emphatic about equality among people. They respect people for who they are, and have little regard for wealth and social status. Therefore, emphasize honesty and forthrightness in negotiations. Avoid hype and ostentation.
- The business atmosphere is slower paced than in the United States, but generally faster than the pace in Australia.
- In general, conservative North American manners will be appropriate in interactions.
- Initial meetings often take place in an office setting. After that, you may suggest meeting over lunch at a restaurant or hotel.
- Lunch appointments are for conducting business. If you receive an invitation for dinner, this will be a more relaxed social evening with spouses. This is not the time to discuss business.

Business Entertaining

- New Zealanders love to entertain in their homes; do not be surprised by an invitation to a meal. Note that there is a difference between "tea" and "afternoon tea." Afternoon tea is served between 3:00 and 4:00 P.M., and tea is the evening meal served between 6:00 and 8:00 P.M. "Supper" is a late night-snack.
- Don't expect much conversation during the meal. Most socializing takes place after you have eaten.
- Good conversation topics are politics and sports. The New Zealanders love the outdoors and are very active in noncompetitive activities such as hiking, fishing, or sailing as well as organized sports.
- Racial topics are best avoided, especially the treatment of the Maori people.
- New Zealanders strive to establish a separate and distinct identity from Australia. There is a strong rivalry between the two countries. Avoid praising Australia or Australians to New Zealanders, and never confuse the two nations.
- New Zealanders are also very opinionated about politics. Hold up your end of the conversation and debate, without becoming insulting or personal. A person who has no apparent beliefs or convictions is not respected in New Zealand. Have some knowledge of New Zealand's nuclear-free policy and how it leads to tension with other nations, notably the United States.

Time
- New Zealand is twelve hours ahead of Greenwich Mean Time (G.M.T. + 12), or seventeen hours ahead of U.S. Eastern Standard Time (E.S.T. + 17).

Protocol

 Greetings

- New Zealanders are very friendly and polite but tend to be reserved and formal. They may wait to be approached but are warm when they are.
- Men shake hands upon introductions and when preparing to leave. The handshake should be firm and accompanied by eye contact.
- New Zealand men usually wait for a woman to extend her hand. Women generally shake hands with other women.
- The formal "How do you do?" is used until a more friendly level is achieved. After that, "Hello" or the New Zealand "G'day" is appropriate for informal settings.

Titles/Forms of Address

- The order of names for European-descended New Zealanders is the same as in the United States: first name followed by surname.
- At first meetings, expect to address New Zealanders by their title or Mr., Mrs., or Miss plus their surname.
- Once a relationship is established, New Zealanders progress to a first-name basis as quickly as possible. But continue to use titles and surnames until you sense that a more informal tone has been set or until you are asked to address someone by his or her first name.

 Gestures

- Chewing gum or using a toothpick in public is considered rude.
- The "V for victory" sign is considered obscene, especially when done with the palm facing inward.
- New Zealanders usually keep their speech soft and find loud voices annoying. They do not open their mouths wide when they speak; indeed, they often seem to be speaking through clenched teeth.
- Expansive behavior of any sort, even when drinking, is looked down upon. New Zealanders maintain more of the traditional British reserve than do Australians.

 Gifts

- When visiting a New Zealand home, you may bring a modest gift of chocolates, flowers, or whiskey, although it is not expected.
- Gifts should be simple and utilitarian. Ostentation is frowned upon.

 Dress

- Dress is similar to North American styles. While general dress is casual, business dress is slightly more formal than in the United States.
- New Zealand is in the Southern Hemisphere, so the seasons are reversed from those of North America. The climate is temperate, not tropical; warm clothes and rain gear are appropriate most of the year.
- Business attire is conservative. Men may wear a dark suit and tie. Businesswomen should wear a dress or a skirt and blouse with a jacket.

MANAGUA

Nicaragua

CULTURAL NOTE

*t*he devastating Nicaraguan earthquake of December 1972 killed or injured 10,000, yet it is best remembered by U.S. citizens for the death of Pittsburgh Pirates baseball player Roberto Clemente. The Puerto Rican-born Clemente—the most famous Hispanic athlete of his generation—had insisted upon flying to Mangua in an overloaded DC-7 full of relief supplies, knowing that only his presence would ensure that the supplies would reach the poor. His plane crashed shortly after takeoff, and the supplies that did reach Managua went directly into the hands of Somoza's National Guard, who sold most of them at a profit.

Country Background

History

The original inhabitants of Nicaragua were Amerindians; the coastal tribes were the first to encounter Europeans when Columbus landed in 1502. The Spanish explorer Francisco Fernández de Córdoba (after whom Nicaragua's currency is named) established settlements in 1523. However, full-scale colonization by Spain did not occur until the following century.

Most of Nicaragua eventually came under Spanish imperial rule. In 1821, Nicaragua became part of the United Provinces of Central America, which declared its independence from Spain. Between 1837 and 1838 the United Provinces of Central America broke up. Independent Nicaragua then experienced a period of instability and violence stemming from a rivalry between the Conservatives, based in Granada, and the Liberals, based in León.

Foreign influence—mostly from the United States and Britain—was strong in the new Nicaraguan state. Shortly after independence, U.S. financier Cornelius Vanderbilt (known as "the richest man in America") was given rights to operate a transportation service across the country, facilitating travel between the eastern states and California. With the southern states of the United States stymied in their efforts to expand slavery in North America, southern leaders began looking toward Central America. Their dreams seemed to be fulfilled in 1855 when a Tennessee adventurer named Walter Walker invaded Nicaragua with a mercenary army. Walker's "Phalanx of Immortals"—all fifty-eight of them—actually conquered the country, and Walker proclaimed himself president of Nicaragua. But Walker incurred the wrath of Vanderbilt, who incited the armies of neighboring Central

American countries to march against him. Walker was forced to flee in 1857, and control of the country returned—at least nominally—to Nicaraguans.

The Conservatives and the Liberals had been switching Nicaragua's capital back and forth between thecities of Granada and León, respectively, but following the Walker interregnum they agreed on Managua as a neutral site for a permanent capital. The Conservatives then took power for thirty years, during which time they persecuted the Liberals and encouraged foreign investment.

The Liberals returned to power after a revolt in 1893 and soon antagonized the United States. The Conservatives were returned to power in 1910 when the United States refused to accept the new Liberal candidate for president. U.S. troops in the form of a 100-man Marine "Embassy Guard" kept the Conservatives in power. Additional troops were brought in as needed, as when the United States kept order during the 1912 elections (which offered only one presidential candidate, a U.S.-backed Conservative).

The United States removed its Marines in 1925; civil war immediately broke out. When President Calvin Coolidge found that many of his constituents were against returning the Marines to Nicaragua, the "Communist threat" was invoked for the first time. Coolidge then sent Henry L. Stimson to Nicaragua as a special envoy to negotiate peace between the warring factions. One Liberal leader, the charismatic General Augusto César Sandino, refused to give up his arms until the U.S. troops left, and conducted a guerrilla war against both the Nicaraguan National Guard and the U.S. Marines. The six years of fighting that followed proved inconclusive, although it gave the U.S. Marine Air Corps the opportunity to be the first in military history to use aerial dive-bombing tactics. When the U.S. military finally left, Sandino stopped fighting, only to be assassinated in Managua in 1933. (Almost thirty years later, the Sandinista rebels named themselves after Augusto Sandino.)

When the U.S. troops withdrew, National Guard Commander Anastasio Somoza García grew in influence. He became president in 1937, and became the wealthiest man in Central America. He or his surrogates ruled Nicaragua until his assassination in 1956. The Somoza family continued to dominate the country through the presidencies of his two sons, Luis Somoza Debayle (1956-1963) and Anastasio Somoza Debayle (1967-1979).

Anti-Somoza sentiment grew with reports of the torture and killing of government opponents, including newspaper editor Pedro Joaquín Chamorro in 1978. The following year, the videotaped fatal shooting of ABC News correspondent Bill Stewart at a National Guard checkpoint in Managua was broadcast. U.S. support for the regime was finally withdrawn.

In 1979, the Marxist Sandinista National Liberation Front (FSLN), which had been fighting a guerrilla war since 1962, succeeded in taking control of the government. Somoza fled, complaining that the United States had let him down.

The pluralistic government gradually became dominated by a single party as the Sandinistas suspended the constitution and elections and began tightening control. The elections of 1984 brought Sandinista leader Daniel Ortega Saavedra to power.

Once again the United States found a Nicaraguan government unsatisfactory and made an effort to remove it. An anti-Sandinista group called the Contras was given massive support, and the U.S. government imposed a trade embargo on Nicaragua. The Contras conducted a guerrilla war against the Sandinista government.

After many years of fighting, the Central American Peace Plan proposed by Costa Rican President Oscar Arias Sánchez was finally adopted. A cease-fire was reached, and free elections were promised if the Contras would disarm. In February 1990, elections took place and Ortega was defeated by Violeta Barrios de Chamorro, wife of the assassinated newspaper editor Pedro Joaquín Chamorro.

Type of Government

The republic of Nicaragua is a unitary multiparty republic that calls for a president, vice president, cabinet, and 96-member National Assembly. The president is both head of state and head of the government.

Relations between Nicaragua and the United States have been strained virtually from the birth of Nicaragua as an independent country. Since the election of Mrs. Violeta Barrios de Chamorro in 1990, relations have improved. The United States backed her election and ended the trade embargo that had crippled the Nicaraguan economy.

The country is predominantly agricultural. Exports include coffee (30 percent), bananas, cotton, and tobacco.

Language

The official language is Spanish, although Garifuna is spoken among the black population, Nicaragua's Amerindians speak a number of Indian languages, and English is often spoken along the Atlantic coast.

Nicaraguan Spanish has a number of unique vocabulary words. It is also noted for its forcefulness; words considered profane in neighboring Costa Rica are in everyday use in Nicaragua, even in the mass media.

*d*espite the lack of educational infrastructure, Nicaraguans love poetry. They pride themselves on having more poets per capita than any other nation in the world. **CULTURAL NOTE**

Religion

There is no official religion. Approximately 85 percent of the population belongs to the Roman Catholic church. The remainder belong to various Protestant denominations.

Demographics

Nicaragua's population of 4 million (1992 estimates) is 69 percent mestizo (a mix of European and Indian), 17 percent European, 9 percent black, and 5 percent Amerindian.

*t*he family (including the extended family) is very important, and constitutes the foundation of social life. It is not uncommon for uncles, aunts, cousins, and grandparents to live together in one house or compound. **CULTURAL NOTE**

Cultural Orientation

Cognitive Styles: How Nicaraguans Organize and Process Information

Nicaraguans are a proud people and are circumspect in their evaluation of external information. Since most of their learning is by rote, they tend to think subjectively and associatively. They look at most situations from a personal perspective and seldom rely on rules or laws to resolve their problems.

Negotiation Strategies: What Nicaraguans accept as Evidence

Faith in several ideologies (the Sandinistas, nationalism, the church) influences the truth, although feelings usually determine the outcome. Objective facts are seldom used to prove a point.

Value Systems: The Basis for Behavior

Nicaragua is still struggling with political conflict, which heightens their awareness of their value systems. The following three sections identify the Value Systems in the predominant culture—their methods of dividing right from wrong, good from evil, and so forth.

Locus of Decision Making

Individual decisions always involve the needs of the family and public group. Since a person's self-identity is based on his or her place in the family and performance in the group, Nicaraguans are never completely free of these influences. Expertise is always subordinate to personal connections and one's ability to be part of the group. About 1 percent of the population controls all resources, but there are various factions within this tiny elite.

Sources of Anxiety Reduction

All classes depend upon an extended family organization—a wide range of relatives who are available for help and support. For the lower classes this is the primary social and psychological support system in the face of constant economic need. The church has little political power, but its precepts and social structure permeate all of life and bring some stability to it.

Issues of Equality/Inequality

A tiny oligarchy, full of factions, sits at the top of a small middle class and a huge lower class. There are extreme contrasts between the rich and the poor, but everyone is trying to gain or maintain power. Machismo is very strong. Even the female guerrilla fighters were subordinate to men when they returned home. The women's movement may have gotten a boost from a female's being elected president.

Business Practices

Appointments

PUNCTUALITY

♦ While punctuality is admired, it is not strictly observed. Punctuality is, however, expected from foreigners.

- Remember that many Europeans and South Americans write the day first, then the month, then the year (e.g., December 3, 1999, is written 3.12.99). This is the case in Nicaragua.
- Business hours are 8:00 A.M. to 6:00 P.M., Monday through Friday, and 8:00 A.M. to noon on Saturday. Government offices are open 7:00 A.M. to 5:00 P.M., Monday through Friday. A two-hour break is generally taken from noon to 2:00 P.M.
- Make appointments one month in advance of your trip by telephone or telex.

- The best time to visit Nicaragua is February through July and September through November. Common vacation times are the two weeks before and after Christmas and Easter, and the month of August.

 Negotiating

- Business will take place at a much slower pace than in the United States. Be patient with delays, and allow for them in your time estimates.
- Business is conducted with friends in Latin America. Therefore, time will be spent on building a relationship before jumping into negotiations.
- Contacts are very important in business, so try to establish them before your visit, and have them arrange introductions for you with major clients. You can find business contacts (*enchufados*) through embassies, banks, and the U.S. International Trade Administration.
- Business is discussed at an office or over a meal in a restaurant. It is not discussed in a home or around family. If you are invited to a Nicaraguan home, this is a social event, not a business opportunity.
- Personal honor and "saving face" are very important to people in Nicaragua. Therefore, never criticize someone, pull rank, or do anything that will embarrass another in public.

 Business Entertaining

- The main meal of the day is at noon. This traditionally includes black beans, tortillas or meat, and fruit and vegetables.
- Business breakfasts or lunches are preferred to dinners.
- Good topics of conversation are Nicaraguan sights, family, job, and sports. Topics to avoid include the political unrest and religion.

CULTURAL NOTE

k now something about the history of the United States' involvement in Nicaragua. The United States has repeatedly involved itself militarily in local affairs, from Walter Walker's mercenary army in the 1850s to support for the Contra guerrillas against the Marxist Sandinista government in the past decade. Nicaraguan opinion of the United States varies widely from person to person, and it is useful to understand the sources of any anti-U.S. feeling.

Time
- Local time is six hours behind Greenwich Mean Time (G.M.T. - 6), or one hour behind U.S. Eastern Standard Time (E.S.T. - 1).

Protocol

 Greetings

- Men shake hands in greeting. Women will often pat each other on the right forearm or shoulder instead of shaking hands. Women who are close friends may hug or kiss each other on the cheek.

- Close male friends may engage in an abrazo, a brief embrace.
- At parties, it is customary to greet and shake hands with everyone in the room individually.

Titles/Forms of Address

- Only children, family members, and close friends address each other by their first names.
- Most Hispanics have two surnames: one from their father, which is listed first, followed by one from their mother. Only the father's surname is commonly used when addressing someone; e.g., Señor Juan Antonio Martínez Garcia is addressed as Señor Martínez and Señorita Ana María Gutiérrez Herrera is addressed as Señorita Gutiérrez. When a woman marries, she usually adds her husband's surname and goes by that surname. If the two people in the above example married, she would be known as Señora Ana María Gutiérrez Herrera de Martínez. Most people would refer to her as Señora de Martínez, or, less formally, Señora Martínez. Similarly, the female president of Nicaragua's name is Señora Violeta Barrios de Chamorro. While in office her title is Señora Presidente, but before her election she was known as Señora de Chamorro, or Señora Chamorro.
- When a person has a title, it is important to use it along with the surname. A Ph.D. or a physician is called *Doctor*. Teachers prefer the title *Profesor*, engineers go by *Ingeniero*, architects are *Arquitecto*, and lawyers are *Abogado*.

Gestures

- Making a fist with the thumb between the index and middle fingers is considered obscene. (This gesture is known as the "fig.")
- The "come here" gesture is done with the palm down, making a scooping gesture with the fingers or the entire hand.
- You will see people waving good-bye as is done in the United States, palm facing out, or with the palm facing in, which looks almost like a person fanning himself or herself.
- Do not photograph individuals or religious ceremonies without prior approval; some people object to having their picture taken. Keep in mind that transportation depots and bridges have military significance, so photographing them may be prohibited.

Gifts

- Business gifts are generally not given on the first trip to Nicaragua. At the end of your trip, ask if there is anything you can bring from the United States on your next visit.
- Secretaries and receptionists can be very influential, so always bring them something from the United States. Perfume or a scarf is usually the best choice.
- If you are invited to a home, bring a small gift of flowers or candy.
- Ask a local florist which types of flowers are appropriate. In general, white flowers are reserved for funerals.

Dress

- Businessmen should wear a conservative dark suit and tie, although a jacket is not required in the hottest season; women should wear a dress or skirt and blouse.
- Lightweight clothing is appropriate for casual wear. Men should wear pants and a shirt in cities, and women should wear a dress. Short pants or jeans are not appropriate for either cities or rural areas. Women in pants or revealing clothing are very uncommon and may offend some people. Men may wish to wear the traditional *guayabera*, a light shirt worn not tucked in.

Norway

*t*he Norwegian Trygve Lie was the first Secretary General of the United Nations.

Country Background

History

The Vikings (also called Norsemen) were feared for their raids throughout northern Europe from the eighth to eleventh centuries. These Vikings eventually became the Norwegians, the Swedes, and the Danes.

Political power became concentrated in Denmark, which came to rule much of Scandinavia, including Norway. Eventually, Sweden became a rival power. Denmark sided with Napoleon during the Napoleonic Wars. To punish Denmark, the postwar Congress of Vienna took Norway from Denmark and gave it to Sweden in 1815.

The fishermen, sailors, and merchants of Norway had little in common with the aristocrats of Sweden. Friction developed. Fortunately for the Norwegians, their rugged, rocky nation could not be divided up into the vast farming estates preferred by the Swedes. After a century of Swedish occupation, Norway peacefully gained its independence in 1905. The Norwegian parliament invited a Danish prince to become their constitutional monarch, so King Haakon VII became the first king of Norway.

Norway remained neutral in World War I. However, despite its neutrality, Norway was occupied by Nazi Germany during World War II. For this reason, the Norwegians shifted from a belief in neutrality to one in collective security. Norway signed the North Atlantic Treaty of 1949 and participated in the foundation of the United Nations.

Type of Government

Norway is a multiparty (hereditary) constitutional monarchy. There are three branches of government. The executive branch is made up of the king, who is chief of state, the prime minister, who is the head of government, and the cabinet, or Council of Ministers. Executive power actually resides in the Council of Ministers in the name of the king, or King's Council. The prime minister sits on this council. The prime minister is chosen by the leading political parties. The legislative branch is a modified unicameral parliament, known as the Storting. Members of the Storting are elected according to a system of proportional representation. They serve for four years. There is a Supreme Court.

Norway became a major oil and gas producer in the 1970s. The income from this sector allowed it to further advance its social welfare system. Today it hopes to make the non-oil sector of its economy more efficient and less dependent on subsidies. The United States is Norway's fourth most important trading partner. Norway is currently deciding whether or not to join the European Union.

t —————————————————————— **CULTURAL NOTE**
he Nobel Peace Prize is awarded in Norway.

Language

The official language of Norway is Norwegian, which is a Germanic language related to Icelandic, Danish, and Swedish. It has two forms, a "book language," known as *Bokmål*, used in schools and broadcasting, and a commonly spoken language, known as *Nynorsk*. According to law, *Nynorsk* must sometimes be used in instruction and in the media. The principal minority language is Lappish (also called "Sami"), spoken by Lapps or Laplanders. This group is also known as the Samis, although some find that term derogatory. Most Norwegians have studied English. English is widely spoken in business circles and in major cities.

a —————————————————— **CULTURAL NOTE**
s in the other Scandinavian languages, Norwegian's additional letters (versions of "ae," "o," and "a" with diacritical marks) are listed at the end of the alphabet. Remember this when searching for words beginning with such sounds or letters in a telephone book.

Religion

Norway has complete religious freedom, but it does have an official state church, the Evangelical Lutheran Church, or Church of Norway. About 94 percent of the people belong to this church.

Demographics

The population of Norway is 4.3 million. About 65 percent of the people live along the coast. Oslo, the capital, has about 456,000 people. Today, many foreign workers and immigrants come to Norway, and about 2,000 people obtain citizenship per year.

Cultural Orientation

Cognitive Styles: How Norwegians Organize and Process Information

The Norwegians are generally cautious toward outside information. New products and new ways of doing things are viewed with circumspection. Their education is becoming more abstractive, and people are beginning to process information conceptually and analytically. Although they are deeply concerned with social welfare, their individualism dictates that all be subject to the same rules and regulations.

Negotiation Strategies: What Norwegians Accept as Evidence

Norwegians' faith in the ideologies of the social welfare state dictates the truth in most cases. This is usually supported by objective facts rather than subjective feelings.

Value Systems: The Basis for Behavior

Norway is a highly nationalistic culture with a liberal philosophy of tolerance for dissent and deviation. The following three sections identify the Value Systems in the predominant culture—their methods of dividing right from wrong, good from evil, and so forth.

Locus of Decision Making

There is a strong belief in individual decisions within the social welfare system. There is an emphasis on individual initiative and achievement, with a person's ability being more important than his or her station in life. Although the dignity and worth of the individual is emphasized, there is a strong feeling of obligation to help those who are not able to help themselves.

Sources of Anxiety Reduction

Life's uncertainties are accepted and anxiety is reduced through a strong social welfare system. Life is given stability and structure by a strong nuclear family. Young people are encouraged to mature early and take risks to develop a strong self-image.

Issues of Equality/Inequality

Nationalism transcends social differences, and a largely homogeneous population minimizes ethnic differences. Norway is a fiercely democratic and egalitarian society in which those at different power levels have an inherent trust in people. It is basically a middle-class society that strives to minimize social differences. Husbands and wives share the responsibilities of child care.

Business Practices

Appointments

───────────────────────────────────── **PUNCTUALITY**

♦ Always be punctual. Tardiness in business is interpreted as a lack of respect.
♦ Punctuality is expected for social events as well.

- Remember that many Europeans and South Americans write the day first, then the month, then the year (e.g., December 3, 1999, is written 3.12.99). This is the case in Norway.
- When you deal with a Norwegian firm, the secretary of the firm will make an appointment for you.
- The workweek is Monday through Friday, 8:00 A.M. to 4:00 P.M. Business people leave their offices promptly and go home for dinner, which is typically held at about 5:00 P.M.
- It is best to avoid business trips to Norway at Easter time and in July and early August—most people take vacations then.

Negotiating

- When writing to a Norwegian firm, it is gracious to use the name of the division head, even if you do not know the person.
- Norwegians are relatively informal (far more so than the neighboring Swedes).
- You can introduce yourself to the executive with whom you are meeting, rather than waiting for the secretary to introduce you.
- It is a good idea to set a time limit on the meeting.
- Norwegians are wary of the American concern with legal matters. Written confirmation of business deals is sufficient; if you must mention bringing in a lawyer, be discreet.
- Scandinavians appreciate knowledge about the differences among the countries of their region.
- Avoid personal topics (employment of you host or family members, salary, and social status).
- Hobbies, politics, sports, and travel are good topics for conversation.
- Avoid criticism of other peoples or systems. The Norwegians stress tolerance. Chastising Norwegians for permitting the hunting of whales will not win you any friends.
- Avoid comparisons between Norway and the United States, especially concerning the cost of living. Norwegians are bored with hearing how expensive their country is.
- Norwegians appreciate nature and are proud of their clean environment.

 Business Entertaining

- If you have a late morning meeting, you can invite your Norwegian colleague to lunch.
- The person who extends the invitation pays for the meal.
- Lunch is a light meal but, if it is used for business, it will usually be a hot meal rather than just sandwiches.
- In most Norwegian restaurants, alcohol is served only after 3:00 P.M. and only from Monday through Saturday.
- You may discuss business at any time during the meal.

CULTURAL NOTE

orwegians enjoy discussing sports—cross-country skiing began in Norway.

- In restaurants, raise your hand to call the waiter over.
- Norwegians usually eat dinner at 5:00 or 6:00 P.M.
- When you go to a Norwegian home, wait to be asked in; wait again until you are asked to sit down. At the table, wait until the host invites everyone to begin eating.
- Some Norwegians have a cocktail before dinner; others do not. It is possible that you will be directed to the dinner table as soon as you arrive. Arrive on time.
- The fork is held in the left hand; the knife remains in the right hand.
- Hands should not be kept in the lap at the table.
- It is preferable to finish what is on your plate.

- A dinner in a Norwegian home may have numerous courses and last several hours. Pace yourself.
- At the end of the meal, people thank the hostess by saying *takk for maten*, or "thank you for the food"; you will please your hosts by saying this in Norwegian.

> *t*—————————————**CULTURAL NOTE**
> here was a turn-of-the-century fashion in Norwegian interior design for disguising interior doors. You may have to search for a door in older homes; do not be surprised if the door is covered by wallpaper. Doors are traditionally kept shut.

- You should initiate your own departure, as your hosts will not. Expect the evening to end around 10:00 P.M. in the winter. However, in the summer, the sun does not set until around midnight. Your hosts may suggest a walk after dinner, followed by a final drink. In the summer, expect to leave around 11 P.M.

Time

- Norway is one hour ahead of Greenwich Mean Time (G.M.T. + 1); or six hours ahead of Eastern Standard Time (E.S.T. + 6).

Protocol

Greetings

- The handshake is the standard greeting for men and women.
- People greet each other by saying "Morn" (which means "morning") at any time of day.
- Norwegians are a fairly quiet people. Avoid speaking loudly.

Titles/Forms of Address

- The order of names is the same as in the U.S.: first name followed by surname.
- The use of first names is not as common as in the United States. Follow the lead of your hosts. Indeed, many men are addressed solely by their surnames, without even a "Mr." in front.
- Among older people, titles are used; among younger people, usage varies. In general, professional titles (Doctor, Engineer, Professor, and so forth) are used, followed by a surname; business titles (Director, President, and so forth.) are not typically used. With government officials, it is appropriate to use titles. Oddly, lawyers and clergymen do not use titles.

Gestures

- A toss of the head means "come here."
- Norwegians do not always rise when another person enters the room. Don't be offended by this.
- However, do rise when you are being introduced to someone.
- Talking with one's hands in one's pockets is considered too casual.

- The North American "O.K." gesture (thumb and forefinger forming a circle) is considered insulting.

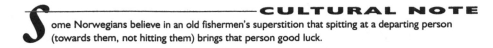

CULTURAL NOTE

*S*ome Norwegians believe in an old fishermen's superstition that spitting at a departing person (towards them, not hitting them) brings that person good luck.

Gifts

- Flowers, liqueurs, wine, liquor, or chocolates are appropriate gifts for your hostess when invited to a Norwegian home.
- When giving flowers, avoid the following, since they are all used only for funerals: lilies, carnations, and all white flowers, as well as wreaths.
- Alcohol taxes are high, so alcohol makes a prized gift.
- It is not appropriate to give a business gift at the first meeting.
- If you give a business gift, be sure it is wrapped in good-quality paper. Make the gift neither too extravagant nor too skimpy.

Dress

- In general, Norwegians dress more informally than American business people; however, visitors should dress as they would in a business context at home.
- Men should always wear a tie for business appointments, but a sports jacket rather than a suit is usually acceptable.
- Women may wear dresses or pants.
- Clean blue jeans and t-shirts are standard casual wear, but torn clothes are unacceptable. Shorts are worn for hiking; they are not common in urban areas.

ISLAMABAD

Pakistan

Country Background

History

The name Pakistan was first used in 1933, and the Pakistani nation was established as a separate Muslim state in 1947 during the British partition of India. However, the land that makes up the country has a history and cultural heritage more than 4,000 years old.

Pakistan was historically known as "the land of the Indus," named for the Indus River, which originates in the Himalaya mountains and flows through the country to empty into the Arabian Sea.

The Aryan tribes who invaded the Indian subcontinent over several centuries built up a sophisticated civilization long before the flourishing of the Greek and Roman Empires. Kingdoms rose and fell, frequently toppled by outsiders. In 712 A.D., the Pakistani province of Sind was the first to be occupied by Muslim invaders. More Muslim invaders came, and the entire subcontinent fell to the Mogul Empire in 1526. In what would become India, the Hindu citizenry often failed to adopt the Islamic faith of their Mogul rulers. However, in Pakistan, the majority of the people accepted Islam.

The Mogul supremacy fell before the technology of the European invaders who began arriving in 1498. Pakistan eventually became part of British-ruled India.

When the British promised independence to India after World War II, Muslim leaders became fearful that the more-numerous, better-educated Hindus would subordinate the Muslim population. Consequently, they insisted on a separate, independent Muslim state. Despite opposition from many Hindu leaders, including Mahatma Gandhi, the predominantly Muslim provinces of Punjab and Bengal became Pakistan (a Dominion within the British Commonwealth) on August 15, 1947. Pakistan proclaimed itself a fully independent republic on March 23, 1956.

At independence, Pakistan consisted of two separate regions; East Pakistan and West Pakistan were separated by over a thousand miles of Indian territory. Smaller East Pakistan sought more autonomy from Islamabad. These efforts resulted in war between the two regions in 1970. East Pakistan was no match for the military might of West Pakistan. Some one million East Pakistanis were slain, and ten million fled into India. This prompted India to declare war in December 1971. Indian troops invaded East Pakistan and routed the West Pakistani occupation army. East Pakistan became the independent nation of Bangladesh.

During the decade-long war in neighboring Afghanistan, Pakistan served as a conduit for massive U.S. military aid to the anti-Soviet Afghan rebels. Now the U.S.S.R. has broken up, the Soviet troops have left, and the world's attention has turned from both Afghanistan and Pakistan. The only positive aspect of the war's end for Pakistan is that the 3.2 million Afghans who sought refuge in Pakistan are gradually returning home.

The failure of the scandal-ridden Bank of Credit and Commerce International (B.C.C.I.), was another blow to Pakistan. The B.C.C.I. failure caused considerable economic distress among Pakistanis at home and abroad. Many Pakistanis blamed B.C.C.I.'s failure on the West, seeing a conspiracy against the third world.

Type of Government

The Islamic Republic of Pakistan is a parliamentary democracy in a federal setting. Pakistan has frequently been ruled by its military, which has been tolerated because Pakistanis feel an urgent need for the military's protection. In Pakistan's short existence as a nation, its military has been involved in battles with China, Bangladesh, and India. Conflict with India continues over the status of the disputed territories of Jammu and Kashmir, which are claimed by both India and Pakistan.

The government consists of a bicameral legislature made up of a 237-member National Assembly (elected directly by the people) and an 87-member Senate (elected by four provincial assemblies). The executive branch consists of the president, who is head of state, and the prime minister, who is head of government. The prime minister is elected by the National Assembly from among its members.

CULTURAL NOTE

*a*s often happens in Islamic nations during times of strife, Pakistan has sought redemption through religion. In May 1991, the National Assembly declared that the Koran—the holy book of Islam—was the supreme law of Pakistan. All aspects of Pakistani life are now subject to Islamic law. This move met with the approval of the masses of impoverished peasantry, who form the majority of Pakistan's 130 million people. Much of the urban elite opposed the adoption of Islamic law, which may result in removal of the Western legal traditions inherited from British colonial rule.

One change centers on the fact that Islam prohibits the levying of interest. Not surprisingly, the adoption of Islamic law is causing great difficulty for the Pakistani banking system.

Language

Urdu and English are the official languages of Pakistan; Urdu is being encouraged as a replacement for English, but English is used by the government and the educated elite. Urdu is spoken by only 7 percent of the population. The provinces are free to use their own regional languages and dialects (such as Punjabi, Sindhi, Pushtu and Baluchi).

Religion

Pakistan was created as a Muslim state, and as a result, religion is an important part of all aspects of life there. About 97 percent of the population are Muslims and belong to either the Sunni or the Shiite branch. Hindus make up only 2 percent of the population, with Christians and adherents of other religions making up the final 1 percent. Muslims are called to prayer five times a day, and you will find men bowed in prayer in shops and airports, as well as the fields. The direction of Mecca is marked in every hotel room.

Demographics

Pakistan is the tenth most populated country in the world, with about 115 million people. About 70 percent of the population live in rural areas.

Cultural Orientation

Cognitive Styles: How Pakistanis Organize and Process Information

In Pakistan, although some ethnic groups are more closed than others, in general there is an openness to information from the West among urban dwellers. Since education is elitist, most people process information subjectively and associatively. Islamic law offers solutions to personal problems.

Negotiation Strategies: What Pakistanis Accept as Evidence

Truth lies in one's faith in the ideologies of the Islamic law. This may be modified by one's immediate feelings about the situation but seldom by objective facts.

Value Systems: The Basis for Behavior

Pakistan is the home of Islam, and all behavior is perceived through the lens of Islamic Law. The following three sections identify the Value Systems in the predominant culture—their methods of dividing right from wrong, good from evil, and so forth.

Locus of Decision Making

The male leader is the center of decision making, but he is expected to consider the family group upon whom the decision is binding. Opinions are determined by the family, the ethnic group, and Islamic law, in that order. Membership in social organizations is the source of identity and pride, and private life is sacrificed to these memberships.

Sources of Anxiety Reduction

Pakistanis believe that their destiny is in the hands of Allah; Westerners often view this as fatalism. Security is found in strong loyalties to family and ethnic groups, but not in national unity. Rules are only guidelines, and maintaining a relationship is crucial to inner peace. A strong military presence ensures internal stability and security from outside attack.

Issues of Equality/Inequality

Inequality follows ethnic lines. The Punjabis dominate the government and the military. A great gulf exists between the rich and the poor; most people live in absolute poverty. There seems to be a tolerance for some deviation in Islamic sects, as common practice differs from formal Islamic law. Prestigious positions are reserved for males, although Pakistan is the only Islamic state to elect a female prime minister. There are strict sex roles based on the Islamic code. Men and women do not generally socialize together.

Business Practices

Appointments

PUNCTUALITY

- ◆ Punctuality: Pakistanis are not time conscious, but they expect foreign visitors to be prompt.
- ◆ Guests traditionally arrive anywhere from fifteen to sixty minutes late to a social event. However, it is the host's responsibility to be prepared for any eventuality. If a guest arrives three hours late with several uninvited family members in tow, the host must graciously accommodate them.
- ◆ The Urdu language uses the same word (*kal*) to describe both yesterday and tomorrow. Not surprisingly, Pakistanis do not share Western concepts of time and punctuality.

- The best time to schedule a business trip to Pakistan is between October and April. Avoid the months of May through August, which is the monsoon season.
- Avoid scheduling trips during major Muslim holidays, such as Ramadan, as business patterns are often interrupted. Dates for these holidays vary from year to year, so you should check with the tourist office, consulate, or embassy before scheduling your visit. (See "Contacts and Holidays.")
- Write or telex for appointments at least a month in advance. If in Pakistan, make appointments a week in advance. For local tradespeople, make appointments a day or two in advance.
- The best times for appointments with government officials and commercial establishments are morning and early afternoon.
- Business hours: 9:00 A.M. to 4:00 P.M., Saturday through Thursday, in winter and 7.30 A.M. to 2.30 P.M. in summer.
- Government office hours: 8:30 A.M. to 4:30 P.M., Saturday through Thursday. Lunch is always taken from 1:00 to 2:00 P.M.
- All offices, banks, and shops are closed on Friday, the Muslim Sabbath. Many offices close on Saturday as well.

 ## Negotiating

- Pakistani businessmen are formal, reserved, and deliberate in business negotiations.
- Business is conducted at a more leisurely pace than in the United States, but a "down to business" attitude is also characteristic.
- If you are negotiating with the government, expect to make several trips to Pakistan. The Pakistani government is the largest potential customer in the country and has many public and semipublic corporations, each with its own bureaucracy.
- Always present your business cards.
- Avoid discussing local politics, religion, Israel and Jews, and Pakistan's relationship with its neighbors (especially India).
- Never discuss or make jokes about sex.
- Pakistanis are a serious, unsmiling people. Jokes and levity have no place in Pakistani business affairs.
- Never call Muslims "Mohammedans"; they believe it makes them sound like followers of a cult figure.

- Women must be aggressive in banks and post offices or men will be waited on first.
- Be sure always to accept the tea you will be offered during an office visit. To refuse is considered rude.
- The most important units of measurement to know when discussing financial or demographic statistics are the *lakh*, which equals 100,000, and the *crore*, which is 100 *lakhs* (1,000,000).
- The official Pakistani fiscal year is July 1 to June 30.

Business Entertaining

- Foreign businesswomen should be aware that it will be very difficult for them to pick up the check when entertaining Pakistani businessmen. It may be preferable to entertain in your hotel restaurant and make prior arrangements to have the meal charged to your room.
- If you wish to invite the wife of a business counterpart to dinner, ask him discreetly if she is in *purdah* (the seclusion of women from public observation—a practice among Muslims and some Hindus).
- If you are invited to a Pakistani's home for a meal, expect to be served very late—perhaps as late as 11:00 P.M. Guests are expected to leave immediately upon completion of the meal.
- Pakistanis normally eat with their hands, but when they entertain guests, they usually provide forks and spoons. Use the fork with your left hand and the spoon in your right, pushing the food with the fork into the spoon.
- If you do eat with your hands, use only the right hand, as the left is considered unclean.
- Muslims do not eat pork.

Time
- Pakistan is five hours ahead of Greenwich Mean Time (G.M.T. + 5), or ten hours ahead of U.S. Eastern Standard Time. (E.S.T. + 10).

Protocol

Greetings
- Men usually shake hands with other men. Although strict Muslim men avoid the touch of women, most Pakistani businessmen will shake hands with a woman.
- Pakistani women do not normally shake hands with other women.
- Men may embrace male friends, and women hug and kiss upon meeting. But people of the opposite sex do not show affection in public.
- Introductions at social gatherings will be done by your host.

Titles/Forms of Address
- Pakistani naming patterns are so complex and unfamiliar that a foreigner must ask how to address a Pakistani.

- Most Pakistanis will introduce themselves with all their names but without any titles. There will usually be three names. The clan name or surname may come first or last; it will not generally be in the middle. Pakistanis should be addressed as Mr. or Mrs. plus surname. An academic or job title may substitute for the Mr. or Mrs.
- The Pakistani equivalent of "Mr." is *Sahib*. The female equivalent is (roughly) *Begum*. These titles follow the surname: Mr. Zia would be called Zia Sahib and Mrs. Hussein would be addressed as Hussein Begum. (However, she could more formally be referred to as Mr. Hussein's Begum.) These titles can also follow academic or job titles (Doctor Sahib or Director Sahib).
- Another complexity is that some Pakistani names make sense only in context, relating a first name to a second name. If the name is broken down into each part, it conveys a different meaning. For example, the name Ghulam Hussein means "slave of (the Islamic martyr) Hussein." To call him simply Ghulam is to address him as slave.
- Do not use a Pakistani's first name until you have been invited to do so.

Gestures

- Gesturing with a closed fist is considered obscene.
- Beckoning is done with the palm down rather than up, waving all the fingers toward the body.
- Using individual fingers to make gestures is considered impolite.
- Never point the bottom of your foot or shoe toward another person.
- Women should never wink.

Gifts

- You are not obliged to bring a gift when you are invited to a meal at a Pakistani's home. If you choose to do so, however, chocolates or flowers are good choices.
- Alcohol is prohibited to Muslims. Do not give alcohol as a gift unless you know that a Pakistani drinks alcohol.
- Pens, Swiss knives, watches, and transistor radios or other gadgets make good business gifts.
- If you are invited to stay at a Pakistani home, hand each servant a small tip before you leave. (Most Pakistanis have servants.)

Dress

- Men should never wear a suit and tie for business from November through March (the jacket can be omitted the rest of the year, except when dealing with government officials). For women, dressy pants are preferable to a short dress. Women should keep their arms covered.
- Men wear a dark suit (no tuxedos) at formal events; women, a street length dress or skirt.
- In casual circumstances, men wear trousers and a shirt; something modest is the key for women. Pants and a shirt or traditional Pakistani dress, *salwar kameez*, is appropriate for tourists.
- Shorts are never appropriate for women. Men should wear them only when jogging. Jeans are acceptable for either sex.

Panama

Country Background

History

Columbus reached Panama in 1502 on his fourth and final voyage to the New World. The country was first explored by Balboa in 1513.

Panamanian history has been heavily influenced by its unique location. European explorers found it to be the quickest path between the Atlantic and Pacific oceans. Panama became a transshipment point; the riches of Spain's Pacific colonies were portaged overland to Panama's Atlantic ports for shipment to Spain. Four hundred years later, the completion of the Panama Canal changed the nature of world trade. As a result, Panama has been heavily influenced by Spain and the United States, as each controlled this route of access.

Most of Central America declared its independence from Spain in 1821. Rather than going it alone, Panama joined the already-independent nation of Colombia. This union was not entirely successful, and many Panamanians sought independence from Colombia.

At the start of the twentieth century, U.S. interests focused on building a canal connecting the Atlantic and Pacific oceans. The Panama isthmus was the favored site, but Colombia refused to grant the required concessions.

Consequently, the United States supported Panamanian independence, in return for concessions (primarily the establishment of the U.S.-controlled Panama Canal Zone). The canal was finally completed in 1914. It is due to return to Panamanian control on December 31, 1999.

Since its independence from Colombia in 1903, Panama has been a republic. The military controlled the government until 1989, when dictator General Manuel Noriega was overthrown by U.S. forces and civil rule was instituted.

Type of Government

Panama is a multiparty republic, with a president, two vice presidents, a cabinet, a unicameral legislative assembly serving five year terms, and a supreme court. The president is the head of state and the head of the government.

Language

Spanish is the official language. The indigenous Amerindians speak a variety of languages. Because of the extensive U.S. influence, most Panamanians are bilingual in Spanish and English.

Religion

The majority of Panamanians (94 percent) are Roman Catholic, although Panama has no official religion. There are also small numbers of Protestants, Muslims, Hindus, and others.

Demographics

Panama's population of 2.4 million people (1990 estimates) is one of the smallest in Central America. It is 70 percent mestizo (a mix of Indian and European), 14 percent West Indian, 10 percent European, and 6 percent Amerindian.

Over a quarter of the people engage in agriculture, growing crops such as bananas, shrimp, coffee, sugar, rice, corn, sugarcane, and livestock.

t——————————————**CULTURAL NOTE**

wo concepts are helpful in understanding Panama. The first is *personalismo*, which can be defined as the trust you put in an individual and his or her personal sense of integrity (as opposed to putting that trust in a business or government). The second is *machismo*, the belief that males should be dominant (a concept that is thankfully changing).

Cultural Orientation

Cognitive Styles: How Panamanians Organize and Process Information

Panamanians are open to all kinds of information. Depending on their party, they may resist any data from the United States. They process information subjectively and associatively, and their personal involvement in any problem makes them unable to appeal to rules or laws to solve it.

Negotiation Strategies: What Panamanians Accept as Evidence

Truth is found in the immediate feelings of the person involved. However, this truth may be influenced by a strong faith in the ideologies of nationalism. Unless they have been educated abroad, Panamanians will seldom let objective facts stand in the way of their desires.

Value Systems: The Basis for Behavior

All value systems in Panama are influenced by their feelings of subjugation to U.S. interests. The following three sections identify the Value Systems in the predominant culture—their methods of dividing right from wrong, good from evil, and so forth.

Locus of Decision Making

The individual makes the decisions, but always in light of their effect on the family or group to which he or she belongs. It is difficult for Panamanians to make a decision, particularly if it is negative. Personal relationships are everything, and Panamanians strive to maintain them at all costs. A small, elite, oligarchy is now in power, and they will make decisions favorable to U.S. interests.

Sources of Anxiety Reduction

The extended family is the surest defense against a hostile and uncertain world. There is a strong work ethic, but little work seems to get done. This is a laid-back society that does not let time dictate its behavior. Panamanians are followers of strong leaders and hesitant to act on their own. The rituals and precepts of the Catholic church give structure to societal behavior.

Issues of Equality/Inequality

There is a large gap between rich and poor, a fairly large middle class, and a large lower class. Panamanians no longer believe that the powerful elite are entitled to unlimited privileges. There is an inherent trust in people, so one needs to cultivate friendships. Machismo is strong. Most believe that the ideal focus for a woman is a home, family, and children.

Business Practices

Appointments

PUNCTUALITY

- Punctuality, although not strictly adhered to in daily living, is expected in business circles—particularly with foreigners.
- If you are invited to a party, never be on time. For dinner parties, it is appropriate to arrive up to one hour late if there are several guests, and up to thirty minutes late if you are alone. At large parties, you may arrive up to two hours late.

- Remember that many Europeans and South Americans write the day first, then the month, then the year (e.g., December 3, 1999, is written 3.12.99). This is the case in Panama.
- Business hours are 8:00 A.M. to 6:00 P.M., Monday through Friday. Government hours are 8:00 A.M. to noon and 12:30 P.M. to 4:30 P.M., Monday through Friday.
- Make appointments by either mail or telex two to four weeks in advance of your arrival in Panama.

 Negotiating

- Contract negotiations take place at a much slower pace than in the United States. Be patient with delays, and be prepared to travel to Panama more than once to finalize a transaction.
- Business is conducted among friends in Panama. Therefore, spend time establishing a relationship with your counterpart before jumping into business discussions. Emphasize the personal compatibility of the two companies and develop a high level of trust, rather than focusing solely on the logical bottom line.
- Although more women are moving into higher managerial positions, they are still relatively rare in such positions. Women should therefore emphasize the

fact that they are part of a team from a company that is strongly committed to doing business in Panama.

- Have business cards and other material printed in Spanish as well as English. Although a Panamanian may speak English well, he or she may read it with some difficulty.
- Adjust your starting price to allow a margin for bargaining.
- Use graphs and other visual aids in making presentations.
- Latin Americans tend to be status conscious. At least one member of the negotiating team should be from a high level of management.

L—————————————————**CULTURAL NOTE**

atin Americans are sometimes sensitive about U.S. influence in their countries. Be careful not to remark how "Americanized" the people are, or refer to U.S. citizens as "Americans," since everyone from North, Central, and South America is an American.

- Panamanians believe in the intrinsic worth of the individual, and treat one another with respect and dignity, regardless of a person's social standing or material wealth. Therefore, it is very important not to pull rank or publicly criticize a person.
- To avoid embarrassment, Panamanians rarely disagree with anyone in public. This can extend to a foreign business person trying to close a deal; a Panamanian may tell a foreigner "yes" simply to be polite. Lukewarm affirmatives, like "maybe" or "we will see," are polite ways of saying "no." A "yes" is not final until a contract is signed.
- A familiarity with Panamanian history, sites, culture, and art will impress your counterparts.
- Senior officials and the elderly are given preferential treatment. They should be greeted first, and may be served before you in a line.

 Business Entertaining

- Always stay at top hotels and entertain your guests at premier restaurants. Ask your client's secretary about any preferences the client may have for restaurants or clubs.
- Good topics of conversation include sports, travel, and local cultural events. Avoid discussions of the Canal Zone and local politics.
- Foreign businesswomen should always include spouses in invitations to business dinners.
- In order to pay for either a lunch or dinner with male clients, women should arrange to take care of the bill privately with the waiter. If the check is brought to the table, the men will strongly resist letting her pay. Give the waiter your credit card beforehand or, if you are hosting a dinner at your hotel, arrange to have the charge added to your hotel bill.

C—————————————————**CULTURAL NOTE**

itizens of the U.S. working in Panama have often remained separate from Panamanians in business and social networks. In order to encourage better cultural and business ties, U.S. businesses should plan and support fully integrated functions.

Time
- Local time is 5 hours behind Greenwich Mean Time (G.M.T. - 5). This is the same as U.S. Eastern Standard Time.

Protocol

Greetings

- Men usually shake hands in greeting. Women will often pat each other on the right forearm or shoulder instead of shaking hands. If they are friends, they may hug or kiss each other on the cheek.
- At parties, it is customary to greet and shake hands with each person in the room.

Titles/Forms of Address

- Titles are very important and should be used whenever possible. When addressing someone directly, use the title alone and do not include a last name (*Profesor*, *Doctor*, and so forth). First names are used only by persons on a familiar basis.
- Persons who do not have professional titles should be addressed as Mr., Mrs., or Miss, plus their surnames. In Spanish these are
  - Mr. = *Señor*
  - Mrs. = *Señora*
  - Miss = *Señorita*
- See the Cultural Note at the beginning of Panama.

Gestures

- Because of the long-standing U.S. presence in Panama, most North American gestures (and insults) are understood.

Gifts

- Gifts are not required in a business setting. However, after the first few meetings, you may want to bring a gift from your home state, such as a local craft or illustrated book. Other good gifts include small electronic gadgets or expensive liquor.
- Gifts are appropriate if you are invited to a Panamanian home or if you are visiting rural areas. Some good options are chocolates, wine, scotch, or local crafts from home. Gifts are not expected, however, and it is enough to extend your thanks and to invite your hosts to a meal in return.

Dress

- Men should wear a conservative business suit for work. Panamanian businessmen in higher positions wear suits; others wear *camisillas* (a lightweight, open-necked shirt that is not tucked inside the trousers). Women should wear a skirt and blouse or a dress.
- Pants, including jeans, and a shirt are appropriate casual wear in the city. Shorts should not be worn by either sex, and women should avoid any revealing clothing. It is rare in rural areas to see women wearing pants, and it may draw some attention.

Paraguay

CULTURAL NOTE

*t*ry to avoid offering any political opinions. When you cannot, wait until your Paraguayan counterpart has voiced his or hers, then choose a position that does not disagree. "Going along" has
been the key to success in Paraguay for many years.

Paraguay has not been known for its political tolerance. Paraguayans in positions of authority have never
had to be tolerant; under the Stroessner regime political dissidents were harassed or thrown in prison.

Country Background

History

The city of Asunción, which today is the capital of Paraguay, was founded in
1537. For a time, Asunción was the capital city of the Spanish colonial provinces of
Paraguay and Río de la Plata (encompassing virtually the bottom third of the continent). But Paraguay lacked the gold and silver sought by the Spanish, so the country was not developed.

A major social experiment was instituted by the Jesuit missionaries, who established a series of self-sufficient missions among the Indians, the famous *reducciónes* (reductions). This pitted the Jesuits against the Spanish-descended settlers,
who wanted cheap Indian labor for their plantations. Unfortunately, the Jesuits
were expelled from the continent in 1776; the *reducciónes* failed, and the Indians
fled into the jungle or were sold into slavery. Power shifted away from Asunción—
notably to Buenos Aires.

Paraguay gained its independence from Spain in 1811 without violence. From
1814 to 1840, its elected "supreme dictator," Dr. José Gaspar Rodríguez de Francia,
cut Paraguay off from the outside world. Paraguay became totally self-sufficient, and
intermarriage with the Indians was encouraged. As a result, Paraguay evolved into a
highly nationalistic, ethnically homogeneous state.

At the time of its independence, Paraguay was about a third larger than it is
today. Part of its land was lost when it became involved in territorial wars with all
of its neighbors. Had Argentina and Brazil been able to agree upon a partition,
Paraguay would have ceased to exist. As it was, the wars of 1865-1870 and 1932-
1935 devastated the population. An astonishing 80 percent of the men in Paraguay
were slain in the first war alone.

In 1954, General Alfredo Stroessner took control of Paraguay in a coup. His reign lasted until another coup, led by General Andrés Rodríguez Pedotti, ousted him in February 1989. Rodríguez was elected president of Paraguay in May 1989, and he restored some civil and political rights.

Type of Government

Technically a constitutional republic, Paraguay has a powerful executive branch, and has usually been under the thumb of one strongman after another. However, Paraguay has managed a peaceful transition of power from one elected president to another since 1989. The president is both the chief of state and head of the government.

Government is divided between the executive branch (headed by a president who is elected for a five-year term), an independent judiciary, and a two-house legislature. Voting is mandatory for all citizens between the ages of eighteen and sixty.

CULTURAL NOTE

Stroessner's thirty five-year reign serves as a sort of paradigm for the Paraguayan condition. There was peace and a modicum of prosperity. Communism was seen as a dire threat, and no effort was spared to keep it out of Paraguay. If most of the people are poor agriculturalists (50 percent work on farms or ranches or in forestry), they are nevertheless proud to be Paraguayans.

Language

Paraguay is unusual in that it has two official languages: Spanish and Guarani (a language of the indigenous Amerindian population). While most writing is done in Spanish, there is some literature in the Guarani language.

Religion

Roman Catholicism is the state religion of Paraguay, and is adhered to by about 97 percent of the populace. The state pays all church salaries and controls all church appointments. However, religious freedom is guaranteed, and the remaining 3 percent are members of Mennonite and other Protestant denominations.

Demographics

Most of the 4.66 million Paraguayans do not live in the cities. Although the population is concentrated in 40 percent of the land area of the country, this rural dispersion makes it difficult to provide social services. Health services in the cities are adequate, but malaria remains a serious problem.

Today, 95 percent of the population is mestizo (mixed European and Guarani Indian ancestry), making Paraguay the most homogeneous nation in South America. The minority population is very small, consisting mostly of Italian, German, and Japanese settlers.

Cultural Orientation

Cognitive Styles: How Paraguayans Oranize and Process Information

In Paraguay very strict government controls have insulated the people from most outside information. Paraguayans process information subjectively and associatively. This makes their solutions subjective and particular, rather than rule-based or law-based.

Negotiation Strategies: What Paraguayans Accept as Evidence

Truth is found in the subjective feelings of the moment. This truth may be influenced by faith in the ideologies of nationalism and religion. One seldom sees objective facts used to prove a point.

Value Systems: The Basis for Behavior

Paraguay has the most homogeneous population (95 percent mestizos) in Latin America. The following three sections identify the Value Systems in the predominant culture—their methods of dividing right from wrong, good from evil, and so forth.

Locus of Decision Making

The male is the decision maker, but he always keeps the interests of the family or group in mind. One's self-identity is based on one's family genealogy and position in the social system. Decisions will always favor friends or family over expertise. There has always been a strong leader (usually a dictator) to make the decisions for the nation.

Sources of Anxiety Reduction

Family and kin, not the community, are the center of the social universe. They give stability and security to the individual. Godparents are a very important part of the web of kinship. Paraguayans like to follow strong leaders, and their nationalism gives them a sense of security. Catholicism is an essential component of social life, with its rituals, fiestas, and holidays all providing continuity and stability.

Issues of Equality/Inequality

There is a tradition of authoritarian rule and a concomitant lack of democratic institutions. There is an extreme contrast between the elite (educated, prosperous, city-based, and city-bred) and the poor. The basic social dichotomy is between small farmers and a narrow stratum of elite families who control all the resources. Machismo is strong.

Business Practices

Appointments

PUNCTUALITY

♦ While punctuality is not a high priority for Paraguayans, the North American is expected to be on time.
♦ Despite their formality, business meetings rarely start on time. It would be unrealistic to expect your Paraguayan counterparts to be prompt.

- Remember that many Europeans and South Americans write the day first, then the month, then the year (e.g., December 3, 1999, is written 3.12.99). This is the case in Paraguay.
- Mornings are best for appointments.
- Business hours are generally 7:00 A.M. to noon and 3:00 to 6:00 P.M., Monday through Friday. Some business people keep office hours on Saturday mornings as well.
- Government offices are open six days a week, but only in the mornings, from 7:00 A.M. to noon, Monday through Saturday.

- Shop hours, in general, are 7:30 A.M. to noon and 3:30 to 7:30 P.M., Monday through Friday.
- The best time of year to conduct business in Paraguay is from June through October. Little business is accomplished during the two weeks before and after Christmas and Easter, or during Carnival. December through February is vacation time in Paraguay, as is May around Paraguay's Independence Day.

 ## *Negotiating*

- The pace of business negotiations in Latin America is usually much slower than in the United States. This is especially true in Paraguay, where the pace can seem extremely slow to North Americans.
- Most Paraguayan men dislike confronting or offending women. Thus, it can be useful to include a female business representative on your team.
- Personal relationships are far more important than corporate ones in Paraguay. Each time your company changes its representative in Paraguay, you will virtually be starting from scratch. A new relationship must be built up before business can proceed.
- Don't assume that each portion of a contract is settled as it is agreed upon. Until the entire contract is signed, each portion is subject to renegotiation.
- While many of the executives you meet will speak English, check beforehand as to whether or not you will need an interpreter.
- All printed material you hand out should be translated into Spanish. This goes for everything from business cards to reports to brochures. You are not expected to translate material into Guarani.
- Paraguayans are great sports fans. Talking about sports is always a good way to open a conversation. Soccer (called *fútbol*) is the most popular sport. U.S.-style football is *fútbol americano*. Basketball, volleyball, and horse racing are also popular.
- Most people in Paraguay are very proud of their country's massive engineering projects, especially their hydroelectric dams. The Itaipu Dam, a joint project of Paraguay and Brazil, is the world's largest. Inquiring about such projects is a safe topic of conversation, and one that will please your counterpart.

 ## *Business Entertaining*

- Business lunches are rare in Paraguay, as the majority of people go home for lunch. However, some Paraguayan executives are beginning to work through the afternoon; consequently, they may consider a business lunch.
- Most business entertaining is done over dinner, which is held late, often at 9:00 or 10:00 P.M. Indeed, most restaurants will not serve dinner before 9:00 P.M.
- Dinner is considered a social occasion; don't try to talk business unless your counterpart brings it up.
- Paraguayans love to have long dinners under the stars. Many restaurants have shows that last until after midnight. There are also several casinos.

 CULTURAL NOTE

t a gathering such as a party, it is important to shake hands with everyone, both as you arrive and when you leave.

- Paraguay is a major cattle producer, so expect a lot of beef to be served in restaurants.

Time
- Paraguay is three hours behind Greenwich Mean Time (G.M.T. - 3), making it two hours ahead of U.S. Eastern Standard Time (E.S.T. + 2).

Protocol

 ### Greetings
- Except when greeting close friends, it is traditional to shake hands firmly with both men and women.
- Close male friends shake hands or embrace upon meeting; men kiss close female friends. Close female friends usually kiss each other.
- Close friends of either sex may walk arm in arm.

 ### Titles/Forms of Address
- Remember that Paraguay has two official languages: Spanish and Guaraní. However, all the business people you meet will be fluent in Spanish, so Spanish titles may be used.
- Most people you meet should be addressed with a title and their surname. Only children, family members, and close friends address each other by their first names.
- Persons who do not have professional titles should be addressed as Mr., Mrs., or Miss, plus their surname. In Spanish, these are
    - Mr. = *Señor*
    - Mrs. = *Señora*
    - Miss = *Señorita*
- Most Hispanics have two surnames: one from their father, which is listed first, followed by one from their mother. Only the father's surname is commonly used when addressing someone; e.g., Señor Juan Antonio Martínez García is addressed as Señor Martínez and Señorita Ana María Gutiérrez Herrera is addressed as Señorita Gutiérrez. When a woman marries, she usually adds her husband's surname and goes by that surname. If the two people in the above example married, she would be known as Señora Ana María Gutiérrez Herrera de Martínez. Most people would refer to her as Señora de Martínez or, less formally, Señora Martínez.
- When a person has a title, it is important to use the title followed by the surname. Everyone who graduates from a university is entitled to be addressed as *Licenciado* (pronounced lee-sehn-SYAH-doh). A Ph.D. or a physician is called *Doctor*. Teachers prefer the title *Profesor*, while engineers go by *Ingeniero* and architects are *Arquitecto*.

Gestures

- As in much of Latin America, people converse at a much closer distance than do U.S. citizens. Restrain yourself from trying to back away; a Paraguayan will probably step forward and close the distance.
- The U.S. "thumbs up" gesture means "O.K." in Paraguay.
- The U.S. "O.K." sign—thumb and index finger in a circle—should be avoided. When done with the wrist bent and the other fingers pointed toward the ground, the gesture is obscene.
- Winking in Paraguay has sexual connotations.
- Tapping one's chin with the top of the index finger means "I don't know."
- A backwards tilt of the head means "I forgot."
- Sit only on chairs, not on a ledge, box, or table. Manners dictate an erect sitting posture; don't slump.
- Don't rest your feet on anything other than a footstool or rail; it is very impolite to place them upon a table.

 Gifts

- Gift giving is problematical in Paraguay, because corruption was widespread during the former regime.
- As in any country, any gift given should be of high quality. If the item is produced by your corporation, the corporate name or logo should appear discreetly, not be emblazoned over the whole surface.
- Avoid giving knives; they symbolize the severing of a friendship.
- Gifts are not expected when invited to a Paraguayan home. However, a gift of flowers, chocolates, wine, or whiskey would certainly be appreciated.

CULTURAL NOTE

realize that Paraguay is a major trading center with plenty of affluent consumers. You may have to search to find something from the United States that isn't for sale in Paraguay. In fact, many gifts can often be bought at a cheaper price in Paraguay if you are prepared to bargain with the merchants.

 Dress

- Business dress in Paraguay is conservative: dark suits and ties for men; white blouses and dark suits or skirts for women. Women are not required to wear nylons during the summer. Men should follow their Paraguayan colleagues' lead as to wearing ties and removing jackets in the summer.
- Dress to handle the heat and humidity of Paraguayan summers. Most local people wear cotton. Don't forget that the seasons in South America are the reverse of those in North America.
- Sweaters are recommended during the winter. Although Paraguay never gets very cold, the heating in buildings is often poor.
- Whatever the season, be prepared for sudden changes in weather and temperature.

- Men may wear the same dark suit for formal occasions (such as the theater, a formal dinner party, and so forth), but women are expected to wear an evening gown. The invitation will specify that the affair is formal.
- Both men and women wear pants as casual wear. If you are meeting business associates, avoid jeans and wear a jacket or blazer. Women should not wear shorts.

CULTURAL NOTE

*d*on't wear anything outside that can be damaged by water during carnival. Drenching pedestrians is a favorite carnival pastime of the young.

LIMA

Peru

CULTURAL NOTE

*P*eru is rich in natural resources, some of which are intriguing to international oil, gas, and space industries. A major natural gas site exists in Camisea, (an eastern jungle), and the high, clear characteristics of Peru's *altiplano* are attractive for space observation and launching concerns.

Country Background

History

Peru was a center of the powerful Inca Empire until Spanish conquistadores under Francisco Pizarro invaded in 1532. Peru then became the richest and most powerful of the Spanish colonies in South America.

Peru declared its independence from Spain in 1821. But the war of independence lasted several years, and a subsequent war with Spain lasted from 1864 to 1866. Independence did not bring a stable government. The first hundred years of Peru's existence is a record of one revolution after another.

Although Peru has had democratically elected governments since 1980, it is still seeking stability and freedom from the threat of revolution. Terrorist activities continue from two major insurgent organizations, the *Sendero Luminoso* (Shining Path) and the *Tupac Amaru Revolutionary Movement* (MRTA).

Type of Government

The Republic of Peru is a unitary multiparty republic with a single legislative house, the Congress. The president is the chief of state and head of the government. In 1991, President Alberto Fujimori dissolved the Congress and suspended the Constitution in an attempt to stabilize the economy.

Language

Peru has two official languages: Spanish and Quechua (an Amerindian language). Besides Quechua, another Indian language, Aymara, is widely spoken in the southern highlands. Although many business people understand English, all written materials are expected to be presented in either Spanish or Spanish and English.

Religion

The Spanish brought Roman Catholicism to Peru, and over 90 percent of the population is considered Catholic. About 5 percent belong to various Protestant faiths.

Religion plays a significant part in Peruvian life, and often reflects a mix of traditional Indian beliefs and Christianity.

Demographics

Nearly one-third of Peru's twenty-three million (1993 estimates) people live in the Lima area. Approximately 40 percent of the population is under fifteen years old.

CULTURAL NOTE

*P*eru is an ethnically diverse country, with descendants from the Incan Empire, Europe, Africa, Japan, and China. Its culture is heavily influenced by two major groups: the Spanish conquistadores and the indigenous Incas.

Cultural Orientation

Cognitive Styles: How Peruvians Organize and Process Information

The culture of Peru is open to most information, but attitudes are not changed easily. Except for the highly educated, information is processed subjectively and associatively. Personal involvement in problems and solutions is more important than having a rule or law that dictates one's approach to life.

Negotiation Strategies: What Peruvians Accept as Evidence

One's personal feelings about a situation are the basis for truth. In Peru, the ideologies that may influence the truth are those of elitism and religion. Faith in either of these may affect the truth. Objective facts do not carry much weight.

Value Systems: The Basis for Behavior

The value systems of Peru are built around ideologies of an elitist system in which each level is controlled by the next step in the hierarchy—only those deemed fit can enter. The following three sections identify the Value Systems in the predominant culture—their methods of dividing right from wrong, good from evil, and so forth.

Locus of Decision Making

Individuals are responsible for their own decisions, but the best interests of the families or groups are dominating factors. A small upper class of the elite oligarchy controls the resources of the country. Personal relationships are more important than one's expertise in business associations. One's self-identity is based on the social system and the history of one's extended family.

Sources of Anxiety Reduction

At every level of society, the family is the cornerstone of relationships. Kinships define the principal areas of trust and cooperation. At the highest levels of society, kinship and marriage reinforce and solidify political and economic alliances.

A system called "the cargo" consists of a series of ranked offices, each of which has specific duties attached to it. Participation in "the cargo" system is essential to validate one's status and wealth in the eyes of the community and to give a person a feeling of security.

Issues of Equality/Inequality

All classes have ranks within them stratified along lines of deep-seated inequalities. Education is the gatekeeper to social advancement in the Peruvian elitist system. It appears that the power holders try to maintain the large gap between the rich and the poor. Machismo is quite strong. There are restrictions on women's social and work behavior.

Business Practices

Appointments

──────────────────────────────────── **PUNCTUALITY**

♦ Punctuality is becoming more important in both private and public sectors. However, do not be put off if your Peruvian contact is late.

- Remember that many Europeans and South Americans write the day first, then the month, then the year (e.g., December 3, 1999, is written 3.12.99). This is the case in Peru.
- Make appointments at least two weeks in advance. Upon arrival, do not make impromptu calls at business or government offices.
- Appointments should be scheduled in the morning and may involve a lunch invitation, so do not plan more than one meeting each morning.
- The workweek is longer in Peru, since businesses are often open six days a week. Business hours generally run from around 8:00 A.M. to 5:00 or 6:00 P.M. People may return home for lunch, so offices sometimes close between 1:00 and 3:00 P.M.
- Government offices and banks work different hours in the summer (January to March) and winter (April to December).
- Many Peruvians go on vacation between January and March, and two weeks before and after Christmas and Easter. Therefore, try not to schedule major appointments then or during national holidays.

 Negotiating

- During negotiations, be prepared to discuss all aspects of the contract concurrently, rather than discussing individual aspects sequentially, and be prepared for seemingly extraneous data to be reviewed and re-reviewed. Try to be as flexible as possible; ask questions and avoid confrontations.
- Include a variety of materials in your presentations (computer demonstrations, attractive graphics, and so forth).

─────────────────────────── **CULTURAL NOTE**

*a*bove all else, do not switch your company's players during the negotiation process, since this may result in the Peruvian negotiation team's calling a halt to the process. Peruvians relate to the person they have come to know, not to the organization.

- If you plan to invite your prospects to dinner or lunch during the negotiations, ask only the vital players. After the deal is completed, invite everyone who was involved in the project.
- You may be received with exceptional warmth since Peruvians are very eager for foreign investment.
- Peruvians may be more comfortable discussing their Spanish heritage than their Indian background; therefore, it may be unwise to inquire about an individual's ancestry. Also avoid making remarks about the Peruvian government, terrorists, or politics in general.
- Peruvians value personal relationships, and relate more to an individual business associate than to a corporation. When approaching a prospect in Peru, it is always better to establish the connection through a local mediator, or *enchufado*. Your *enchufado* will be able to navigate through the maze of networks that make up Peruvian business and government.
- Have your business cards and all company materials printed in both Spanish and English.

 Business Entertaining

- Entertain at prestigious restaurants, and include spouses in the invitations if it will be a dinner.
- Discussing business over dinner is not common.
- Most dinner invitations will be for 9:00 P.M., which means dinner will probably be served around 10:30 P.M. Arrive around thirty minutes late, and stay about thirty minutes after dinner ends.
- Imported alcohol is very expensive.
- Stay at a first-class hotel, and feel free to use it to host a meeting or luncheon, particularly if you will be communicating with the United States by fax or telex. (Be careful not to touch anything metal when taking a shower, since shower heads are connected to electrical heating units.)
- An invitation to tea at a private residence is usually for 6:00 to 8:00 P.M.

Time
- Peru is five hours behind Greenwich Mean Time (G.M.T. - 5), or the same as U.S. Eastern Standard Time.

Protocol

 Greetings

- Men and women shake hands both in greeting and in parting.
- Once a friendship has been established, men may greet each other with a hug, and women may kiss one another on the cheek.

 Titles/Forms of Address

- Titles are very important in Peru. Address a person directly by using his or her title, such as *Profesor*, or *Doctor* and last name or surname. First names are used only by people on familiar terms. Wait for your counterpart to intitiate this switch to first names.

- Persons who do not have professional titles should be addressed as Mr., Mrs., or Miss, plus their surnames. In Spanish these are
  - Mr. = *Señor*
  - Mrs. = *Señora*
  - Miss = *Señorita*
- Most Hispanics have two surnames: one from their father, which is listed first, followed by one from their mother. Only the father's surname is commonly used when addressing someone; e.g., Señor Víctor Antonio Nuñez Martínez is addressed as Señor Nuñez and Señorita María Elena Gutiérrez Herrera is addressed as Señorita Gutiérrez. When a woman marries, she usually adds her husband's surname and goes by that surname. If the two people in the above example married, she would be known as Señora María Elena Gutiérrez Herrera de Nuñez. Most people would refer to her as Señora de Nuñez or, less formally, Señora Nuñez.

Gestures

- Peruvians communicate in close proximity. When they stand nearby, do not back away, as you will offend them. And do not be surprised if your Peruvian associates take your arm as you walk — men often walk arm in arm with other men, as do women with other women.
- To signal "come here," hold your hand vertically and wave it back and forth with the palm facing out, or put your palm face down, and wave the fingers back and forth.
- Crossing your legs by resting the ankle of one leg on the knee of the other is inappropriate; however, you may cross your legs at the knee.
- When eating out, be sure to rest both hands on the table, rather than leaving one in your lap.
- "I'm thinking" is represented by tapping your head.
- "Go away" is shown by holding your hand flat and flicking the fingers toward the irritation.
- "Pay me" is signified by an eyebrow raise, or by sweeping your hand toward your body.

Gifts

- Giving a gift is not required at the first meeting. Instead, buy lunch for your prospect to cement the relationship, then consider the individual's tastes for future gift giving.
- Wait until after the formal meeting is over to present a gift. A relaxed social situation is the best time.
- A gift with a significant connection to your home state will be remembered (for example, a Texas belt buckle, native folk art, or an illustrated book).
- Keep company logos small.
- Appropriate gifts are ones that "represent" the firm; e.g., a cigarette company might present lighters that incorporate stone quarried from the state where it is headquarted.
- Small electronic gadgets, such as calculators, electronic address books, and day-timers, are appropriate, particularly since import taxes would normally

have to be paid on these items. Have items customized with your contact's initials when possible.

- Inexpensive cameras and name brand pens are appreciated, as are ties, scarves, or other accessories in natural fabrics. (It is often too hot for manmade weaves.)
- When invited to a home, bring wine, whiskey or other liquors, or chocolates. Bring gifts for the children: U.S. university T-shirts, caps, cassette tapes, and so forth.
- Sending roses after a dinner is appropriate if they are not red (these have romantic connotations). Any other flower is regarded as cheap.
- Avoid sending thirteen of anything, any purple or black objects (which have connotations of religious ceremonies), knives (which can signify cutting off a relationship), or handkerchiefs (which represent grief).
- If you intensely admire one of a Peruvian's possessions, he or she may feel obligated to present it to you as a gift.
- There are some social idiosyncrasies in Peru related to the "caste" system. Various levels of family history, social standing, and education may influence the gifts exchanged. Be aware of these sociological issues.

 Dress

- For business meetings, always dress in formal, well-tailored suits.
- Invitations to official parties normally require tuxedos and cocktail dresses or evening gowns.
- Foreigners should not wear native Indian clothing, even if they intend to honor the local culture.

CULTURAL NOTE

*I*n the United States, gift giving for business is less commonplace than in other countries. U.S. gift giving often symbolizes an emotional attachment and is done only at Christmas or at retirement parties. However, in Latin America, giving gifts is a normal part of business protocol.

Peruvians sometimes consider it ironic that the U.S. business people feel hesitant about giving a well-thought-out gift to a Peruvian prospect or client, yet will insist on being overtly friendly by immediately calling the Peruvian by his or her first name. (Among Peruvians, a first-time basis would not be normal until gifts have been exchanged.)

Philippines

CULTURAL NOTE

Culturally, Filipinos are unique. Although the majority are of Malay stock, most have Hispanic surnames, are Roman Catholic (this is the only Christian nation in Asia), and speak some English which makes the Philippines the fourth-largest English-speaking country in the world, after the United States, the United Kingdom, and India.

Country Background

History

The Philippine Islands have been inhabited throughout human history. To this day, one can find human cultures at every level of technology living there. Many Filipinos live in modern, bustling Pacific Rim cities, while others live in isolated tropical jungles at a stone-age level of civilization. (The Tasaday tribe of hunter-gatherers on Mindanao Island only came into contact with the outside world in 1971.)

This cultural diversity began in the tenth century A.D., when the Chinese began to trade with the Filipinos. Eventually, some Chinese stayed in the Philippines. Although the ethnic Chinese today represent only 3 percent of the Philippine population, they control about half of the nation's commerce and banking. While many prominent Filipinos have Chinese ancestry (including Corazon Aquino), there is considerable hostility toward the Chinese dominance of business.

Arab traders introduced Islam to the Philippines in the fourteenth century. Concentrated in the southern islands, these Muslims fiercely resisted both Spanish and American authority. Their refusal to yield to colonial overlords is a source of pride to many Filipinos, Muslim and Christian alike.

The Portuguese navigator Magellan led a Spanish fleet to the Philippines in 1521 and named the islands after King Philip II of Spain. The Spaniards subsequently ruled for 350 years and brought Catholicism to the islands, as well as the Latino attitudes and traditions that are now a major part of the Filipino makeup. Filipino nationalism also manifested itself under Spanish domination; for example, Filipino-born clergy agitated for equality with the Spanish clergy in the nineteenth century. The Spanish language and culture never became totally dominant in the Philippines, perhaps because Spain did not rule directly. The Philippines were overseen indirectly, via Mexico.

After the Spanish-American War, the Philippines were ceded to the United States in 1899. Already fighting against their Spanish overlords, the Filipinos had no desire to be ruled by another colonial power. The so-called Philippine insurrection against the United States lasted over twelve years and cost the lives of hundreds of thousands of Filipinos. But after the war, the United States brought infrastructure development to the country. It was in the U.S.-built public schools that English became the language of education. Under U.S. control, the nation became the Commonwealth of the Philippines in 1935.

The Japanese conquered the Philippines in 1941, demonstrating to the Filipinos that the United States was not unbeatable. The Philippines were liberated in 1945 by Allied troops, both U.S. and Filipino. Full independence for the Philippines came in 1946.

Type of Government

The Philippines have been inhabited since before recorded human history, but only since 1946 has the Republic of the Philippines been an independent nation. Many Filipinos see their history as a struggle against foreign domination, first by Spain, then by the United States.

The Republic of the Philippines is a unitary republic patterned after the United States. The president of the Philippines is both head of state and head of the government. There are two legislative houses: a 24-seat Senate and a 250-seat House of Representatives (50 of the House seats are nonelective, allocated to various sectoral interests).

The first Philippine constitution dates back to 1935, when the Commonwealth of the Philippines came into being under control of the United States. Japan conquered the Philippines in the Second World War, and the United States realized that it could not reassert control over the Philippines after the war. The Philippines became an independent republic, although the United States maintained a sizable military presence.

U.S. military bases were a source of contention, a constant reminder of colonial domination. Furthermore, the United States exerted tremendous influence, as when it helped to keep the corrupt dictatorship of Ferdinand Marcos in power. The end of the cold war reduced the importance of the two major U.S. bases in the Philippines, Clark Air Force Base and Subic Bay Naval Base. While the U.S. and the Philippine governments were negotiating over the future of the bases, the Mount Pinotubo volcano erupted in June 1991. Buried under volcanic ash, Clark Air Force Base was rendered unusable. A new deal was negotiated to allow Subic Bay Naval Base to remain open. President Corazon Aquino agreed to the deal, but the Philippine Senate rejected it. The Philippine people themselves were split over the issue; had it been put to a referendum, the majority might have voted to allow U.S. forces to remain at Subic Bay Naval Base.

Now the Philippines face a future relatively free of foreign influences, but without the millions of dollars the U.S. military presence pumped into the economy. The country was already struggling with high unemployment, a stagnant economy, and a huge debt load, not to mention recent earthquake and volcano disasters.

Language

English and Pilipino (based upon Tagalog) are the official languages of the Republic of the Philippines, although over seventy languages and dialects are spoken.

Religion

Approximately 83 percent of Filipinos profess to be Roman Catholics, but traditional beliefs remain strong. While only 9 percent of Filipinos are Protestant, that percentage is growing, with Evangelical sects growing fastest. Some 6 percent belong to the Philippine Independent Church, a Catholic sect that has broken with

Rome. Muslims number about 5 percent of the population, and are concentrated in the southern islands.

Demographics

Today, the sixty-two million Filipinos are approaching an even split between urban and rural life: 43 percent live in the cities, 57 percent in the country. The population of Manila, the capital and largest city, is about ten million.

Cultural Orientation

Cognitive Styles: How Filipinos Organize and Process Information

In the Philippines one will find a culture that loves to converse. Filipinos are open to information but do not change their attitudes readily. Because most of their education is by rote, they tend to process information subjectively and associatively. They become personally involved in problems rather than using rules and laws to solve them.

Negotiation Strategies: What Filipinos Accept as Evidence

Most of the truth comes from immediate feelings. Although some truths may rest on faith in ideologies, such as those of the Catholic church, very few can be traced back to objective facts.

Value Systems: The Basis for Behavior

The culture of the Philippines is rich in diverse influences. China, the Muslims, Spain, and the United States all left their marks on this culture. The following three sections identify the Value Systems in the predominant culture—their methods of dividing right from wrong, good from evil, and so forth.

Locus of Decision Making

Individuals act in the context of a group (the family is the most important group). Thus, they must seek the consensus of the group, as the individual never feels that he or she has the final say on anything. Decisions are made from a relational perspective. Filipinos must get to know you, and this involves asking about your family and personal background. Rather than presenting their own ideas, they more often react to the input of others. It is difficult for them to confront and to give an outright "no."

Sources of Anxiety Reduction

The nuclear and extended family is the main source of support and stability. The whole family may be shamed by the action of one member. Much of the stability of life is found in the adherence to tradition, especially the observance of rituals that maintain relationships. Many of these are connected with religion. Interpersonal relationships bring with them a sense of obligation. Reciprocity in relationships is practiced on all levels, and paying one's obligations binds the persons involved more closely.

Issues of Equality/Inequality

Filipino politics is a system that serves its players, not the people. However, Filipinos are strongly in favor of democracy, individual freedom, education, and freedom of the press. Filipinos are very status-conscious. This sometimes extends to issues of race—for example, the lighter the skin, the higher the status. Whites can often get things done that darker-skinned people cannot. Things that are foreign can be seen as better than indigenous things. There is a preoccupation with chastity and safety.

Business Practices

Appointments

PUNCTUALITY

- ◆ Foreigners are expected to be on time for all business appointments. Filipinos tend to be reasonably punctual for business meetings.
- ◆ Most Filipino social events do not begin at the stated time. Indeed, it would be impolite to arrive on time to a party. The more important the guests, the later they are expected to arrive. This could range from fifteen minutes to as much as two hours late. In general, foreign executives should arrive fifteen to thirty minutes late.
- ◆ The exception to the socially correct delay is the Filipino wedding. Guests are expected to arrive on time. Only the bride may be late.

- Appointments can be scheduled up to one month prior to your arrival in the Philippines.
- When introducing yourself to a new customer, letters of introduction from either friends or business associates can be useful.
- English is the language of most business transactions and virtually all business or government correspondence in the Philippines.
- Without introductions, it is very difficult to meet with decision makers, who are always at the top of organizations.
- In order to reach the decision maker, one may have to meet many times with subordinates. Not only must you progress through levels of influence, but you must progress in meetings through levels of formality—from introductions at social events, to semiofficial luncheons, to scheduled business meetings.
- A skilled go-between is often hired to cut through several levels of interference to get to the decision maker.
- Mid-mornings or mid- to late afternoons are usually best for appointments.
- Business hours are generally from 8:00 A.M. to 5:00 P.M., Monday through Friday. Most offices close during the lunch break, which is usually from 12:00 noon to 1:00 P.M. but can easily stretch for two hours. Some offices may open from 8:00 A.M. to 12:00 noon on Saturdays.
- Government offices keep an 8:00 A.M. to 5:00 P.M. schedule Monday through Friday. Many senior government officials work late, and some accept phone calls after hours—but only at their offices, never at home. (By contrast, many business people can frequently be reached at home.)

Negotiating

—————————————————————————**CULTURAL NOTE**

*f*ilipinos smile constantly. However, as with the Japanese, smiles and laughter do not necessarily indicate happiness or amusement.

Filipinos may smile or laugh in situations that Westerners consider inappropriate. Smiles hide embarrassment and discord. Filipino businessmen may laugh at the most serious part of a business meeting; a Filipino physician may smile while telling a patient he is seriously ill.

- While foreigners are not expected to smile as much as Filipinos, they are expected to restrain their temper. As in Japan, one who expresses anger in public has shamefully lost face and respect. Furthermore, since the Philippines is a more violent country than Japan, expressing anger at someone can easily provoke a similar response. Foreigners can unintentionally push a Filipino into a public outburst, since the Filipino feels he must act to regain his honor—whatever the cost. If you must reprimand a Filipino employee, do it calmly and in private.
- Filipinos consider everyone worthy of respect. The more important you are, the more you are expected to be humble and generous. Even the requests of a Filipino beggar are rejected with the phrase *Patawarin po* (Forgive me, sir). The Filipino is literally apologizing to the beggar for not giving anything. If you brusquely dismiss a beggar, you are risking a loss of face.
- Speak in quiet, gentle tones. Filipinos revere harmony. The only time you are likely to hear loud Filipinos is when they are boisterously happy.
- The pace of business negotiations in the Philippines is much slower than in the United States.
- It would be unusual to complete a complicated business deal in only one trip to the Philippines. Expect to take several trips over a period of months.
- Because Filipinos avoid conflict, they are likely to say what they think the other person wants to hear. Filipinos try hard not to say "no."
- Since a Filipino wants to please the person he or she is speaking to, he or she is liable to say "yes" to an offer. This simply means that the Filipino does not want to offend you with an outright "no." In the Philippines, "yes" can mean anything from "I agree" to "maybe" to "I hope you can tell from my lack of enthusiasm that I really mean 'no'."
- To ensure that a Filipino "yes" really means "yes," you must get it in writing. If possible, try to get written agreement at each stage in your negotiations. A Filipino feels honor-bound to fulfill a written commitment.
- Expect to see your Filipino business partners often at social situations. Never decline an invitation to a social event.
- When you interrupt a Filipino during a meal, he or she is obliged to ask you to join in. This is a formality; just thank the Filipino and decline, saying that you have already eaten.
- Remember that social contacts are more important in the Philippines than business ones. A Filipino must like you and be comfortable with you, in order to do business. This relationship does not extend to your company. If your company replaces you with another executive, the new executive will have to forge this relationship anew (unless the new executive is a blood relative of yours).
- Business cards may be printed in English; it is not necessary to translate them into Pilipino. The exchange of business cards is more casual than in other parts

of Asia; a Filipino business person to whom you have given a card may—or may not—give you one of his or hers. The visiting business person should be the first to offer a card.

- If a Filipino gives you a business card with their home phone handwritten upon it, take that as an invitation to telephone. Business in the Philippines evolves out of social interaction, most of which takes place outside the office.
- Once you become accepted, Filipinos are very sociable and love to talk. Expect to be asked very personal questions, such as "Why are you not married?" They will also ask how much you paid for something, out of concern that you may have been cheated.

Business Entertaining

- Food is vitally important in Filipino culture. Social occasions always involve food. Indeed, the standard Pilipino greeting, *Kumain ka na ba?* translates as "Have you eaten?"

CULTURAL NOTE

*O*ne rite of passage that will endear you to Filipinos consists of eating one of the few local dishes that foreigners are squeamish about. These include the foul-smelling shrimp paste called *bogoong*, or the boiled duck egg called *balut* (which has a half-incubated duck embryo inside). However, the years of Spanish and American influence have rendered most Filipine cuisine very palatable to Westerners.

- Celebrate the conclusion of a business deal by inviting your Filipino partners to a restaurant. The person who issued the invitation always pays—unless it was a woman, in which case most Filipino businessmen will insist upon paying.
- Invite the wives of your business partners to dinner, but not to a luncheon.
- Expect to be invited to dinners and parties at the home of your Filipino partner (unless he or she is Chinese; Chinese rarely entertain at home). Such parties traditionally have numerous guests, including many relatives. Remember to show respect for elders. You may or may not be individually introduced to everyone.
- Most households have servants, including a cook. Compliment the hostess on the decor, but be aware that she probably did not prepare the food herself.
- Desserts are very popular in the Philippines at both lunch and dinner. If you are hosting a luncheon, be sure to provide a dessert.

CULTURAL NOTE

*n*ever appear too eager to begin eating at a party; allow the hostess to ask you several times to sit down. A person who jumps at food is considered uncouth and greedy.

This need to be asked several times extends to invitations. It is not enough to invite someone once to a dinner or a party; he or she will give a polite "yes" without feeling committed. Reconfirm the invitation at least once. Do not be surprised if someone declines via a third party. You can try sending out a written invitation with an R.S.V.P, but since Filipinos feel honor-bound by written commitments, few will return R.S.V.P. cards.

- Social events often end with dancing and singing. Expect to be invited to sing.
- Despite boisterous partying and hard drinking (by men), Filipinos find public drunkenness shameful. Do not get out of control.

Time

- The Philippines are eight hours ahead of Greenwich Mean Time (G.M.T. + 8), or thirteen hours ahead of U.S. Eastern Standard Time (E.S.T. + 13).

Protocol

Greetings

- Foreign businessmen should expect to shake hands firmly with Filipino men, both upon introduction and at subsequent meetings.
- Traditionally, there is no physical contact between men and women in public. Men should wait for a Filipino woman to offer her hand, which most Filipino businesswomen will do.
- Foreign businesswomen may initiate a handshake with Filipino men or women.
- Close female friends in the Philippines hug and kiss upon greeting. Similarly, close male friends may exhibit extended physical contact, such as holding hands or leaving an arm around a friend's shoulder.

*a*mong Filipinos, much can be communicated via eye contact and eyebrow movement. Filipinos may greet each other by making eye contact followed by a raising and lowering of the eyebrows.

A traditional Filipino may demonstrate respect upon greeting an elder by placing the elder's hand or knuckles on his or her forehead.

Titles/Forms of Address

- Most people you meet should be addressed with a title and their surname. Many professionals have titles, since Filipino companies often reward employees with titles instead of additional pay or responsibilities.
- Persons who do not have professional titles should be addressed, in English, as Mr., Mrs., or Miss, plus their surname.
- Wives of persons with important titles are sometimes addressed as "Mrs. plus (husband's title)," e.g., Mrs. Senator or Mrs. Mayor.
- Upper-class Filipinos may follow the Hispanic tradition of having two surnames: one from their father, which is listed first, followed by one from their mother. Only the father's surname is commonly used when addressing someone; e.g., Mr. Juan Antonio Martínez Garcia is addressed as Mr. Martínez and Miss Ana María Gutiérrez Herrera is addressed as Miss Gutiérrez. When a woman marries, she may add her husband's surname and go by that surname. If the two people in the above example married, she would be known as Mrs. Ana María Gutiérrez Herrera de Martínez. Most people would refer to her as Mrs. de Martínez or, less formally, Mrs. Martínez.

CULTURAL NOTE

*m*any Filipinos did not have surnames until the mid-nineteenth century. In 1849, the Spanish governor ordered all Filipinos to adopt Hispanic surnames. Families chose surnames from lists provided by the government, and the first letter of every surname on a list was specific to a particular area. Thus, people from one town or area all had surnames beginning with the letter A, the next town used B, and so on. Even today, the first letter of a person's surname can provide information about where his or her family originally came from.

- Most Filipinos have nicknames, many of which sound incongruous to foreigners. Once a Filipino invites you to address him or her by a nickname, you are expected to do so. After such an invitation, you should invite a Filipino to address you by your nickname (if you don't have one, make one up).
- Flattery by means of "verbal promotion" is common in the Philippines. A police officer may be referred to as Captain, and a police captain called Major, and so on. Foreigners are not expected to participate in such verbal games.

 Gestures

- Because of the years of U.S. military presence in the Philippines, most North American gestures are recognized.
- The foremost obscene gesture in both the United States and the Philippines involves an extended middle finger. However, in the Philippines, that finger is pointed at the person or thing being insulted.
- Since pointing can easily be taken for an insulting gesture, Filipinos rarely indicate objects or directions by pointing with their fingers. Instead, they indicate with a glance or by pursing their lips.
- Indicating "two" with the fingers is done by holding up the ring and little finger, instead of the forefinger and middle finger. The thumb is not used to count numbers in the Philippines.
- Staring has various nuances in the Philippines, most of them negative. Foreigners should avoid staring at Filipinos, who can easily interpret a stare as belligerence. If you are stared at, look away.
- As in much of the world, to beckon someone you hold your hand out, palm downward, and make a scooping motion with the fingers. Beckoning someone with the palm up and wagging one finger, as in the United States, can be construed as an insult.
- To stand tall with your hands on your hips—the "arms akimbo" position—is always interpreted as an aggressive posture. Worse, it expresses an aggressive challenge—and in the Philippines, belligerence is often met with belligerence.
- Looking down is useful to avoid giving offense when making one's way through a crowd or between two people who are conversing. This may also be accompanied by an outstretched, flat hand (like a karate chop) or with both hands clasped together; the hand(s) are in front, preceding the direction of motion.
- A Filipino may try to attract your attention by brushing a finger against your elbow.

 Gifts

- Gift giving is an important part of Filipino society. Flowers and food are the most common gifts, although there are situations in which a handful of small coins is traditional.
- When invited to a Filipino home, bring (or have sent before you arrive) flowers or a delicacy, such as candy or chocolates, to your hostess. Avoid bringing alcohol or a substantial food, as this may imply that your host cannot serve enough to satisfy guests. However, exceptions are made for a specialty dish or food that only you can provide, such as a recipe from your home country. A thank-you note is appropriate afterwards; some people also send a small gift.
- After a dinner party, Filipinos often give their guests extra food to take home, an ancient tradition called *pabalon*.

- At Christmas, you will be expected to give a token gift—such as a company calendar—to seemingly everyone you know or do business with. Your list should include everyone who works for you, all service personnel you deal with regularly (your postal clerks, your security guards), and anyone who could make your life difficult if they refused to cooperate with you, such as the secretary of an important client.
- Filipinos follow the Asian habit of not opening gifts in the presence of the giver. Traditionally, if the recipient is not happy with the gift, he or she avoids embarrassment by opening it away from the giver. Furthermore, Filipinos abhor appearing greedy; to open a gift immediately would give this impression. Do not be dismayed if your gift is casually set aside and ignored; you will be thanked for it at a later date.

f————————————————**CULTURAL NOTE**

oreigners are honored in the Philippines by being invited to family events: weddings, anniversaries, baptisms, and so on. It is an even greater honor to be asked to participate in such events, as a sponsor in a wedding or a godparent in a baptism. Bring a gift, whether you are a guest or a participant. These events are part of establishing the personal relationships that are all-important in Filipino business practices.

At some events—notably at Filipino baptisms—it is traditional to toss a handful of small coins to the children. There is also a rural wedding tradition whereby guests attach currency (usually small-denomination peso bills) to the clothing of the bride and groom with pins.

 Dress

- Because of the heat and humidity, business dress for Filipinos is often casual: dark trousers and white, short-sleeved shirts for men, sans tie; white long-sleeved blouses and skirts for women. Despite this simplicity, these clothes will be neat, clean, and fashionable. Filipinos are very style-conscious.
- As a foreigner, you should dress more conservatively until you are sure what degree of formality is expected. Men should expect to wear a suit and tie; businesswomen wear white blouses and dark suits or skirts.
- Many Filipino men wear an embroidered shirt called a *barong tagalog*. It is worn without a tie and hangs outside the trousers, not tucked in. Long-sleeved ones are often worn to work and to semiformal occasions; short-sleeved ones are only for casual wear.
- Men may wear a business suit for formal occasions, such as the theater, a formal dinner party, and so forth, but women are expected to wear a short cocktail dress. Long evening gowns are required only on rare occasions, such as for diplomatic functions.
- Neither men nor women should wear shorts or sandals in public, except at the beach.
- Since Filipinos are so competitively fashionable, many offices, including banks and the government, require their workers to wear uniforms.
- Don't wear anything outside that can be damaged by water during a fiesta. Drenching pedestrians is a favorite fiesta pastime.

WARSAW

Poland

Country Background

History

The very existence of Poland is a testament to the tenacity of the Polish people, for this country has disappeared from the face of Europe several times.

The Slavic tribes that would later become the Polish people settled in this northern corner of Eastern Europe more than two thousand years ago. The nation took its name from one of these tribes, the Polane (the people of the plain). The Polish nation dates its existence to the tenth century, with the ascension of King Mieszko I in 963 A.D. Mieszko adopted the Roman Catholic faith in 966, and the country has remained staunchly Catholic to this day.

Poland flourished culturally and economically, but not politically. The country's flat, fertile plains and lack of defensible frontiers have made it a constant target for its aggressive neighbors. In 1386 the Polish state opted for unification with neighboring Lithuania, and for a time Polish fortunes were strengthened. But again political decline set in, and the country was partitioned three times between the German, Russian, and Austrian Empires. By 1795, the time of the third partition, Poland had vanished.

The 1815 Congress of Vienna decreed that a Kingdom of Poland still existed, but only within the confines of the Russian Empire, where it was legally ruled by the Russian czar. For the next hundred years the Poles continually worked for independence, with the Poles' Catholicism serving as a rallying point against their Russian Orthodox overlords.

It was World War I that returned Poland to the map. When Russia sued the Central Powers for peace, the Treaty of Brest-Litovsk in 1918 dismembered the Russian Empire. Poland reemerged as an independent state. But this independence proved to be short-lived. World War II began when Nazi Germany overran Poland. Over 6 million Poles, including virtually the entire population of Polish Jews, died during the occupation. The Germans were pushed out by the Soviet Army in 1945, and the Polish borders were redrawn in their current configuration.

But Poland was not yet free. Instead, Poland became a Communist state under Soviet domination. Again the Poles protested against their Russian overlords.

The first glimmering of success came in 1981 with the organization of the Solidarity labor union. Martial law was unable to stifle the will of the people, and—after the Polish regime ascertained that the Soviets would not intervene—Solidarity was legalized in 1989. Political liberalization and a transition to a market economy were followed by the election of Solidarity leader Lech Walesa as the leader of the Polish Republic in late 1990.

Type of Government
The Republic of Poland is a multiparty democracy. The president is the chief of state; the prime minister is the head of government. There are two legislative houses: the Senate with 100 seats and the Diet with 460.

Language
Polish is the official language. Closely related to Czech, Polish is placed in the Slavic branch of the Indo-European linguistic family (English is also part of this family). Polish is written in a modified Latin alphabet, not the Cyrillic alphabet of Russian. However, Polish is often considered the most difficult Indo-European language for native speakers of English to master.

Religion
The vast majority of Poles are Roman Catholics. About 1.5 percent of the population is Orthodox.

CULTURAL NOTE

Since the overthrow of the Communist regime, religious holidays have been celebrated openly. Poles take great pride in the fact that Pope John Paul II is Polish. However, there is some opposition to the influence the Catholic church has gained in secular matters.

Demographics
The population of Poland is about 38.5 million. The country is very homogeneous; 98 percent of the population is ethnic Polish. Ukrainians constitute a very small minority.

Cultural Orientation

Cognitive Styles: How Poles Organize and Process Information
The Polish culture has always been open to information from the West. With the demise of Communism, many aspects of education in Poland are in a state of flux. Poles are abstractive, processing information conceptually and analytically, however, they value relationships as much as the law.

Negotiation Strategies: What Poles Accept as Evidence
In Poland, truth rests more on objective facts than on the subjective feelings of the moment. Faith in ideologies that may change one's perspective on the truth is

changing, shifting from the ideologies of the Communist party to those of national-ism and democracy.

Value Systems: The Basis for Behavior

With the fall of the Iron Curtain and the rise of democracy, the value systems of Poland are being influenced more and more by those of the West. The following three sections identify the Value Systems in the predominant culture—their meth-ods of dividing right from wrong, good from evil, and so forth.

Locus of Decision Making

As the movement toward freedom and privatization advances, more decision-making responsibility is being placed on the shoulders of the individual. There is a strong sense of individualism and democracy, plus a belief that all citizens should influence the way the society is governed. In many instances, the individual may transfer decision-making responsibility to the group as a whole or to a consensus of privileged individuals.

Sources of Anxiety Reduction

Post-Communist freedom is perceived as threatening most of the structures the Poles have depended upon for stability and security. However, since most Poles are Catholics, the church is a significant factor in filling this need. Polish Catholicism has been described as emotional and traditional, and the Poles are considered the most devout of all European Catholics. A strong extended family also helps to give structure and security.

Issues of Equality/Inequality

The removal of Communist party control has allowed resentments over inequality to surface. Internal disputes arise over power and control. Although Poland has a largely homogeneous population, the drive for power will be seen at all levels of government, business, and society. This drive for power threatens to undercut the humanitarian belief in equality. There is some disjunction between private and public morality.

Although Poland is a male-dominated society, it is not necessary to hide one's emotions. There is a history of sensitivity to the feelings of others; intentions, feelings, and opinions are openly expressed.

Business Practices

Appointments

PUNCTUALITY

- As a foreigner, you are expected to be on time for all appointments.
- Punctuality was not required under the Communist regime. Do not be surprised if your Polish coun-terpart is very late.

- The Polish work day starts early. Appointments at 8:00 A.M. are not unusual.
- Business lunches are often held quite late, around 4:00 or 5:00 P.M.
- Requests for appointments should be made in writing when possible. Translating the request into Polish will make a good impression.

- Most businesses have a 5 1/2-day workweek: 8:00 or 9:00 A.M. to 2:00 or 3:00 P.M., Monday through Friday, and 8:00 A.M to 1:30 P.M. Saturdays.

Negotiating

- It is difficult to predict how long it will take to negotiate a business deal. Under the former regime, deals would take months. Even today, if the government is involved, you can expect negotiations to proceed slowly. On the other hand, some of Poland's new entrepreneurs are anxious to move quickly. With small enterprises, this is sometimes possible.
- A local Polish representative will be vital to successful operations. Everything from office space to restaurant reservations is in short supply, and only a local "fixer" will be able to arrange them for you.
- Bring plenty of business cards and give one out to everyone you meet.
- It is not necessary to have your business card translated into Polish.
- Proposals, reports, and promotional materials should be translated into Polish. If graphics are included in this material, make sure they are well done and neatly printed. Poland has long had some of the best graphic artists in the world.

CULTURAL NOTE

*P*oland's relations with its neighbors have not always been cordial; Poland was partitioned between the German, Russian, and Austro-Hungarian Empires. Do not bring up your background if you are of German, Hungarian, or Russian descent.

Anti-Semitism is also a subject to avoid. Remember that the Nazis located most of the death camps on Polish soil, not in Germany itself.

Polish is still a male-dominated society. Most of the business persons you meet will be male, and admonishing Poles for sexist attitudes, real or perceived, will not help your relationship.

- If possible, keep the conversation away from politics.
- Food, sports, and sightseeing are good topics to bring up.

Business Entertaining

- Business lunches and dinners are popular, but breakfast meetings are virtually unknown in Poland.
- Poland suffers from a major housing shortage. Because apartments are very cramped, do not expect a Polish business person to invite you home. Almost all entertaining is done in clubs and restaurants.
- The person who issues the invitation to a restaurant is usually the one who pays the bill.
- As a foreigner, you will probably get more attention and better service in restaurants and clubs than Poles—but only if people realize that you are a foreigner. Speak English.
- Despite having to go to work early, Poles love to stay up late, talking and drinking. Leaving early may insult them, so be prepared for a long night.
- Although there is an effort to promote beer as an acceptable drink (most Poles consider beer a chaser), vodka is still the drink of choice. Don't get trapped in a vodka-drinking contest with Poles; you'll lose. Expect your glass to be refilled every time it is empty until the vodka runs out.

Time

- Poland is one hour ahead of Greenwich Mean Time (G.M.T. + 1), and thus six hours ahead of U.S. Eastern Standard Time (E.S.T. + 6).

Protocol

 Greetings

- Shake hands when you meet a Pole and when you leave. Be sure to shake hands when you are introduced to someone for the first time.
- Wait for a Polish woman to extend her hand before offering to shake hands. Old-fashioned Polish men may kiss a woman's hand; foreign men are not expected to do this. If you feel an additional expression of respect is called for, simply make a short bow.
- Close Polish friends or relatives may greet each other effusively, with much hugging and kissing of cheeks.

 Titles/Forms of Address

- As in some other Slavic cultures, the final letter in a woman's surname may be different from that of a man's. Where this is the case, a woman's surname will end in the letter 'a'—thus, it is Mr. Solski and Mrs. Solska.
- The simplest way to address a Polish professional is by using Mr., Mrs., or Miss and their job title.
  - Mr. = *Pan* ("pahn")
  - Mrs. = *Pani* ("pah'-nee")
  - Miss – *panna* ("pah'-nah")
  - Mr. Executive = *Pan Dyrektor*   Mr. Reporter = *Pan Redaktor*

————————————————————CULTURAL NOTE

*I*f a Pole lacks a title, be sure to address him as Mr. plus (surname). Only close adult friends will address each other by their first names. You will know if a Pole wishes you to use his first name; there is a whole ceremony (the *bruderschaft*) that celebrates the decision to go to a first-name basis.

 Gestures

- In social situations, when a Pole flicks his finger against his neck, he is inviting you to join him for a drink (probably vodka).
- Do not chew gum while speaking to someone.
- Do not litter; Poles are shocked at the sight of anyone throwing trash anywhere but in a trash receptacle.
- Avoid loud behavior in public; Poles tend to be a quiet people. You will notice that Poles speak more softly than North Americans.
- Polish men tend to have traditional views of acceptable female behavior. Women who speak forthrightly may encounter resistance from Polish men.

- When asking directions from strangers, a woman should approach either a policeman or another woman. Approaching a man will probably be interpreted as flirting.

Gifts

- A foreign gift is appropriate the first time you meet a Polish businessman. Liquor (anything except vodka) is a good choice.
- Always bring a gift when visiting a Polish home, even for a brief visit. Flowers are the most common gift. Give the flowers, unwrapped, to your hostess. Always bring an odd number of flowers, and avoid red roses (used for courting) and chrysanthemums (used at funerals).
- Items that are in short supply in Poland are always appreciated as gifts or tips, but which items are scarce varies. Coffee, perfume, and American cigarettes are usually a good bet. Even if you don't smoke, bring cigarettes.

Dress

- Business dress is the same as in the United States: suits and ties for men, dresses for women. Colors tend to be conservative.
- For casual wear, jeans are ubiquitous for both men and women. Jeans with a dressy shirt or blouse will get one through most nonbusiness situations. Exceptions are
    - expensive restaurants (these require suits and ties or dresses);
    - theater and the opera (these require suits and ties or dresses);
    - dinner invitations in a Polish home (these require jackets and ties or dressy pants or skirts); and
    - formal invitations, as on New Year's Eve (these require tuxedos or gowns).

LISBON

Portugal

t———————————**CULTURAL NOTE**

hough Portuguese is related to Spanish, and many Portuguese understand Spanish, foreigners should not assume that knowledge of Spanish is enough. The Portuguese consider it insulting when foreigners constantly try to communicate in Spanish.

Country Background

History

Over the course of history, Portugal's coastline has been populated by a succession of cultures. Ancient Phoenicians, Carthaginians, and Greeks preceded the Romans, who conquered the region in 27 B.C. Subsequently, the Visigoths and the Moors governed until the twelfth century. In 1140, Portugal became an independent nation under King Alfonso Henriques. During the fourteenth and fifteenth centuries, Portuguese explorers immensely expanded their empire. Both Spain and France temporarily ruled Portugal before the Republic of Portugal was established in 1910.

t———————————**CULTURAL NOTE**

he Portuguese overseas Province of Macao lies about 40 miles southwest of Hong Kong. Both Hong Kong and Macao will return to Chinese sovereignty in 1997.

Type of Government

From 1974 to 1976 Portugal underwent a nearly bloodless transition from an authoritarian government to a constitutional democracy. Today, Portugal is a multi-party parliamentary democracy.

The parliament is known as the Assembly of the Republic. It is unicameral, and its members are elected by direct universal suffrage. Deputies serve for four years. The president is the chief of state, while the prime minister is the head of the government.

The 1976 constitution was revised in 1982 and 1989. It placed the military under civilian control and eliminated the Marxist rhetoric and socialist goals of the first document. This has led to privatization of many sectors of the economy, such as banks. It also calls for increasing decentralization of the administration.

Portugal joined the European Community (now the European Union) in January of 1986. Membership has stimulated liberalization of economic policy. This has resulted in one of the best economic performances and one of the lowest unemployment rates in Europe.

Language
Portuguese, a Romance language, is spoken throughout Portugal. Some English is spoken in tourist centers, and French is often used in business.

Religion
Most Portuguese are Roman Catholic (97 percent). However, there is no official religion in Portugal. Freedom of religion is guaranteed in the constitution. There are very small numbers of Protestants, Jews, and Muslims.

Demographics
The population of Portugal is 10.4 million.

CULTURAL NOTE

*I*n addition to Portugal's ten million, there are two million Portuguese residing abroad, as emigrants or as temporary workers. Portugal strives to retain ties with Portuguese communities overseas and to protect workers abroad.

Cultural Orientation

Cognitive Styles: How the Portuguese Organize and Process Information
In Portugal information is readily accepted for the purpose of discussion, but negotiations may be extensive with little movement from the initial perspective. Teaching is formal and innovation is discouraged, which fosters a subjective, associative mode of information processing. Since interpersonal relationships are of major importance, Portuguese are more inclined to maintain a relationship than to abide by rules and laws.

Negotiation Strategies: What the Portuguese Accept as Evidence
Truth is found in the personal feelings of those involved in a situation. While faith in the ideologies of humanitarianism and the church may modify the truth, the Portuguese will seldom let objective facts influence them.

Value Systems: The Basis for Behavior
The Portuguese's value systems are still in transition from the old authoritarian political and economic systems to the present democratic and capitalistic systems. The following three sections identify the Value Systems in the predominant culture—their methods of dividing right from wrong, good from evil, and so forth.

Locus of Decision Making
Individuals are responsible for their decisions, but they are always subject to the pressures of the family or the working group. The elite control all seats of power, intermarry for stability, and rely on extended kinship ties for control. One's self-identity comes from the history of one's extended family and one's position in society. One's connections are much more important than one's expertise when finding a job.

Sources of Anxiety Reduction

Most Portuguese are members of the Catholic church, and its teachings and social structure provide stability and security to the individual. Friendship and patronage networks are the cement of Portuguese society and the primary means of communication within and between social classes. The family is the primary unit of social interaction, and it is one's role in the social structure and the presence of the extended family that give a sense of stability and security to life.

Issues of Equality/Inequality

There is ethnic and linguistic homogeneity in Portugal, and this brings a sense of equality to the people. Although there are extreme contrasts between rich and poor, with a small upper class, a larger middle class, and a massive lower class, in general people feel that they are all equal because they are all unique. Failures are often attributed to external circumstances rather than personal inadequacies. It is a strongly macho society.

Business Practices

Appointments

PUNCTUALITY

* Punctuality is not a high priority in Portugal. Although foreigners are expected to be punctual, your Portuguese counterpart could easily be thirty minutes late.

- Remember that many Europeans and South Americans write the day first, then the month, then the year (e.g., December 3, 1999, is written 3.12.99). This is the case in Portugal.
- Prior appointments are necessary.
- The workweek is 9:00 A.M. to 5:00 or 5:30 P.M., Monday through Friday. Lunch is from noon to 2:00 P.M. Try to avoid appointments between noon and 3:00 P.M.
- Shops are open Monday through to Friday, 9:00 A.M. to 1:00 P.M. and again from 3:00 to 7:00 P.M.

 Negotiating

- Establishing a strong rapport through constant personal contact is essential.
- Emphasize your commitment to your clients; frequent visits are highly recommended. Do not expect negotiations to proceed at a rapid pace.

*P*ersistence and patience are vital. Nothing is accomplished quickly in Portugal. The Portuguese do not consider themselves slaves to the clock. Until you learn to appreciate their viewpoint, you will have difficulty conducting business there.

CULTURAL NOTE

- After-sale service of your product is necessary. You must prove to your clients that this service will be provided.

- Good topics of discussion are the family, positive aspects of Portuguese culture, and personal interests.
- Avoid discussing politics and government.
- Avoid sounding too curious about others' personal matters.
- Many Portuguese study British-English, so avoid idioms from the U.S.
- Business cards are used. It is best to have yours translated, so that English is on one side and Portuguese on the other.
- Present your business card to your colleague with the Portuguese side facing him or her.

 Business Entertaining

- Lunch is the main meal of the day and is eaten at approximately 1:00 P.M. Business lunches are common.
- Wine is the typical beverage consumed with meals.
- If you are invited out to lunch or dinner, be certain to reciprocate; however, do not mention that you "owe" the other person the favor.
- Women eating alone in a restaurant may be approached unless they obviously take work with them.
- The fork is held in the left hand and the knife remains in the right hand.
- Hands should not be kept in the lap at the table.
- It is impolite to eat while walking down the street.
- People often meet at tea houses (*casas de cha*).

Time

- Portugal is one hour ahead of Greenwich Mean Time (G.M.T. + 1), or six hours ahead of U.S. Eastern Standard Time (E.S.T. + 6).

Protocol

 Greetings

- A warm, firm handshake is the standard greeting.
- For social occasions, men greet each other with an embrace.
- Women kiss on both cheeks when greeting each other.

 Titles/Forms of Address

- The order of names is the same as in the United States: the first name is followed by the surname.
- Use of first names is reserved for close friends.
- Some professionals are introduced as *Doctor* or *Doctora* even if they are not officially doctors.

 Gestures

- "Come here" is indicated with the hand down and fingers or hand waving.

- It is considered impolite to point.
- To call a waiter to your table in a restaurant, simply raise your hand.

 Gifts

- It is not appropriate to give a business gift at the first meeting.
- When you give a business gift, do not include your business card; instead, include a handwritten card.
- Do not make your gift too extravagant or too skimpy.
- The gift should not be a vehicle for your company logo.
- It is not necessary to bring a gift when you are invited to a home. Instead, you may invite your hosts out at a later date.
- If you do wish to give something to your Portuguese hosts, fine chocolates or other candy is the preferred gift.
- If you send flowers to your Portuguese hosts, do not send thirteen of them. This is considered bad luck. Do not send chrysanthemums or roses. Do make sure that the bouquet is impressive; a gift of cheap flowers will have a negative effect.

 Dress

- Conservative, formal dress is essential. Portuguese men wear jackets and ties even when going to the movies!
- Despite the hot Portuguese weather, men should not remove their jackets unless their Portuguese colleagues do so first.
- Portuguese businesswomen usually wear dresses in subdued colors rather than suits.

BUCHAREST

Romania

CULTURAL NOTE

*t*he Romanians consider themselves a Mediterranean people who just happen to live in Eastern Europe.

Country Background

History

Romania is a younger nation than the United States; it only achieved full independence from the Ottoman Empire in 1878. However, the name Romania means "land of the Romans," and the Romanian people lived in this area of Eastern Europe even before it was a province of the Roman Empire.

CULTURAL NOTE

*t*he current preferred spelling of the country's name is "Romania," rather than the older "Rumania" or "Roumania."

Despite their central European location, the Romanians identify more closely with Italy and France. The Romanian capital, Bucharest, is known as "the Paris of the East."

After the popular overthrow of the Ceausescu regime in 1989, an interim government called the National Salvation Front took control. The National Salvation Front leader, Ion Iliescu, was elected president in May of 1990, despite his Communist background and close ties to the Ceausescu government.

Type of Government

Romania is now a multiparty republic with two legislative bodies. The Romanian Senate has 143 seats; the Assembly of Deputies has 341. The president is the chief of state. The prime minister is the head of the government.

As one of the poorest countries in Europe, Romania's main concern is the economy. Romania has recently attracted international attention over human rights, its proximity to the warring Yugoslav state of Serbia, and the Moldova problem.

CULTURAL NOTE

*M*uch of Moldova, formerly known as the Republic of Moldavia in the U.S.S.R., was creat-ed from captured Romanian lands. The Soviets kept the area under tight control and attempted to convince the ethnic Moldavians that they were a separate people from their brothers across the Prut and Danube Rivers in Romania. The Soviets even forced the Moldavians to write their Romanian dialect in the Cyrillic alphabet, instead of the Latin alphabet used in Romania. These efforts failed; after the dissolution of the U.S.S.R., the western portion of Moldova clamored for union with Romania. Ethnic Russians in eastern Moldova (aided by Moscow) took up arms, threatening to create their own "Trans-Dniester Republic" (which would contain most of Moldova's resources).

Faced with such opposition, the Moldovans decided not to pursue immediate union with Romania. Since Romania is no better off financially than Moldova, there was no economic advantage to such a union.

Language

Romanian, the official language, is derived from Latin; it is in the same linguis-tic family as Italian, French, Spanish, and Portuguese. Indeed, it is alleged that a flu-ent speaker of Italian can communicate fairly well with the Romanians—especially if the speaker knows the Italian dialect used around Genoa.

Religion

Some 90 percent of the population belongs to the Romanian Orthodox Church. The remainder of the population is Roman Catholic, Jewish, Calvinist, Islamic, or atheist.

Demographics

The current population of Romania is about twenty-three million. Romania's population is 89 percent ethnic Romanian. The largest minority (8 percent) consists of Hungarians (Magyars), as the traditionally Hungarian province of Transylvania was placed within Romania's borders after World War I. A sizable German popula-tion shrank in the late 1980s when emigration to Germany was allowed. Other minorities include Ukrainians, Russians, Serbs, Croats, Turks, and Gypsies. The presence of ethnic Romanians in adjacent countries, notably Moldova, is a source of occasional friction.

Cultural Orientation

Cognitive Styles: How Romanians Organize and Process Information

The people in Romania have always been independent (even under Communist rule) and are open to outside information. Their basic education fos-ters associative thinking, but most of them are now processing information con-ceptually and analytically. They are also returning to personal involvement in situa-tions rather than following the rules of a party line.

Negotiation Strategies: What Romanians Accept as Evidence

The more educated the participants are, the more they will use objective facts to define the truth. Subjective feelings are still strong, but faith in an ideology, other than freedom, does not cloud the issue of truth.

Value Systems: The Basis for Behavior

The Romanians share a Latin heritage and hold to many of the same values of equality and humanitarianism as other Latin cultures. The following three sections identify the Value Systems in the predominant culture—their methods of dividing right from wrong, good from evil, and so forth.

Locus of Decision Making

As the movement toward freedom and privatization advances, it puts the responsibility for decision making on the shoulders of the individual. The individual may, in turn, transfer this power to the group as a whole or to selected experts within the group. It is not clear yet who will be the beneficiary of the individuals' decision-making skills: the decision maker or the people as a whole. It seems that the Romanians' tendency is to work for the betterment of the people.

Sources of Anxiety Reduction

Family cohesion is the basic social unit that gives identity and security to the individual. However, this is now breaking down because more women are working outside the home. Romanians are very nationalistic and have always pursued an independent course in both their internal development and their foreign relations. It may be that the church will be able to fill the need for structure left by the departure of Communist rule.

Issues of Equality/Inequality

A discernible hierarchy of classes has evolved, from the peasant to the bureaucratic elite. Although egalitarianism is favored, some resentment is found among the various ethnic and social groups. The Hungarian and German minorities are very distinct, with their own languages, and present potential social and political problems. The ethnic Romanians do not hide their emotions, and tend to express their intentions, feeling, and opinions freely. In marriage both spouses have equal rights, and their roles are not clearly differentiated.

Business Practices

Appointments

————————————————————— PUNCTUALITY

◆ Romanians tend to be very punctual; be on time.

- Appointments should be made well in advance.
- Appointments may be requested by mail. Business letters should be sent in English. Not only do Romanians expect to translate foreign letters, but such a letter is accorded more respect and attention than one written in Romanian.
- An interpreter will be necessary for the meeting unless you are positive that you and your Romanian counterpart are fluent in a common language.

————————————————————— CULTURAL NOTE

*a*lthough Romanian is quite similar to the Genoese dialect of Italian, some 12 percent of the Romanian vocabulary is derived from Slavic languages; do not expect to be able to conduct business by speaking Italian to your Romanian-speaking client.

- Because many Romanian students study at French universities, French is the most widely spoken foreign language. Hungarian is frequently spoken in

Transylvania; Russian is common near the Romanian-Russian border. Among Romanian business people, the older ones tend to speak some German, while the younger ones are learning English. Major hotels and resorts have English-speaking staff members.
- Business and government office hours are 8:00 A.M. to 4:00 P.M., Monday through Friday, and 8:00 A.M. to 12:30 P.M., Saturday. Shops keep even longer hours.

 Negotiating
- Patience is necessary in establishing business contacts in Romania; the process often seems glacially slow. However, once the connection is established, one can expect to do business with the Romanians for a very long time.
- It is generally preferable to stay at one of the more prestigious international hotels. Staying elsewhere will diminish your importance in the eyes of Romanians.
- Be prepared to hand out a large number of business cards. Your cards need not be translated into Romanian; a card in English or French is satisfactory. Your title and any advanced degrees should be listed on the card.

 Business Entertaining
- Remember that Romania is the poorest country in Europe after Albania. As a foreigner, your hard currency gives you priority access to available goods. You should also bring some gift items with you from home. The easiest way to please Romanians is to treat them to something that they can't get themselves.
- The items that are in short supply in Romania change frequently, but may include coffee, good soap, candy (especially chocolate), perfume, light bulbs, and cigarettes. Even if you don't smoke, you should bring your duty-free limit of two hundred American cigarettes (Kent is the preferred brand). A pack of American cigarettes as a tip will improve service everywhere from taxis to restaurants.
- Your Romanian colleagues will do the majority of the entertaining. However, if you wish to reciprocate, start by inviting them to lunch or dinner at your hotel. This simple step may take several invitations to accomplish, as business contacts were usually confined to business offices during the Ceausescu regime.

Time
- Romania is on Central European Time, two hours ahead of Greenwich Mean Time (G.M.T. + 2) and seven hours ahead of U.S. Eastern Standard Time (E.S.T. + 7).

Protocol

 Greetings
- Romanians shake hands constantly: when they are introduced, when they leave someone, and every time they meet. No matter how many times they run into each other during the day, they will shake hands each time. Men should wait for a woman to extend her hand first. Some older Romanians will kiss a woman's hand.

- If seated, men should rise when being introduced to someone; women may remain seated.
- Good friends will greet each other expansively. Men may kiss each other on both cheeks or the mouth.
- At social gatherings, wait for your host to introduce you to everyone there.

 ## *Titles/Forms of Address*

- The order of names in Romania is the same as in the United States: first name followed by surname.
- Only close adult friends and relatives address each other by their first names. Adults address the young by their first names.
- Always address Romanian professionals by their title (Doctor, Engineer, Professor, and so forth) and surname.

 ## *Gestures*

- Businessmen in Romania wear hats. It is considered polite to remove one's hat when indoors, even in the lobby of a large building. Romanian farmers wear Tyrolean hats similar to the type worn by Chico Marx in the old Marx Brothers movies; do not insult them by laughing at their head gear.
- Romanian gestures tend to be expansive, reflecting both Italian and Slavic influences.
- To call someone a cuckold, a Romanian extends his first and little fingers (the same "hook 'em horns" gesture used by University of Texas football fans).
- The "fig" gesture—the thumb between the index and middle fingers of a clenched fist—is an insult.

 ## *Gifts*

- For business dealings, inexpensive gifts such as pens, calculators, or lighters discreetly imprinted with your company name are appropriate to celebrate Christmas or a contract signing.
- If you are invited to dinner at a private home, bring wine, liquor, or wrapped flowers. When bringing flowers, be sure you have an odd number (three or more); carnations and roses (but not red roses) are good choices.
- If you are staying at a Romanian home, try to find out in advance which items are currently in short supply (frequently it will be coffee, perfume, light bulbs, or cigarettes) and bring those. Offer to help with some household chore, although your offer will probably be refused. You may be allowed to purchase (and pay for) groceries.

CULTURAL NOTE

*I*f your hosts were educated in France and are wealthy enough to have a large house, they may have picked up the French habit of segregating rooms into "guest" and "nonguest" rooms. Never barge into a room you have not been into before. This is especially true of the kitchen.

Dress

- Casual Western-style dress is common; jeans are everywhere. However, business people are still expected to dress in conservative business apparel. Men wear dark suits except in summer, when short-sleeved shirts with ties are acceptable; women wear suits and heels. Make sure your shoes are well polished.
- Don't bother to bring formal wear (tuxedos and evening gowns); business wear will suffice for formal occasions.
- Shorts are appropriate only for the country or the shore, not in the cities.
- Unless specified otherwise, assume that invitations to a Romanian house or restaurant call for the same clothes you wear for business.
- Women should wear a skirt and have their shoulders covered when entering an Orthodox church. Covering up one's hair is not required.

MOSCOW
•

Russia

CULTURAL NOTE

*W*estern business people have learned how important restraint is when negotiating with the Japanese; never lose your temper when dealing with Japanese. The Russians are the exact opposite. Russian negotiations almost always involve temper tantrums, dire threats, and walkouts. Loss of temper during negotiations is expected by the Russians. Only in one crucial area are the Russians and Japanese alike: They both have tremendous patience. Both cultures prize endurance, which often puts impatient North Americans at a disadvantage.

Country Background

CULTURAL NOTE

*t*he breakup of the U.S.S.R. added fifteen new independent nations to the map of the world. Since Russia undeniably controlled the U.S.S.R., many nations that shared a border with the U.S.S.R. felt that they essentially shared a border with Russia. Since the breakup, this is no longer the case. Russia historically insulated itself from foreigners by creating client "buffer states" between Russia and the outside world. These buffer states are now independent. Thus, Russia today shares no borders with any former Warsaw Pact nation except Poland. Russia today shares no borders with Afghanistan, a nation in which thousands of Soviet troops fought during the 1980s. Russia today does not even share borders with six of the former republics of the U.S.S.R!

However, territorial disputes are widespread throughout the former U.S.S.R. Border adjustments may continue for years to come.

History

The U.S.S.R., also known as the Soviet Union, lasted from 1917 through 1991. Before 1917, most of the territory in the U.S.S.R. was part of the Russian Empire. The Russian Empire expanded outward from Moscow, the historic capital of the Russian Republic and of the Soviet Union itself. (Czar Peter the Great moved the capital in 1712 from Moscow to Saint Petersburg—Peter's "window on the West"— but the Communists moved the capital back to Moscow in 1918.)

Russia was the most powerful of the fifteen republics in the U.S.S.R. Indeed, it is not incorrect to say that the U.S.S.R. was ruled by Russia for Russia's benefit.

The authoritarian, one-party rule of the Communists collapsed with surprising speed. Theories for this collapse abound, ranging from impoverishment caused by the arms race to the inability of any totalitarian government to control information in an era of computers, faxes, and modems. One thing is clear: The Communist leaders underestimated the bitterness the fourteen other republics felt toward Moscow's domination.

The precipitating event was the August 1991 coup attempt, when hard-line Communist leaders briefly imprisoned President Mikhail Gorbachev. Faced with resistance on all sides (from Gorbachev, who refused to acknowledge their authority; from Russian President Boris Yeltsin, who became a popular hero for facing down tanks in the streets; and from thousands of Russians who took to the streets in protest), the coup failed in less than a week. The coup attempt ended the careers of the coup leaders (the "gang of eight") and of Gorbachev as well; Gorbachev had appointed the very men who had plotted against him.

In disarray, Moscow was unable to prevent the non-Russian republics from leaving the Soviet Union. The U.S.S.R. ceased to exist on December 25, 1991. The Russian Federation is still the largest and most powerful of the former republics.

d—————————————————————**CULTURAL NOTE**

*d*espite their mistrust of Moscow, most of the former republics have united in a vague alliance called the Commonwealth of Independent States. (The exceptions are the three Baltic states of Lithuania, Latvia, and Estonia, which direct their attention toward Europe, not Moscow.) Thus, although Moscow no longer rules the U.S.S.R., it retains great influence (and responsibilities) in most of the former constituent republics.

The central Asian republics are particularly dependent upon Moscow for aid, both economic and military. Furthermore, the presence of ethnic Russians in every republic gives Moscow an excuse for intervention, as it did to "protect" ethnic Russians in Moldova.

Type of Government

Russia is nominally a federal republic, but many areas of Russia itself are in revolt against Moscow. Non-Russian ethnic enclaves within the Russian Federation are agitating for autonomy and even independence. The Russian president is the chief of state. The Russian prime minister is the head of the government.

The laws and policies of Russia are currently in a state of flux.

Language

Russian is the official language. Note that the use of Russian has become unpopular in those ethnically non-Russian areas of the Russian Federation that are clamoring for independence.

Education

Education is compulsory and free between the ages of seven and seventeen; literacy is almost 100 percent. Instruction is conducted in many languages, and English is sometimes taught as early as the third grade. Students must pass rigorous exams to gain admittance to college.

Religion

The U.S.S.R. was officially an atheist nation; religion was suppressed, and some 50 percent of the population considered themselves nonreligious or atheist. Religious worship is now permitted. Many religions are represented in Russia, including Russian Orthodoxy, Protestantism, Islam, and Judaism. Religious participation is increasing since the Communist system (which had several characteristics of a religious belief system) has been discredited.

Demographics

Russia is not only the largest nation on earth, it is also one of the most populous, with some 150 million citizens. Its largest cities have populations exceeding those of some small European countries: 8.7 million in Moscow and 4.5 million in Saint Petersburg.

Cultural Orientation

Cognitive Styles: How Russians Organize and Process Information

Historically, Russians have not been open to outside information. With the breakup of the U.S.S.R. and the downfall of Communism, many Russians acknowledge that they must learn new ways. But it is a struggle, and they may once again close themselves off from outside information. Their tendency is to process information subjectively and associatively. Their experience teaches them to follow the universal rules and laws of the Communist Party line. Some Russians are able to transfer this allegiance to the abstract rules of science and technology.

Negotiation Strategies: What Russians Accept as Evidence

The more educated managers will let objective facts dictate the truth. However, many will still look to faith in some ideology or their own personal feelings to guide them to the truth.

Value Systems: The Basis for Behavior

Russia is currently going through a tremendous struggle to exchange the values of Communism for those of a free-market economy and democracy. The following three sections identify the Value Systems in the predominant culture—their methods of dividing right from wrong, good from evil, and so forth.

Locus of Decision Making

Although the Russians are by nature collectivistic, Communist Party rule put decision making in the hands of the party. Soviet executives made their decisions in line with party policy; as long as the party rules were followed, the decision could not be wrong. Now these individuals have to make decisions on their own—and even take responsibility for those decisions! In many instances, executives are delegating this authority to the group as a whole or to specialists within the group.

Sources of Anxiety Reduction

The demise of Communism has abolished many of the structures the people depended upon for stability. This stability is now being sought in the church, social groups, the family, or elsewhere. The transition to a free-market economy and democracy will not succeed unless the people can be shown that these changes provide increased security and stability.

Issues of Equality/Inequality

Despite the Communist premise of equality, there has always been a great deal of inequality in this culture. There is currently a power struggle between free-market economists and extremist nationalists in Russia. Since the nationalists are xenophobic and racist, the Russian people seem to have a choice of promoting equality or inequality.

Ethnic differences are also coming to the fore and threatening to disrupt social stability. And, while there is a semblance of legal equality of the sexes, Russian women still struggle for equality with men. Sexual harrassment is rampant in business and government.

Business Practices

Appointments

PUNCTUALITY

♦ Always be punctual, but do not be surprised if the Russians are not. It is not unusual for Russians to be one or two hours late to an appointment.
♦ Punctuality was not considered essential under the Soviet system, since employment was guaranteed and no one could be fired for tardiness.
♦ Even today, patience, not punctuality, is considered a virtue in Russia.
♦ Allow plenty of time for each appointment. Not only may they start late, but they may run two to three times longer than originally planned.

■ Remember that the date is written differently in many countries. In Russia and the CIS, the day is normally listed first, then the month, then the year. For example, 3.12.99 or 03.12.99 means December 3, 1999, not March 12, 1999.
■ Obtaining an appointment can be laborious. Be patient and persistent. Once your appointment is scheduled, make every effort to avoid a cancellation.
■ Business hours are generally from 9:00 A.M. to 5:00 P.M., Monday through Friday.

Negotiating

■ It is said that Russians are great "sitters" during negotiations. Russians regard compromise as a sign of weakness; compromise is morally incorrect. Russians would rather out-sit the other negotiator—and gain more concessions from the other side.
■ Be certain that all members of your negotiating team know and agree on exactly what you want out of the deal. Write this down (perhaps adding a few "nice to haves" that can be given away later) and bring it with you. Do not show the Russians anything other than unity among your team.
■ Be factual and include all levels of technical detail.
■ You may be asked to sign a *Protokol* after each meeting. This is a joint statement that delineates what was discussed. It is not a formal agreement.
■ "Final offers" are never final during initial negotiations. Be prepared to wait; the offer will be made more attractive if you can hold out.
■ If you or your negotiators have not walked out of the negotiating room in high dudgeon at least twice during the negotiations, you're being too easy. Russians expect walkouts and dire proclamations that the deal is off. Think of how often the Soviet delegation to the United Nations walked out in a huff but always came back. Play hardball; they will.
■ Until you have a signed, formal agreement, do not get overconfident about the deal at hand. And never expect that you can renegotiate later for a better deal. This contract is as advantageous as you will ever get.

- The Russians may request that some funds be paid to them directly in cash, or to an account in a foreign bank. This is because of their concern over the oppressive Russian tax system and the rarity of being paid in cash. Be prepared to propose various options, since very few Russians will be familiar with Western trade, banking, and business regulations.
- One current Russian tactic is to allow (after long negotiation) the foreign partner to own 51 percent of a joint venture. However, contracts usually require unanimity among the partners for major decisions anyway, so 51 percent is not a controlling interest.
- Include a clause requiring the joint venture partners to submit to arbitration in a neutral country if they can't come to an agreement. Sweden is the most popular choice for third-country arbitration.
- Russian regulations represent the biggest liability to a successful joint venture. Since these regulations are in constant flux (reforms are being made all the time), don't count on your Russian partner to have a full grasp of the legal issues involved. Get your own expert in Russian law. Don't be surprised when something you did yesterday is disallowed tomorrow; many laws are nebulous, and their interpretation is subject to change.
- Appearances can be deceiving. Russian firms may try to make themselves look prosperous and full of potential. Select a partner based upon full knowledge of the assets it owns or controls.

---

*b*e sure to take enough business cards. They are very important, especially since telephone books are not easily available; the phone book published in Moscow in 1990 issued only 250,000 copies— obviously not sufficient for a city of 9 million! Therefore, many people depend upon their business card files. There are now a variety of telephone books available, but their scope and circulation are narrow.

Do not be surprised if you do not receive a Russian's business card in exchange for yours. They may not have them.

- In many countries—such as Japan—people tend to respond to a question by saying "yes." In the U.S.S.R. the tendency used to be just the opposite; managers and bureaucrats said "no" at every opportunity. However, Russian businessmen now often say "yes" to proposals—even if they lack the authority to arrange the project. They make promises in order to continue the contacts they want with foreigners.
- Historically, there were many reasons why Russians said "no" to business proposals. One was that innovation had been discouraged. People were afraid that if they gave the go-ahead and a project failed, they would be held responsible. Another reason had to do with the position of an individual in a rigid, hierarchical bureaucracy. You rarely met a Russian bureaucrat who had the power to push a project forward without the agreement of others. But one individual could cancel a project, all by himself or herself. The ability to say "no" was the only real power many bureaucrats possessed; not surprisingly, they used it frequently.

*P*eace, international relations, the changes in Russia, and difficult economic situations are all common topics of conversation.

People will ask what you think of Russia and what life is like in the United States. The questions may sound somewhat bizarre, but they are usually sincere. For example, visitors were asked to verify something that had been broadcast on Russian television: a documentary on U.S. farm life that showed a veterinarian inoculating pigs with disposable needles. This astonished the Russians, who don't have enough disposable needles to use for humans!

 Business Entertaining

- Always have a good supply of soft drinks, tea, coffee (not in plastic cups!), danish, cookies, snacks, and so forth, on the meeting table. Russians try hard to provide a variety of refreshments when conducting business, and appreciate your reciprocating in kind.
- At Russian hotels and restaurants, the doormen must try to let in only certain people. Don't be surprised if they are not friendly.
- In restaurants, you may have a long wait for food. Ignore the menus; perhaps only a third of the items listed will actually be available. You must ask the waiter (if he or she speaks English) what is being served that day.
- Restaurants tend to have large tables set for many people. If your party consists of just two or three people, you may have to share a table with others.

*t*wo bottles will be on the table: one has water, the other vodka. Be aware that once you open a bottle of vodka, the concept is to drink it all at one sitting! Many vodka bottles do not have resealable caps.

Russians are very confident of their ability to drink heavily and still remain "clear." They may prefer conducting business when you are drunk. Mixed drinks are not popular.

- Dinners are held early (about 6:00 P.M.).
- It is a great honor to be invited to a Russian home. It is also a great burden for the host. Russian tradition demands that you be served a lunch or dinner that far exceeds everyone's appetite and, often, the financial capabilities of the hosts. For example, caviar might be served with huge spoons.
- It is good to know a few toasts. The most common is *Nah-zda-ROE-vee-ah*.
- In a restaurant or nightclub, Russians may invite you to dance or to come over to their table. It is best to accept graciously.

Time

- Moscow and Saint Petersburg are both in the westernmost time zone, three hours ahead of Greenwich Mean Time (G.M.T + 3), or eight hours ahead of U.S. Eastern Standard Time (E.S.T. + 8).
- The huge Russian federation spans eleven time zones. Daylight saving time changes usually occur on a Saturday night at the end of March and October.

Protocol

t—————————————————————**CULTURAL NOTE**
he Russian word *nyekulturny* (literally, "uncultured" or "bad mannered") signifies the wrong way
to do something. Foreigners are often judged by the same standards Russians apply to themselves. Some *nyekulturny* behaviors are

- Wearing your coat (and heavy boots) when you enter a public building—particularly the theater. You
  are expected to leave your coat in the *garderob* (cloakroom). One does not sit on one's coat at a concert, restaurant, and so forth. Many office buildings also have a *garderob*.
- Standing with your hands in your pockets, or generally lounging around. This is especially true in public buildings.
- Wearing business clothes that are less than conservative—for example, pastel shirts with white collars.
- Speaking or laughing loudly in public.
- Not only is whistling indoors considered *nyekulturny*, but there is a superstition that it will cause a loss
  of money.

Greetings

- Only during greetings do Russians display affection in public. Relatives and good
  friends will engage in a noisy embrace and kiss each other on the cheeks.
- Except at formal or state occasions, Russians usually greet a stranger by shaking hands and stating their name, rather than uttering a polite phrase (such as
  "How do you do?"). Respond in the same way.

Titles/Forms of Address

- Russian names are listed in the same order as in the West, but the Russian
  middle name is a patronymic (a name derived from the first name of one's
  father). Thus, Fyodor Nikolaievich Medvedev's first name is Fyodor (a Russian
  version of Theodore), his last name is Medvedev, and his middle name means
  "son of Nikolai."
- Russian women add the letter "a" on the end of their surnames; Medvedev's
  wife would be Mrs. Medvedeva.
- Unless invited to do so, do not use first names. If a Russian has a professional
  title, use the title followed by the surname. If he or she has no title, use Mr.,
  Miss, Mrs., or Ms. plus the surname.
- Among themselves, Russians use a bewildering variety of diminutives and nicknames. They also address each other by first name and patronymic, which can
  be quite a mouthful. As you establish a relationship with them, you will be
  invited to call them by one of these. This is the time to invite them to call you
  by your first name.
- Despite the length of their names, there are relatively few variations of first
  names and surnames in Russia. Indeed, some names (e.g., Ivan Ivanovich
  Ivanov) are so common that you will need additional information to be able to
  refer to the correct one. In official circles, Russians use a person's birth date to
  differentiate between identically named individuals.

Gestures

- Russian is a language abundant in curses, and there are quite a number of obscene gestures as well. Both the American "O.K." sign (thumb and forefinger touching in a circle) and any shaken-fist gesture will be interpreted as vulgar.
- Whistling is not taken as a sign of approval in a concert hall; it means you did not like the performance.
- The "thumbs up" gesture indicates approval among Russians.
- Do not sit with the legs splayed apart or with one ankle resting upon the knee.

a **CULTURAL NOTE**

s a society historically subject to police surveillance, the Russians evolved gestures that would foil eavesdroppers. For example, to avoid saying the name of Brezhnev, Russians would touch a finger to an eyebrow (a reference to Brezhnev's hairy eyebrows). The free speech that has accompanied glasnost has reduced the need for such gestures, but they have not entirely disappeared. Nowadays, a gesture may be used to refer to a member of the Russian Mafia.

- Some common traditions or superstitions include sitting for a minute before leaving a home, knocking three times on wood to avoid bad luck, and spitting three times behind the shoulder to prevent bad news.

Gifts

- Not surprisingly, items in demand make prized gifts; these often include baseball caps, rock or country and western cassettes, ballpoint pens, picture books or art books, perfume, good soaps, American cigarettes, lighters, plastic bags, and gum. Other good gifts include solar-powered calculators, well-made business card holders, VCR tapes, cameras, watches, and inexpensive jewelry.
- Take flowers, liquor, or a food item currently in scarce supply if invited to a Russian home.
- Feasting is also a part of religious holidays. Remember that the Russian Orthodox church follows the Julian calendar, not the Gregorian calendar in official use throughout the Western world. Currently, the Julian calendar is generally running thirteen days behind the Gregorian one.

Dress

- If you go to Russia during the winter, bring very warm clothes or buy Russian-style hats and gloves upon arrival. In addition, bring a pair of shoes or boots with skid-resistant soles.
- Bring your own shoe polish, since Russian streets can be muddy all year round. Women in high heels will have a difficult time if they have to run around outside on many errands.
- When buying Russian clothes, keep in mind that it is generally advantageous to look like a foreigner, as foreigners get preferential treatment almost everywhere.
- Since Russian buildings are usually well heated, a layered approach is best in clothing, allowing you to take off clothes to be comfortable while inside.
- Business dress is conservative. Russian clothing styles tend to lag years behind the West.
- While shorts are frowned upon for casual wear, you will note that Russians strip down to as little as possible on those rare days when it is sunny enough to sunbathe.

RIYADH

Saudi Arabia

CULTURAL NOTE

*g*uests in Saudi Arabia, whatever their nationality, are subject to the same rigorous Islamic law as Saudis. It is not uncommon for Westerners to be imprisoned in Saudi Arabia for possessing an illegal substance. (Alcohol, pornography, pork, and narcotics are all highly illegal.) Saudi law is draconian; thieves still have their hands amputated, and capital crimes are punished by public beheadings. Not surprisingly, the populace is quite law-abiding.

Country Background

History

Although the Arabian Peninsula has been occupied for thousands of years, the Saudi Arabian nation was only founded in 1932. In that year, after thirty years of fighting, Abdul-Aziz al-Saud united the tribes of the Peninsula.

Most of the day-to-day running of Saudi Arabia is left in the hands of foreign workers. Technical and managerial workers tend to come from North America, Europe, and Japan. Manual and unskilled laborers are primarily from Africa and Asia. The Saudis have been replacing the Middle Eastern workers that formerly constituted a large part of their foreign workforce; these Palestinians and Lebanese are not considered politically reliable by the Saudi government. Guest workers may not become citizens, no matter how long they stay in Saudi Arabia.

While most of the citizens of Saudi Arabia are quite well off, some segments of the population have not benefited from the country's wealth. Some nomadic Bedouins still maintain their traditional lifestyle. But the Bedouins are given the opportunity to change, whereas the Shiite minority is not. Fearful of the Shiite power in Iran, the Saudi government keeps its Shiite citizenry poor and powerless.

The 1990 invasion of neighboring Kuwait by Iraq proved a traumatic experience for Saudi Arabia. Iraqi Scud missiles struck Saudi territory, and a Saudi border town was briefly occupied by Iraqi troops.

To support the allied liberation of Kuwait, Saudi Arabia found itself hosting troops from thirty-three nations. Both foreign troops and Saudis had to adjust. (In deference to Western sensibilities, public beheadings were delayed until after the effective conclusion of the war; upon resumption of the executions, sixteen men were beheaded in one day.) Contrary to the expectations of some observers, however, the Saudi government did not find itself forced to initiate liberal reforms.

Type of Government

Saudi Arabia is an Islamic monarchy. It was united, is ruled, and is run by the house of Saud (al-Saud). There is no written constitution, although it is traditional to say that the Koran is the constitution of Saudi Arabia.

Abdul-Aziz al-Saud (known incorrectly in the West as Ibn Saud) united the Arabian peninsula in 1932. Saudi Arabia was named after him, and he became the new country's first king. All of the successive kings have been sons of Abdul-Aziz; indeed, the majority of government officials are members of the al-Saud family. (Abdul-Aziz united his kingdom by marriage and by conquest. He married more than 300 times and has thousands of descendants.)

The king of Saudi Arabia is also prime minister, making him both the head of state and head of government. An appointed Council of Ministers advises the king. There is no elected government. The only codified restraint on the power of the king is Islamic law. In practice, however, the king is careful not to alienate either the religious fundamentalists or his people.

CULTURAL NOTE

*W*hile Saudis are thankful for the protection of the United States and the Western Alliance in the Gulf War with Iraq, the government and much of the populace are ambivalent about the West. Western values are seen as decadent and threatening to the Saudi way of life. Any change in this attitude will come very slowly.

Language

Arabic is the official language. Foreign-educated Saudis usually speak English.

Education

A massive education campaign has raised the literacy level to 57 percent. Many older, rural Saudis are still illiterate; most post offices are surrounded by scribes who write letters for the illiterate. Educational levels for males are far above those for females, as Wahabi tradition dismissed education for girls as counterproductive.

Religion

Saudi Arabia is an Islamic nation. Saudi citizens are Muslim and are not permitted to change religions. Westerners are frequently surprised to learn that Saudi Arabia is a more fundamentalist nation than the Islamic Republic of Iran.

The official religion of Saudi Arabia is the Wahabi branch of Sunni Islam. Wahabism is a rigid, ultrapuritanical sect that reflects Islam as it was practiced during the lifetime of Mohammed, over 1,300 years ago.

Many Western observers believe that Wahabism is insufficiently flexible for the wealthy, modern state that Saudi Arabia has become. However, it is firmly entrenched, and adherence to its precepts is enforced daily by the *Matawain* (religious police).

Saudi Arabia is home to the two holiest cities of Islam: *Makkah* (Mecca) and *Madinah* (Medina). Hundreds of thousands of Muslims from all over the world make the pilgrimage to *Makkah* each year. Entry into *Makkah* and *Madinah* is prohibited to non-Muslims.

Demographics

The population is just over fourteen million, not including more than two million guest workers. About 90 percent of the citizens are Arabs, the majority belonging to the Wahabi branch of Sunni Islam. The remaining 10 percent are mostly African or Asian, descendants of Islamic settlers who have been coming to the Arabian Peninsula for generations. (Modern guest workers, Islamic or not, are not permitted to become citizens.)

Cultural Orientation

Cognitive Styles: How Saudi Arabians Organize and Process Information

Saudis find it difficult to accept any outside information that does not reflect Islamic values. Most Saudis are trained to think associatively. However, the majority of Saudis complete their higher education in the United States, where they learn to process information conceptually and analytically. They do become personally involved in all situations rather than using rules or laws to solve problems.

Negotiation Strategies: What Saudi Arabians Accept as Evidence

Generally, a Saudi's faith in Islamic ideologies shapes the truth, but it is also affected by the immediate feelings of the participants. Objective facts seldom overrule one's thinking.

Value Systems: The Basis for Behavior

Saudi Arabia is a very strong Islamic state and finds it difficult to integrate Western ideas into its value systems. The following three sections identify the Value Systems in the predominant culture—their methods of dividing right from wrong, good from evil, and so forth.

Locus of Decision-Making

The male leader is the decision maker, but he does so through consensus of the group or collective. The individual is always subordinate to the family, tribe, or collective. Solutions to all problems are found in the correct interpretation and application of divine law. Leadership and identity come from one's lineage and one's ability to protect the honor of the extended family.

Sources of Anxiety Reduction

Tribal membership remains the cornerstone of the individual's social identity, and security is found in family loyalty and absolute submission to Islamic law. There is a strong sense of fatalism, with one's destiny in the hands of Allah. One can do nothing about this, so one tends to accept the status quo. Loyalty to the house of Saud, not nationality, brings a feeling of national security.

Issues of Equality/Inequality

Within Islam all believers are equal and united in the ulma. There is cultural homogeneity among tribes. Most are Sunni Muslims adhering to Wahabi religious tenets. There are a great number of foreign workers who are accepted with varying degrees of bias. Men and women are seen as qualitatively different in emotion and intellect. Public life is the exclusive domain of men. There are very few occupations open to Saudi women.

Business Practices

Appointments

PUNCTUALITY

+ Punctuality is not considered a virtue in Saudi Arabia. Your client may be late for an appointment or not show up at all. You, however, should endeavor to be prompt.

+ It is standard practice to keep supplicants, including foreign business people, waiting. Do not expect to be able to keep more than one appointment per day.

- You will need a Saudi sponsor before you may enter Saudi Arabia. This sponsor will act as intermediary and arrange appointments with the appropriate individuals.

n

CULTURAL NOTE

on-Muslims may not enter Saudi Arabia without an invitation, which usually involves being sponsored by a prominent Saudi. Once you enter the country, realize that you are beyond the protection of your government. You are subject to Saudi Islamic law, and something as innocuous (to Westerners) as dressing immodestly in public can result in your being arrested or even whipped. Study the rules for acceptable behavior carefully. Also be aware that you may not leave Saudi Arabia without an exit permit, no matter what the emergency.

As for businesswomen, the limitations on allowable behavior are so stringent that, even if a businesswoman is given a visa, there will be little that she will be permitted to do.

- An appointment is rarely private. Expect your visit to be interrupted by phone calls and visits from your client's friends and family. Westerners frequently find these distractions infuriating; try to maintain your equanimity.
- Saudi officials are prohibited by tradition from working more than six hours per day. Mornings are usually best for appointments.
- Because of the summer heat, some Saudi business people work after dark. They may request an evening appointment at any time up to midnight.
- Friday is the Muslim holy day; no business is conducted. Most people do not work on Thursdays, either. The workweek runs from Saturday through Wednesday.
- Government hours are 7:30 A.M. to 2:30 P.M., Saturday through Wednesday.
- Banking hours tend to be 8:30 A.M. to 12 noon and 5:00 to 7:00 P.M., Saturday through Wednesday. Some banks keep Thursday morning hours as well.
- Business hours vary widely, but most businesses close for much of the afternoon and reopen for a few hours in late afternoon.
- Holidays: Remember that the Islamic calendar uses lunar months of 28 days, so an Islamic year of 12 months is only 354 days long. Holidays will thus be on different dates by the Western calendar every year. Paperwork should carry two dates, the Gregorian (Western) date and the Hijrah (Arabic) date.
- Check with your Saudi sponsor as to which holidays will be observed by the persons you intend to meet. However, two important holidays are observed by everyone, and no business will be conducted during them. They are
  'Aid-al-Fitr—The festival of breaking fast. This is a three-day feast celebrating the end of the fasting of the month of *Ramadan*.

'Aid-al-Adha—The feast of the sacrifice. This is a three-day festival beginning on the tenth day of the month of *Zul-Hijiah*.

 Negotiating

- The pace of business is much slower in Saudi Arabia than in the West. Be patient.
- Business meetings always start slowly, with long inquiries into one's health and journey.
- Decisions will take a long time to be made.
- A clever Saudi contact will sound out the opinions of various decision makers before you meet with them. Then, he will put you in contact only with the ones most likely to favor your proposal. Do not rush your contact into introducing you to decision makers. To do so is to risk having your proposal turned down because you met with the wrong persons.
- Your Saudi contact-sponsor is the single most important key to success in Saudi Arabia. You must find one that has the right temperament and influential friends or relatives. If you do not yet have a contact, inquire about one through banks doing business in Saudi Arabia or the U.S. International Trade Administration. Once you choose a sponsor, you will not be permitted to switch.
- Business cards should be printed in English on one side and in Arabic on the other.
- Many Saudis have unlisted telephone numbers. When a Saudi gives you his business card, record all the information on the card.
- Be prepared to leave multiple copies of all brochures and materials. The person you spoke to might not be the real decision maker, and your proposal may have to be relayed to one or more persons.
- Saudis speak at a much closer distance than North Americans are used to. Do not back up or shy away. There is also more physical contact. Conversations usually involve touching.
- Coffee is often served toward the end of a business meeting. This is a signal that the meeting will soon conclude. Incense is often lit at this time as well.
- Saudi men often walk hand in hand. If a Saudi holds your hand, take it as a sign of friendship.
- Arabic is a language of hyperbole. When a Saudi says "yes," it usually means "possibly." Be encouraged by this, but do not assume that the negotiating is over.
- Saving face and the avoidance of shame are vital to Saudis. You may have to compromise on some issue to protect someone's dignity even if there is no substantive reason to do so.
- Do not bring up the subject of women unless your Saudi counterpart does so first. Do not even inquire as to the health of a Saudi's wife or daughter.
- The topic of Israel should similarly be avoided.
- Sports are a good topic of conversation. Soccer (football), horse and camel racing (with betting prohibited), hunting, and falconry are the most popular Saudi sports.

 Business Entertaining

- Hosting visitors is considered a virtue among Saudis, so they will take care of all of the entertaining within their country.
- Be prepared to remove your shoes before entering a building. Follow the lead of your host.

- Remember that alcohol and pork are illegal, and that eating is done with the right hand only. Even if you are left-handed, eat with your right hand.
- If you cannot keep up with Saudi appetites during a meal, try to nibble on something while they finish eating.
- Expect to encounter eating utensils only in the most Westernized of Saudi homes.
- Also expect constant inquiries of "How are you?" Your host will be concerned that you have everything you want to eat or drink, and this is a common way of asking.

Time
- Saudi Arabia is three hours ahead of Greenwich Mean Time (G.M.T. + 3) or eight hours ahead of U.S. Eastern Standard Time (E.S.T. + 8).

Protocol

Greetings
- As there are several styles of greeting currently in use in Saudi Arabia, it is safest to wait for your Saudi counterpart to initiate the greeting, especially at a first meeting.
- Westernized Saudi men shake hands with other men.
- Some Saudi men will shake hands with Western women. Saudi women take no part in business. When a veiled Saudi woman is with a Saudi man, it is not traditional to introduce her. Again, follow the Saudi's lead.
- A more traditional Saudi greeting between men involves each grasping the other's right hand, placing the left hand on the other's right shoulder, and exchanging kisses on each cheek.

Titles/Forms of Address
- Westerners frequently find Arabic names confusing. The best solution is to ask your Saudi sponsor to provide you with the names—written in English—of any Saudis you will have to meet, speak to, or correspond with. Find out their full names for correspondence and how they are to be addressed in person.
- Saudi names are written in Arabic. In part because short vowels are not written in Arabic, translating from Arabic to other alphabets is not an exact science. Arabic names may be spelled several different ways in English (e.g., the leader of Libya's name is variously rendered Colonel Muammar al-Qaddafi, Mu'ammar al-Qadhafi, and so forth).
- In general, Saudi names are written in the same order as English names: title, given name, middle name (often a patronymic), and surname (family name). Thus, the current ruler of Saudi Arabia is King Fahd bin Abdul Aziz al-Saud; his title is King, his given name is Fahd, bin Abdul-Aziz is a patronymic meaning "son of Abdul-Aziz," and al-Saud is the family name.
- The term *bin* (sometimes spelled *ibn*) literally means "from" in Arabic, so it is not immediately apparent whether a name like *bin* Mubarak indicates "son of Mubarak" or "from the town of Mubarak." However, most Saudis use it as a patronymic.

- If an Arab's grandfather is (or was) a famous person, he sometimes adds his grandfather's name. Thus, Dr. Mahmoud bin Sultan bin Hamad Al Muqrin is "Dr. Mahmoud, son of Sultan, grandson of Hamad, of the House (family) of Muqrin."
- Westerners frequently mistake *bin* for the name Ben, short for Benjamin. Obviously, *bin* has no meaning by itself, and one cannot address a Saudi as *bin*.
- The female version of *bin* is *bint*. Thus, Princess Fatima bint Ibrahim al-Saud is "Princess Fatima, daughter of Ibrahim, of the house of Saud."
- Most Saudis should be addressed by title and given name (e.g., Prince Khalil), just as you would address a member of the British aristocracy (e.g., Sir John). They can also be addressed as "Your Excellency." In writing, use their full name.
- In Saudi Arabia, the title *Sheikh* (pronounced "shake") is used by any important leader well versed in the Koran; it does not designate membership in the royal family.

Gestures

- The left hand is considered unclean in the Arab world. Always use the right hand in preference to the left (unless you are handling something considered unclean). Never eat with the left hand; eat only with your right hand. Avoid gesturing with the left hand.
- Although Arabs constantly gesture with their hands while speaking, they do not point at another person. This would be considered impolite.
- As a general rule, keep both feet on the ground. Arabs do not cross their legs when sitting. Never show the bottom of your foot to an Arab; this is considered offensive.
- The "thumbs up" gesture is offensive throughout the Arab world.

Gifts

- Saudi hospitality is legendary. However, you are not expected to bring any gift when invited into a Saudi home.
- Traditionally, every Saudi who must broker or approve a business deal takes a percentage. Be careful that you do not run afoul of the U.S. Foreign Corrupt Practices Act.

Dress

- While foreigners are not exempt from Saudi standards of dress, do not adopt native clothing [for men, a *ghotra* (headdress) and *thobe* (flowing white robe); for women, a veil and an *abaya* (black head-to-foot robe)]. Saudis may find it offensive to see foreigners dressed in their traditional clothes.
- Foreigners should wear Western clothes that approach the modesty of Saudi dress. Despite the heat of the desert, most of the body must remain covered.
- Men should wear long trousers and a shirt, preferably long-sleeved. A jacket and tie are usually required for business meetings. Keep shirts buttoned up to the collarbone. Saudi law prohibits the wearing of neck jewelry by men, and Westerners have been arrested for violating such rules.
- Women must wear modest clothing. The neckline should be high, and the sleeves should come to at least the elbows. Hemlines should be well below the knee, if not ankle-length. The overall effect should be one of baggy con-

cealment; a full-length outfit that is tight and revealing is not acceptable. Therefore, pants or pantsuits are not recommended. While a hat or scarf is not always required, it is wise to keep a scarf at hand. The suitability of your attire will be apparent as soon as you venture out; if Saudi men stare lewdly at you, your dress is not sufficiently modest. These same stares are used to determine when a Saudi girl is old enough to start wearing an *abaya*.

t———————————————**CULTURAL NOTE**

he *Matawain* (religious police) enforce the modesty of dress in public. They have full civil authority to arrest violators. Indeed, where the jurisdiction of the civil and religious police overlap, the civil authorities generally defer to the *Matawain*. While the ranks of the *Matawain* include a surprising number of foreign-educated Saudis, the ones enforcing Islamic law on street corners—and there are many—are usually uneducated zealots brandishing camel whips. Western women with skirts that are too short can expect to have their legs whipped by a *Matawah*. Most Westerners fall afoul of them sooner or later. The *Matawain* can be neither reasoned with nor bribed, only endured.

Singapore

Singapore remains a booming center of capitalism in Southeast Asia. It is considered very safe (even antiseptic), but visitors should be warned that Singapore's myriad laws apply to natives and foreigners equally. Before arrival, travelers should become familiar with these laws, e.g., no littering, no chewing gum, no illegal drugs, no pornographic materials, no weapons, no jaywalking, no spitting, no smoking in most public places. And be sure to flush a public toilet after you use it; the fine for not doing so is $150.

Country Background

History

A crossroads of trade for centuries, Singapore was annexed by the British in 1819. British rule was to last some 120 years, and gave the island British legal traditions and the English language. During World War II, the Japanese occupied Singapore from 1942 to 1945. After the war Singapore became a British Crown Colony, but the power of the British Empire was fading.

Singapore's first election was held in 1959. The People's Action Party (PAP) took the election and has remained in power ever since. The first prime minister was Cambridge-educated Lee Kuan Yew. Singapore experienced tremendous development under Lee and the PAP.

Singapore joined the Malayan Federation in 1963, but it seceded just two years later. Since 1965 it has been a separate, sovereign nation and a member of the British Commonwealth.

Many did not believe that Singapore could survive as an independent country. The tiny island had no natural resources aside from its harbor, and no way to defend itself against populous and often aggressive neighbors. Realizing that Singapore's people were its greatest national asset, Prime Minister Lee Kuan Yew's government embarked upon social engineering on a grand scale. The people would be educated, and capitalism would be encouraged. Old traditions were suppressed, and Singapore was turned into a true meritocracy.

No aspect of life was considered beyond the reach of the government. The "3-S Plan" of Social Responsibility, Social Attitude, and Skill became an official credo. Citizens were constantly reminded of the threat from Singapore's populous neighbors, and internal dissent was silenced. Tiny Singapore built up defense forces with the most up-to-date technology in the world. However, opponents of the government were sometimes jailed without trial, and overly critical foreign journalists were deported, and any publication that employed such a journalist was liable to be banned from sale in Singapore.

Type of Government

The Republic of Singapore is a parliamentary democracy that has been ruled by one party since the nation achieved independence from Malaysia in 1965. The government exhorts its people to accept stringent limitations on freedom in return for peace and prosperity. These limitations often make Singapore more attractive from a business standpoint. (For example, Singapore's citizens have a high rate of savings, since participation in the Central Provident Fund—a pension program—is mandatory for all citizens.)

The leaders of Singapore are fond of saying that their island's only resources are the wit, industry, and inventiveness of the Singaporean people. They have successfully turned a developing nation into a center of capitalism.

Singapore has a unicameral 87-seat parliament. The prime minister is the head of government. The chief of state is the president.

Language

Singapore has four official languages: Malay, Tamil, Chinese, and English. To unify Singapore's three fractious ethnic groups—the Chinese, Malays, and Indians—English (native to none of these groups) became the language of instruction, business, and government. (This process has not ended; to unify the diverse Chinese populations, only Mandarin Chinese movies may be shown—despite the fact that most Singaporean Chinese speak Cantonese, not Mandarin.)

Religion

Most of the indigenous Malay are Muslim, but not all Muslims are Malay. The Muslims account for over 15 percent of the population. Similarly, Christianity is adhered to by several different ethnic groups (totaling almost 13 percent). Those Singaporeans who trace their roots to the Indian subcontinent come from many different ethnic groups; they may be Hindu, Muslim, Christian, Zoroastrian, Sikh, or adherents of yet another religion. The majority Chinese may profess to follow Buddhism, Confucianism, Taoism, none of these, or several of the above simultaneously. Wisely, Singapore has no official religion.

Demographics

Almost 2,800,000 people live in this tiny nation. As a prosperous trading center, Singapore attracted many races. The indigenous Malay now constitute only 15 percent of Singapore's citizenry. Numerous ethnic groups from the Indian subcontinent call Singapore home; together they make up 7 percent of the population of Singapore. Europeans were attracted to Singapore, especially when it was a British colony. But Europeans now constitute less than 1 percent of Singapore's population. The vast majority (76 percent) of Singaporeans are Chinese.

Cultural Orientation

Cognitive Styles: How Singaporeans Organize and Process Information

In Singapore we find a culture closed to all but select information. Singaporeans' basic education teaches them to think associatively, but higher education brings in conceptual and analytical thinking. They have strong loyalties to nation, companies, and groups, but particular relationships are more important than personal values.

Negotiation Strategies: What Singaporeans Accept as Evidence

Immediate feelings have a strong influence on the truth. This is usually biased by faith in the ideologies of nationalism, and supplemented by the accumulation of objective facts.

Value Systems: The Basis for Behavior

The strong Malay and Indian subcultures have different value systems from those of the Chinese. The following three sections identify the Value Systems in the predominant culture—their methods of dividing right from wrong, good from evil, and so forth.

Locus of Decision Making

Individuals must work within the consensus of the group and forgo personal triumphs. The person with the highest ethos in the group (usually the oldest member) is the de facto leader. One must not lose face or cause another to lose face, so Singaporeans would rather use polite vagaries than say an outright "no." There is a very strong authoritative structure that demands impartiality and obedience. One must build a relationship with the participants of a group before one can conduct business.

Sources of Anxiety Reduction

The family is the most important unit of social organization. Political power, wealth, and education are the criteria for social status. There is a very strong work ethic in which emotional restraint is prized and aggressive behavior is frowned upon. Although this is a multiracial society with strong national identity, the social structure continues to change, and this leads to uncertainty. Multiracial housing has fostered feelings of insecurity, not community.

Issues of Equality/Inequality

Businesses are more competitive and ethnocentric than in the United States. Emphasis is on competence, merit, and team play. Performance, progress, excellence, and achievement are highly prized for the group. There is an inherent trust in people of the same ethnic group, with a strong feeling of interdependency among members of a group or business. There is some evidence of ethnic bias among the dominant Chinese against the Malays and the Indians. There are clearly differentiated sex roles in society, but Western style equality is creeping in. Men still dominate in all public situations.

Business Practices

Appointments

 ———————————————————————— **PUNCTUALITY**

◆ It is important to be on time for all business appointments. Making a Singaporean executive wait is insulting and impolite.

CULTURAL NOTE

*I*n Singapore, social events can involve different rules for different cultural groups. In general, when invited to a social event, most Singaporeans arrive on time or slightly late. Traditionalists are concerned that arriving on time to a dinner may make them appear greedy and impatient.

Once a close friendship has been established, guests may arrive a few minutes early to a social occasion. If you are the host and your guests are close friends, it is important to be ready early.

- Try to schedule appointments at least two weeks in advance. Executives are quite busy and travel frequently—especially to conferences in their area of specialization.
- English is the language of most business transactions and virtually all business or government correspondence in Singapore. However, the English spoken often has native inflections, syntax, and grammar, which can easily lead to misunderstandings.
- Business hours are generally 9:00 A.M. to 5:00 P.M., Monday through Friday. However, many offices stagger their work hours, with workers arriving any time from 7:30 A.M. to 9:30 A.M. Some offices will be open for a half day on Saturdays, generally in the morning.
- The traditional lunchtime was from 12:00 noon to 2:00 P.M. Efforts have been made to reduce this to a single hour, from 1:00 to 2:00 P.M.; nevertheless, many people will take longer than an hour for lunch. Friday is the Muslim holy day, and Muslims who work on Fridays will take a two-hour break at lunchtime.
- Remember that Singapore is a meritocracy. Few people get ahead, either in business or in government, without hard work and long hours. Executives will often work far longer days than their subordinates.

Negotiating

- The pace of business negotiations in Singapore is much slower than that in the United States. Be patient.
- It would be unusual to complete a complicated business deal in only one trip to Singapore. Expect to take several trips over a period of months.
- Since politeness demands that a Singaporean not disagree openly, the word "no" is rarely heard. A polite but evasive "yes" is simply a technique to avoid giving offense. In Singapore, "yes" can mean anything from "I agree" to "maybe" to "I hope you can tell from my lack of enthusiasm that I really mean 'no'."
- A clear way to indicate "no" is to suck in air through the teeth. This sound always indicates a problem, no matter what words are said.
- Evading is indicative of a "no," even if the person has said neither "yes" nor "no." The person may even pretend that the question was never asked.
- Remember that a Singaporean must like and be comfortable with you personally in order to do business. This relationship does not extend to your company. If your company replaces you with another executive, the new executive will have to forge this relationship anew (unless the new executive is a blood relative of yours).
- Politeness is the single most important attribute for successful relationships in Singapore. This politeness in no way hinders the determination of Singaporean business people to get their own way.

CULTURAL NOTE

*S*tandards of polite behavior vary widely between cultures. Many Singaporeans will ask you highly personal questions (such as "Why aren't you married?" or "How much do you earn?) without realizing that Westerners find such questions intrusive. Simply smile and explain that such topics are not discussed openly in your culture—and be aware that you, too, will unknowingly violate local standards of polite behavior.

- People in Singapore may smile or laugh in situations that Westerners consider inappropriate. Smiles may hide embarrassment, shyness, bitterness, discord, and/or loss of face. Singaporean businessmen may laugh at the most serious part of a business meeting; this may be an expression of anxiety, not frivolity.
- In Singapore, one who expresses anger in public has shamefully lost face. A person who loses his or her temper is considered unable to control himself or herself. Such a person will not be trusted or respected.
- It is considered polite among Singaporean Chinese to offer both the positive and negative options in virtually every decision. Even when speaking in English, they are likely to add a "yes/no" pattern to a question. Rather than asking "Would you like to have dinner?" they are likely to ask "You want dinner or not?" The phrases involved ("want or not want?" "good or not?" "can or cannot?") are direct translations of Chinese phrases into English. They often sound unduly aggressive to Western ears.
- Be cautious in asking Singaporean Chinese a question. English speakers would give a negative answer to the question "Isn't my order ready yet?" by responding "no" (meaning, "No, it's not ready"). The Chinese pattern is the opposite: "yes" (meaning, "Yes, it is not ready").
- Age and seniority are highly respected. If you are part of a delegation, line up in such a way that the most important persons will be introduced first. If you are introducing two people, state the name of the most important person first (e.g., "President Smith, this is Engineer Wong").
- Speak in quiet, gentle tones. Always remain calm. Leave plenty of time for someone to respond to a statement you make; people in Singapore do not jump on the end of someone else's sentences. Politeness demands that they leave a respectful pause (as long as ten to fifteen seconds) before responding. Westerners often assume that they have agreement and resume talking before a Singaporean has a chance to respond.
- Business cards should be printed (preferably embossed) in English. Since ethnic Chinese constitute the majority of Singaporeans (and an even higher percentage of business people), it is a good idea to have the reverse side of your card translated into Chinese (gold ink is the most prestigious color for Chinese characters).
- The exchange of business cards is a formal ceremony in Singapore. After introductions are made, the visiting business person should offer his or her card. Make sure you give a card to each person present. With both hands on your card, present it to the recipient with the print facing him or her, so that he or she can read it. The recipient will receive the card with both hands, then study it for a few moments before carefully putting it away in a pocket. You should do the same when a card is presented to you. Never put a card in your back pocket, where many men carry their wallets. Do not write on someone's business card.
- Topics to avoid in conversation include any criticism of Singaporean ways, religion, bureaucracy, or politics. Also avoid any discussion of sex.
- Good topics for discussion include tourism, travel, plans for the future, organizational success (talking about personal success is considered impolite boasting), and food (while remaining complimentary to the local cuisine).

Business Entertaining

- Take advantage of any invitations to social events. Establishing a successful business relationship hinges on establishing a social relationship as well.
- Food is vitally important in Singapore culture. Social occasions always involve food. Indeed, the standard Chinese greeting literally means "Have you eaten?"
- Respond to written invitations in writing. Among the Chinese, white and blue are colors associated with sadness; do not print invitations on paper of these colors. Red or pink paper is a good choice for invitations.
- Generally, spouses may be invited to dinners but not to lunch. However, no business will be discussed at an event where spouses are present.
- Singapore's anticorruption laws are so strict that government officials may be prohibited from attending social events.

Time
- Singapore is eight hours ahead of Greenwich Mean Time (G.M.T. + 8), making it thirteen hours ahead of U.S. Eastern Standard Time (E.S.T. + 13).

Protocol

Greetings

- Singapore has three major ethnic groups, each with its own traditions: Chinese, Malay, and Indian.
- With younger or foreign-educated Singaporeans, a handshake is the most common form of greeting. The standard Asian handshake is more of a handclasp; it is rather limp and lasts for some ten or twelve seconds. (By contrast, most North American handshakes last for only three or four seconds.) Often, both hands will be used.
- In Singapore, Westernized women may shake hands with both men and women. Singaporean men usually wait for a woman to offer her hand. It is perfectly acceptable for a woman to simply nod upon an introduction rather than offer her hand. Women should offer their hands only upon greetings; too-frequent handshaking is easily misinterpreted as an amorous advance. (Among themselves, men tend to shake hands on both greeting and departure.)
- Among Singaporean Chinese, the traditional greeting was a bow. However, most now shake hands or combine a bow with a handshake. Chinese men are likely to be comfortable shaking hands with a woman—more so than other ethnic groups of Singapore.
- Singaporean Malay are generally Muslim. Traditionally, there is no physical contact between Muslim men and women. Indeed, if a religious Muslim male is touched by a woman, he must ritually cleanse himself before he prays again. Because of this, women should not offer to shake hands with Malay men nor should men offer to shake hands with Malay women. Of course, if a Westernized Malay offers to shake hands, do so.
- The traditional Malay greeting is called the *salaam*, which is akin to a handshake without the grip. Both parties stretch out one or both hands, touch each other's hand(s) lightly, then bring their hand(s) back to rest over their heart.

This greeting is done only between people of the same sex. However, if cloth such as a scarf or shawl prevents actual skin-to-skin contact, then Malay men and women may engage in the salaam.

- Many, but not all, Singaporean Indians are Hindu. They avoid public contact between men and women, although not as vehemently as most Muslims. Men may shake hands with men, and women with women, but only Westernized Hindus will shake hands with the opposite sex.
- The traditional Indian greeting involves a slight bow with the palms of the hands together (as if praying). This greeting, called the *namaste*, will generally be used only by older, traditional Hindus. However, it is also an acceptable alternative to a handshake when a Western businesswoman greets an Indian man.

 Titles/Forms of Address

- Most people you meet should be addressed with a title and their name. If a person does not have a professional title (President, Engineer, Doctor), simply use Mr. or Madam, Mrs., or Miss, plus their name.
- Each of the three major ethnic groups in Singapore has different naming patterns.
- Chinese names generally consist of a family name followed by two (sometimes one) personal names. In the name Chang Wu Jiang, Chang is the surname (or clan name). He would be addressed with his title plus Chang (Mr. Chang, Dr. Chang).
- Chinese wives do not generally take their husband's surnames, but instead maintain their maiden names. Although Westerners commonly address a married woman as Mrs. plus her husband's family name, it is more appropriate to call her Madam plus her maiden family name. For example, Li Chu Chin (female) is married to Chang Wu Jiang (male). Westerners would probably call her Mrs. Chang. She is properly addressed as Madam Li.
- Thankfully, many Chinese adopt an English first name so that English speakers can have a familiar-sounding name to identify them by. Thus, Chang Wu Jiang may call himself Mr. Wally Chang. Others use their initials (Mr. W. J. Chang).
- If many Chinese seem to have similar clan names, it is because there are only about 400 different surnames in China. However, when these surnames are transcribed into English, there are several possible variations. For example, Wong, Wang, and Huang are all English versions of the same Chinese clan name.
- Malays do not have family names. Each Muslim is known by a given name plus *bin* (son of) plus their father's name. For example, Osman bin Ali is "Osman, son of Ali." He would properly be called Mr. Osman, not Mr. Ali—Mr. Ali would be Osman's father.
- A Malay woman is known by her given name plus *binti* (daughter of) plus her father's name. For example, Khadijah binti Fauzi is "Khadijah, daughter of Fauzi." She would be known as Miss Khadijah or, if married, Mrs. Khadijah. For business purposes, some Malay women attach their husband's name. Thus, if Khadijah was married to Osman, she might choose to be known as Mrs. Khadijah Osman. Note that in English, *binti* may also be spelled *binte*.
- Some Westernized Malays drop the *bin* or *binti* from their name.
- Indians in Singapore may follow several different traditions. While they did not traditionally have surnames, some have now adopted a family name that all members of their family use, generation after generation.
- Traditional Indians have no family surname. An Indian male will use the initial of his father's name first, followed by his own personal name. For example, V.

Thiruselvan is "Thiruselvan, son of 'V.'" For legal purposes, both names would be written out with an "s/o" (for "son of") between the names: Thiruselvan s/o Vijay. In either case, he would be known as Mr. Thiruselvan. However, long Indian names are often shortened. He may prefer to be called either Mr. Thiru or Mr. Selvan.

- Indian female names follow the same pattern: father's initial plus personal name. When written fully out, "d/o" ("daughter of") is used instead of "s/o." When an Indian woman marries, she usually ceases to use her father's initial; instead, she follows her personal name with her husband's name. For instance, when S. Kamala (female) marries V. Thiru (male), she will go by Mrs. Kamala Thiru.

- With so many complexities, it is best to ask a Singaporean what you should call him or her. Repeat it to make sure you have it correct. Be forward in explaining what they should call you (they may be equally unsure as to which is your sur- name), but choose the same degree of formality. Don't tell a Singaporean to "just call me Bob" when you are calling him Dr. Gupta.

 Gestures

- Aside from handshakes, there is no public contact between the sexes in Singapore. Do not kiss or hug a person of the opposite sex in public—even if you are husband and wife. On the other hand, contact is permitted between people of the same sex. Men may hold hands with men or even walk with their arms around each other; this is interpreted as nothing except friendship.

- Among both Muslims and Hindus, the left hand is considered unclean. Eat with your right hand only. Do not touch anything or anyone with your left hand if you can use your right hand instead. Accept gifts and hold cash in the right hand. (Obviously, when both hands are needed, use them both.)

- The foot is also considered unclean. Do not move anything with your feet, and do not touch anything with your feet.

- Do not show the soles of your feet or shoes. This restriction determines how one sits: You can cross your legs at the knee, but you cannot sit with one ankle on the other knee. Also, do not prop your feet up on anything not intended for feet, such as a desk.

- It is impolite to point at anyone with the forefinger. Malays use a forefinger only to point at animals. Even pointing with two fingers is impolite among many Indians. When you must indicate something or someone, use the entire right hand (palm out). You can also point with your right thumb, as long as all four fingers are curled down. (Make sure all your fingers are curled—older Malays would interpret a fist with the thumb and little finger extended as an insult.)

- Pounding one fist into the palm of your other hand is another obscene Malay gesture to be avoided.

- The head is considered the seat of the soul by many Indians and Malays. Never touch someone's head, not even to pat the hair of a child.

- Among Indians, a side-to-side toss of one's head indicates agreement, although Westerners may interpret it as a nod meaning "no." Watch carefully; the Indian head toss is not quite the same as the Western negative nod (which leads with the jaw).

- As in much of the world, to beckon someone, you hold your hand out, palm downward, and make a scooping motion with the fingers. Beckoning someone with the palm up and wagging one finger, as in the United States, can be con- strued as an insult.

- Standing tall with your hands on your hips—the "arms akimbo" position—is always interpreted as an angry, aggressive posture.
- The comfortable standing distance between two people in Singapore varies with the culture. In general, stand as far apart as you would if you were about to shake hands (about 2 to 3 feet). Indians tend to stand a bit further apart (3 or 3 1/2 feet).

 Gifts

- Singapore prides itself on being the most corruption-free state in Asia. Consequently, it has strict laws against bribery. Government employees may not accept any gift at all.
- Gifts are given between friends. Do not give a gift to anyone before you have established a personal relationship with that person. Otherwise, the gift may have the appearance of a bribe.
- It is not the custom to unwrap a gift in the presence of the giver. To do so would suggest that the recipient is greedy and impatient. Worse, if the gift is somehow inappropriate or disappointing, loss of face would result. Expect the recipient to thank you briefly, then put the still-wrapped gift aside until you have left.
- The Chinese traditionally decline a gift three times before accepting; this prevents them from appearing greedy. Continue to insist; once they accept the gift, say that you are pleased that they have done so.
- Gifts of food are always appreciated by Chinese, but avoid bringing food gifts with you to a dinner or party unless it has been agreed upon beforehand. To bring food may imply that your host cannot provide enough. Instead, send food as a thank-you gift afterwards. Candy or fruit baskets are good choices.

t────────────**CULTURAL NOTE**

he Chinese associate all of the following with funerals—do not give them as gifts:

- Straw sandals
- Clocks
- A stork or crane (although the Western association of storks with births is known to many young Chinese)
- Handkerchiefs (often given at funerals; they symbolize sadness and weeping)
- Gifts or wrapping paper where the predominant color is white, black, or blue

Also avoid any gifts of knives, scissors, or cutting tools; to the Chinese, they suggest the severing of a friendship.

Although the Chinese only brought flowers to the sick or to funerals, Western advertising has popularized flowers as gifts. Make sure you give an even number of flowers; an odd number would be very unlucky.

- At Chinese New Year, it is customary to give a gift of money in a red envelope to children and to the nongovernmental service personnel you deal with on a regular basis. This gift is called a *hong bao*. Give only new bills in even numbers and even amounts. Many employers give each employee a hong bao equivalent to one month's salary.
- Since pork and alcohol are prohibited to observing Muslims, do not give them as gifts to Malays. Other foods make good gifts, although meat products must be *halal* (the Muslim equivalent of kosher). The prohibition against pork and alcohol also precludes pigskin products and perfumes containing alcohol.
- Malays consider dogs unclean. Do not give toy dogs or gifts that picture dogs.

- Among Indians, the frangipani flower (used by Hawaiians to make leis) is used only for funeral wreaths.
- Should you give money to an Indian, make sure it is an odd number (just the opposite of Chinese tradition). Usually this is done by adding a single dollar; for example, give $11 instead of $10.
- Observant Hindus do not eat beef or use cattle products. This eliminates most leather products as gifts.

 Dress

- Singapore is only some 85 miles (136.8 km) north of the Equator. It is hot and humid all year long, with a temperature range of 75 to 88°F (24 to 31°C), and humidity above 90 percent.
- The rainy season is November through January, but sudden showers occur all year long. Many people carry an umbrella every day.
- Because of the heat and humidity, business dress in Singapore is often casual. Standard formal office wear for men is dark trousers, light-colored long-sleeved shirt, and tie, without a jacket. Many businessmen wear a short-sleeved shirt with no tie.
- Businesswomen wear a light-colored long-sleeved blouse and a skirt. Stockings and business suits are reserved for more formal offices. Fashions for businesswomen tend to be more frilly and decorative than those worn by U.S. businesswomen.
- As a foreigner, you should dress more conservatively until you are sure what degree of formality is expected. Men should expect to wear a suit jacket and tie, and remove them if it seems appropriate. Whatever you wear, try to stay clean and well-groomed; bathe several times a day if necessary.
- Many Singaporean men wear an open-necked batik shirt to work. These are also popular for casual wear. Jeans are good for casual wear, but shorts should be avoided.
- In deference to Muslim and Hindu sensibilities, women should always wear blouses that cover at least their upper arms. Skirts should be knee length or longer.

SEOUL

South Korea

*W*hile there are many religions in Korea, Confucianism exerts the strongest influence on society. It is not a religion centered around the worship of a supreme deity, but rather a rigid ethical and moral system that governs all relationships. It was established by Confucius, a Chinese scholar and statesman who lived during Chinese feudal times over 2,000 years ago.

Country Background

History

Korea's original name, *Choson*, meant "land of the morning calm." The country's history has been shaped by frequent invasions from its neighbors. Korean history is divided into three main periods: the Silla (668-935), Koryo (935-1392), and Yi (1392-1910) dynasties. The name "Korea" is derived from the middle dynasty of Koryo. Foreign influence—direct and indirect—occurred throughout these dynasties. All of Korea's foreign overlords—Mongolian, Chinese, and Japanese—instituted a closed-door policy in order to solidify their rule. This isolation earned Korea the name of the Hermit Kingdom.

In 1910, Japan annexed Korea and enforced ruthless control, outlawing Korean culture and language. Despite resistance, several generations grew up more familiar with Japanese than with Korean customs. At the Yalta Conference at the end of World War II, the United States and the Soviet Union jointly established temporary administrative trusteeship over Korea until democratic elections could be held. Japanese forces south of the thirty-eighth parallel surrendered to the United States and forces in the north surrendered to the U.S.S.R. The Soviets blocked attempts to hold nationwide elections, and the two sides became deadlocked. When authorities in the north ignored a United Nations resolution for supervised elections in 1948, a pro-Western government was established in the south (the Republic of Korea). Later the Soviet Union established the Democratic People's Republic of Korea in the north. In June 1949, U.S. troops withdrew.

One year later, North Korean forces invaded South Korea. A United Nations-backed coalition of sixteen member nations sent assistance to South Korea. The resulting war lasted three years and ended in a stalemate. On July 27, 1953, an armistice agreement was signed and a Military Armistice Commission with five members for each side was set up to supervise the implementation of the armistice. Since neither the United States nor South Korea ever signed the agreement (although they respect the terms as members of the United Nations), a state of war is formally still in effect.

The United States still maintains a military presence in South Korea, although feelings that this should end are growing there. The two countries remain strong allies and trading partners.

P——————————————————————————**CULTURAL NOTE**
rior to the 1950s, North Korea was the industrial heartland of the peninsula. However, modernization has come quickly to South Korea. Seoul is now a glitzy modern city, not the drab village depicted in the *M*A*S*H* series on television. The people are more independent and individualistic than their Asian neighbors. Koreans are the most straightforward of all Asians but can also be defensive, a trait stemming from a history of invasion by their neighbors.

Type of Government

South Korea is a unitary multiparty republic, governed by a president, prime minister, deputy prime minister, and State Council (cabinet). There is also a 299-seat unicameral National Assembly and a supreme court.

The prime minister is the head of the government. The chief of state is the president, who is elected to a five-year term. Members of the National Assembly serve a four-year term.

Language

Korean is the official language of South Korea. English is widely taught in schools. Therefore, business people are often familiar with English, especially in urban areas.

Religion

Dominant religions include Confucianism, Christianity (28 percent of the population), Buddhism, Shamanism (spirit worship), and Chondokyo (religion of the heavenly way).

C——————————————————————————**CULTURAL NOTE**
onfucius taught that the basic unit of society is the family. In order to preserve harmony in the home, certain reciprocal responsibilities must be preserved in relationships. These relationships are between those ruler and subjects, between husband and wife, between father and son, between elder brother and younger brother, and between friends. Since all but the last are hierarchical, rank and age are very important in all interactions. While all actions of the individual reflect upon the family, filial piety is of utmost importance. Virtues of kindness, righteousness, propriety, intelligence, and faithfulness are also revered.

Demographics

The forty-three million people of South Korea are ethnically homogeneous (99.9 percent Korean with a very small Chinese minority.)

Cultural Orientation

Cognitive Styles: How South Koreans Organize and Process Information

In South Korea one finds a culture that is closed to almost all foreign influences. Its basic education teaches one to think associatively and subjectively. In all situations, personal involvement is stronger than the rules and laws one might use to control behavior.

Negotiation Strategies: What South Koreans Accept as Evidence

One's personal feelings about an issue are perceived as the truth about that issue. Faith in the ideologies of nationalism may have some influence on the truth, and the use of objective facts is becoming more common in negotiations.

Value Systems: The Basis for Behavior

The Koreans are strong adherents of Confucianism. They strive to build a society in which each individual is aware of his or her relative position, fulfills his or her obligations to superiors with obedience and respect, and recognizes his or her responsibility to treat inferiors with justice and benevolence. The following three sections identify the Value Systems in the predominant culture—their methods of dividing right from wrong, good from evil, and so forth.

Locus of Decision Making

This is a collectivistic culture in which the individual may speak for the group, but decisions are made by a consensus of the group, with deference given to the one in the group who has the highest ethos—usually the oldest member. Loyalties to kin always supersede those to friends, neighbors, or the state. The self is downplayed, but Western-style individualism is beginning to be felt. One must save face and not cause another to lose face, so an outright "no" is not used.

Sources of Anxiety Reduction

The nuclear family is the basic unit of society, but the extended family gives stability and security to its members. There is a very strong work ethic, but intragroup harmony must also be maintained. Giving gifts to acquire favors is a common practice in the workplace, and reciprocity is expected. Friends expect to rely on each other for everything. They spend a lot of time together, and friendships last a lifetime.

Issues of Equality/Inequality

In business, the emphasis is on entry-level skills and team play. There is an inherent trust in people because of the homogeneity of the populace and social pressure. This produces a strong feeling of interdependency among members of a group or business. Age is revered. Respect and deference are directed from the younger to the older, and authority and responsibility from the older to the younger. There are clearly differentiated sex roles in society, but Western-style equality is creeping in and there is a strong feminist movement. Men still dominate in public situations.

Business Practices

Appointments

PUNCTUALITY

- ◆ Be punctual to meetings. This is expected from foreigners as a sign of good business practice. Do not get upset, however, if your counterpart is late.
- ◆ Punctuality is also expected at social events.

- Koreans often arrange one-on-one business meetings (as opposed to the Japanese, who prefer group meetings). Nevertheless, this one Korean business person will have to sell your proposal to his or her entire company. It is important that you establish a strong relationship with your contact person.
- Age and rank are very important in Korea. It is sometimes easier to establish a rapport with a business person your own age.
- When entering a group meeting, the senior member of your party should enter the conference room first, then the next-highest-ranking person, and so on. The Koreans will be lined up inside in order of importance.
- English is the most widely studied foreign language. Your business meetings can be conducted in English. Promotional materials and correspondence may be in English as well.
- Business hours are 9:00 A.M. to 5:00 P.M., Monday through Friday, and often 9:00 A.M. to 1:00 P.M. on Saturday.
- The best times for business meetings are 10:00 to 11:00 A.M. and 2:00 to 3:00 P.M. Prior appointments are necessary. Business dinners are common, and meetings may take place in a local coffee shop, but business breakfasts are rare.
- Korean business people vacation from mid-July to mid-August; avoid trying to schedule appointments at this time of year. Other bad times include early October, a time of many holidays, and Christmastime.

 Negotiating

t

CULTURAL NOTE

he basis for a successful business relationship in Korea is a respectful rapport between individuals. Personal relationships take precedence over business. Businesses are basically conservative and have a strong work ethic. Harmony and structure are emphasized over innovation and experimentation. Be sincere and honest in business dealings. Meet face to face and keep in touch after your trip by mail and telephone.

- At each meeting, take time to talk to your counterpart. The first meeting should be solely for that purpose; never jump right into business discussions. Expect tea to be served at the beginning of the meeting; it is good manners to accept this sign of hospitality. Retain your formality as long as your counterpart does; do not become "chummy."
- Do not be fooled into thinking that Korea is completely Westernized because of its facade of modernization. While the younger generation is becoming

more open to globalization, traditional values run deep, especially with the older generation. You may find younger executives easier to negotiate with, since they will follow more Westernized patterns.

- Business will tend to take place at a slower pace than in North America or Europe. Be patient with delays in decision making. Often, this is a tactic to wear down the other side. Therefore, do not talk about your deadlines. Expect to make several trips to Korea before reaching an agreement.
- Do not be surprised if a Korean executive does not call you back immediately when you notify his or her office of a problem. Korean employees are very protective of their boss's harmony, and traditionally will not upset their boss with a problem until the timing is just right. This is especially true at the start of the workday.
- Find out who will be included in the negotiating team for the other side and match the rank of the persons represented. Status is very important, and a mismatch may prove embarrassing to both sides. Generally, representatives should be older and hold senior positions in the company.

a——————————————————**CULTURAL NOTE**

Korean man has a higher social status than a Korean woman; do not be surprised to see women open doors for men and allow them to pass through first. Western businesswomen are excluded from these rules.

It is still rare to have women participate in business in Korea. This means that women will have the additional challenge of overcoming this initial hesitancy. It is best to carefully consider this factor and mention to your Korean contact that a woman will be included in the team. This will allow them some time to adjust to the situation.

- Negotiations in Korea will be much more emotional than in Western countries that stress logic and the bottom-line cost. Mutual trust and compatibility will be the basis of a good business relationship. Also be prepared for the style to be aggressive at times, with emotional outbursts from your counterpart during negotiations. Koreans are much more direct and quicker to express anger or frustration. Remain calm yourself, and do not take everything said during these sessions seriously.
- Consider sending your proposals in advance of your visit for your host to preview. At a presentation, recap the major points at the beginning and the end. Break the information up into small segments with pauses and question-and-answer periods in between. Be patient with extensive questioning. Address the chief negotiator occasionally, even if he does not speak English. Do not use triangular shapes in your promotional material, since triangles have negative connotations.
- Look for cues that your counterpart did not understand you. Silence is one such sign. Do not ask or expect Koreans to tell you when this happens, since it will cause them embarrassment. Instead, rephrase your statement or inquire if they would like more information. The use of a translator is recommended to avoid these miscommunications.
- Make a beginning bid that will leave you plenty of room to negotiate. Your counterparts will start off with an extreme position but will be prepared to meet you in the middle. This way both sides come away having gained a lot of ground.
- Brute honesty is not appreciated in Korea. While a direct "no" is more accepted in Korea than in other Asian countries, Koreans are not as direct as North Americans. In order to avoid saying "no," Koreans will often give the answer they think the other wants to hear. It is more important to leave you with good feelings than to be accurate and cause displeasure. Therefore, learn to listen to

subtleties by asking questions that do not require a yes or no answer. A "yes" or nod of the head may mean "maybe" or "I understand." A "maybe" usually means "no." A negative response is sometimes indicated by a squint of the eyes or by tipping the head back while drawing air in through the teeth and waiting for you to speak again.

- Be sensitive to the overall length of the meeting. If the Koreans appear curious, take this lead and pursue it. If they return to social chit-chat, take this as a sign that they are finished discussing business for the day.
- Bow at the beginning and end of a meeting. An exit bow that is longer than the greeting bow is an indication that the meeting went well.
- Avoid being loud and boisterous around Koreans. Although they are more direct than most Asians, they dislike rowdy behavior.
- Treat the elderly with respect. Acknowledge them first in a group, and do not smoke or wear sunglasses when they are near. If you meet in a doorway, allow the older person to pass through first.
- Modesty is very important in Korea. Do not enter a home or office until you are invited, and do not seat yourself until you are asked to do so. Wait for the invitation to be extended several times before accepting. Be modest about your position and accomplishments in your company, and if you receive a compliment, politely refute it. Expect others to do the same. This should not stop you from complimenting another, however, since compliments are appreciated.
- Protecting "face"—the dignity of another person—is a very important and delicate matter. Therefore, never embarrass another person, especially in public. Never criticize your competition or admit that you do not know the answer to a question; these will cause you to lose face.
- Do not confuse Korean history and culture with those of any of its Asian neighbors. Korea has a distinctive language, history, and culture, and Koreans are very proud of this. This pride and sense of history is quite strong and constitutes a large part of their self-image. Koreans are especially sensitive about Japan, so do not bring gifts from Japan or make reference to personal contacts there.
- If the Korean national anthem is played in a public place, stand at attention out of respect.
- Be careful not to overly admire an object belonging to another person. He or she may feel obliged to give it to you.
- Contacts are important in Korea. Koreans tend to be suspicious of people they do not know or people with whom they do not have a mutual contact. Try to obtain a personal introduction from a bank, the Commerce Department, or the Korea Trade Promotion Corporation (KOTRA).
- Be prepared to give out a lot of business cards. Have your name, company, and title printed in English on one side and in Korean on the reverse. Cards are very important, since they indicate your rank and are a key to the respect you deserve in their culture. Offer your card with your right hand. Never place a Korean's card in your wallet if you intend to put your wallet in your back pocket. Never write on a business card.
- Do not sign a contract or write a person's name in red ink. This indicates that the person is deceased.
- Do not be surprised if you are asked personal questions, such as how much you paid for something or your salary. These questions are not considered in bad taste in Korea and often reflect an attempt to determine your rank and status.
- Attempts by foreigners to adhere to Korean modes of etiquette will not go unnoticed and may be instrumental in your eventual business success.

Business Entertaining

- The largest meal of the day is taken in the evening, usually between 6 and 8 P.M. Entertaining is most often done in a restaurant or coffee shop; rarely is it done at home. If you are invited to a home, consider this an honor. Do not discuss business during a meal unless your host brings it up first. Do not expect to be shown around the house, and do not wander about the home or look in such rooms as the kitchen.

- Remove your shoes when entering a Korean home, restaurant, or temple building. Leave them with the toes pointing away from the building. When putting your shoes back on, do not sit with your back toward the temple.

- Call ahead before visiting a home. When taking your leave, express your thanks and bow slightly. Send a thank-you note to your host after a meal. It is polite to reciprocate by inviting your host to a meal of equal value at a later date.

- It is common to be invited out after business hours to a Kisaeng house, bar, or dinner where there will be a lot of alcohol. This is an important part of establishing an informal relationship and judging the character of the other person. The alcohol is a stimulus to expression of more direct opinions, however, all comments and promises made during these times will be taken seriously afterwards. Do not refuse these invitations, and do not bring your spouse. Try to reciprocate before you leave.

- The person who invites the other(s) is expected to pay for the meal. It is polite for the younger to pay for the older. In all cases, a good-natured argument over who will pay is expected.

- Koreans eat a lot of garlic in their food. The smell is emitted from the skin and becomes very strong. In getting used to this, remember that Koreans find the odors emitted from red meat eaters offensive.

- When sitting on the floor for a meal, men should cross their legs while sitting on the cushion. Women (and men) may sit with their legs to the side, but never straightened out under the table.

- Koreans use chopsticks for eating and a porcelain spoon for soup. Your attempts at using chopsticks will be appreciated. When you are finished, set your chopsticks on the table or on the rest. Placing them parallel on top of your bowl is considered a sign of bad luck, and leaving them sticking out of rice is in bad taste, since this is how offerings are made to ancestors.

- Pass food with your right hand, supported by your left. Do not be shocked to see such foods as chicken feet. It is polite to refill your neighbor's cup and soy sauce bowl when empty; expect the same. Drinking partners will often trade filled cups to drink. If you do not want a refill, do not finish your glass.

- Do not put food taken from a serving dish directly into your mouth. Transfer it to your plate or bowl first. Never pick up food with your fingers. Even fruit is eaten in slices with chopsticks. Covering bowls or lids are placed on the floor under your place. Bones and shells are placed on the table or a spare plate; they are never placed in your rice bowl or on your plate.

- When eating a meal, do not finish everything on your plate. This indicates that you are still hungry and that the host did not provide enough for you. The host will offer more food several times. Even if you want more, refuse at least twice before accepting more. If you are hosting a party, offer food at least three times.

- At the end of a meal, there may be singing. It is impolite to refuse to sing if asked. If you are asked to sing but do not like to do so, have ready a traditional Western song in English, such as "I'm a Yankee Doodle Dandy" or "You Are My Sunshine."

- Good topics of conversation include the Korean cultural heritage (which is extensive), kites, sports (especially the Olympics), and the health of the other's family (although family inquiries on topics other than health are considered an intrusion). Topics to avoid are local politics (discussions of which are often forbidden by the government for reasons of national security), socialism, Communism, Japan, and your host's wife.

Time
- Local time is nine hours ahead of Greenwich Mean Time (G.M.T. + 9), or fourteen hours ahead of U.S. Eastern Standard Time (E.S.T. + 14).

Protocol

Greetings
- Korean men greet each other with a slight bow and sometimes an accompanying handshake while maintaining eye contact. Indicate added respect by supporting your right forearm with your left hand during the handshake.
- The junior person will initiate the greetings and be the first to bow. The senior person will be the first to offer his hand. A weak handshake or nod of the head may be sufficient in business circles. Women rarely shake hands. Western men should not try to shake hands with a Korean woman; Western women will have to initiate a handshake with Korean men.
- Elderly people are very highly respected, so it is good manners to greet and speak to them first, and spend a few minutes with them.
- A compliment on an elder's good health is always appreciated.
- Wait to be introduced to another at gatherings and parties. Avoid introducing yourself, and employ a third person if there is someone you wish to meet.
- When writing letters, address the recipient as "To my respected" with the title and full name. The family name is not sufficient by itself.

Titles/Forms of Address
- Korean names are different from Western names. A person has a family name, a generational or clan name, and also a given name (in that order). For example, Kim Hyong Sim has the family name of Kim, the generational name of Hyong, and a given name of Sim. While this is confusing to Westerners, our system is equally confusing to them, so they too will mix Western names around.
- Korean family names tend to be one-syllable, while generational names are more likely to be two-syllable.
- The most common family names are Kim, Park, and Lee. Note that these names can be transliterated into English in several ways; Lee in English might be Rhee, Yi, Li, or Lee.
- Address people by their title alone or by both their title and their family name. Kim Hyong Sim would be referred to as Mr. Kim, Kim *Sonsaengnim* (meaning "Mr." or "teacher") or Kim*ssi*, with the suffix *-ssi* added, which can mean Mr., Mrs., or Miss. Given names are strictly not used unless permission is granted to do so.

- Married women will retain their maiden names. If you do not know a woman's maiden name, it is permissible to refer to her as Madame with her husband's family name.

 Gestures

- Do not put your arm around another person's shoulders. People of the same sex will often hold hands. Physical contact is inappropriate with older people, with people of the opposite sex, or with people who are not good friends or family.
- Feet are considered dirty and should not touch other people or objects. Men should keep their feet flat on the floor during formal situations. At other times men should take care that the soles of their shoes are pointing down. Women are permitted to cross their legs.
- Show respect to older people by touching your left hand, palm up, lightly to your right elbow when shaking hands or passing objects such as food or documents.
- Get someone's attention by extending your arm palm down and moving your fingers up and down. Beckoning a person by moving a single finger toward you is very rude.
- Cover your mouth when yawning or using a toothpick. It is not necessary to cover your mouth when laughing, as Korean women do.
- Blowing your nose in public is considered bad manners. If the highly spiced Korean food makes your nose run, get up and move away from the table before blowing your nose.
- If embarrassed, a Korean may laugh excessively.
- Eye contact is important to convey sincerity and attentiveness to the speaker.

 Gifts

- When visiting a family, it is appropriate to bring a gift of fruit, imported coffee or quality tea such as ginseng, chocolates, or crafts from home. Liquor may be given to a man but never to a woman.
- Gift giving is often practiced within a business setting. Good gifts for a first trip include impersonal products with your company logo on them. (Be sure these gifts were not produced in Korea or Japan.)
- When giving or receiving a gift, use both hands. The gift is not opened in the presence of the giver. A gift of money should be put in an envelope. Expect initial resistance to receiving a gift. This is good manners, so be persistent.

i───────────────────────**CULTURAL NOTE**

*I*t is customary to reciprocate a gift with one of similar value. Therefore, choose a gift that takes into account the receiver's economic means. If you receive such an extravagant gift that you cannot reciprocate, send it back, being very careful not to offend the sender. Indicate that the sender's generosity is great and the gift is too much.

 Dress

- Men should wear a conservative suit and tie and a white shirt for business; women should wear a conservative skirt and blouse or dress. Avoid tight skirts, since many people sit on the floor in homes and restaurants.
- Dress modestly for informal times. Revealing clothing for women will be a mark of poor character. Shorts are appropriate for young people. Avoid the colors yellow and pink.

MADRID

Spain

*t*he year 1492 holds great significance for several different cultures. In the United States, as in Spain, it marks the year Columbus "discovered" America. However, it marks two other important events in the history of Spain. It is the date of the reconquest of Spain from the Moors (Islamic invaders from North Africa). But the Spaniards proved to be less tolerant than the Moors: 1492 was also the year that the Jews were expelled from Spain.

Country Background

History

Spain was settled by Iberians, Celts, and Basques. Its development was subsequently influenced by conquering Carthaginians, Romans, Visigoths, and Moors. The fifteenth century reconquest of Moorish held Spain not only united Spain for the first time under a Christian king but marks the beginning of Spanish nationalism. Spain began its development of a colonial empire in 1492.

Over the next few centuries, Spain gained colonies, then gradually lost them in a series of conflicts. These losses included Mexico, most of Central and South America, the Netherlands, parts of Italy and Germany, Cuba, the Philippines, and Puerto Rico. Defeat in the Spanish-American War of 1898 ended Spain's global ambitions, although Spain retained a few African colonies until recent times.

In 1939, Francisco Franco became dictator of Spain after the bloody three-year Spanish Civil War. Spain remained neutral in World War II, but maintained good relations with the Nazis. As a result, Spain was not permitted entrance into the United Nations until 1955. Franco remained in power until his death, and tried to ensure political stability by designating Prince Juan Carlos as the future king of Spain in 1969.

Prince Juan Carlos became king of Spain in 1975, and soon had to put down an attempted military coup. He rapidly and independently mustered the support of many other parts of the military, allowing Spain to remain under civilian rule.

Type of Government

The current constitution was written in 1978 and makes Spain a constitutional monarchy. The king is the chief of state. Legislative power resides in the *Cortes*, or parliament, consisting of two chambers: the Congress of Deputies and the Senate. Deputies and senators are elected by universal suffrage and serve for four years.

The executive branch consists of a prime minister (who is the head of the govern-ment), his deputy, and ministers, all of whom are responsible to the *Cortes*.

Spain granted autonomy to Catalonia and the Basque country in 1980. However, political violence continues—mainly in the Basque region in the north, where some Basques seek total independence from Spain.

Spain continues to request the return of Gibraltar, which has been under British control since 1704.

t————————————————————**CULTURAL NOTE**

he 1980s showed rapid economic growth in the private sector and high levels of economic sup-port from other countries, especially since Spain gained membership in the European Community in 1986. Changes for the better are expected to continue for Spain—particularly in light of the positive results of 1992. Spain successfully hosted the Olympic Games in Barcelona and Expo '92 in Seville, and celebrated the country's five hundredth anniversary of Columbus' voyage to the New World.

Language

The official language of Spain is Spanish, with the Castilian dialect used by the majority of Spaniards. It is the standard for business throughout every region of Spain.

In addition, the Basques of the north, the Galicians of the northwest, and the Catalans of the extreme northeast all speak their own languages.

Religion

Although Spain is an overwhelmingly Catholic country, Spain has no official religion. Today, 97 percent of Spaniards practice Catholicism.

S————————————————————**CULTURAL NOTE**

paniards observe many holidays and rituals associated with the Catholic church. One of the elabo-rate processionals during the week before Easter is the famous pilgrimage to Santiago de Compostela. Santiago is Spanish for "St. James," and the apostle's tomb is believed to be located under the church. During the Middle Ages, the relics made Santiago de Compostela the most important city of pilgrimage after Jerusalem and Rome. The saint's relics are still credited with miracles.

Demographics

The population of Spain is almost thirty-nine million. The capital, Madrid, has almost five million people in its metropolitan area.

In recent years, urbanization has occurred on a large scale.

Cultural Orientation

Cognitive Styles: How Spaniards Organize and Process Information

The culture of Spain opened up with the fashioning of a working democracy. Spaniards are open to information on all issues but do not change their attitudes easily. Most information is processed associatively and subjectively. Spaniards' per-sonal involvement with issues does not let them use more abstract rules and laws to solve their problems.

Negotiation Strategies: What Spaniards Accept as Evidence

One's subjective feelings on an issue are the ultimate source of truth. However, faith in the ideologies of the church or nationalism may help to formulate this truth. Seldom do Spaniards use objective facts to prove a point.

Value Systems: The Basis for Behavior

Spain is the home of the philosophy that all people are equal because each person is unique. Thus one must get to know each person as an individual. The following three sections identify the Value Systems in the predominant culture—their methods of dividing right from wrong, good from evil, and so forth.

Locus of Decision Making

The individual shoulders responsibility for his or her decisions, but the best interests of the family or group are always kept in mind. Self-identity is obtained from the family name and one's position in society. Relationships (both kinships and friendships) are more important than one's expertise in obtaining a job. The elite at the top of the social scale is a privileged minority group with substantial control over economic resources.

Sources of Anxiety Reduction

Although the Catholic church has lost most of its direct influence, the more educated a person is, the more likely he or she is to be a practicing Catholic. The church's teachings are basic to most of the population and are a source of structure, stability, and security. The extended family is being replaced by the nuclear family as a source of security. There is a strong belief in nationalism.

Issues of Equality/Inequality

Society is differentiated along class, occupational, and professional lines, with an expanding middle class and a decreasing proportion of rural poor. Changes in the system were made by revolutions or military coups in the past, but now the democratic form of government seems to be well in place. Machismo is still very strong. However, women are beginning to figure more prominently in education, politics, and the workforce. Women have complete equality with men before the law.

Business Practices

Appointments

 ———————————————— **PUNCTUALITY**

- ◆ While you should be on time for all business appointments, Spaniards are not always punctual. Be prepared to wait.
- ◆ Social events rarely begin at the scheduled time. Try to ask what time you are really expected to arrive; it is likely to be from fifteen to thirty minutes after the scheduled time.
- ◆ It is said that only the bullfights start on time in Spain

- ▪ Remember that many Europeans and South Americans write the day first, then the month, then the year (e.g., December 3, 1999, is written 3.12.99). This is the case in Spain.
- ▪ Always make business appointments well in advance, and confirm them by letter just before your arrival.

- The workweek is forty hours in Spain, but hours of operation may vary.
- In Madrid, businesses are open from 9:00 A.M. to 1:30 P.M. and again from 3:00 to 6:00 P.M., Monday through Friday. In July and August, when most people take their vacations, hours may change to 8:30 A.M. to 2:30 P.M., Monday through Thursday, and 8:30 A.M. to 2:00 P.M. on Friday.
- Government offices are usually open to the public from 9:00 A.M. to 1:00 P.M., Monday through Friday.
- If a holiday falls on a Thursday or Tuesday, many people take a four-day weekend. Most Spaniards have thirty days paid vacation per year, and usually take them in July or August. Also avoid scheduling appointments around Easter or Christmas.
- Business can be conducted over meals, but many Spaniards go home for lunch, so do not be surprised if your invitation is politely declined.
- Do not schedule breakfast meetings before 8:30 A.M.

 Negotiating

- Personal contacts are essential for business success in Spain. Select your Spanish representatives with great care, since once a representative is associated with you, it is very difficult to switch to another person.
- To the Spanish, information is considered a valuable commodity. For this reason, they may not be anxious to share useful facts with you, no matter how encouraging they may seem.
- Be warm and personal during your negotiations, yet retain your dignity, courtesy, and diplomacy. Your Spanish counterparts may initially seem restrained and indirect, but this is normal until your relationship has been established.
- Do not expect to discuss business at the start of any meeting.
- Politics, sports, and travel are good topics of conversation. Avoid discussions of religion.
- Bullfighting is considered an art, and should not be judged on any but Spanish terms; derogatory remarks about bullfighting are inappropriate.
- The Spanish give advice to one another and to foreigners freely; don't be offended by this.
- Have business cards printed up in Spain, with English on one side and Spanish on the other. Present your card with the Spanish side facing your Spanish colleague.
- Expect protracted negotiations.

CULTURAL NOTE

Spaniards are known for their pride and personal sense of honor. However, foreign business people are sometimes surprised that business acumen and expertise are not always highly regarded in Spain. (As with the upper-class English, to call someone "clever" in Spain is a veiled insult.) Spaniards often take more pride in personal characteristics than in business skills.

 Business Entertaining

- If your prospect accepts your invitation to lunch, this can be a good time to discuss business. However, do not bring up business matters until coffee is served following the meal.

- Always invite Spanish clients to excellent restaurants, since many Spaniards are very knowledgeable about gourmet food and vintage wines.
- At around 5:00 or 6:00 P.M., many Spaniards go out for hors d'oeuvres, called *tapas*. These *tapas* are eaten at a series of bars (called *tabernas*, *bars*, *mesones*, or *cafés*) and can vary from salted almonds and olives to octopus and potato omelets. Spaniards will walk from bar to bar, eating *tapas*, drinking sherry, and visiting friends for an hour or two.
- Dinner is not served until 9:00 or 10:00 P.M.
- You will probably not be invited to a Spanish home, as this type of socializing is reserved for intimate friends. You might, however be invited out to dinner.
- If an invitation to a Spanish home is offered, you may decline at first, and accept it only when pressed; first invitations are often only for politeness. If the invitation is extended again, you may accept.
- In the continental style of eating, the fork is held in the left hand and the knife in the right, and they are never switched. Push food onto the fork with the knife. When you are finished, place knife and fork side by side on the plate; if they are crossed or on opposite sides of the plate, you will be offered more food. Hands should be kept above the table. Pay compliments to your host (and to the waiters in a restaurant).
- If you have been invited out, reciprocate at a later date, being careful not to mention "repaying" your hosts.
- Be aware that many restaurants close for a month of vacation.

Time
- Spain is one hour ahead of Greenwich Mean Time (G.M.T. + 1), or six hours ahead of U.S. Eastern Standard Time (E.S.T. + 6).

Protocol

 Greetings
- A handshake is a normal greeting.
- You will note that among close friends, Spanish men will add a pat on the back or a hug to the handshake.
- Women lightly embrace and touch cheeks while kissing the air. A professional woman may also greet a Spanish man who is a close colleague in this way.

 Titles/Forms of Address
- First names are appropriate among friends and young people only. Always wait for your Spanish counterpart to initiate the use of first names or the use of the familiar form of address (*tú*) as opposed to the formal form (*Usted*).

i ——————————————————**CULTURAL NOTE**

*I*n Spain, the use of the familiar (*tú*) and formal (*Usted*) forms of address are different from their usage in Latin America. For example, Spaniards always speak to domestic servants in the formal (*Usted*) manner; they feel this confers dignity and shows respect for the servant as a person. Also, the informal (*tú*) form is more likely to be used by colleagues in a Spanish office than in a Latin American office. Sometimes employees even speak to their bosses using the *tú* (informal) form. This would border on insubordination in other Spanish-speaking countries.

- Most people you meet should be addressed with a title and their surname.
- Persons who do not have professional titles should be addressed as Mr., Mrs., or Miss, plus their surname. In Spanish, these are
  - Mr. = *Señor*
  - Mrs. = *Señora*
  - Miss = *Señorita*
- Most Spaniards have two surnames: one from their father, which is listed first, followed by one from their mother. Only the father's surname is commonly used when addressing someone; e.g., Señor José Antonio Martínez de García is addressed as Señor Martínez and Señorita Pilar María Nuñez de Cela is addressed as Señorita Nuñez. When a woman marries, she usually adds her husband's surname and goes by that surname. If the two people in the above example married, she would be known as Señora Pilar María Nuñez Cela de Martínez. Most people would refer to her as Señora de Martínez or, less formally, Señora Martínez.
- As a general rule, use only one surname when speaking to a person, but use both surnames when writing.
- It is important to address individuals by any titles they may have, followed by their surnames. For example, teachers prefer the title *Profesor*, and engineers go by *Ingeniero*.

Gestures

- There are many gestures used in daily Spanish conversation. Their significance may vary from region to region, so observe local behaviors, and ask if you are unsure.
- To beckon another person, turn the palm down and wave the fingers or whole hand.
- Snapping the hand downward is used to emphasize a point.
- The A-O.K. gesture (making a circle of the first finger and thumb) is rude.

Gifts

- Generally, if you are given a gift, you should open it immediately.
- If you are invited for a meal at a Spanish home, it is appropriate to bring chocolates, pastries, or flowers (but not dahlias or chrysanthemums, which are associated with death).
- Don't give thirteen flowers—it is considered bad luck.
- Business gifts should not be given at a first meeting.
- If you give a business gift, choose it carefully; it should not be a vehicle for your company logo (although a fine pen with your company name is acceptable).
- Local crafts or illustrated books from your region are appropriate; university or sports team shirts and caps are good gifts for children.

- Gifts should always be name-brand items of high quality, and should be beautifully wrapped.

 Dress

- The Spanish are highly aware of dress. This goes along with their concern for projecting an impression of good social position.
- Always select well-made conservative attire. Name brands will be noticed. Dress in subdued colors.
- Men dress conservatively, while women are expected to be stylish.
- Shorts are not acceptable in public.

COLOMBO

Sri Lanka

a────────────**CULTURAL NOTE**
lthough its influence is declining, a caste system still exists in Sri Lanka. This system dictates a person's social standing, occupation, and even marriage possibilities. While there are only four traditional castes, these are broken down into thousands of subcastes.

Country Background

History/Date of Origin

The first Sinhalese immigrants to Sri Lanka arrived in the sixth century from northern India. Three hundred years later, Buddhism was brought with the Indian Prince Mahinda, son of the great Buddhist King Asoka. The religion flourished and became central to the culture.

The Portuguese were the first Europeans to arrive in Sri Lanka in the sixteenth century; they brought Catholicism with them. The Dutch followed in the next century, and finally the British arrived and declared it the British colony of Ceylon in 1815. During this colonial period, tea, rubber, and coconut plantations were established in the northern part of the island, and labor was brought over from the Tamil Nadu province in India. Sri Lanka's independence was peacefully obtained on February 4, 1948.

Since that time, free elections have been the vehicle for transfer of power, with the exception of the assassination of Prime Minister Bandaranaike in 1959. In 1971, an uprising of a Maoist group caused the government, under Bandaranaike's widow, to declare a state of emergency and suppress the insurrection. Although the revolt was put down in a few weeks, the state of emergency lasted six years. Partially in response to the turbulence, a new constitution was written that changed the country to a republic and its name to Sri Lanka. In addition, it created a presidency (appointed by the prime minister) and initiated economic policies that were highly socialistic.

In 1977, a change in political parties brought a new constitution and an open economy under J. R. Jayewardene. At that point, the Tamils' demand for more equalization at the federal level changed to a demand for an independent state of Tamil Eelam. The extremist Liberation Tigers of Tamil Eelam resorted to force to achieve their goals. In 1983, the deaths of thirteen Sinhalese soldiers caused violent confrontations. Bloodshed, terrorism, and accusations of human rights violations occurred on both sides.

In 1987, the situation was deadlocked. India became involved by sending peacekeeping troops to help resolve the crisis. An accord was signed that made concessions to some of the militants' demands, including giving official status to the Tamil language. But the militant troops backed out on their agreement to surrender to the Indian peacekeeping force. The fighting continued, and Indian troops remained in northern Sri Lanka for two years.

After the negotiated Indian withdrawal occurred in 1990, elections were held in the newly restructured provinces. With the resulting victory in Tamil strongholds and the seats won in the National Assembly, the militants halted activities. However, fighting broke out again in June 1990. Several hundred people were killed before a cease-fire was declared.

Type of Government

The Democratic Socialist Republic of Sri Lanka is a unitary multiparty republic. Under the constitution of 1978, there is a strong executive president, elected for a six-year term, and a prime minister. The unicameral National Assembly has 225 seats. The president is head of both the state and the government.

Internationally, Sri Lanka maintains a nonaligned foreign policy. Relations with India, which have been tense in the past, remain a focus of attention.

Language

Sri Lanka has two official languages, spoken by the two dominant ethnic groups. The Sinhalese speak Sinhala, and the Tamils speak Tamil. English, a legacy from the colonial period, is the language of commerce and is spoken by about 10 percent of the population. It is spoken in tourist areas, and most business people and senior civil servants speak it fluently.

Religion

When Buddhism went into decline in India, Sri Lanka emerged as a Buddhist stronghold in southern Asia. The majority of the population (69 percent) claim Buddhism as their religion. Of the remaining 31 percent, 15 percent are Hindu, 8 percent are Christian, and 8 percent are Muslim.

Demographics

Of Sri Lanka's seventeen million inhabitants, 74 percent are Sinhalese, 18 percent are Tamil, 8 percent are Moor, and 1 percent are Burgher (descendants of Dutch colonists), Malay, and Vedda. The Veddas are a small remnant of the island's original inhabitants who have assimilated into Sri Lankan society and lost all traces of their original culture and history. Ethnic divisions between the Sinhalese and the Tamils run deep, and violent strife has been a problem since 1983. Tamils are generally concentrated in the "tea country," the northern part of the island.

Cultural Orientation

Cognitive Styles: How Sri Lanka's Citizens Organize and Process Information

In Sri Lanka both the Sinhalese and the Tamils are open to new methods and innovations, except when those methods or innovations come from the opposite ethnic group. Most education is skill training, and there is little abstraction.

Generally, Sri Lankans tend to behave in ways that are dictated by tradition and the situation of the moment. Interpersonal relationships are more important than abstract rules in the conduct of business.

Negotiation Strategies: What the citizens of Sri Lanka Accept as Evidence

Both the Sinhalese (Buddhists) and the Tamils (Hindus) will use faith in the ideologies of their religion as a foundation for truth, modified by their personal feelings about an issue. They seldom resort to objective facts to find the truth.

Value Systems: The Basis for Behavior

In Sri Lanka there are two strong ethnic groups, the Sinhalese and the Tamils, whose values and goals are clashing constantly. The following three sections identify the Value Systems in these predominant cultures—their methods of dividing right from wrong, good from evil, and so forth.

Locus of Decision Making

The concern of the Sinhalese is with one's responsibility to self and to interpersonal relationships, while the Tamils' concern is with one's responsibility to the collective—family, group, religion. Identity for both is found in the social system. Thus, individual decisions are made with social position in mind. There is a need for prestige within the group, so ranking is important.

Sources of Anxiety Reduction

The family is the central social unit in both groups and gives the individual the most security. Religious and ethnic affiliations (nearly synonymous terms) give the individual and his or her family the structure for their life. A strong patrilineal kinship system assures continuity and family stability. A high level of religious tolerance helps to offset the anxiety of ethnic differences.

Issues of Equality/Inequality

There is a strong feeling of inequality between the majority Sinhalese and the minority Tamils, leading to active insurrection and terrorism. The caste system exists but is not rigidly adhered to. Although ethnic groups desire segregation, government policy is to treat all people as equals. Men dominate all aspects of business and public life and are the heads of their family units. There are clear and classic role differences between the sexes.

Business Practices

Appointments

 PUNCTUALITY

- Punctuality is considered important and expected from Westerners. Do not be surprised, however, if your counterpart is late or keeps you waiting.
- Urban areas in Sri Lanka have heavy traffic during rush hours. Allow plenty of time between appointments for travel.
- Sri Lankans have a much more relaxed attitude about time than do North Americans. Most Sri Lankans would not object to a two- or three-hour wait before seeing an important person. Do not display anger if you are made to wait.

- Business hours are 8:30 A.M. to 4:30 or 5:00 P.M., Monday through Friday. Many companies close for lunch between noon and 2:00 P.M. Government offices observe regular business hours.
- As a foreigner, you must make appointments at least one week in advance. Also, reconfirm your appointments a day or two before. (Native Sri Lankans, however, often drop in on one another without appointments.)
- Sri Lankans take a "tea break" both in the morning and in the afternoon. Don't expect help from any employees during their tea break, even if they are sitting at their desks. No business is conducted during the tea break.
- Many introductory business appointments are held over meals. To meet for lunch in a restaurant is a common first appointment, but lunch or dinner in a Sri Lankan home is not unusual.
- Most Sri Lankan holidays are connected with the country's four main religions: Buddhism, Hinduism, Islam, and Christianity.

Negotiating

- It is important to establish a rapport with your counterpart before jumping into business discussions. Therefore, take time to talk socially before starting negotiations. Be patient with delays, and do not expect business to move as quickly as in Western countries. Several trips to Sri Lanka may be necessary to finalize a business deal.
- If you are served tea at the beginning of a meeting, always accept this as a goodwill gesture and make a compliment on its quality.
- A first meeting will typically be held at a restaurant for lunch.
- Be prepared for your Sinhalese counterparts to consult with an astrologer before making any important commitments.
- Women in high business positions are still rarities, although not as unusual as in neighboring India or Pakistan.
- Business cards are often exchanged at first meetings. Have your cards printed in English. Having the local language printed on the reverse side is a good idea only if you can distinguish between a Tamil and a Sinhalese. Since this is often difficult for foreigners, it is better to leave it off.
- The caste system is still the way of life in many areas. It is important to respect this aspect of the culture and realize that there are places and activities where some people are not accepted. Do not pressure a person to violate this set of beliefs.
- The left hand is considered taboo for most purposes, since it is used for hygienic purposes. Therefore, do not use this hand when eating, passing food or objects, or touching another person.

t———————————————————**CULTURAL NOTE**

reat religious objects with the utmost respect. Do not sit or stand on large statues of Buddha or otherwise handle images of Buddha sacrilegiously. Do not give Buddhist monks money directly, since they are forbidden to touch it; instead, place donations in the box found at the entrance to the temple. Hand any other object to a monk with both hands.

When visiting a mosque or temple, wear clothing that covers your legs and arms (both men and women), and remove your shoes and hat at the door. Remember, leather articles are often restricted and always impolite.

Business Entertaining

- It will not be uncommon for you to be invited to a local home for a visit or a meal. If this happens, it is good manners to reciprocate with a meal in a restaurant in your hotel.
- It is not impolite to drop by unannounced, especially if the family has no phone. The best times to visit are between 4:00 and 7:00 P.M.
- Meal times are 7:00 to 8:00 A.M. for breakfast, noon to 2:00 P.M. for lunch, and 7:00 to 10:00 P.M. for dinner.
- Be prepared for as much as two or three hours of talking and socializing before a meal. It is advisable to have a small snack before going.
- At a meal, communal dishes are placed in the center of the table and each person serves himself or herself. Do not let the serving utensils touch your plate, and never use your left hand. There usually will be no utensils, since people eat with their hands. Bread and rice balls are used to scoop up curries and vegetables. Watch your host. This technique takes a bit of practice. If your meal is served on a plantain leaf, do not eat it; that plantain leaf is your plate!
- Do not serve yourself large portions, but leave room to compliment your host and hostess by returning for two or three helpings. When you are finished, politely refuse additional servings.
- Buddhists are vegetarians, Hindus do not eat beef, and Moslems do not eat pork.
- When eating out, the person who initiates the invitation is the one who will pay for the entire meal.
- Good topics of conversation include families, home, schools, and sights of Sri Lanka. Topics to avoid include the ethnic strife between the Tamils and Sinhalese, relations with India, religion, the caste system, and sex.

Time

- Local time is 5 1/2 hours ahead of Greenwich Mean Time (G.M.T. + 5 1/2), or 10 1/2 hours ahead of U.S. Eastern Standard Time (E.S.T. + 10 1/2).

Protocol

Greetings

- The traditional greeting is to place your hands together at chin level, bow slightly, and say *namaste*, meaning "I salute the god-like qualities within you." *Aaibowan* is the Sinhalese greeting. Foreigners are not expected to initiate this gesture, but returning it will be appreciated.
- As a result of British influence, the Western mode of greeting, shaking hands, is also appropriate for either sex.
- At a party, greet and shake hands with everyone in the room.

Titles/Forms of Address

- It is customary to address a Sinhalese person as Sir (*Mahattaya*) or Madam (*Nona*) following their last names, or simply by this title alone. Tamils have no titles such as this, so they will use *Aiyaa* (father) or *Ammaa* (mother) instead to an older person, connoting respect.

- Use the title Doctor for medical doctors or those holding degrees.
- Each of Sri Lanka's many cultures has different naming patterns. It is best to ask someone how he or she prefers to be addressed. (See the chapter on India for further details on naming patterns.)

 Gestures

- Nonverbal signals for agreement are reversed from those in Western countries. A nod of the head means "no," and shaking your head from side to side indicates "yes."
- Pointing with your finger is considered rude. Beckon a person by waving your fingers with the hand extended, palm down.
- Smiling can be considered as flirtatious.
- The head is considered sacred, and the feet are dirty. Therefore, do not touch another's head and do not prop your feet up on desks or chairs.

 Gifts

- If you are invited to a home for a meal, a gift is not expected but will be appreciated. Good gifts include fruit, imported chocolates, and crafts from home.
- Before giving liquor, be certain that the recipient drinks alcohol; if so, then a bottle of imported whiskey would be a good choice.

 Dress

- Business dress is usually conservative, but cool, in consideration of the climate. Men should wear a light shirt and pants. Jackets and ties are rarely worn. Women should wear a modest, light blouse and skirt. Your Sri Lankan counterpart will probably dress conservatively.
- Nice, yet cool clothing is appropriate for casual wear. Shorts; low-cut, revealing, or sleeveless clothing; and bathing suits are inappropriate for women except in resort areas or on the beach. Western dress is common among youth.

STOCKHOLM

Sweden

Country Background

History

The Vikings (also called Norsemen) were feared for their raids throughout northern Europe from the eighth to eleventh century. These Vikings eventually became the Swedes, the Norwegians, and the Danes.

Political power was concentrated first in Denmark, which came to rule much of Scandinavia, conquering Sweden in 1520. Many prominent Swedes were slain by the Danes in this "Stockholm Bloodbath." But Sweden broke away from Denmark in 1523 and became a rival power. The Kingdom of Sweden dates from 1523. Rather than heading west to battle Denmark, Sweden's armies marched east and conquered most of the Baltic lands. Sweden's military supremacy ended in 1700, when a coalition of Denmark, Poland, and Russia forced Sweden to yield its captured Baltic territory.

Sweden and Denmark fought on opposite sides during the Napoleonic Wars. To punish Denmark for supporting Napoleon, the postwar Congress of Vienna took Norway from Denmark and gave it to Sweden in 1815.

Sweden had become an aristocratic nation of landed noblemen, and had little in common with the fishermen, sailors, and merchants of Norway. Friction developed. Fortunately for the Norwegians, their rugged, rocky nation could not be divided up into the vast farming estates preferred by the Swedes. In 1905, after a century of Swedish occupation, Sweden gave Norway its independence.

Sweden remained neutral in both world wars.

Type of Government

The Kingdom of Sweden is a parliamentary state under a constitutional monarchy. Sweden's current constitution was adopted in 1975. In the executive branch, the cabinet (which consists of the prime minister and the advising ministers) is responsible to parliament. The parliament has one house, the Riksdag. Its members are elected by universal suffrage and serve three years. There is a Supreme Court. The king is the chief of state, while the prime minister is the head of the government.

Sweden has a free-enterprise economy, while maintaining an extensive social-welfare system. State benefits include child care, health care, and extensive pension plans.

Sweden historically maintained neutrality and felt that membership in the European Union would not be consistent with this policy. However, the end of the cold war put Sweden's entire foreign policy into question. There is no longer a need for Sweden to maintain a strict neutrality between NATO and the now-defunct Warsaw Pact.

Language

The official language is Swedish, which is a Germanic language related to Danish, Norwegian, and Icelandic. The native minority group, known as the Lapps or Laplanders, speak their own language. The term *Sami* is a somewhat derogatory term for this group. The language most commonly learned in school is English, and you will find that most Swedes can speak English; if you plan to do business outside of the major metropolitan areas, German is useful.

Religion

The majority (over 90 percent) of Swedes are Lutheran, but other Christian denominations are represented, as are Jews. The Evangelical Lutheran church is supported by the state, but there is complete religious freedom.

Demographics

The population of the Kingdom of Sweden is 8.7 million. Stockholm, the capital, has over 1.5 million people in its metropolitan area. Sweden is highly urbanized. One-eighth of the population is foreign-born.

Cultural Orientation

Cognitive Styles: How Swedes Organize and Process Information

The Swedes a proud people. Their education teaches them to think conceptually and analytically, and they tend to look to universal rules or laws to solve their problems.

Negotiation Strategies: What Swedes Accept as Evidence

All truth is subject to one's faith in the ideologies of the social welfare state. These truths are supported by objective facts rather than subjective feelings.

Value Systems: The Basis for Behavior

Sweden is a humanitarian culture, with the quality of life and environmental issues given top priority. The following three sections identify the Value Systems in the predominant culture—their methods of dividing right from wrong, good from evil, and so forth.

Locus of Decision Making

There is a strong belief in individual decisions within the social welfare system and with the consensus of all concerned. Although there is a strong self-orientation, there is also a need to help those who are not able to help themselves, and a need for teamwork. Swedes place an emphasis on individual initiative and achievement, with one's ability being more important than one's station in life. They feel that they have a right to a private life that is not to be discussed in business situations.

Sources of Anxiety Reduction

Life's uncertainties are accepted, and anxiety is reduced through a strong social welfare system; but a "spiritual unease" makes Swedes very serious about life. A strong nuclear family gives stability and structure to life. The need for social organization and ritual allows Swedes to remain uncommitted and uninvolved with others.

Issues of Equality/Inequality

Sweden is basically a middle-class society that strives to minimize social differences, so there is very little evidence of poverty or wealth. Nationalism transcends social differences, and a largely homogeneous population minimizes ethnic differences. However, there is a deep need to find a challenge in life, since most of the necessities are taken care of. This is an androgynous society in which husbands and wives share the responsibility of child care.

Business Practices

Appointments

PUNCTUALITY

♦ Be punctual at all times, to both business and social events. It is not appropriate to be "fashionably late" to dinners.

- Appointments should be made two weeks in advance.
- Remember that many Europeans and South Americans write the day first, then the month, then the year (e.g., December 3, 1999, is written 3.12.99). This is the case in Sweden.
- The workweek is 8:30 or 9:00 A.M. to 5:00 P.M., Monday through Friday. There is one hour for lunch, and many people go to lunch between 11:30 and 1:30 P.M.
- The minimum vacation per year is five weeks.
- Most people take their vacations in July, so this is not a good time for business in Sweden.
- During the Christmas holidays (from December 22 to January 6), many Swedish business people are unavailable.

 Negotiating

- In business meetings, the Swedes do not begin with small talk, but get right down to business.
- Do not show emotion during negotiations.
- The Swedes value consensus and avoid confrontation.
- In presentations, be very precise and concrete; do not exaggerate or expect the Swedish imagination to do part of the work.
- Humor is not usually part of negotiations. Swedes tend to be serious in general, and may appear downright stuffy in business.

- Many business people are fluent in English, especially in the large cities, such as Stockholm, Göteborg, and Malmö.
- Avoid criticism of Swedish culture, Swedish politics, or the Swedish sense of humor (which North Americans often find incomprehensible).
- Swedes avoid arguing over sensitive topics in general, especially with foreigners. If a discussion of this type begins, don't be offended if the Swede cuts it off abruptly.
- Do not be too open in expressing emotion (for example, "I'm so happy to be here" should be said calmly).
- Similarly, appearing reserved or even slightly shy can give a positive impression to your Swedish hosts.
- Avoid conducting a private conversation in public areas.
- Do not ask personal questions or be offended if Swedes do not inquire about your family, work, and so forth.
- Avoid superficiality in conversation.
- Silence is accepted with ease by Swedes; don't rush to fill in pauses in the conversation.
- There is much pride in local regions. Visitors should not praise one area over another.
- Scandinavians appreciate knowledge of the differences among the people of Finland, Norway, Sweden, and Denmark.
- The Swedes have an intense appreciation of nature.
- Relaxation is important to the Swedes. This includes breaks in their work schedule. Don't try to rush a Swede who is taking a long coffee break or an even longer lunch break, even if you are inconvenienced by it.

 Business Entertaining

- Business lunches and dinners are quite popular. Make reservations in advance. Formal restaurants are recommended for business meals.
- Invite spouses to business dinners, but not to lunches.
- It is not uncommon for businesswomen to pick up the check in Sweden, especially if they are on an expense account.
- The Swedes generally do not socialize with coworkers after working hours, although they do consider their colleagues to be good friends.
- If you are invited to a Swedish home, you should bring flowers for the hostess.
- The toast is more formal in Sweden than elsewhere in Northern Europe.
- Allow your host and those older than you to toast you before proposing a toast to them.
- *Skoal* is the Swedish "cheers."
- Wait until your host has said *skoal* before touching your drink.
- If you are seated next to the hostess as the guest of honor, you may be expected to make a speech.
- The *smörgåsbord* is a buffet (hot and cold) served year round, and especially during Christmas and Easter.

Time
- Sweden is one hour ahead of Greenwich Mean Time (G.M.T. + 1), or six hours ahead of U.S. Eastern Standard Time (E.S.T. + 6).

Protocol

Greetings

- The handshake is the standard greeting.
- Good friends (especially among the young) who see each other often do not bother to shake hands.

> # CULTURAL NOTE
>
> *O*lder, upper-class people may be very formal. Be sure to shake their hands when greeting and when leaving. Note that they often avoid the pronoun "you," but instead refer to people in the third person (e.g., when greeting Mr. Jarl, they will say "How is Mr. Jarl today?"). To be properly formal, you should respond in the same way, although few young people use this mode of speech.

- When you meet someone after you have been a guest at his or her house, thank him or her immediately.
- Usually a third person will introduce you to a group, but if this doesn't happen, go around the room, shaking hands and telling your name to each person.

Titles/Forms of Address

- The order of names in Sweden is the same as in the United States: first name followed by surname.
- Expect to address everyone by their surname unless you are invited to do otherwise. Young people are more likely to go to a first-name basis quickly.
- People without a professional title should be addressed as Mr., Mrs., Miss, or Ms., plus surname.
- Persons with professional titles should be addressed by that title, plus surname (e.g., Professor Olson). Such titles include Doctor, Engineer, Professor, and so forth.

Gestures

- The Swedes do not use many gestures; you should be restrained as well. Avoid talking with your hands.
- A toss of the head means "come here."
- In dealing with the Swedes, keep your voice tone modulated. Swedes are a relatively quiet people.
- Look people directly in the eye when you speak to them.
- Swedes do not like physical contact with anyone except close friends, except for the handshake. Do not touch, backslap, embrace, or put an arm around a Swede.
- While Swedes are known for their sexual openness, do not mistake a Swedish woman's forwardness for a sexual invitation. Swedish women often speak to strangers, especially foreigners when they want to practice the foreigner's language.
- Hats are commonly worn in cold weather. Men should tip their hat when passing someone they know, and remove it when speaking to a woman.

Gifts

- Liquor is very expensive in Sweden, and so is a highly appreciated gift. Fine liquor or wine from the United States makes a good business gift.
- Flowers, liquor, wine, cake, or chocolates are appropriate gifts for your hostess when you are invited to a Swedish home. You may also bring candy for the children.

Dress

- Conservative dress is appropriate. For business appointments, men should wear suits and ties, while women should wear suits or dresses.
- Swedes are usually fashionably well-dressed in public.

BERN

Switzerland

S———————————————————**CULTURAL NOTE**

witzerland has four official languages: French, Italian, German, and Romansch. In addition to one or more of these languages, most business people in the cities also speak English as well.

Country Background

History

Switzerland's history goes back to 1291 when a number of cantons in the Holy Roman Empire federated. This Swiss Confederation achieved independence from the Holy Roman Empire in 1648. Switzerland's borders were fixed in 1815 by the Congress of Vienna, which also guaranteed Switzerland's neutrality. Several Catholic cantons tried to secede from the Swiss Confederation in 1847. But a new Swiss Constitution in 1848 gave each canton enough control over its local affairs that the nation held together.

Type of Government

The Swiss Confederation is a federal state of twenty-eight sovereign cantons. The president is head of both the state and the government. There are two legislative houses: the 46-seat Council of States and the 200-seat National Council.

Switzerland has a policy of permanent neutrality. It did not enter into either world war; indeed, it has not been involved in a war since Napoleon invaded it in 1815. Yet national defense is taken seriously, and all men must serve in the military.

Language

Linguistically, Switzerland is complex. There are four official languages. Around Lake Geneva (in the southwest), French is spoken. Italian is spoken by about 10 percent of the population of the country, concentrated in the Ticino. In 65 percent of the country, German is spoken. The fourth language, Romansch, is a Romance language spoken by only 1 percent of the population. The Swiss take the preservation of traditional languages and cultures quite seriously. In the cities, finding some-one who speaks English does not pose a problem.

Religion

Most Swiss are Christian, with 48 percent being Roman Catholic and 44 percent Protestant.

Demographics

Switzerland has a population of approximately 6.8 million. Bern, the capital, has a population of about 300,000 in its metropolitan area; Geneva has almost 400,000. Zürich is the largest city, with 840,000 in the metropolitan area.

Cultural Orientation

Cognitive Styles: How the Swiss Organize and Process Information

In Switzerland we find a culture that is very ethnocentric and circumspect toward outside influence. The younger generation is becoming more open. The German and French segments of Switzerland process information conceptually and analytically; the rest tend to think associatively. The German and French portions will use universal rules to solve problems, while the others tend to become personally involved in each situation.

Negotiation Strategies: What the Swiss Accept as Evidence

The German and French segments rely on objective facts to determine the truth, while the rest use subjective feelings. In both cases, faith in the ideologies of nationalism and utopian ideals may influence the truth.

Value Systems: The Basis for Behavior

The culture of Switzerland is made up of four subcultures with differing value systems: The German, French, Italian, and 1 percent of indigenous population who speak Romansch. The following three sections identify the Value Systems in these predominant cultures—their methods of dividing right from wrong, good from evil, and so forth.

Locus of Decision Making

The individual is the decision maker. Although he or she may defer to the interest of the family, the company, or the state, he or she is still responsible. Decision making is a slow and involved process in which a relationship must be developed between the negotiators. Ethnocentric values may shape the decision. In families there is joint decision making between parents and older children.

Sources of Anxiety Reduction

Four languages and two religions are all very important to the Swiss, but they have come to terms with all cleavages and do not find them sufficient cause for civil unrest. They may acquire this ability to live together in the Swiss military, where all of the groups are brought together in a well-integrated force. The nuclear family is the basic social unit, and there is a very high feeling of ethnocentrism—languages and religions mix and work together as Swiss.

Issues of Equality/Inequality

Although there is a history of disagreement among the groups, the central government has been able to negotiate acceptable conditions for all. Equal rights for men are guaranteed by law, and those who feel discriminated against use the law to work out their problems. A Swiss motto is "Unity, yes; uniformity, no." The Swiss are competitive, responsible, tolerant, materialistic, proud, and private. There are still some classic role differences between the sexes, and discrimination against women still exists in some cantons.

Business Practices

Appointments

PUNCTUALITY

◆ The Swiss reputation for promptness is deserved. Always be punctual. This applies to both business and social events.

- Remember that many Europeans and South Americans write the day first, then the month, then the year (e.g., December 3, 1999, is written 3.12.99). This is the case in Switzerland.
- The work week is generally Monday through Friday from 7:30 A.M. to 5:30 P.M., with a one- or two-hour lunch break.
- Stores are open from 8:00 A.M. to noon and from 1:30 to 6:30 P.M., Monday through Saturday. Some close on Saturday or Monday mornings. The bigger stores do not close for lunch.
- Most people take their vacations in July and August. It is not advisable to try to schedule important appointments at this time.

 Negotiating

- Business is a serious and sober undertaking. Humor has little purpose in negotiations.
- Expect deliberations to proceed slowly. High-pressure tactics inevitably fail; there is no way to speed up decisions.
- Generally, the Swiss take a very long time to establish personal relationships. Be patient. A good relationship will help immensely down the road.
- German Swiss tend to get right down to business. The French and Italians will expect some small talk first.
- If you use an interpreter, speak slowly and clearly. Avoid idioms. Frequently confirm that what you have said has been understood.
- Since many people speak English, it is not necessary to translate your business cards.

CULTURAL NOTE

*i*f your firm is an old one, put the year it was established on your business card. The Swiss respect age.

- When arriving for an appointment, give your business card to the secretary. When you meet your client, give him or her a business card as well; the secretary will keep yours on file.

- Good topics of conversation are sports, positive aspects of Switzerland, travel, and politics.
- The Swiss attribute their independence to their military preparedness, which includes universal military conscription. Opinions on this subject are passionately held. Bringing the topic up can result in an argument.
- It is not appropriate to talk about dieting, especially while eating. Avoid personal questions and talk about work.
- Keep your wrists on the table at meals. Never put your hands in your lap.
- The elderly are respected in Switzerland. On public transportation, younger people are expected to relinquish their seat to the elderly.
- In the German areas of Switzerland, men tip their hats when passing acquaintances on the street.
- When entering a Swiss shop, say "Hello" to the clerk.
- It is not unusual for passersby to admonish strangers for "improper behavior" in the street. This is more common in German areas.

 Business Entertaining

- Business lunches and dinners are popular, but business breakfasts are uncommon.
- Business lunches are often quite informal, sometimes taking place in the company cafeteria.
- Business dinners are the time to impress your client with a meal at a fine restaurant.
- The Swiss rarely invite business associates into their homes.
- Toasting is a formal process. After your host has proposed a toast, look directly at him or her and respond verbally ("To your health" covers most occasions, but try to say it in the local language), then clink glasses with everyone within reach—preferably the whole table. Only then may you drink.

Time
- Switzerland is one hour ahead of Greenwich Mean Time (G.M.T. + 1), or six hours ahead of U.S. Eastern Standard Time (E.S.T. + 6).

Protocol

 Greetings

- The standard greeting is the handshake. Even children are encouraged to shake hands.
- Always rise to be introduced to someone. Wait to be introduced by a third person.
- In the German areas of Switzerland, women sometimes embrace, but men do not.
- In the French and Italian areas, both men and women may embrace. The French also kiss each other twice on the cheek.

Titles/Forms of Address

- The order of names is the same as in the United States: first name followed by surname.
- Only children address each other by their first names. Always address Swiss adults by their title or Mr., Mrs., or Miss, plus their surname.

Gestures

- It is impolite to talk with one's hands in one's pockets.
- Gum chewing in public is inappropriate.
- Do not sit with one ankle resting on the other knee.
- Backslapping is not appreciated.

Gifts

- Flowers or chocolates are good gifts when you are invited to a Swiss home.
- Red roses are only for lovers.
- Interpreters or guides appreciate personalized gifts rather than a tip.

Dress

- Conservative dress is always expected of business people.
- The Swiss appreciate discretion regarding wealth. Do not wear ostentatious jewelry and so forth.

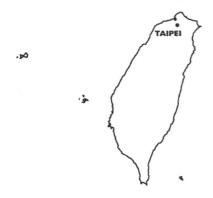

Taiwan

Country Background

History

Migration to Taiwan from mainland China began in A.D. 500. Dutch traders claimed the island as a base for their trade in 1624 and administered it until 1661. In 1664, loyalists from the Ming Dynasty fled to Taiwan to escape the Manchu invasion, and in 1683 it came under Manchurian control. When Taiwan became a Chinese province three years later, migration increased to the point where the Chinese dominated the aboriginal population. In 1895, following the first Sino-Japanese war, Taiwan was annexed to Japan. During the next fifty years, Taiwan underwent agricultural development and the construction of a modern transportation network. At the end of World War II, Taiwan again became governed by China.

A revolution founded the Republic of China (ROC) under Sun Yat-sen's Kuomintang (KMT) party. However, a civil war was waged in China between the KMT forces (led by Chiang Kai-shek after the death of Sun in 1925) and the Communist forces of Mao Tse-tung. The KMT was defeated, and the refugees fled to Taiwan. The provisional government they established claimed to be the only legitimate government over both the mainland and Taiwan. This claim is still in effect today.

Many countries supported Taiwan as the legitimate government until 1971, when the People's Republic of China was admitted to the United Nations in place of the Republic of China. The United States opened relations with the mainland government in 1979.

The United States retains unofficial relations with Taiwan through a nongovernmental agency, the American Institute in Taiwan (AIT). A peaceful solution to the Chinese situation is still being sought. Debate continues over Taiwan's retaining its claim to mainland China or becoming a separate, independent country.

After his death in 1975, Chiang Kai-shek was succeeded by his son Chiang Ching-kuo. Extensive modernization efforts have created a growing and prosperous economy in Taiwan. Martial law was lifted in 1987, and political opposition was legalized in 1989, opening the way for multiparty democratic elections.

Relations with the United States and other countries are good, and extensive trading continues.

> ## 𝓶 ————————————— CULTURAL NOTE
> odernization has come swiftly to Taiwan, making it one of the wealthiest countries in East Asia. Fast food restaurants, Western-style clothing, and modern appliances are evident. This is attributed in part to the long-term stability of the government and the strong feelings of solidarity and nationalism. The Taiwanese are generally quiet and reserved, yet friendly and courteous to strangers.

Type of Government

The nation's official name is Republic of China. It is often known as Nationalist China.

After years as a one-party presidential regime, Taiwan is now a multiparty republic. Political opposition parties were legalized in 1989.

The chief of state is the president. The head of government is the premier, who is appointed by the president. There is a National Assembly of some 400 seats, plus a unicameral legislative *yuan* of 220 seats. There are other *yuans* (or cabinets): a judicial *yuan*, a control *yuan* that monitors public service and corruption, and an examination *yuan* that serves as a civil service commission.

Language

The official language of Taiwan is traditional Mandarin Chinese, although Taiwanese (a southern Fukien dialect) is spoken more and more frequently. The Taiwanese do not use the modernized Chinese script currently used in the People's Republic of China. English is a popular language to study in school, and many business representatives can speak, understand, and correspond in English.

Religion

The religious distribution is 93 percent Buddhist, Confucian, and Taoist; 4.5 percent Christian; and 2.5 percent other religions.

> ## 𝓒 ————————————— CULTURAL NOTE
> onfucianism, although not a religion in the Western sense, has a great influence on Chinese society. Confucius was a Chinese scholar and statesman who lived during feudal times over 2,000 years ago. He established a rigid ethical and moral system that governs all relationships.
>
> Confucius taught that the basic unit of society is the family. In order to preserve harmony in the home, certain reciprocal responsibilities must be preserved in relationships. These relationships are between ruler and subjects, between husband and wife, between father and son, between elder brother and younger brother, and between friends. Since all but the last are hierarchical, rank and age are very important in all interactions. The concepts of face and not causing shame to another are paramount. And since all actions of the individual reflect upon the family, filial piety is of utmost importance. The virtues of kindness, righteousness, propriety, intelligence, and faithfulness are also revered.

Demographics

Taiwan's population of 20.5 million is primarily Taiwanese and mainland Chinese. Only 2 percent of the population consists of the aboriginal inhabitants of Taiwan. Although they live together amicably, there is some tension between the groups.

Almost 55 percent of Taiwanese are under age thirty.

Cultural Orientation

Cognitive Styles: How the Taiwanese Organize and Process Information

In Taiwan we find a culture that is generally closed to outside information but willing to consider data that conforms to its vital interests. Taiwanese are trained to think associatively and to stress wholeness over fragmentation. They are more apt to let their personal involvement in a problem dictate its solution than to use rules or laws.

Negotiation Strategies: What the Taiwanese Accept as Evidence

One's immediate feelings are the source of truth. This may be biased by faith in the ideologies of nationalism. The Taiwanese are moving toward the use of more and more facts to justify their decisions.

Value Systems: The Basis for Behavior

Confucianism has a great influence on Chinese society. It generates a rigid ethical and moral system that governs all relationships. The following three sections identify the Value Systems in the predominant culture—their methods of dividing right from wrong, good from evil, and so forth.

Locus of Decision Making

Decisions are made by consensus of the group, which defers to those who have the most ethos—usually the oldest members. It is the individual's duty not to bring shame on any unit of which he or she is a member—family, group, or organization. Individuals must also be very careful not to cause someone else to lose face. Thus, Taiwanese may speak in vague politeness rather than saying "no." There is a strong authoritative structure that demands impartiality and obedience.

Sources of Anxiety Reduction

The family is the most important unit of social organization, and life is an organization of obligations to relationships. The Taiwanese are highly ethnocentric with a natural feeling of superiority and confidence in their political system. This gives them a feeling of national and personal security. One must work for harmony in the group, so emotional restraint is prized and aggressive behavior is frowned upon.

Issues of Equality/Inequality

There is a strong feeling of interdependence among members of the family, group, or organization. Businesses are very competitive and put heavy emphasis on entry level skills and one's ability to get along in the group. There is some bias against native Taiwanese. Taiwan is still a male-dominated society with clearly differentiated sex roles. There is a strong women's movement.

Business Practices

Appointments

PUNCTUALITY

♦ Be punctual to meetings. This is expected from foreigners and is a sign of good business practices. Do not get upset, however, if your counterpart is late.

- Business hours are 8:30 A.M. to noon and 1:00 to 5:00 P.M., Monday through Friday, and 8:30 A.M. to noon on Saturday. Government offices are open 8:30 A.M. to 12:30 P.M. and 1:30 to 5:30 P.M., Monday through Friday, and 8:30 A.M. to noon on Saturday.
- Many business people nap between 1:30 and 2:00 P.M., and may not be fully awake for a 2:00 appointment.
- Evening entertainment is an important part of doing business in Taiwan, so expect to be out late. It is wise to schedule morning appointments for late morning. This gives both you and your client a chance to rest.
- Plan a visit to Taiwan between April and September. Many business people vacation from January through March.
- Traffic in Taipei is very congested. Unless your next appointment is so close that you can get there on foot, plan for long travel times between appointments.

Negotiating

- The basis of a business relationship in Taiwan is respect and trust. Take time to establish a rapport with your counterpart. Initially, you will have to overcome the Taiwanese distrust of Westerners. Meet face to face as often as possible, and keep in touch after your trip is over.
- Taiwan is relatively similar to other East Asian countries. The Chinese in Taiwan are capitalists with the same motivations for doing business as the Japanese. However, while Taiwan may seem very Westernized, the heart of the culture is still very traditional. Westernization is often a veneer, and the older generation still retains the decision-making authority in society.
- Business will tend to take place at a slower pace than in North America or Europe. Be patient with delays. Often, this is a tactic to wear down the other side. Therefore, do not talk about your deadlines. Expect to make several trips before reaching an agreement.
- Your negotiating team should include persons with seniority and a thorough knowledge of your company. Most importantly, include an older person. The Chinese revere age and status—sending a senior executive shows that a company is serious about starting a business relationship.
- It is still rare to have women participate in business in Taiwan. Foreign women will have the additional challenge of overcoming this initial hesitancy. When women are to be included in the teams, be certain to discuss this with your Chinese contact. Allow him some time to adjust to the idea.

- Brute honesty is not appreciated in Taiwan. A direct "no" is considered rude. Learn to speak in and listen to subtleties. A "yes" or nod of the head may mean "maybe" or "I understand." A "maybe" usually means "no."
- When negotiating, be sincere and honest. Humility is a virtue, and a breach of trust, since trust is a vital factor in business relationships, will not be taken lightly. (Most proposals and potential business partners will be thoroughly investigated.)
- Emphasize the compatibility of your two firms, your personal amicability, and your desire to work with your counterpart. Profits are very important, but harmonious human interaction precedes them in importance. Avoid high-pressure tactics.
- Protecting "face" or individual dignity is a very important and delicate matter. Therefore, never embarrass another person, especially in public.
- Never criticize your competition, or avoid admitting that you do not know the answer to a question.
- Consider sending your proposals in advance of your visit for your host to preview. At a presentation, recap the major points at the beginning and at the end. Look for cues that your counterpart did not understand you. Do not expect him or her to tell you when this happens, since this will cause embarrassment. Break the information up into small segments with pauses for question-and-answer periods. Be patient with extensive questioning. Address the chief negotiator occasionally, even if he does not speak English.
- Avoid using your hands when speaking. Chinese rarely use their hands while speaking and become distracted by a speaker who does.
- Business is competitive in Taiwan. Be prepared to discuss all parts of your proposal in detail. Bargaining is also a way of life, so be prepared to make concessions.
- Be sure to have products patented or registered in Taiwan to protect yourself against imitation.
- Have written materials translated by a Taiwanese expert. It is not acceptable to use the simplified Chinese script used in the People's Republic of China.
- Treat the elderly with respect. Acknowledge them first in a group, and do not smoke or wear sunglasses when they are near. When going through a doorway, allow older people to pass first. If they refuse, gently insist upon this point of etiquette.
- Modesty is very important in Taiwan. Do not enter an office until you are invited, and do not seat yourself until you are asked to do so. If you receive a compliment, politely refute it and expect others to do the same. This should not stop you from complimenting another person, however, since compliments are always appreciated.
- Avoid being loud and boisterous around the Taiwanese/Chinese. They dislike this behavior, since they interpret strong emotions, either positive or negative, as a loss of self-control. Westerners are stereotyped in Taiwan as being loud and emotional.
- Try to obtain a personal introduction from a bank or through the Commerce Department, since local contacts are extremely important.
- Be prepared to give out a lot of business cards. Your name, company an title should be printed in English on one side, and in Mandarin Chinese on the reverse side. (Gold ink is the most prestigious color for the Chinese side.) Cards are very important, since they indicate your rank and are a key to the respect you deserve in their culture. Never place a person's card in your wallet and then put it in your back pocket.
- For meetings, you will probably be taken to an informal sitting area and served coffee and tea. At the table, the member of your team with the highest seniori-

ty should sit in the middle of one long side. The second-ranked person will sit at his right, the third-ranked person to his left, and so forth. The Chinese delegation will do the same, so you will be able to identify key players on their team. If you are sitting on a sofa and chairs, follow the same pattern.

- Be careful not to overly admire an object belonging to another person. He or she may feel obliged to give it to you.
- Remove your shoes when entering a home or a temple building.
- Do not be surprised if you are asked personal questions. You may be asked how much you paid for something, or what your salary is. These questions are not considered in bad taste in Taiwan. If you don't want to answer, politely explain that it is not your custom to reveal such things.
- Important issues to be aware of include observing hierarchy, respecting the elderly, modesty, and reciprocating gestures of goodwill.

 Business Entertaining

- Hospitality is very, very important. Expect to be invited out every night after hours. This will entail visiting local night spots and clubs, often until late at night.
- The largest meal of the day is taken in the evening, at about 6:00 P.M. Entertaining is most often done in a restaurant and rarely in a home. If you are invited to a home, consider this an honor. Do not discuss business during a meal unless your host brings it up first.
- Never visit a home unannounced. Before leaving, express your thanks and bow slightly. Send a thank-you note to your host after a meal. It is polite to reciprocate by inviting your host to a meal of equal value at a later date.
- If you are the guest of honor at a round table, you will be seated facing the door. This is a custom carried over from feudal times that signified trust and goodwill on the part of the host, since the guest would be the first to see an attack and the host would be the last. It is also customary for the guest to be the first to sample a dish before anyone else starts eating.
- At a meal, eat lightly in the beginning, since there could be up to twenty courses served. Expect your host to keep filling your bowl with food whenever you empty it. Finishing all of your food is an insult to your host, since it means that he did not provide enough and that you are still hungry. Leaving a full bowl is also rude. The trick is to leave an amount somewhere in the middle.
- Chinese use chopsticks for eating and a porcelain spoon for soup. Your attempts at using chopsticks will be appreciated. When you are finished, set your chopsticks on the table or on the rest. Placing them parallel on top of your bowl is considered a sign of bad luck.
- Sticking your chopsticks straight up in your rice bowl is rude, since they will resemble the joss sticks used in religious ceremonies. Hold your rice bowl near your mouth to eat.
- Do not put food taken from a serving dish directly into your mouth. Transfer it to your plate or bowl first. Bones and shells are placed on the table or a spare plate; they are never placed in your rice bowl or on your plate.
- Leave promptly after the meal is finished.
- Good topics of conversation include Chinese sights, art, calligraphy, family, and inquiries about the health of the other's family. Topics to avoid are the situation with mainland China and local politics. Generally, conversation during a meal focuses on the meal itself and is full of compliments to the preparer.

Time
- Local time is eight hours ahead of Greenwich Mean Time (G.M.T. + 8) or thirteen hours ahead of U.S. Eastern Standard Time (E.S.T. + 13).

Protocol

Greetings
- When meeting someone for the first time, a nod of the head is sufficient. When meeting friends or acquaintances, a handshake is appropriate and will be expected from Westerners. Show respect by bowing slightly with your hands at your sides and your feet together.

> ***W***——————————————**CULTURAL NOTE**
> ith younger or foreign-educated Taiwanese, a handshake is the most common form of greeting. The standard Asian handshake is more of a handclasp; it is rather limp and lasts for some ten or twelve seconds. (By contrast, most North American handshakes last for only three or four seconds.) Sometimes both hands will be used.

- Chinese women will rarely shake hands. Western men should not try to shake hands with Chinese women. Western women will have to initiate a handshake with Chinese men.
- Elderly people are very highly respected, so it is polite to speak with them first. A compliment on their good health is always appreciated.
- Don't be surprised if you are asked if you have eaten. This is a common greeting, originating during the famines of feudal times. This phrase is comparable with "How are you?" in the West. A polite response is "yes," even if you have not eaten.
- Wait to be introduced to another at gatherings and parties. Avoid introducing yourself. Instead, employ a third person if there is someone you wish to meet.

Titles/Forms of Address
- Names are listed in a different order from Western names. Each person receives a family name, a generational name, and a given name at birth—in that order. Generational and given names are often separated by a hyphen. For example, President Li Teng-hui has the family name of Li, a generational name of Teng, and a given name of Hui.
- Most people you meet should be addressed with a title and their name. If a person does not have a professional title (President, Engineer, Doctor), simply use Mr. or Madam, Mrs., or Miss, plus their name.
- Chinese wives do not generally take their husband's surnames, but instead maintain their maiden names. Although Westerners commonly address a married woman as Mrs. plus her husband's family name, it is more appropriate to call her Madam plus her maiden family name. For example, Li Chu-chin (female) is married to Chang Wu-jiang (male). Westerners would probably call her Mrs. Chang. She is properly addressed as Madam Li.

- Thankfully, many Chinese adopt an English first name so that English speakers can have a familiar-sounding name to identify them by. Thus, Chang Wu-jiang may call himself Mr. Wally Chang. Others use their initials (Mr. W. J. Chang).
- If many Chinese seem to have similar clan names, it is because there are only about 400 different surnames in China. However, when these surnames are transcribed into English, there are several possible variations. For example, Wong, Wang, and Huang are all English versions of the same Chinese clan name.

Gestures

- Do not wink at a person, even in friendship.
- Do not put your arm around another's shoulders. While young children of the same sex will often hold hands, it is inappropriate for others to do so or to make physical contact with people who are not good friends or family.
- Do not touch the head of another person's child. Children are considered precious, and it is believed that they may be damaged by careless touching.
- Feet are considered dirty and should not touch things or people. Men should keep their feet flat on the floor, while women are permitted to cross their legs.
- Chinese point with their open hands, since pointing with a finger is considered rude. They beckon by extending their arms palm down and waving their fingers.
- While Westerners point to their chests to indicate the first person, "I," Chinese will point to their noses to indicate the same thing.

Gifts

- Gift giving is often practiced within a business setting. Good gifts for a first trip include items with small company logos on them. Be sure the products were not manufactured in Taiwan.
- Other popular gifts to business people include imported liquor, gold pens, and magazine subscriptions.
- When giving or receiving a gift, use both hands. The gift is not opened in the presence of the giver.
- The Chinese traditionally decline a gift three times before accepting; this prevents them from appearing greedy. Continue to insist; once they accept the gift, say that you are pleased that they have done so.
- Gifts of food are always appreciated by Chinese, but avoid bringing food gifts with you to a dinner or party (unless it has been agreed upon beforehand). To bring food may imply that your host cannot provide enough. Instead, send food as a thank-you gift afterwards. Candy or fruit baskets are good choices.
- The Chinese associate all of the following with funerals—do not give them as gifts:
  - Straw sandals
  - Clocks
  - A stork or crane (although the Western association of storks with births is known to many young Chinese)
  - Handkerchiefs (often given at funerals; they symbolize sadness and weeping)
  - Gifts (or wrapping paper) where the predominant color is white, black, or blue—red, pink, and yellow are happy, prosperous colors
- Also avoid any gifts of knives, scissors, or cutting tools; to the Chinese, they suggest the severing of a friendship.

- Flowers were traditionally associated only with the sick, with weddings, and with funerals. Should you have cause to bring flowers as gifts, make sure you give an even number of flowers. An odd number of flowers would be very unlucky.
- At Chinese New Year, it is customary to give a gift of money in a red envelope to children and to the service personnel you deal with on a regular basis. This gift is called a *hong bao*. Give only new bills in even numbers and even amounts. Many employers give each employee a *hong bao* equivalent to one month's salary.
- It is customary to reciprocate a gift with one of similar value. Therefore, choose a gift that takes into account the receiver's economic means.

 Dress

- For business, men should wear a conservative suit and tie. A jacket may be removed during meetings if your Chinese counterpart does so first. Women should wear a conservative skirt and blouse or suit.
- Dress modestly for casual activities. Revealing clothing for women is considered a mark of poor character. Shorts are appropriate for young people. Neatness and cleanliness are important.

BANGKOK

Thailand

Country Background

History

Like other countries of Southeast Asia, Thailand was peopled in prehistoric times through successive migrations from central Asia. Evidence of Bronze Age civilizations in northeast Thailand illustrate the high level of technology achieved by prehistoric people in Southeast Asia.

During the eleventh century, the Thai people began migrating from southern China. (Some research indicates that they were forced out by the Han Chinese.)

From the thirteenth century to the early twentieth century, the country was called Siam. The name was changed to Thailand in 1939.

Thailand was ruled by an absolute monarchy until a group of foreign-educated Thais directed a military and civilian coup d'etat in June of 1932 and replaced the absolute monarchy with a constitutional monarchy. The current nation can be dated to that period.

In 1941 Japan occupied Thailand. After World War II, Thailand followed a pro-Western foreign policy.

Since the Second World War, a balance of power has been established between the military and the civilian leaders, with the king occasionally mediating. Whenever the military has felt threatened, it has seized power. This has become more difficult as a growing political consciousness has developed in the Thai people. The Thais hope that the days of military coups are now over.

Type of Government

The Kingdom of Thailand is a constitutional monarchy.

Thailand has a prime minister and a parliament with two legislative houses, but their power has been limited by the military. Membership in the lower house is by election, but in the upper house it is by appointment, and the military is well represented. Generally, the upper house has supported the military, while the lower house has been more likely to oppose it.

Language
Thai, which is linguistically related to Chinese is the official language. Several other languages are spoken, including Chinese, Lao, Khmer, and Malay.

Religion
About 95 percent of the Thais are Theravada Buddhists (the Theravada school of Buddhism is an early form of Buddhism). About 3 percent of the population are Muslims, with the remaining 1 percent split between other religions (including Christianity).

Demographics
Thailand has a population of about 57 million. Nearly 10 percent of the population lives in Bangkok, the country's capital and largest city. About 78 percent of the people are ethnic Thais, 13 percent are Chinese, and the remaining 9 percent are a mixture of other Asians and non-Asians.

Cultural Orientation

Cognitive Styles: How Thais Organize and Process Information
The Thais cultivate alternatives and so are open to information on most issues. They live in a concrete, associative, pragmatic world where the present is more important than the future and the person takes precedence over the rule or law.

Negotiation Strategies: What Thais Accept as Evidence
The truth develops from subjective, fatalistic feelings on the issue modified by faith in the ideologies of Theravada Buddhism. Thais with higher education from European or U.S. universities may develop their truths from objective facts.

Value Systems: The Basis for Behavior
Religion plays a very important part in a Thai's life, but it does not dictate his or her every move. There are no absolute demands because their form of Buddhism permits selective conformity. They are free to choose which precepts of Buddhism, if any, they will follow.

Locus of Decision Making
The individual is responsible for his or her decisions. Thais are nonassertive, as well as being very conscious of the feelings of others and their position in the social hierarchy. Decision making revolves around the hierarchical, centralized nature of authority and the dependence of the inferior upon the superior. Thus, the typical supervisor is authoritarian. The superior makes decisions autonomously, and the inferior unquestioningly obeys. A benevolent superior and a respectful inferior is the Thai ideal.

Sources of Anxiety Reduction
The extended family is the basic social unit, with structure provided by the family, the village, and the *wat* (temple). The king is the primary provider of social cohesiveness. Thais refrain from developing specific expectations whenever possible because fate and luck play a major role in any event. You cannot plan because you cannot predict, so Thais live with a great deal of uncertainty. There is a high sense of self-reliance—what a person is depends on his or her own initiative.

Issues of Equality/Inequality

Status is of primary importance, as hierarchical relations are at the heart of Thai society. However, people gain their social position as a result of karma, not personal achievement. The royal family and the nobility are the only real class-conscious segment, although a class-conscious society is emerging. Regional and ethnic differences are socially and politically significant. This is a male-dominated society.

Business Practices

Appointments

PUNCTUALITY

* Punctuality is a sign of courtesy. Foreigners are expected to be on time.
* Traffic is extremely heavy in Bangkok, and floods make travel even worse. Allow plenty of time between appointments, especially during the rainy season.

- The best time to schedule a visit to Thailand is between November and March. Most business people vacation during April and May. Avoid the weeks before and after Christmas, and the month of April. Thailand's Water Festival is held in April, and businesses close for an entire week.
- Write a month or two in advance to arrange appointments.
- Arrange for a letter of introduction, and try to have an intermediary.
- Business hours are 8:30 A.M. to 5:00 P.M., Monday through Friday.
- Shops are open from 10:00 A.M. to 6:30 or 7:00 P.M., Monday through Saturday. Smaller shops open earlier and close later.

Negotiating

- Your initial meeting with Thai business people may be over lunch or drinks, so that they can get to know you. However, do not expect to discuss business over lunch.
- Because of the Thai deference to rank and authority, all requests and correspondence must pass through many layers before reaching top management.
- Be flexible and patient in your business dealings. Recognize that the Thais do not follow the same relentless work schedule that other cultures do. Allow sufficient time to reach your goal.
- Never lose control of your emotions, and don't be overly assertive; that is considered poor manners.
- Thais avoid confrontation at all costs. They will never say "no," but will instead make implausible excuses or pretend that they don't understand English. They may even tell you that they must check with someone at a higher level, when such a person doesn't exist. Likewise, they find it difficult to accept a direct negative answer.
- Always present your business card, preferably with a translation printed in Thai on the opposite side. (You can have these printed in Bangkok.)
- Thai business people will be impressed if you learn even a few words of Thai.

- If someone begins laughing for no apparent reason in a business meeting, change the subject. He or she is embarrassed.

_____**CULTURAL NOTE**

*d*irect confrontation is considered very impolite. Do not ask questions that require a value judgment (e.g., "Which of these competing products is the best?"). Such questions are much too blunt. Use more subtle questions, and slowly work your way toward the answer ("Which of these competing products do you use?"). But don't make assumptions about the answer (e.g., "So you use this one because it is best?" will probably elicit a "yes," even if the true reason for the preference is because a relative sells that brand).

 Business Entertaining

- To entertain a small group, take them to a Western restaurant in a large hotel. Arrange a buffet supper for a large group. Always include Thai wives in business dinners.
- Expect to eat with Western-style forks and spoons. Keep the fork in the left hand and the spoon in the right (reverse this if you are left-handed). Cut with the side of the spoon, not the fork. Use the fork to push food onto the spoon.
- Never finish the last bit of food in a serving dish. Wait until it is offered to you and then refuse politely the first time. When it is offered again, accept; it is considered an honor to have the last bit of food.
- Drink tea or beer with meals. Drink water only if you have seen it being poured from a bottle.
- Many Thais smoke after dinner, but don't be the first to light up. Always pass cigarettes around to the men at the table. Although traditional Thai women do not smoke or drink in public, it is acceptable for Western women to do so.

Time
- Thailand is seven hours ahead of Greenwich Mean Time (G.M.T. + 7), or twelve hours ahead of U.S. Eastern Standard Time (E.S.T. + 12).

Protocol

 Greetings

- Press your hands together as though in prayer, keeping arms and elbows close to your body, bow your head to touch your fingers, and say *Wai* (pronounced like "why"). This traditional greeting is used for both meeting and departing.
- Thais will shake hands with Westerners, but they will be pleased if you greet them with their traditional greeting.
- When introduced to a monk, never touch him; simply give a verbal greeting without shaking hands.

 Titles/Forms of Address

- Titles are very important to Thais.

- Many Thai business people are Chinese.
- Chinese names generally consist of a family name, followed by two (sometimes one) personal names. In the name Chang Wu Jiang, "Chang" is the surname (or clan name). He would be addressed with his title plus Chang (Mr. Chang, Dr. Chang).
- Chinese wives do not generally take their husband's surnames, but instead maintain their maiden names. Although Westerners commonly address a married woman as Mrs. plus her husband's family name, it is more appropriate to call her Madam plus her maiden family name. For example, Li Chu Chin (female) is married to Chang Wu Jiang (male). Westerners would probably call her Mrs. Chang. She is properly addressed as Madam Li.
- Thankfully, many Chinese adopt an English first name so that English speakers can have a familiar-sounding name to identify them by. Thus, Chang Wu Jiang may call himself Mr. Wally Chang. Others use their initials (Mr. W. J. Chang).
- Ethnic Thais predominate in government positions, but they will also be found in the business world.
- Since the adoption of surnames in the 1920s, ethnic Thais generally have two names. Their given name will come first, then their surname.
- Address people by their title (or Mr./Mrs.) and their given (first) name. The short Thai term for Mr., Mrs., or Miss is *Khun* (although there are longer forms as well). Thus, former Prime Minister Chatchai Choonhavan could be addressed as Khun Chatchai.
- Nicknames are popular in Thailand. Don't be surprised if the Thais give you a nickname, particularly if your name is hard for Thais to pronounce.

 Gestures

- Public displays of affection between members of the opposite sex are not condoned. However, members of the same sex may touch or hold hands with one another.
- Never point your foot at anyone; it is considered extremely rude. Don't cross your legs with one leg resting on the other knee, and never cross your legs in front of an older person.
- Never touch anyone—especially children—on the head.
- Always give up your seat on a bus or train to a monk who is standing.
- Never walk in front of Thais praying in a temple.
- Beckoning is done with the palm down and the fingers waved toward the body.

 Gifts

- Gifts are not opened in the presence of the giver.
- If you are invited for a meal, bring flowers, cakes, or fruit. Don't bring marigolds or carnations, however, as they are associated with funerals.
- Other popular gifts include women's cosmetics or perfume, brandy, neckties and clips, cigarettes, illustrated books from your area, dolls in native dress, and stationery.

Dress

- For business, men should wear a lightweight suit or slacks and a jacket, white shirt, and necktie; women should wear a plain, conservative dresses or suits. Women should not wear black dresses, a color the Thais reserve for funerals or mourning.
- Dress for success. The Thais are impressed with appearance because it indicates that you are of the upper class. Businesswomen usually wear full eye makeup.
- Men should wear slacks and shirts, with or without ties in casual settings; women should wear light dresses or skirts and blouses. Short-sleeved blouses are acceptable, but sleeveless ones are not. Both sexes may wear jeans (but may find them too hot). Shorts are acceptable on the streets, but not in the temples.
- Men should wear traditional summer formal attire for formal occasions—white jacket, black pants, and black tie; women should wear long dresses. Black is acceptable to wear at a formal event if it is accented with color.
- Wear old or inexpensive shoes when visiting temples. You must remove them before entering, and sometimes they are stolen from outside the temple.
- Never wear rubber thongs on the street; they are considered very low class.

Turkey

*t*urkey occupies one of the most strategic locations in the world. Turkey controls access to the Black Sea. Russia's only warm-water ports lie on the Black Sea; Bulgaria, Romania, Ukraine, and Georgia also depend upon their Black Sea ports. Access out of the Black Sea into the Mediterranean is via the straights of the Bosporus and the Dardanelles, both of which lie entirely in Turkish territory. Furthermore, as the only member of NATO in direct proximity to Russia, Iran, and Iraq, Turkey's strategic importance cannot be underestimated.

Country Background

History

The Republic of Turkey is the successor to a series of empires that have existed on the Anatolian peninsula since the dawn of recorded history.

The current state emerged from the dissolution of the Ottoman Empire after its defeat in the First World War. A war hero, Mustafa Kemal (later known as Kemal Atatürk), held the ethnically Turkish areas of the empire together. Despite invading armies, fundamentalist opposition, and the total absence of a democratic tradition, he turned the core of this crumbling Islamic empire into a secular republic. Founded in 1923, this Turkish Republic has survived and prospered to this day.

*t*he history of modern Turkey is inseparable from the biography of one man Kemal Atatürk, Turkey's national hero.

At the time of his birth in 1881, the Ottoman Empire had been reduced to a Middle Eastern dominion. Possessions in North Africa, the Caucasus, and Europe had been taken away (in Europe alone, the countries of Hungary, Romania, Bulgaria, Greece, Yugoslavia, and Albania were all once occupied by the Ottomans). But the beleaguered empire was still a power, and Mustafa Kemal attended the War College and rose through the ranks of the military. He was an energetic student and officer, and one of his teachers nicknamed him *Kemal* (excellence). He became involved in a nationalist reform group known as the Young Turks. The Young Turks finally achieved power, but failed to liberalize the government. Disappointed, Kemal broke with the Young Turks.

Since Russia (Turkey's traditional enemy) was allied with Britain and France, Turkey allied itself with the Central Powers in World War I. Kemal was then a lieutenant colonel of the infantry. He emerged as his country's greatest war hero, providing one of the Ottoman Empire's few victories by repulsing an overwhelming British attack at Gallipoli, saving the Ottoman capital of Istanbul (formerly known as Constantinople) from invasion.

After the defeat of the Central Powers, the victorious Allies proceeded to dismember the Ottoman Empire. A Turkish nationalist army was formed with Kemal as its leader, and a struggle that became known as the Turkish War of Independence was underway. After building the army up to a point where it threatened the Allied Occupation Forces, Kemal quit to become president of the new Turkish nationalist parliament in Ankara. Turkey then had two opposing governments: Kemal's nationalists in Ankara, and one in the old capital of Istanbul, under the thumb of the Allied Occupation Forces.

Unwilling to fight further, the Allies eventually recognized the new government in Ankara as the legitimate leaders of the Turkish areas of the Ottoman Empire. The modern Republic of Turkey was born on October 29, 1923, with Kemal as its president.

Kemal remained in power until his death fifteen years later and initiated an astonishing number of reforms. To Kemal, modernization meant Westernization. Turkey became a democratic secular state—no easy feat in a Muslim land. The old titles were abolished, and all Turks were ordered to adopt surnames. Kemal was awarded the surname *Atatürk* (father of the Turks) by the parliament. Illiteracy was reduced by replacing Arabic script with the easier-to-master Roman alphabet. These and other reforms were not accomplished without considerable opposition. For most of his tenure, Kemal Atatürk found it necessary to rule Turkey as a one-party state. But the government he founded was strong enough to endure even after his death.

Turkey managed to remain neutral in World War II. Choosing to ally itself with the West in the cold war, Turkey sent an infantry contingent to fight in Korea in 1950 and joined NATO in 1952. Political turmoil following the introduction of multiparty elections sometimes resulted in the Turkish military involving itself in government. But throughout it all, Turkey has maintained a more stable, pro-Western government than most countries with Islamic majorities.

The 1990 invasion of Kuwait by Iraq put enormous strains upon Turkey. Turkey was a major trading partner of neighboring Iraq, but it supported both the embargo against Iraq and the multinational coalition that liberated Kuwait in 1991. Although Turkish troops did not serve in the liberation, the use of Turkish air bases was considered vital. Turkey experienced economic problems from both the embargo and high inflation during the Gulf crisis, although these were partially offset by $4 billion in grants and credits from Turkey's grateful allies.

In June 1992, Turkey initiated the Black Sea Economic Cooperation Treaty. Signed by Turkey, Greece, Bulgaria, Romania, and several ex-Soviet republics, the treaty is designed to enhance trade within the region.

Type of Government

The Republic of Turkey is a multiparty democracy. The president is the chief of state. The presidency was traditionally a largely ceremonial office, but the late President Turgut Ozal (who was also a former prime minister) turned it into a forum for directing Turkey's international affairs. The prime minister is the head of the government.

There is one legislative house, the 450-seat Grand National Assembly.

The Gulf crisis thrust Turkish President Turgut Ozal into the international spotlight. However, Ozal's foreign policies were not universally popular within Turkey. Opposition leaders accused him of exceeding his authority by involving Turkey in a war against Iraq. Problems increased with the establishment of the coalition-protected Kurdish zone in northern Iraq. Turkey's own Kurds agitated for autonomy, and the secessionist Kurdish Workers' Party took advantage of the protected zone to establish bases from which they attacked Turkish security troops. A government program to meet some Kurdish demands failed to halt the rising violence.

Turkey is also concerned about wars in various regions of the former U.S.S.R., especially between Armenia and Azerbaijan (centered on the autonomous region of Nagorno-Karabakh). The Muslim Azeris are considered friends of Turkey, but there is historic animosity between the Turks and the Christian Armenians. Should the Armenians win this war, Turkey reserves its historic right to intervene in conflicts on its border.

CULTURAL NOTE

*W*ith the breakup of the former U.S.S.R., Turkey and Iran are in a battle for influence over the Islamic republics of the former Soviet Union. This battle is being waged on numerous fronts—even over which alphabet to use. All of the Muslim ex-Soviet republics wish to drop the Russian Cyrillic alphabet, which was forced upon them by Moscow. Whether they adopt the Arabic alphabet used by Iran or the Roman alphabet used by Turkey is a matter of great debate. Turkey and Iran are trying to influence the decision by sending books and typewriters using their respective alphabets to the Muslim republics.

Language

Turkish is the official language. It is a member of the Ural-Altaic linguistic group, and thus totally unlike any Indo-European language (such as English, German, or the Romance tongues). Turkish used to be written in Arabic script, but in 1928 the Latin alphabet was officially adopted. This made education much simpler, and today the literacy rate has increased to over 70 percent. English is a popular second language.

Religion

Turkey has no official religion, although 90 percent of the Turkish population is Sunni Muslim. The remaining 10 percent are mostly other Muslim sects, plus some Christians and Jews.

Demographics

Of Turkey's 55.3 million inhabitants, some 85 percent are ethnic Turks. There are a significant number of minorities, including Greeks, Armenians, Jews, and Arabs, but the largest minority group (12 percent) is the Kurds.

Cultural Orientation

Cognitive Styles: How Turks Organize and Process Information

Historically, Turks are generally closed to outside information. This is ameliorated somewhat by Turkey's position as a bridge between East and West. Turks are trained to process information subjectively and associatively. Turkey is a secularized Islamic nation, and one's personal involvement is more important than rules or laws.

Negotiation Strategies: What Turks Accept as Evidence

On any question, the answer comes from a combination of immediate feelings and faith in the ideologies of Islam. Among Turks, truth seldom comes from the accumulation of objective facts.

Value Systems: The Basis for Behavior

Turkey's territory lies both in Europe and Asia, and its value systems have always been an amalgam of East and West. The following three sections identify the Value Systems in the predominant culture—their methods of dividing right from wrong, good from evil, and so forth.

Locus of Decision Making

The male leader is the decision maker, but he always considers the family group upon which the decision is binding. Private life is overwhelmed by family, friends, and organizations, and these determine one's opinions. A relationship between participants must be established before any formal negotiations can take place. Identity is based on the social system, and education is the primary vehicle for moving up the social ladder.

Sources of Anxiety Reduction

Stability and identity in life come from one's role in the social structure, plus the presence of a strong family orientation. There is a deeply ingrained work ethic, but time is not a major source of anxiety. Pride in one's country, society, and family bolsters one's self-image and self-esteem. Emotions are shown, assertiveness is expected, and risks are taken to develop self-reliance.

Issues of Equality/Inequality

There is a definite social hierarchy, with some bias against classes, ethnic groups (especially the Kurds), and religions. The privileged elite control the country, with conspicuous consumption and education being the status symbols. There is not a lot of trust in people outside of the family and intimate friends. The old dominate the young, and men try to dominate women even though they have equal rights by law. Men and women historically had separate social subsocieties and did not mix in public, but this is changing rapidly.

Business Practices

Appointments

PUNCTUALITY

♦ You are expected to be punctual for all business appointments.
♦ Traffic jams are frequent in both Istanbul and Ankara, so allow yourself plenty of travel time.

- Arrange appointments by mail well in advance. A personal introduction (or at least a letter of introduction) will be of great help to you in gaining acceptance.
- Turkish business people who deal internationally are usually able to communicate in one or more foreign languages. English is commonly understood, as are German and French. Given advance notice, your Turkish colleagues should be able to conduct business in English; they probably have an English-speaking person on their staff. Business letters may also be in English. However, Turks will appreciate the effort if you learn at least a few phrases in Turkish.
- Do not expect to get right down to business in a meeting with a Turkish business person. The seemingly interminable small talk that precedes business allows him or her to get to know you.

- Business and banking hours: 9:00 A.M. to 12 noon and 2:00 P.M. to 5:00 P.M., Monday through Friday. (Note that business executives generally arrive between 9:30 and 10:00 A.M. and return from lunch around 2:30 P.M.)
- Although Friday is the Muslim holy day, business is still conducted on that day. Sunday is the government-mandated "day of rest."
- Business appointments can rarely be made during the months of June, July, and August; most Turkish business people take extended vacations during this time.
- Obviously, you cannot expect to conduct business on a Turkish holiday. Be aware that many people will begin the holiday around noon the day before.

CULTURAL NOTE

*b*oth secular and Islamic holidays are celebrated in Turkey.

November 10 is a secular holiday remembering the death of the founder of modern Turkey, Kemal Atatürk, in 1938. It is a serious insult not to observe the moment of silence at 9:05 A.M., the time of Atatürk's death.

These Muslim holidays will fall on different dates each year:

- *Ramazan* (called *Ramadan* in other Muslim countries), the holy month. Observers fast from dawn until dusk. Dusk is announced by a cannon shot. The faithful are awakened before sunrise by drummers who roam the streets, reminding them to eat before dawn. It is impolite for nonbelievers to eat, drink, or even smoke in the presence of those who are fasting; be discreet. Office hours may be curtailed. No surprisingly, fasting people may be short-tempered, especially when Ramazan falls during the sweltering days of summer. This is called *Ramazan kafasi*, or Ramazan irritability (literally, "Ramazan head").
- *Sheker Bayram*, the three-day festival at the end of the Ramazan fast. Children go door to door asking for sweets; Muslims exchange greeting cards, feast, and visit one another. Banks and offices are closed for all three days.
- *Kurban Bayram*, the feast of the sacrifice. Celebrating the traditional story of Abraham's near-sacrifice of his son Isaac, this is the most important religious and secular holiday of the year. The holiday lasts for four days, but many banks and businesses close for an entire week. Resorts and transportation will be booked solid.

Negotiating

- In a family-owned business, the decision maker may be quite elderly. Remember that elders are always deferred to in Turkey. Never lose your temper or shout at an elder.
- The pace of negotiation is much slower in Turkey than it is in the United States. Politeness is important, and negotiations may take place over innumerable cups of tea or coffee. Meetings start slowly, with many inquiries as to your background, your education, and so on. Many of these questions will seem irrelevant to the purpose of your visit, but it is a serious breach of etiquette to cut them short.
- Business cards need not be translated into Turkish. Bring plenty of them, and give them to everyone you meet. When you enter an office and hand the receptionist your card, the receptionist will probably keep it rather than sending it in to announce you, so give another to the business person you have come to see.
- In conversation, avoid taking sides in any Turkish political question or on the Turkish-Greek dispute over Cyprus. Safe topics include families, personal hobbies and interests, professions, and noncontroversial international affairs. Always ask a Turkish father about his family; few subjects give a Turk more pride than his sons.
- Tobacco is everywhere in Turkey. No-smoking zones are virtually nonexistent. If you are allergic to tobacco smoke, you will have a difficult time in Turkey.

Business Entertaining

- By and large, most business entertaining will take place in restaurants. This is not a drawback, as Turkish cuisine is one of the finest in the world. However, you may not get the chance to act as host; Turkish hospitality is legendary, and your colleagues may insist upon doing (and paying for) all of the entertaining. When your colleagues invite you to a restaurant, you will not be allowed to pay for even part of the meal.
- Only when you issue an invitation to a meal will you be allowed to pick up the tab—and even then you may have to fight off your colleagues' efforts to grab the check.
- In general, restaurants in the international hotels are bland and uninteresting compared to the average Turkish restaurant. However, Western-style alcoholic drinks are more readily available in such hotels.
- Turks use the same eating utensils that Americans use. The fork is held in the left hand and the knife in the right; the knife is used for cutting and to push food onto the fork.
- Service in Turkish restaurants is very quick. Except in the international hotel restaurants, Turks do not usually order the entire meal at once. Instead they order the courses one at a time, deciding what to eat next only after finishing the last course.
- Turks usually smoke between courses.
- A toothpick is usually offered at the end of the meal. You may use it at the table, but be sure to cover your mouth with your hand.

CULTURAL NOTE

*t*ea, rather than coffee, is the national drink. A concentrated tea is poured into small, tulip-shaped glasses (hold the glass by the rim to avoid burning your fingers), and water is added to dilute the tea to your taste. Sugar may be added to tea, but never milk. As the glasses are small, you will probably go through many of them during a meeting. Outdoor tea gardens are common, and quite pleasant.

Turkish coffee is strong, and is best appreciated as an after-dinner drink. Each cup is brewed individually, and the sugar is added at the time of the brewing, so you must indicate whether you want it plain or with little, medium, or lots of sugar. (U.S. palates usually require medium sugar.) Don't drain the cup; there will be coffee grounds at the bottom. Milk is not usually added to Turkish coffee but is generally available with instant coffee or the less concentrated American-style coffee.

Time

- Turkey is on Eastern European Time, which is two hours ahead of Greenwich Mean Time (G.M.T. + 2)—except between April and September, when Turkish clocks are advanced one hour. It is seven hours ahead of U.S. Eastern Standard Time, (E.S.T. + 7).

Protocol

Greetings

- Shake hands firmly when greeting or being introduced to a Turkish man. It is not customary to shake hands again upon departure.
- Turks may greet a close friend of either sex with a two-handed handshake and/or a kiss on both cheeks.
- Elders are respected in Turkey; if you are seated, rise to greet them when they enter a room. When being introduced to a group of men, shake hands with each one, starting with the eldest.
- Remember that Turkey is primarily a Muslim country, so the vast majority of your business contacts will be male. Women are usually kept out of business affairs by ethnic Turks. Do not address a Turkish woman unless she has been formally introduced to you. If this happens, wait for her to extend her hand before offering to shake hands. Any businesswomen you meet will probably be Greek or Armenian rather than Turkish.

t——————————————————**CULTURAL NOTE**

he traditional Turkish greetings are *"Merhaba"* (MEHR-hah-bah; Hello) and *"Nasilsiniz?"* (NAHS-sulh-suh-nuhz; How are you?). The response to the latter is *"Iyiyim, teshekur ederim"* (ee-YEE-yihm, tesh-ek-KEWR eh-dehr-eem; I'm fine, thank you!). Turks will appreciate any effort you make to speak their language.

Titles/Forms of Address

- The easiest and most respectful way to address a Turkish professional is by his occupational title alone. Simply say "Doctor" (*Doktor*) or "Attorney" (*Avukat*). If the professional is a woman, add the word Bayan after the title (e.g., Mrs./Miss Attorney is Avukat Bayan).
- When your Turkish colleague does not have a title, the situation becomes more complicated. Realize that most Turks did not have surnames until they were made mandatory by the 1934 Law of Surnames. The order of names is the same as in the United States: first name followed by the surname.
- The traditional mode of address was to use a Turk's first name, followed by *bey* (for men) or *hanim* (for women). Use this form with older people unless instructed otherwise.
- Most of the Turks you will do business with use the modern form of address. The modern way is to use the surname, preceded by *Bay* (for men) or *Bayam* (for women). For example, Cengiz Dagci, a male novelist, would traditionally be addressed as Cengiz bey. The modern form of address is Bay Dagci (note the difference in spelling: *bey* vs. *bay*). Nezihe Meric, a female author, would traditionally be addressed as Nezihe hanim. The modern form of address is Bayam Meric.

Gestures

- It is safest to keep both feet flat on the ground when sitting. Displaying the soles of your shoes (or feet) to someone is insulting. It is discourteous for women to cross their legs while facing another person.
- It is rude to cross your arms while facing someone.
- Keep your hands out of your pockets while speaking.
- Avoid blowing your nose in public, especially in a restaurant. If you must, turn away from others and blow as quietly as possible.
- Do not kiss, hug, or even hold hands with someone of the opposite sex in public.
- While Turks indicate "yes" by nodding their heads up and down (the same way as in the United States), the gestures for "no" are different. Two ways to indicate "no" are as follows:
    1. Raising the eyebrows is a subtle way to indicate "no." This arch look may be accompanied by the sound "tsk."
    2. A broader way to indicate "no" is to accompany the eyebrow-arching with a backward tilting of the head and lowering of the eyelids (rather like someone trying to peer through the lower half of a pair of bifocals).
- The U.S. gesture for "no" (wagging the head from side to side) is a Turkish gesture for "I don't understand." If you inadvertently make this gesture in response to a question, a Turk will probably assume that you did not comprehend the language and will ask the question in another tongue.
- Describing a desired length by holding the palms apart in midair (in the manner of a fisherman describing "the one that got away") will not be understood in Turkey. The Turks approximate length by extending one arm and placing the flat of the other hand on the arm; the length indicated is measured from the fingertips of the extended arm up to the side of the hand.
- To attract attention, Turks wave (palm out) with an up-and-down motion, rather than from side to side.
- The Turkish "follow me" gesture is done with the entire curled hand moved in a downward "scooping" motion, not by curling an upraised index finger. It is considered rude to point your finger directly at someone.

 Gifts

- Your gift-giving responsibilities are very limited as long as your Turkish colleagues entertain you only in public places like restaurants. If you know that your colleague drinks, a fine whiskey or liqueur is appropriate.
- If you are invited to a Turkish home—and an invitation may come more quickly from someone you meet socially than from a business colleague—a gift will be expected. If you are not the only guest, your hostess may not open the gift in your presence; seeing to the comfort of the guests takes priority.
- Again, wine or liquor is appropriate if you are sure your hosts drink alcohol. Other suitable gifts are candy, pastries, roses, or carnations. Glassware, such as a vase, goblet, or decanter is a prized gift.
- If your invitation is for an extended stay (rather than a meal), further gifts are advisable. Items such as records or books in English are prized, as they are hard to find in Turkey. Be sure to bring gifts for the children, such as candy (especially chocolate) or small toys.

- Orthodox Islam prohibits alcohol and depictions of the human body (including photographs and drawings). Ascertain whether your hosts adhere to these strictures before giving such gifts.

 Dress

- Business dress is conservative: dark suits for men; suits and heels for women. However, Turkey is very hot in the summer. Jackets and even ties may be removed in the heat. Women's clothing may be comfortable but should remain modest; even in severe heat, necklines may not be low and skirts may not be short.
- Formal dress is required to attend the balls held during New Years and the Turkish national holiday (October 29). Men need dark suits or tuxedos; women wear long gowns.
- Casual dress should also be modest. Shorts are appropriate only at seaside resorts. Jeans are acceptable for both men and women, but they should not be torn or frayed.

CULTURAL NOTE

Should you enter a mosque, your clothing should be appropriate; it can be casual, but it must be modest. Expect to leave your shoes at the door, as one does not walk on mosque carpets in shoes. If you wish, you may rent slippers from an attendant at the mosque for a small fee. Pants are usually acceptable for women, but women are expected to cover their heads, shoulders, and arms. If your clothing is judged unacceptable, an attendant may offer you the loan of a long robe. A small donation to the mosque is always appreciated. Avoid visiting during prayer times or on Fridays (the Muslim holy day).

Ukraine

CULTURAL NOTE

*t*he name Ukraine means "borderland," and Ukraine has often constituted the border of several empires. This also resulted in the use of the definite article before Ukraine. English speakers said "the Ukraine" just as they said "the Bronx" or "the Netherlands." Current usage omits the article; the country is now just "Ukraine" or "Republic of Ukraine."

Country Background

History

Slavic peoples populated Ukraine at least 2,000 years before Christ. Kiev, the capital, dates to about the eighth century A.D.—some four hundred years before Moscow. One of the oldest and most important of Slavic cities, Kiev is often considered the "mother" city of Ukraine, of the Russian Empire, and of the Slavic Orthodox churches. Christianity came to Ukraine (and from there spread to Russia) when Prince Vladimir of Kiev was converted to Orthodoxy by Byzantine missionaries from Constantinople in A.D. 988. For hundreds of years Kiev was the leading city of the Orthodox Slavic lands.

Ukraine's flat, fertile expanses historically made it difficult to defend. The Mongols sacked Kiev in 1240, and from this point on, Moscow became the dominant Slav city. (Orthodox Russians see a progression of "holy cities of Orthodoxy," from Constantinople to Kiev to Moscow.)

Ukraine has been a prize coveted by many warring peoples. The Mongols were eventually driven back eastward, but other rulers took their place. The Lithuanians conquered Ukraine around 1392. When Lithuania and Poland merged in 1569, Polish influence became dominant. Under Polish rule, the Ukrainian farmers were forced into serfdom. Those who resisted began to band together and became known as Cossacks. They lived a harsh existence in frontier areas, and gave only nominal allegiance to the Polish king.

In the 1600s, Polish Jesuits began to impose Catholicism on the Ukrainians by force. This rallied the Orthodox Cossacks, and in 1648 the Cossacks drove the Poles out of part of Ukraine. (This also left a legacy of hatred of Jesuits among both Ukrainians and the Russian Orthodox. Even today, paranoid Orthodox Slavs envision Jesuit conspiracies, and right-wing Nationalist propaganda includes Jesuits in its lists of enemies.)

397

Fearing that their independent state was too weak to stand alone, the Cossacks requested that Moscow rule them in 1654. The Cossacks believed that they could trust the Orthodox Muscovites; they were mistaken. Moscow tightened its grip on the Ukrainians decade after decade, reducing the Cossacks' power and completing the process of enserfment. Ukrainian mistrust of Russians dates back to this period.

Whether Czarist or Soviet, Russian leaders came to view Ukraine as an integral possession of Russia. Many Russians accepted the loss of the Baltics and the Asian republics after the 1991 breakup of the U.S.S.R., but there are Russians who still do not accept Ukraine as a separate state. Ukraine constituted 20 percent of the population of the U.S.S.R., and was second only to Russia in size.

Type of Government

Ukraine is a multiparty republic with a single legislative house, called the Supreme Council. The head of government is the prime minister. The president is the chief of state.

Ukraine remains a member of the Commonwealth of Independent States, despite its mistrust of Russia.

Language

The official language of Ukraine is Ukrainian, which is similar—but not identical—to Russian. Modern Ukrainian has Polish linguistic influences that are absent in Russian. Today, Ukrainian and Russian are about as close as Dutch and German. Although the languages are different, native speakers can manage some communication. (However, foreigners who learn Russian usually report that they cannot understand Ukrainian without study.)

Religion

The majority of Ukrainians are Ukrainian or Russian Orthodox. Less than 5 percent of the population is Baptist or Jewish. About 10 percent of Ukrainians belong to the Uniat church, a Byzantine Orthodox branch that accepts the authority of the Catholic Pope. There is no official religion.

Demographics

The population of Ukraine is about 52 million.

Cultural Orientation

Cognitive Styles: How Ukrainians Organize and Process Information

The Ukrainians have traditionally maintained freedom of discussion and have been open to outside information. At the same time, they hold to their beliefs strongly and are quick to confront. They excel in the sciences, with higher education teaching abstractive and conceptual thought. However, their emotions bind them to the associative and the particular.

Negotiation Strategies: What Ukrainians Accept as Evidence

Truth is usually found in the accumulation of objective facts. However, Ukrainians' ability to reason analytically and objectively is sometimes held captive to their subjective feelings about the issue being discussed. Perhaps the only ideology in which they have faith is that of nationalism.

Value Systems: The Basis for Behavior

The Ukrainian culture is one of contrasting value systems—Ukrainians are deeply idealistic, but just as deeply attached to the personal and subjective. The following three sections identify the Value Systems in the predominant culture—their methods of dividing right from wrong, good from evil, and so forth.

Locus of Decision Making

To the Ukrainian, the individual is the primary unit for decision making. He or she may be so independent that it is difficult to reach a consensus. Ukrainians tend to repudiate all forms of communal life that call for strict obedience. Decisions are not fixed on objective reality, but on idealistic reality containing many elements of imagination and fancy. Ukrainians tend to confront reality with emotion, make decisions on the spur of the moment, and intermix theoretical and practical issues.

Sources of Anxiety Reduction

With the Communist party no longer in control, the church is regaining its importance as the focal point for external structure and stability. The Ukrainians are deeply religious but not fundamentalist; they look for ways to comprehend the essence of a creed rather than being fixated on dogma. Strong family ties help to ease the feelings of uncertainty. However, since feelings take precedence over reason, a person may go from deep love to great hatred or from great enthusiasm to deep despair in a short time. Thus, the system may never seem to be in a stable condition.

Issues of Equality/Inequality

Ukrainians possess strong moral courage. They have a desire for harmony and an inclination to compromise and tolerate differences. Without a strong central government, the quest for control is being seen on all levels of society. This may lead to both ethnic and class disputes. Poetic by nature, they associate love not with eroticism but with a more philosophical, maternal love. There is a genuine softness of character that is expressed in politeness and high regard for the female sex. Women are considered the moral leaders of the nation.

Business Practices

Appointments

——————————————————— PUNCTUALITY

* Always be punctual, but do not be surprised if the Ukrainians are not. It is not unusual for Ukrainians to be one or two hours late to an appointment.
* Punctuality was not considered essential under the Soviet system, since employment was guaranteed and no one could be fired for tardiness.
* Even today, patience, not punctuality, is considered a virtue in Ukraine.
* Allow plenty of time for each appointment. Not only may they start late, but they may run two to three times longer than originally planned.

- Remember that the date is written differently in many countries. In Ukraine, the day is listed first, then the month, then the year. For example, 3.12.99 means December 3, 1999—not March 12, 1999.

- Obtaining an appointment can be a laborious process. Be patient and persistent. Once you have obtained an appointment, make every effort not to allow it to be canceled.
- Business hours are generally from 9 A.M. to 5 P.M., Monday through Friday.
- Major stores are open from 9 or 10 A.M. to 8 or 9 P.M., Monday through Saturday. Smaller shops usually close by 7 P.M. Most stores close for an hour at lunchtime. Food stores are also open on Sunday.

Negotiating

- Be factual and include technical details.
- Until you have a signed agreement, do not get overconfident about the deal at hand. Never expect that you can renegotiate later, either; the existing contract is as advantageous as you will ever get.
- Never accept the first "no" as an answer. "No" is a quick and automatic response. Remain pleasant, try to establish a personal rapport, and ask again in a different way.
- "Final offers" are never final during initial negotiations. Be prepared to wait; the offer will be made more attractive if you can just hold out.
- If you or your negotiators have not walked out of the negotiating room in high dudgeon at least twice during the negotiations, you're being too easy. Ukrainians, like Russians, expect walkouts and dire proclamations that the deal is off. Play hardball; they will.
- Foreigners can use two approaches to dealing with Ukrainian theatrics in negotiations: They can be patient and wait them out, or they can respond with equal shouting and dramatics. Either method is usually acceptable.
- Haste always puts you at a disadvantage. If you give the impression that you cannot wait out your counterpart, you will inevitably lose.
- Any time you can get Ukrainians to come to the West to negotiate, you have an advantage. In the West they are away from home, spending hard-currency dollars in hotels and restaurants. This puts the Ukrainians under time pressure.
- North Americans view negotiation as an exercise in compromise. However, the traditional Russian view is that compromise equals weakness. If they can avoid compromising, they will. To yield on even an insignificant matter is something to be avoided. While Ukrainians in general are more easygoing than Russians, Ukrainian negotiators have been trained in Russian techniques.
- Ukrainian negotiators tend to speak with one voice. Foreign negotiators need to be in agreement among themselves and present a unified front to the Ukrainians.

CULTURAL NOTE

*U*krainians are fairly status-conscious. They will probably have several people at any negotiation. They prefer you to have an executive whose rank is equivalent to that of their top negotiator at the discussions. A lone foreign executive in a room with a team of Ukrainians will have a difficult time.

- Joint ventures with Ukrainians are the current preferred type of business deal. Countertrade (such as PepsiCo trading soda for Stolichnaya vodka) opportunities are vanishing. The Ukrainians have learned that anything of theirs that a foreign firm can sell on the open market, the Ukrainians themselves can sell.

- Include a clause requiring the joint venture partners to submit to arbitration in a neutral country if they can't come to an agreement. Sweden is the most popular choice for third-country arbitration.

- Ukrainian regulations represent the biggest liability to a successful joint venture. Since these regulations are in constant flux (reforms are being made all the time), don't count on your partner to have a full grasp of the legal issues involved. Get your own expert on Ukrainian law. Don't be surprised if they way you did something yesterday isn't allowed tomorrow; many laws are nebulous, and their interpretation is subject to change.

- Unfortunately, Ukraine is currently lagging behind even the Russian Republic in free-market reforms. This makes for a difficult business climate.

- Be sure to have enough business cards to hand out. Since telephone books are not easily available, businesses depend upon their business-card file. However, do not be surprised if you do not receive a business card in return. Ukrainians may not have any to give out.

- Traits that many Ukrainians and North Americans have in common include a respect for nature and the outdoors, a fascination with technology and gadgets, and a tendency towards building things "big." All of these make good topics for conversation.

- In many countries—such as Japan—people tend to respond to a question by saying "yes." In Ukraine the tendency used to be just the opposite; managers and bureaucrats said "no" at every opportunity. However, businessmen now often say "yes" to proposals in order to continue the contacts they want with foreigners. Be aware that they may not be able to carry out everything they promise.

- Historically, there were many reasons why Ukrainians said "no" to business proposals. One reason was that innovation was discouraged. People were afraid that if they gave the go-ahead and a project failed, they would be held responsible. Another reason had to do with the position of an individual in a rigid, hierarchical bureaucracy. You rarely met a bureaucrat who had the power to push a project forward without the agreement of others. But one individual could cancel a project, all by himself or herself. The ability to say "no" was the only real power many bureaucrats possessed; not surprisingly, they used it frequently.

- A positive response usually requires groundwork. Before making a decision, the bureaucrat should know who you are, what you want, what your project is, and which other bureaucrats have agreed to it so far. This information is best communicated through a third person, but a letter will sometimes serve.

- Pessimism is characteristic of the Russian (and, to a lesser extent, Ukrainian) mentality. They expect things to go wrong. Do not be surprised if they fail to respond enthusiastically.

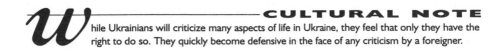

CULTURAL NOTE

hile Ukrainians will criticize many aspects of life in Ukraine, they feel that only they have the right to do so. They quickly become defensive in the face of any criticism by a foreigner.

Business Entertaining

- Business success in Ukraine hinges upon establishing a personal rapport with your Ukrainian partners. Much of this will evolve out of social events.

- Doormen of hotels and restaurants must try to let in only certain people, and may require proof that you belong. Don't be surprised if they are not friendly.

- In restaurants, you may have a long wait for food. Ignore the menus; perhaps a third of the items listed are actually available. You must ask the waiter what is being served that day.
- Ukrainian restaurants tend to have large tables set for many people. If your party consists of just two or three, you may have to share a table with other people.
- Two bottles will be on the table: one has water, the other has vodka. The vodka will not have a resealable lid—once it is opened, Ukrainians expect your party to drink it all.
- Besides vodka, Ukrainians also drink a lot of champagne.
- Dinners are early (about 6:00 P.M.).
- It is a great honor to be invited to a Ukrainian home.
- Ukrainians do not feel obligated to phone before dropping by a friend's house. Once you have established true friendship, a Ukrainian may stop by at any time—even late at night if a light is visible in your window.
- Guests are always offered food and drink (usually alcohol).
- Expect to do a lot of drinking—mostly vodka, champagne, and cognac.
- In a restaurant or nightclub, Ukrainians may invite you to dance or to come over to their table.

Time
- Ukraine is in the westernmost time zone of the C.I.S., three hours ahead of Greenwich Mean Time (G.M.T. + 3). This is eight hours ahead of U.S. Eastern Standard Time (E.S.T. + 8).

Protocol

Greetings
- Ukraine is home to several ethnic groups, notably Ukrainians, ethnic Russians, Belarussians, Moldavians, and Poles. While each group has its own cultural traditions, their similarities are greater than their differences.
- Throughout Ukraine, men shake hands with other men upon meeting and leaving.
- Allow women to take the initiative on handshaking.
- Although ethnic Ukrainians are generally less inhibited than Russians, both cultures are rather dour and sedate in public. Smiles are reserved for close friends.
- Only during greetings do Ukrainians and Russians display affection in public. Relatives and good friends will engage in a noisy embrace and kiss each other on the cheeks.
- Ukrainians and Russians often greet a stranger by shaking hands and stating their name, rather than uttering a polite phrase (such as "How do you do?"). Respond in the same way.

Titles/Forms of Address
- Ukrainian and Russian names are listed in the same order as in the West, but the middle name is a patronymic (a name derived from the first name of one's father). Thus, Fyodor Nikolaievich Medvedev's first name is Fyodor (a Slavic

version of Theodore), his last name is Medvedev, and his middle name means "son of Nikolai."

- Ukrainian and Russian women traditionally add the letter "a" on the end of their surnames; Medvedev's wife would be Mrs. Medvedeva.
- The variety of Russian names (both first and last) is quite limited. Ethnic Ukrainian names have somewhat more variety; surnames ending in "-enko" are characteristically Ukrainian. Even so, it can be difficult to track down a person in Ukraine by a name alone. Additional data, such as birth date and place of birth, is often necessary.
- Unless invited to do so, do not use first names. Call Ukrainians and Russians by their surname preceded by Mr., Miss, Mrs., or Ms. If they have a professional title (e.g., Doctor), use their title followed by their surname.
- It is considered quite respectable to address someone, even an elder, by their first name and patronymic, although many foreigners find this to be quite a mouthful. Do not be surprised to be asked what your father's first name was, and to have that name scrambled into an unrecognizable patronymic.
- Among themselves, Ukrainians and Russians use a bewildering variety of diminutives and nicknames. As you establish a relationship with them, you may be invited to call them by a nickname or just their first name. This is the time to invite them to call you by your first name.

 Gestures

- Ukrainians and Russians stand about one arm's length away from each other when conversing.
- Ukrainian, like Russian, is a language abundant in curses, and there are quite a number of obscene gestures as well. Both the American "O.K." sign (thumb and forefinger touching in a circle) and any shaken-fist gesture will probably be interpreted as vulgar.
- The "thumbs up" gesture indicates approval.
- Do not sit with the legs splayed apart or with one ankle resting upon the other knee.
- The "fig" gesture—a clenched fist with the thumb protruding between the knuckles of the index and middle fingers—means "nothing" or "you will get nothing" in Ukraine. It is definitely not considered obscene, as it is in the Mediterranean. Indeed, a Ukrainian parent may use this gesture to his or her own child to indicate that the child cannot have something.
- When going to your seat in a Ukrainian theater, it is very impolite to squeeze in front of seated patrons with your back to them. Always face seated people as you move past them.

 Gifts

- Any item currently in short supply makes a prized gift.
- There are many clothing items that can be appropriate for gifts, from good dress shirts and ties to children's shoes in wide sizes—the quality and selection of clothes is quite limited in Ukraine.
- Other good gift ideas include cigarette lighters, stationery products (from highlighters to Post-it notes), inexpensive watches, and thermos-type products (Ukrainians usually take all the food and drink they will need with them on trips).

- If you are invited to a Ukrainian home, try to bring flowers, liquor, or a food item that is scarce.
- The only hard liquors that are easily available in Ukraine are vodka, champagne, cognac, and a Ukrainian honey-based cordial. Ukrainians may be curious about other types of alcohol, although they may not know a fine bourbon or tequila from a poor one.
- Foreign cigarettes are so valuable as gifts and bribes that no one should come to Ukraine without them. Marlboro and Kent are the most prized brands.

CULTURAL NOTE

*W*hile birthdays are not traditionally celebrated, a Ukrainian's "name day" (the feast day of the saint he or she was named after in the Orthodox church) is often commemorated by a special dinner. A gift of a hard-to-find food item for such a celebration will be gratefully accepted.

Feasting is also a part of religious holidays. Remember that the Orthodox church follows the Julian calendar, not the Gregorian calendar in official use throughout the Western world. Currently, the Julian calendar is generally running thirteen days behind the Gregorian one. Thus, Orthodox Christmas will fall thirteen days after Christmas in most Western religions.

Dress

- While parts of Ukraine are quite cold in winter, the country is generally warmer than Russia. In fact, the Ukrainian Crimea, which can be comfortable even in winter, was the major vacation area for all of the U.S.S.R.
- If you go to Ukraine during the winter, bring warm clothes or buy Russian-style hats and gloves upon arrival. In addition, bring a pair of shoes or boots with skid-resistant soles.
- When buying Ukrainian clothes, keep in mind that it is generally advantageous to look like a foreigner, as foreigners get preferential treatment almost everywhere.
- Since Ukrainian buildings are usually well heated, a layered approach is best in clothing, allowing you to take off clothes to be comfortable while inside.
- Business dress is conservative. Ukrainian clothing styles tend to lag behind those in the West.
- Women should not bring their best high heels with them, since the streets are so old and muddy. Comfortable dress flats will be much more practical. Bring your own shoe polish.

WASHINGTON, D.C.

United States of America

Country Background

History

The United States was assembled out of colonies owned primarily by the British, French, Russian, and Spanish Empires. Virtually all of this land had previously been occupied by the indigenous people known as Indians, who suffered greatly from this influx of Europeans. (Many Indians nowadays prefer the term Native American; in the north, many Eskimos prefer Inuit.)

The United States of America was formed following its Declaration of Independence from England in 1776. The Constitution dates to 1787. There have always been free elections.

Type of Government

The government is a federal republic system; individual states have sovereignty over their own territory. The president is both chief of state and head of the government, and is elected for a term of four years. An electoral college of delegates from each state elects the president—an unwieldy system that gives disproportionate power to the most populous states. The legislative branch is elected by universal direct suffrage. It is made up of a bicameral Congress, consisting of the 435-seat House of Representatives and the 100-seat Senate.

Language

English is the official language. Spanish is the most widely used second language.

t━━━━━━━━━━━━━━━━━━━**CULTURAL NOTE**

he level of literacy in the United States is in dispute, with estimates of "functional literacy" running between 85 and 95 percent. Education is compulsory in most states from age five to age sixteen. It is free up through the secondary school level, although a large number of private schools exist. Schools provide services other than teaching academic subjects, including recreation, team sports, music and arts training, and social events.

Religion

Church and state have always been separate in the United States; however, over three-quarters of U.S. citizens belong to a religious group. Most are Christian. Judaism and Islam each account for about 2 percent of the population.

Demographics

The population of the United States is about 255 million. Since the breakup of the U.S.S.R., the United States ranks as the third most populous nation in the world. The largest city is New York, which has over 7 million people within its boundaries, and more in its surrounding area.

There are people of many different ethnic groups in the United States. The majority are Caucasians of European origin, including English, French, German, Irish, Scandinavian, Polish, Russian, and so forth. However, as the United States is a nation of immigrants, virtually every nation on Earth is represented. Blacks (many of whom prefer the term African-American) constitute 12 percent of the population. Other large minorities are Asians, Hispanics, and Native Americans.

Cultural Orientation

Cognitive Styles: How U.S. Citizens Organize and Process Information

In the United States the culture is very ethnocentric, and so it is closed to most outside information. It is very analytical, and concepts are abstracted quickly. Innovation often takes precedence over tradition. The universal rule is preferred, and company policy is followed regardless of who is doing the negotiating.

Negotiation Strategies: What U.S. Citizens Accept as Evidence

In negotiations, points are made by the accumulation of objective facts. These are sometimes biased by faith in the ideologies of democracy, capitalism, and consumerism, but seldom by the subjective feelings of the participants.

Value Systems: The Basis for Behavior

It is often said that Judeo-Christian values are the basis for behavior in the United States. However, these seem to be eroding and being replaced by ego- and ethnocentrism. The following three sections identify the Value Systems in the predominant culture—Their methods of dividing right from wrong, good from evil.

Locus of Decision Making

Although the United States is probably the most individualistic of all cultures, each person becomes a replaceable cog in the wheel of any organization. There is a high self, as opposed to other, orientation emphasizing individual initiative and achievement. People from the U.S. do not find it difficult to say "no." The individual has a life of his or her own that is generally private and not to be discussed in business negotiations. Friendships are few and specific to needs.

Sources of Anxiety Reduction

There is low anxiety about life, as external structures and science provide answers to all important questions and isolate one from life. Anxiety is developed over deadlines and results because recognition of one's work is the greatest reward. The work ethic is very strong, so that it appears that one lives to work. There are established rules for everything, and experts are relied upon at all levels.

Issues of Equality/Inequality

There is structured inequality in the roles people take, but personal equality is guaranteed by law. There is considerable ethnic and social bias against some minorities. Competition is the rule of life, but there is a strong feeling of the interdependency of roles. Excellence and decisiveness are prized characteristics. Material progress is more important than humanistic progress. Traditional sex roles are changing rapidly, but women are still fighting for equality in pay and power.

Business Practices

Appointments

PUNCTUALITY

- ♦ Punctuality is highly emphasized. In some cities, such as Houston, Los Angeles, or New York, extreme traffic can cause delays. Be sure to allow enough driving time to your destination. If you are delayed, call to let your contact know.
- ♦ If you are invited for a meal, you should arrive promptly.
- ♦ If you are invited to a cocktail party, you can arrive a few minutes late; you do not need to call ahead even if you will be a half hour late.

- People in the United States write the month first, then the day, then the year; e.g., December 3,1999, is written 12/3/99. This is very different from many Europeans and South Americans, who write the day first, then the month, then the year (e.g., December 3,1999, is written 3.12.99).
- Prior appointments are necessary.
- The workweek is Monday through Friday, 8:30 or 9 A.M. to 5 or 6 P.M. Many people work overtime.
- Many "convenience" stores (stores that carry frequently purchased products like gasoline, milk, and snacks, and so forth) are open twenty-four hours.

Negotiating

- Business is done at lightning speed in comparison to many cultures. U.S. sales-people may bring final contracts to their first meeting with prospective clients. In large firms, contracts under $10,000 can often be approved by one middle manager in one meeting.
- While knowing the right people and having many contacts in an industry is valu-able, it is not seen as being as important for a salesperson as a good history of sales. Sales staff are evaluated and compensated on their "track records" rather than the potential for exploiting their contacts.
- The "bottom line" (financial issues), new technology, and short-term rewards are the normal focus in negotiations.
- U.S. executives begin talking about business after a very brief exchange of small talk, whether in the office, at a restaurant, or even at home.
- Whether a colleague is a man or a woman should be ignored, except when it comes to personal questions. Women should not be asked if they are married. If a woman mentions that she is married, you should simply ask a few polite questions about her husband or children.
- Remember that the United States is the most litigious society in the world. There are lawyers who specialize in every industry and segment of society, from corporate tax attorneys to "ambulance chasers."
- The standard U.S. conversation starter is "What do you do?"—meaning "What kind of work do you do, and for whom?" This is not considered at all rude or boring.
- Compliments are exchanged very often. They are often used as conversation starters. If you wish to chat with someone, you can compliment something that person has (e.g., clothing) or has done (a work or sports-related achievement).
- Until you know a person well, avoid discussing religion, money, politics, or other controversial subjects (e.g., abortion, race, or sex discrimination).
- Some common topics of conversation are a person's job, travel, foods (and dieting), exercise, sports, music, movies, and books.
- Before smoking, ask if anyone minds, or wait to see if others smoke. Smoking is increasingly prohibited in public places: in airplanes, in office buildings, even in stadiums. Large restaurants usually have a section where smoking is permit-ted. Many hotels designate rooms as smoking and non-smoking.
- Most business people have business cards, but these cards are not exchanged unless you want to contact the person later.
- Your card will not be refused, but you may not be given one in exchange. Don't be offended by this.
- Your card will probably be put into a wallet, which a man may put in the back pocket of his pants. This is not meant to show disrespect.

Business Entertaining

- Business meetings are very often held over lunch. This usually begins at 12:00 noon and ends at 2:00 P.M. Lunch is usually relatively light, as work continues directly afterward. An alcoholic drink (usually wine or beer) may be ordered.
- Dinner is the main meal; it starts between 5:30 and 8 P.M., unless preceded by a cocktail party.
- Business breakfasts are common, and can start as early as 7:00 A.M.

- On weekends, many people enjoy "brunch," a combination of lunch and breakfast beginning anywhere from 11 A.M. to 2 P.M. Business meetings can be held over brunch.
- When eating out, the cost can be shared with friends. This is called "splitting the bill," "getting separate checks," or "going Dutch."
- If you are invited out for business, your host will usually pay.
- If you are invited out socially, but your host does not offer to pay, you should be prepared to pay for your own meal.
- If you invite a U.S. counterpart out socially, you must make it clear whether you wish to pay.
- Before going to visit a friend, you must call ahead.
- Most parties are informal, unless the hosts tell you otherwise.
- If you are offered food or drink, you are not obliged to accept. Also, your host will probably not urge you to eat, so help yourself whenever you want.
- U.S. co-workers or friends will probably enjoy learning a toast from your country.
- The fork is held in the right hand and is used to cut food. The knife is used only to cut or spread something. To use it, the fork is switched to the left hand or is laid down; to continue eating, the fork is switched back to the right hand.
- Many foods are eaten with the hands; take your lead from others, or if you are uncomfortable, do as you like.
- It is not considered rude to eat while walking; many people also eat in their cars (even while driving). There are many fast-food and drive-in restaurants.
- At a fast-food restaurant, you are expected to clear your own table.

Time
- The contiguous forty-eight states of the United States have four time zones. New York is five hours behind Greenwich Mean Time (G.M.T. - 5). The state of Hawaii is 10 hours behind G.M.T.; most of the state of Alaska is 9 hours behind G.M.T. In most states, daylight saving time is in effect from mid-spring to mid-autumn.

Protocol

 ### Greetings
- The standard greeting is a smile, often accompanied by a nod, wave, and/or verbal greeting.
- In business situations, a handshake is used. It is very firm. Weak handshakes are taken as a sign of weakness. Men usually wait for women to offer their hand before shaking.
- Good friends and family members usually embrace, finishing the embrace with a pat or two on the back.
- In casual situations a smile and a verbal greeting is adequate.
- If you see an acquaintance at a distance, a wave is appropriate.
- The greeting "How are you?" is not an inquiry about your health. The best response is a short one, such as "Fine, thanks."

Titles/Forms of Address

- The order of most names is first name, middle name, last name.
- To show respect, use a title such as Dr., Ms., Miss, Mrs., or Mr. with the last name. If you are not sure of a woman's marital status, use Ms. (pronounced "Miz").
- When you meet someone for the first time, use a title and their last name until you are told to do otherwise (this may happen immediately). Sometimes you will not be told the last name; in this case just use the first name or the nickname. Nicknames may be formal names which have been shortened in surprising ways (e.g., Alex for Alexandra, or Nica for Monica).
- Be sure your U.S. acquaintances know what you wish to be called.
- The letters "Jr." stand for Junior and are sometimes found after a man's surname, e.g., Jeff Morrison, Jr., or first name (e.g., Jeff Jr.). Both indicate that he was named after his father.
- The Roman numeral III, or IV indicates a third- or fourth-generation scion, with the same name as his predecessors (e.g., Patrick Evans III).

Gestures

- The standard space between you and your conversation partner should be about two feet. Most U.S. executives will be uncomfortable standing closer than that.
- In general, friends of the same sex do not hold hands. If men hold hands, it will probably be interpreted as a sign of sexual preference.
- To point, you can use the index finger, although it is not polite to point at a person.
- To beckon someone, wave either all the fingers or just the index finger in a scooping motion with the palm facing up.
- To show approval, there are two typical gestures. One is the "O.K." sign, done by making a circle of the thumb and index finger. The other is the "thumbs up" sign, done by making a fist and pointing the thumb upward.
- The "V-for-victory" sign is done by extending the forefinger and index finger upwards and apart. The palm may face in or out.
- The backslap is a sign of friendship.
- To wave good-bye, move your entire hand, palm facing outward.
- Crossing the middle and index fingers on the same hand has two meanings: either to bring good luck, or (when hidden) to indicate that the statement the person is making is untrue. Both gestures are used more often by children than by adults.
- There are many ways to call a waiter/waitress over: make eye contact and raise your eyebrows, briefly wave to get his or her attention, or mouth the word for what you want, such as "water" or "coffee." To call for the check, make a writing gesture or mouth the word "check."
- Direct eye contact shows that you are sincere, although it should not be too intense. Some minorities look away to show respect.
- When sitting, U.S. citizens often look very relaxed. They may sit with the ankle of one leg on their knee or prop their feet up on chairs or desks.
- In business situations, maintain good posture and a less casual pose.
- When giving an item to another person, one may toss it or hand it over with only one hand.

Gifts

- Business gifts are discouraged by the law, which allows only a $25 tax deduction on gifts.
- When you visit a home, it is not necessary to take a gift; however, it is always appreciated. You may take flowers, a plant, or a bottle of wine.
- If you wish to give flowers, have them sent ahead so as not to burden your hostess with taking care of them when you arrive.
- If you stay in a U.S. home for a few days, a gift is appropriate. You may also write a letter of thanks.

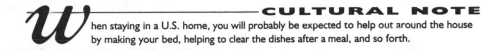

CULTURAL NOTE

hen staying in a U.S. home, you will probably be expected to help out around the house by making your bed, helping to clear the dishes after a meal, and so forth.

- At Christmastime gifts are exchanged. For your business associates, you can give gifts that are good for the office, or liquor or wine. Most stores gift-wrap at Christmas.
- A good time to give a gift is when you arrive or when you leave. The best gifts are those that come from your country.
- Personal gifts such as perfume or clothing are inappropriate for women.
- Gifts for children are a good idea, but take into account the belief system of the parents. Pacifists (such as most Quakers) would probably object to your giving a toy gun to their child. As U.S. citizens tend to be wretched at geography, any gift that describes the location of your country is a good choice: a colorful map, an inexpensive globe, or even a balloon with a map on it.
- Business gifts are given after you close a deal. Unless the giver specifies a time at which the gift is to be opened (as may happen with a gift at Christmastime), gifts are usually unwrapped immediately and shown to all assembled.
- You may not receive a gift in return right away; your U.S. friend might wait a while to reciprocate.
- Taking someone out for a meal or other entertainment is a common gift.

CULTURAL NOTE

oreigners who watch U.S. films and television may assume that U.S. business people don't wrap gifts—they enclose them in colorful, easy-to-open boxes. But this is cinematic fiction. Gifts in the U.S. are wrapped just as they are in other countries.

 Dress

- In cities, conservative business attire is best.
- In rural areas and small towns, clothing is less formal and less fashionable.
- When not working, dress casually. You may see people dressed in torn clothing or in short pants and shirts without sleeves.
- If you wish to wear traditional clothing from your country, feel free to do so.

MONTEVIDEO

Uruguay

*t*he flag of Uruguay is quite distinctive. Its general design was inspired by the stars and stripes of the United States' flag. The background is white, the stripes are blue, and there is a sun design in the upper left-hand corner. Although Uruguay is a popular tourist destination, the sun-faced symbol is not intended as a promise of sunny vacations. The symbol is the "sun of May" and represents the sunlight that broke through the clouds and to shine upon the first colonists who demonstrated against their Spanish overlords in May, 1810.

Country Background

History

The first Europeans to settle in Uruguay were the Portuguese, who founded the town of Colonia in 1680. The Spanish established a fort at Montevideo in 1726, and the two groups fought for control of the area. Portugal ceded its claim to Uruguay in 1777. When Napoleon conquered Spain in 1808, Buenos Aires (in Argentina) declared itself in command of the Viceroyalty of Río de la Plata, which included Uruguay. However, the Uruguayans had no desire to submit to Argentine domination.

José Gervasio Artigas, a captain of Spanish forces in the interior of Uruguay, gathered an army and fought Buenos Aires for control of the area. His efforts, lasting from 1810 to 1814, came to be known as Uruguay's war of independence. Neither Spain nor Argentina was ever to regain control of Uruguay, and Artigas is now revered as the father of his country.

However, Uruguay still had to defend its independence. The country was occupied by Brazilian troops in 1820; Artigas and many others were forced to flee. But in 1825, some 33 exiles—immortalized as the "33 Orientals" or "33 patriots"—returned and led Uruguay in a successful revolt. Uruguay had established itself as an independent country.

Despite this, neither Brazil nor Argentina gave up claims to Uruguay. Renewed warfare threatened to disrupt international trade, so in 1828 British gunboats enforced recognition of Uruguay as an independent buffer state between Brazil and Argentina.

The first Uruguayan constitution was signed on July 18, 1830; the main downtown avenue in Montevideo is named for this date.

Uruguay developed into one of the most stable and wealthiest nations on the continent. Its political stability earned it the nickname of "the Switzerland of South America."

However, in the 1950s, Uruguay began to slip into an economic crisis. High tariffs, low productivity, inflation, debt, corruption, and other problems made life difficult for many Uruguayans. Social unrest increased. A Communist guerrilla group, the Tupamaros, became active in the late 1960s. For a time, their activities (jailbreaks of captured members, kidnappings of corrupt officials, and so forth), scarcely impeded by police attempts to stop them, provided an entertaining sideshow for a generally sympathetic populace.

But when the Tupamaros started killing government officials and police, the situation became much more serious. The military (some of them U.S.-trained) took over antiterrorist activities from the civil police. Political activities were banned in 1970. The military took over more and more government functions until, by 1973, they were essentially running the country. In 1976 the military ousted the last elected president and openly ruled Uruguay.

The years of military rule were bloody and brutal. Since the Tupamaros had enjoyed widespread popularity before they turned violent, the junta seemed to regard the entire populace of Uruguay as enemies. Of a total population of under three million Uruguayans, some 5,000 were imprisoned, and between 300,000 and 400,000 fled the country.

Initially, the junta's foreign economic advisers brought a measure of prosperity to Uruguay, and some speculators made millions. But soon the economic experiment turned sour, and the economy was in worse shape than before. The military decided to turn the government back to the civilians. General elections were finally held in 1984, and the military stepped down the following year.

Type of Government

The Oriental Republic of Uruguay has returned to democracy. It has two legislative houses: a 31-seat Senate and a 99-seat Chamber of Representatives. The president is both the chief of state and the head of the government.

The military continues to hover in the background, exerting influence but taking little direct action. However, human rights have been restored, and Uruguay is once again a democracy.

Language

Spanish is the official language.

Religion

Uruguay is one of the most secularized states in Latin America. Church and state are strictly separated, and only 70 percent of the population is classified as belonging to a religious sect. Most of these are Roman Catholic; Protestants and Jews each number 2 percent of the population.

Demographics

Today, the original Indian inhabitants of Uruguay are all but gone. About 88 percent of the population of Uruguay is of European descent (primarily Spanish or Italian, with some German and English as well).

t ——————————————————————**CULTURAL NOTE**

he European ancestry of Uruguay's population is unusual. In most other South American countries, the majority of the population is mestizo (of mixed Indian and European ancestry). Only 8 percent of Uruguayans are mestizos, while 4 percent are descended from black slaves imported by the Spanish.

Cultural Orientation

Cognitive Styles: How Uruguayans Organize and Process Information

The culture of Uruguay has a spirit of moderation and compromise, and tolerance of other people and other social groups. It is open to outside information in discussion of most issues. Uruguayans are trained to think subjectively and associatively. Their educational system does not encourage abstraction, and they will maintain personal loyalty rather than obey a rule or law.

Negotiation Strategies: What Uruguayans Accept as Evidence

Uruguayans find the truth in the immediate subjective feelings one has on an issue. This is sometimes biased by a faith in humanitarian ideologies. Uruguayans seldom resort to objective facts to prove a point.

Value Systems: The Basis for Behavior

The Uruguayans extol humanistic, spiritual, and aesthetic values, but take a pragmatic, utilitarian, and materialistic approach to life. The following three sections identify the Value Systems in the predominant culture—their methods of dividing right from wrong, good from evil, and so forth.

Locus of Decision Making

The individual is responsible for his or her decisions and is the only concern in decision making. Uruguayans respect individualism, regard the family as important, and tend to adopt fatalistic attitudes. One's self-identity is based on one's role in the social system and the history of one's extended family. Since expertise is less important than one's ability to fit into the group, kinships and friendships play a major role in business transactions.

Sources of Anxiety Reduction

The nuclear family is smaller and the kinship relationships fewer than in any other Latin American country, yet the family establishes the individual's position in society. Many Uruguayans disdain manual labor, and time does not rule their lives. There is a high need for personal relationships, as friendship networks are important to security, jobs, and socializing. Catholicism is an integral part of the national culture, giving structure and security.

Issues of Equality/Inequality

People are equal because each person is deemed unique. There is an inherent trust in people and a strong belief in social justice. The small upper class, which is extensively intermarried, controls most of the wealth and commerce. However, the large middle class is very influential. Men hold the dominant positions in society, but women are often involved in national life. They are considered equal in most respects. Women enjoy substantial freedom, are independent and emancipated.

Business Practices

Appointments

PUNCTUALITY

* Punctuality is not a high priority in Uruguay.
* Business meetings rarely start on time, so you will not be penalized for being a few minutes late. It would also be unrealistic to expect your Uruguayan counterparts to be prompt.

- Remember that many Europeans and South Americans write the day first, then the month, then the year (e.g., December 3, 1999, is written 3.12.99). This is the case in Uruguay.
- Business hours are from 8:30 A.M. to noon and 2:30 to 6:30 P.M., Monday through Friday.
- Government offices have different hours in the summer and the winter: 12 noon to 6:30 P.M., Monday through Friday from mid-March through mid-November and 8:00 A.M. to 1:30 P.M., Monday through Friday from mid-November through mid-March.
- Shop hours, in general, are 9:00 A.M. to noon and 2:30 to 7:00 P.M., Monday through Friday.
- The best time of year to conduct business in Uruguay is from May through November. Little business is accomplished for two weeks before and after Christmas and Easter, as well as during Carnival. January through April is summer in Uruguay, and one or another of the decision makers is liable to be off on vacation during this period.

Negotiating

- The pace of business negotiations in Latin America is usually much slower than in the United States. However, most executives are accustomed to U.S. business techniques. Many Uruguayans will adopt a quicker, more direct negotiating style when dealing with executives from the United States.
- Most Uruguayan executives will be experienced and sophisticated; they may well have studied overseas.
- Despite their cavalier attitude toward punctuality, most successful Uruguayan business executives put in a very long workday.
- Uruguay is a nation of immigrants. While many of the business executives you encounter will be of Spanish descent, others will be German, Italian, or Jewish.
- Although many executives speak English, check beforehand as to whether or not you will need an interpreter.
- All printed material you hand out should be translated into Spanish. This goes for everything from business cards to brochures.
- Uruguayans are great sports fans. Talking about sports is always a good way to open a conversation. Soccer (called *fútbol*) is the most popular sport. (U.S.-style football is *fútbol americano*.) Uruguay is a popular South American tourist spot, so ask about sights to see.

*a*void asking questions about family unless prompted by your Uruguayan counterpart. ━━━━━**CULTURAL NOTE**

Remember that the country has been through over fourteen years of brutal military dictatorship, during which more than 10 percent of the population fled into exile and one out of every fifty of the remainder was detained for interrogation (or worse). You don't want to ask a Uruguayan businessman about his family, only to be told that they were victims of the dictatorship.

Again, because of exile, imprisonment, or "political unreliability," a highly competent Uruguayan executive may be working at a lower level than one would expect (e.g., a forty-year-old junior executive). Don't be surprised, and don't ask.

 Business Entertaining

- Uruguayans are comfortable conducting business over lunch. Dinner, however, is a social occasion; don't try to talk business at dinner unless your counterpart brings it up.
- While you are in Uruguay, your counterpart will probably offer to take you out to—and pay for—lunch and dinner.
- Should you wish to reciprocate, the best choice will be an upscale French, Chinese, or Uruguayan restaurant.
- A good choice of location for a business dinner is the restaurant at an international hotel.
- Uruguay is a major cattle producer, and its restaurants serve some of the best beef in the world.
- If a Uruguayan invites you to his home for coffee after dinner—a common practice—don't stay late when the next day is a business day. Be alert for cues that your host is tired and wishes to end the evening.
- Be aware that Uruguay abounds in casinos; your counterpart may invite you out to see them.

Time

- Uruguay is three hours behind Greenwich Mean Time (G.M.T. - 3), making it two hours ahead of U.S. Eastern Standard Time (E.S.T. + 2).

Protocol

 Greetings

- Except when greeting close friends, it is traditional to shake hands firmly with both men and women.
- Close male friends shake hands upon meeting, but men kiss close female friends. Close female friends usually kiss each other.

 Titles/Forms of Address

- Most people you meet should be addressed with a title and their surname. Only children, family members, and close friends address each other by their first names.

- Persons who do not have professional titles should be addressed as Mr., Mrs., or Miss, plus their surname. In Spanish, these are
  - Mr. = *Señor*
  - Mrs. = *Señora*
  - Miss = *Señorita*
- Most Hispanics have two surnames: one from their father, which is listed first, followed by one from their mother. Only the father's surname is commonly used when addressing someone; e.g., Señor Juan Antonio Martínez García is addressed as Señor Martínez and Señorita Ana María Gutiérrez Herrera is addressed as Señorita Gutiérrez. When a woman marries, she usually adds her husband's surname and goes by that surname. If the two people in the above example married, she would be known as Señora Ana María Gutiérrez Herrera de Martínez. Most people would refer to her as Señora de Martínez or, less formally, Señora Martínez.
- When a person has a title, it is important to address him or her with that title followed by the surname. Everyone who graduates from a university—at any level—is entitled to be addressed as *Doctor*. Teachers prefer the title *Profesor*, and engineers go by *Ingeniero*.

Gestures

- While most Latin Americans converse at a much closer distance than U.S. citizens are used to, Uruguayans are generally aware that close proximity makes Yankees nervous. Consequently, most Uruguayan business people give U.S. citizens more "breathing room" than fellow Uruguayans.
- The U.S. "thumbs up" gesture means "O.K." in Uruguay.
- Curling the fingers around so that they touch the thumb indicates doubt. This gesture is usually done with the right hand.
- Sit only on chairs, not on a ledge, box, or table.
- Don't rest your feet on anything other than a footstool or rail; it is very impolite to place them on a table.
- Avoid yawning in public. Yawning is a signal that it is time to adjourn.

Gifts

- Gift giving is not a major aspect of doing business.
- When you are given advance notice of an invitation to a Uruguayan home, bring (or have sent before you arrive) flowers or chocolates to your hostess. Roses are the most appreciated type of flower.
- Don't worry about a gift if an invitation is proffered on short (or no) notice. After business dinners in Uruguay, it is common practice to adjourn to someone's home for coffee. Guests are not expected to stay long if the following day is a work day.

Dress

- Business dress in Uruguay is conservative: dark suits and ties for men; white blouses and dark suits or skirts for women. Women sometimes do not wear nylons during the summer. Men should follow their Uruguayan colleagues' lead with regard to wearing ties and removing jackets in the summer.

- Uruguayans do not favor the bright colors popular elsewhere in Latin America. Choose demure colors for your wardrobe.
- Men may wear the same dark suit for formal occasions (such as the theater, a formal dinner party, and so forth), but women are expected to wear an evening gown.
- Both men and women wear pants in casual situations. If you are meeting business associates, avoid jeans and wear a jacket or blazer. Women should not wear shorts.

*t*ourism is a major industry in Uruguay, and tourists dress as they please. Feel free to do so when away from your Uruguayan business colleagues.

- Don't wear anything outside that can be damaged by water during Carnival because drenching pedestrians is a favorite Carnival trick of the young.
- Summertime can be humid as well as warm, and winters are rainy and chilly. Bring appropriate clothing—and don't forget that the seasons in South America are the reverse of those in North America.

CULTURAL NOTE

*i*f you graduated from the University of Chicago, leave your class ring at home. During Uruguay's military rule, the generals took their economic policy from the "Chicago boys"—free-market economic advisers largely trained by Milton Friedman at the University of Chicago. The Chicago boys are not popular; some Uruguayans feel that they treated Uruguay as an economics experiment, enforced by the guns of the military. Opponents of the regime had a saying that "In Uruguay, people were in prison so that prices could be free."

CARACAS

Venezuela

*V*enezuela considers Simón Bolívar a national treasure, since he was not only the catalyst for Venezuela's independence from Spain but a liberator for much of South America. There is a *Plaza Bolívar* in the center of most Venezuelan cities, and it is important to behave respectfully in that plaza. Venezuela also named its currency the *bolivar*.

Country Background

History

Venezuela was originally inhabited by several Indian tribes, including the Caracas, Arawaks, and Cumanagatos. After Columbus "discovered" the area in 1498, the Spanish began conquering the coastal regions and offshore islands. Alonso de Ojeda named the land Venezuela, or "little Venice," because many Indian homes around Lake Maracaibo and the coast were built on stilts—which reminded him of Venice. Spain controlled Venezuela until 1821, when the forces of Simón Bolívar (a Venezuelan) were victorious at the Battle of Carabobo, and a republic was declared.

The Republic of Greater Colombia originally contained Venezuela, Ecuador, and Colombia. In 1830 Venezuela seceded and became independent.

Type of Government

Since 1958, Venezuela has had progressive, freely-held democratic elections. It is a federal multiparty republic, with a president who is both the head of government and the chief of state. The cabinet, or Council of Ministers, has twenty-six members. There is a bicameral congress, composed of the Chamber of Deputies and the Senate, and the judiciary is represented by the Supreme Court. Elections are held every five years.

Language

Spanish is the official language. English and a variety of Amerindian dialects are also spoken.

Religion

Venezuela has no official religion, but the vast majority of people are Roman Catholic (96 percent).

Demographics

The population of Venezuela is 20.2 million. The capital, Caracas, has approximately 3.2 million people within its city limits. The ethnic makeup consists of mestizo (about 70 percent), Spanish, Italian, Portuguese, Arab, German, and African. Only 2 percent of the population is full-blooded Amerindian.

Cultural Orientation

Cognitive Styles: How Venezuelans Organize and Process Information

In Venezuela, outside information is accepted on most issues for purposes of discussion. However, Venezuelans do not change their attitudes easily. Their educational system trains them to process information subjectively and associatively. Their personal involvement in a situation is more important than the rules or laws that might be used to solve the problem.

Negotiation Strategies: What Venezuelans Accept as Evidence

The truth is usually found in the immediate subjective feelings of the participants. This may be influenced by their faith in the ideologies of humanitarianism, but not by the accumulation of objective facts.

Value Systems: The Basis for Behavior

Venezuela lost some of its humanitarian values when the oil market dropped and it had to increase taxes to maintain its economy. The following three sections identify the Value Systems in the predominant culture—their methods of dividing right from wrong, good from evil, and so forth.

Locus of Decision Making

Individuals are responsible for their own decisions and any impact they may have upon their families or groups. The family, extended family, and friends are very important, and one must do nothing to shame them. Expertise is less important than one's ability to get along with the group, so one usually has to make friends with the participants before meaningful negotiations can take place. The upper class dominates the economic structures of commerce and industry, but the middle class dominates politics.

Sources of Anxiety Reduction

Religion is not a strong force in their daily life, but Venezuelans are emotionally attached to the church, and this gives them a sense of stability. The presence of the extended family helps the individual to have a sense of security. Venezuelans also seem to gain security by following charismatic leaders. Although they are always working on one or more projects, finishing them does not seem to be a goal. Time does not create anxiety.

Issues of Equality/Inequality

There are extreme contrasts between rich and poor, and Venezuelans feel that power holders are entitled to the privileges that come with the office. There is a small white elite, a large mestizo population, and a small black population. One notices some class and ethnic bias. Machismo is very strong. Women have some restrictions on their social and work behavior.

Business Practices

Appointments

PUNCTUALITY

♦ It is better to be a few minutes early than a few minutes late for appointments in Venezuela, so allow yourself plenty of time to compensate for traffic—which can be a serious problem in Caracas.

- Remember that many Europeans and South Americans write the day first, then the month, then the year (e.g., December 3, 1999, is written 3.12.99). This is the case in Venezuela.
- The workweek is Monday through Friday 8:00 A.M. to 5:00 P.M., with at least an hour break for lunch (many executives take a two-hour lunch).
- Stores are open from 9:00 A.M. to noon and again from 2:00 or 3:00 P.M. to 6:00 P.M. or later. Shopping malls stay open later.
- Avoid scheduling appointments two or three days before a holiday.

Negotiating

- Initiate business contacts through local intermediaries. They can make introductions for you at the correct levels and in the appropriate social circles. The U.S. Embassy in Caracas can help you contact Venezuelan representatives (called *enchufados* in Spanish).
- Letters, brochures, and other documents should be translated into Spanish.
- Letters should be followed up with a phone call made during the morning business hours in Venezuela.
- If you receive a reply from a Venezuelan in English, you may begin using English in correspondence.
- In a business meeting, begin by getting to know everyone. Don't rush into a discussion of the deal. At the same time, do not try to be instant friends with your prospects.

CULTURAL NOTE

*i*n Venezuela, there are usually two types of business people, with distinct differences in their styles of conducting business. Among the older generation, people will want to get to know you personally first and will respond to you as an individual, rather than to your company and your proposal. Among the younger generation, your contact may have been educated in the United States, and may relate more to your firm, the proposal you are presenting, and so forth, than to you personally.

- It is best to send an individual rather than a team for the first contact with a Venezuelan prospect. Later, you should send other members of your team.
- Negotiations proceed more slowly in Venezuela than in the United States.
- Avoid dominating the conversation or putting pressure on your Venezuelan colleagues. Venezuelans like to be in control.
- Do not mention bringing in an attorney until negotiations are complete.

- After the first business contact in Venezuela, it is appropriate for the senior executive of the U.S. firm to write to the senior executive of the Venezuelan firm expressing thanks.
- The focus of the business deal should be long-term, not solely geared to immediate returns.
- Topics to avoid discussing are the government, personal relationships, and the influence of the United States on South America.
- It is rude to ask direct questions about a person's family.
- It will be appreciated if you learn about Venezuela's political and cultural history.
- Present your business card immediately following an introduction. Treat business cards with respect.
- Have your business card printed in Spanish on one side and English on the other. Be sure your position is clearly indicated.

 Business Entertaining

- It is good practice to follow up morning appointments with an invitation to lunch, where you can continue your business discussions.
- Arrange with the waiters to have all restaurant and entertainment bills given to you if you have initiated the invitation. This is particularly important for women, since they may encounter some resistance from their male Venezuelan counterparts in paying the check.
- Unlike lunch, dinner is for socializing, not for business.
- Dinner begins at 8:30 P.M. or later, and lasts until midnight.
- Spouses are usually invited to dinner.
- Businesswomen should be aware that going out alone with Venezuelan businessmen may be misconstrued.
- The two senior executives should sit facing each other.
- The senior visiting business person may give a toast offering good wishes for the negotiations, adding a memorized Spanish phrase about the pleasure of being with Venezuelans.
- If you are invited for a meal at a Venezuelan home, be aware that this a sign of close friendship and is not to be taken lightly.

Time
- Venezuela is four hours behind Greenwich Mean Time (G.M.T. - 4), or one hour ahead of U.S. Eastern Standard Time (E.S.T. + 1)

Protocol

 Greetings

- A firm handshake is the standard greeting.
- While shaking hands, announce your full name; the Venezuelan will do the same.

Titles/Forms of Address

- Persons who do not have professional titles should be addressed as Mr., Mrs., or Miss, plus their surnames. In Spanish these are
  - Mr. = *Señor*
  - Mrs. = *Señora*
  - Miss = *Señorita*
- Most Hispanics have two surnames: one from their father, which is listed first, followed by one from their mother. Only the father's surname is commonly used when addressing someone; e.g., Señor Juan Antonio Martínez García is addressed as Señor Martínez and Señorita Ana María Gutiérrez Herrera is addressed as Señorita Gutiérrez. When a woman marries, she usually adds her husband's surname and goes by that surname. If the two people in the above example married, she would be known as : Señora Ana María Gutiérrez Herrera de Martínez. Most people would refer to her as Señora de Martínez or, less formally, Señora Martínez.

Gestures

- Venezuelans greet friends with a brief embrace called an *abrazo*, a squeeze of the arm, and sometimes a kiss on the cheek.
- Venezuelans converse in very close proximity to one another. Try not to flinch or move away, as this will be interpreted as rejection.
- During a conversation, Venezuelans often touch each other's arms or jacket.

Gifts

- It is best to postpone giving business gifts until you have established a friendly relationship.
- The best time to present a business gift is during a long lunch. Do not present a gift during business hours.
- For business, bring high-quality gifts that are somewhat useful—for example, a lighter with your company name, small electronics, carefully selected books, or an imported liquor like a twelve-year old scotch.
- Perfume and flowers (particularly orchids, the national flower) are good gifts for women, and are not considered too personal.
- You may give gifts to the children of your colleagues; this will be greatly appreciated.
- In preparation for subsequent visits, ask colleagues if there is something from the United States that they would like you to bring back.
- Women should not give gifts to businessmen.
- When going to a Venezuelan home, never arrive empty-handed.

Dress

- Venezuelan women are very fashionable. Women should pack their best business clothes and one cocktail dress.
- Details such as high-quality watches or jewelry are impressive to the Venezuelans.
- Men should dress conservatively, in dark business suits of tropical-weight wool.

Contacts and Holidays

Contacts

Some useful numbers for any U.S. traveler going abroad have been listed. Because of the extremely dynamic nature of global assignments in government, industry, and education, the following information providers should be consulted for the most up-to-date information on international business contacts, travel advisories, official holidays, medical information, passports, etc.

Getting Through Customs

Box 136
Newtown Square, PA 19073
Tel: (610) 353-9894
Fax: (610) 353-6994

Produces the PASSPORT SYSTEM, an online database with information on foreign and U.S. embassies, chambers of commerce, Department of State and Department of Commerce officers, foreign political leaders, official holidays, business practices, and protocol. PASSPORT is available through various networks.

Department of State Citizens' Emergency Center

Bureau of Consular Affairs
Room 4811 N.S.
U.S. Department of State
Washington, DC 20520
Tel: (202) 647-5225

Provides travel warnings and consular information sheets.

Bureau of Consular Affairs Fax Services

Tel: (202) 647-3000

Provides the same data via fax.

Bureau of Consular Affairs Electronic Bulletin Board

Tel: (202) 647-9225

Besides travel warnings and consular information sheets, the CABB has data on emergencies involving U.S. citizens abroad, travel information, etc.

Visa information

Tel: (202) 663-1225

Holidays

Make it a practice to contact the U.S. Embassy in each foreign country you visit. U.S. embassies can assist U.S. companies by arranging appointments with local business and government officials; providing counsel on local trade regulations, laws, and customs; and identifying importers, buyers, agents, distributors, and joint venture partners for U.S. firms. They also provide economic, political, technological, and labor data. An inexpensive directory of U.S. Embassies abroad is the Key Officers of Foreign Service Posts—available through the Superintendent of Documents. Call (202) 783-3238.

Every country in the world celebrates holidays, and little or no work is conducted during these celebrations. However, holidays are always subject to change. Governments frequently add, delete, or move certain official holidays. Furthermore, the dates for many holidays do not fall on the same day in the Western (Gregorian) calendar each year. This may be because they are dated using a calendar that does not correspond to the Western calendar [for example, the Arabic (Hijrah) calendar is only 354 days long]. Or, it may happen because the date of the holiday is computed from a variable occurrence, such as sightings of the phases of the moon. Whatever the reason, the only way to be sure your business trip is not interrupted by a local holiday is to contact a reliable, up-to-date source: the country's embassy, your travel agent, the U.S. State Department, etc.

When holidays fall on Saturday or Sunday, commercial establishments may be closed the preceding Friday or the following Monday. Also, remember that in the Muslim world, the Sabbath is celebrated on Friday. Many Islamic nations have their "weekend" on Thursday and Friday, with Saturday as the start of the workweek.

These Muslim holidays will fall on different dates each year:

Ramazan (also called Ramadan): the Holy Month

Observers fast from dawn until dusk. Dusk is announced by a cannon shot. The faithful are awakened before sunrise by drummers who roam the streets, reminding them to eat before dawn. It is impolite for nonbelievers to eat, drink or even smoke in the presence of those who are fasting; be discreet. Office hours may be curtailed. Not surprisingly, fasting people may be short-tempered, especially when Ramazan falls during the days of summer. This is called *Ramazan kafasi* and means Ramazan irritability (literally, "Ramazan head").

Sheker Bayram: The three-day festival at the end of the Ramazan fast

Children go door to door asking for sweets; Muslims exchange greeting cards, feast and visit one another. Banks and offices are closed for all three days.

Kurban Bayram: The Feast of Sacrifice

Celebrating the traditional story of Abraham's near-sacrifice of his son Isaac, this is the most important religious and secular holiday of the year. The holiday lasts for four days, but many banks and businesses close for an entire week. Resorts and transportation will be booked solid.

Medical
Information

Preparations

If possible, schedule physical and dental examinations well before leaving, as some vaccinations must be given over a period of time. You should have current medical documentation with you when you go. List any chronic conditions and current prescription drugs (including dosages). In order to avoid problems at customs, carry all medications in their original containers. Also, take an extra set of glasses, contacts, or prescriptions. Include in your bags the name, address, and phone number of someone to be contacted in case of an emergency.

Prepare a basic medical travel kit, which may include aspirin, a topical antibiotic, bandages, a disinfectant, 0.5 percent hydrocortisone cream (for bites, sunburn), a sunblock, a digital thermometer, and diarrhea medication. Pack the kit in your carry-on luggage. An excellent source of supplies can be found in *Magellan's Catalog of Travel Supplies*. Call 1-800-962-4943.

Also confirm that you have sufficient travel medical insurance. There are two main types of travel insurance: 1) policies that make direct payments for medical care and provide assistance, and 2) policies that reimburse you for emergency expenses (not as helpful an option since you must file a claim after you return home, and many hospitals and doctors will require substantial payments immediately, in local currency!)

Some travel medical insurance companies that provide direct payments, plus assistance include:

TravMed	1-800-732-5309 or 301-296-5225
HealthCare Abroad	1-800-237-6615 or 703-281-9500
Travel Assistance International	1-800-821-2828 or 202-331-1609
Access America	1-800-284-8300 or 212-490-5345
WorldCare Travel Assistance	1-800-253-1877 or 213-749-1358
CareFree Travel Insurance	1-800-645-2424 or 516-294-0220
International SOS	1-800-523-8930 or 215-244-1500

Certain companies specialize in Air Ambulance Services. They provide aircraft, flight doctors and nurses, trip coordinators, and global communications capabilities. Many also arrange stretcher transportation on commercial airlines. Some include:

National Jets	1-800-327-3710
International SOS	1-800-523-8930
North American Air Ambulance	1-800-322-8167
AirAmbulance Network	1-800-387-1966
AirAmbulance International	1-800-227-9996
LifeFlight	1-800-231-4357

Consider lining up emergency medical assistance with English-speaking doctors through your family physician or through the International Association for Medical Assistance to Travelers (IAMAT), 417 Center Street, Lewiston, NY 14092; telephone

(716) 754-4883; fax (519) 836-3412. This is a non-profit organization that offers members a listing of English-speaking physicians in 140 countries.

Finally, the International Traveler's Hotline at the Centers for Disease Control at (404) 332-4559 can give you current information on a variety of medical issues, such as immunizations, epidemics in specific countries, etc.

International Electrical Adaptors

Information and drawings courtesy of *Magellan's Catalog of Travel Supplies*, 1-800-962-4943; teleDaptor drawings courtesy also of TeleAdapt, Ltd., England, 44 (0) 814214444.

The electricity used in much of the world (220-250 volts) is a different voltage from that used in North America (110-125 volts). Electrical appliances designed for North America may need converters to "step down" this higher voltage to the level required to operate. Some appliances can not be converted for use elsewhere because they require 60 cycles-per-second (again, found primarily in North America), or have other requirements. These include TVs, VCRs, clocks, microwave ovens, older typewriters and vacuum cleaners.

Electrical wall sockets found around the world are also likely to differ in shape from the sockets used in North America. Electrical adaptor plugs are available to slip over the plugs of North American appliances for use in such sockets (see charts below). If the appliance being taken overseas has a polarized plug (one blade wider than the other), be certain that the adaptor will accept such a plug. If it has a third grounding prong, it would be wise to obtain slip-on adaptor plugs that also provide grounding in the foreign sockets.

Slip-on Adaptor Plugs

- "A" Pattern.   Flat, parallel blades. Used in Western Hemisphere, several North and Central Pacific countries. Good for adapting European plugs to North American sockets, and for adapting polarized plugs to non-polarized sockets (e.g., Japan).

- "B" Pattern.   Round pins, shorter and closer than D (below). Used in Great Britain, parts of Africa, Far East and Middle East, primarily as bathroom "shaver" plug.

- "C" Pattern.   Three rectangular prongs. Generally found in Great Britain and in her former and present colonies.

- "D" Pattern. Thin, round pins. The most common plug pattern around the world. Also valuable as an extension for step-down converters in recessed sockets.

- "E" Pattern. Flat, angled blades. Encountered throughout the South Pacific, Australia, New Zealand and China.

- "F" Pattern. Three round prongs. Found in Hong Kong, Indian Subcontinent, some of Africa, former British colonies.

- "H" Pattern. Three large, round, widely-spaced prongs, used almost exclusively in South Africa.

Slip-on Grounding Adaptor Plugs

Pattern of appliance plug	Pattern of socket	Countries where socket found
		• "Schuko" sockets of Continental Europe and elsewhere; France, Belgium (4.8 mm prongs)
		• Great Britain, Ireland, Singapore, present and former colonies of England
		• South Pacific (Australia, New Zealand, Fiji); China
		• North America (for appliances *from* Continental Europe and elsewhere (4.8 mm "Schuko" sockets)
		• North America (for appliances *from* Great Britain, Ireland, Singapore, former colonies of England)
		• North America (for appliances *from* Australia, New Zealand, Fiji, China)
		• "Schuko" sockets of Continental Europe and elsewhere; France, Belgium, Eastern Europe, former U.S.S.R. (4.0 mm prongs) for appliances *from* Great Britain, Ireland, etc.
		• Great Britain, Ireland, Singapore, present and former colonies of England, for appliances *from* Continental Europe and elsewhere (4.8 mm sockets)

Guide to World Outlets and Electricity

Voltage around the world is primarily 220 volts. Those countries that use 110 volts, totally or partially, are marked with *. There are many countries that use both 220 volts and 110 volts, depending on the area of the country. Similarly, many countries use more than one wall socket shape because of the influence of modern trade or, perhaps, former colonial status.

Afghanistan - D/F
Algeria* - D/F
Andorra - D
Angola - D
Antigua - A/B/C
Argentina - D/E
Australia - E
Austria - D
Azores - D/F
Bahamas* - A
Bahrain - B/C/F
Balearic Islands* - D
Bangladesh - D/F
Barbados* - A
Belgium - D
Belize* - A
Benin - D/F
Bermuda* - A/C/E
Bolivia* - A/D
Botswana - B/C/F
Brazil* - A/D
Brunei - B/C
Bulgaria - D
Burkina Faso - D
Burundi - D
Cameroon* - D
Canada* - A
Canary Islands - D
Cape Verde, Rep. of - D
Cayman Islands* - A
Central African Rep. - D
Chad - D/F
Chile - D
China, Peo. Rep. of - C/D/E
CIS - D
Colombia* - A/D
Comoros - D
Congo - D
Cook Islands - E
Costa Rica* - A
Cote d'Ivoire - D
Cuba* - A
Cyprus - B/C
Czech Republic - D
Denmark - D
Djibouti - D
Dominica - B/C
Dominican Rep.* - A
Ecuador* - A/D
Egypt - D

El Salvador* - A
England - B/C
Equatorial Guinea - D
Eritrea - D/F
Estonia - D
Ethiopia - D/F
Fiji - E
Finland - D
France - D
French Guiana - D
French Polynesia* - A/D
Gabon - D
Gambia - B/C
Germany - D
Ghana - B/C/D/F
Gibraltar - B/C/D
Greece - D
Greenland - D
Grenada - B/C/D/F
Grenadines - D
Guadaloupe - D
Guam* - A
Guatemala* - A
Guinea - D
Guinea Bissau - D
Guyana* - A/B/C/D/F
Haiti* - A
Honduras* - A
Hong Kong - C/F
Hungary - D
Iceland - D
India - C/D/F
Indonesia* - D
Iran - D
Iraq - B/C/D/F
Ireland, Northern - B/C
Ireland, Rep. of - B/C
Israel - D
Italy - D
Jamaica* - A
Japan* - A
Jordan - B/C/D
Kampuchea - D
Kenya - B/C/F
Kiribati - E
Korea* - A/D
Kuwait - B/C/D/F
Laos - A/D
Latvia - D
Lebanon* - D
Lesotho - D/F

Liberia* - A/B/C
Libya* - D/F
Liechtenstein - D
Lithuania - D
Luxembourg - D
Macao - D/F
Madagascar* - D
Madeira - D/F
Malawi -B/C
Malaysia - B/C
Maldives - D/F
Mali - D
Malta - B/C
Martinique - D
Mauritania - D
Mauritius - B/C/D
Mexico* - A
Monaco* - D
Montserrat - A/B/C
Morocco* - D/F
Mozambique - D
Myanmar - B/C/D/F
Namibia - D/H
Nepal - B/D/F
Netherlands - D
Neth. Antilles* - A/D
New Caledonia - D
New Hebrides - E
New Zealand - E
Nicaragua* - A
Niger - D
Nigeria - B/C/F
Norway - D
Okinawa* - A
Oman - B/C/F
Pakistan - D/F
Panama* - A
Papua New Guinea - A/E
Paraguay - D
Peru* - A/D
Philippines* - A/D
Poland - D
Portugal - D/F
Puerto Rico* - A
Qatar - B/C/F
Romania - D
Rwanda - D
Russia - D
St. Kitts-Nevis - B/C/F
St. Lucia - B/C
St. Maarten* - D

St. Vincent - B/C
Samoa, American* - A/D/E
Samoa, Western - E
Saudi Arabia* - A/D
Scotland - B/C
Senegal* - D
Seychelles - B/C/F
Sierra Leone - B/C/F
Singapore - B/C/D/F
Slovak Republic - D
Solomon Islands - E
Somalia - D
South Africa, Rep. of - C/H
Spain* - D
Sri Lanka - D/F
Sudan - B/C/D
Surinam* - D
Swaziland - D/H
Sweden - D
Switzerland - D
Syria - D
Taiwan* - A
Tanzania - B/C/F
Thailand - A/D
Togo* - D
Tonga D/E/F
Trinidad & Tobago* - A/B/C/F
Tunisia* - D
Turkey - D
Turks & Caicos Islands* - A
Uganda - B/C/F
Ukraine - D
United Arab Emirates - B/C/F
United States of America* - A
Uruguay - D/E
Venezuela* - A
Vietnam* - A/D
Virgin Islands (British) - B/C
Virgin Islands (US)* - A
Wales - B/C
Yemen - A/B/C/D/F
Yugoslavia (former) - D
Zaire - D
Zambia - B/C
Zimbabwe - B/C/F

International Telephone Adaptors

Information and drawings courtesy of *Magellan's Catalog of Travel Supplies*, 1-800-962-4943; teleDaptor drawings courtesy also of TeleAdapt, Ltd., England, 44 (0) 814214444.

Approximately thirty-five different patterns of modular telephone sockets can be found in use around the world. This can be an obstacle for the business traveler who wishes to communicate from foreign countries through a computer modem, and is in the habit of merely plugging into common North American RJ-11 telephone jacks. Fortunately, adaptor plugs exist, individually and in money-saving packs, to convert these foreign modular telephone sockets to the popular RJ-11 pattern. The user merely unplugs the foreign telephone from the wall, inserts one of these adaptor plugs, and then plugs the cord from the computer's modem into the RJ-11 socket that these adaptors provide. In many cases, the foreign telephone can be reinserted into the wall over the top of these adaptors, allowing for simultaneous voice and data transmission (especially valuable when forced to route transmissions via telephone operators or other non-touchtone systems).

The drawings below show the various patterns of the world's telephone sockets. They are described by their "primary country of use," but in many cases, several countries have adopted the modular plug pattern of another. (For example, the Italian plug is used in Ethiopia, the Danish pattern is found in Malawi and elsewhere, and the U.K. plug pattern is found in over twenty countries.)

TeleDaptors

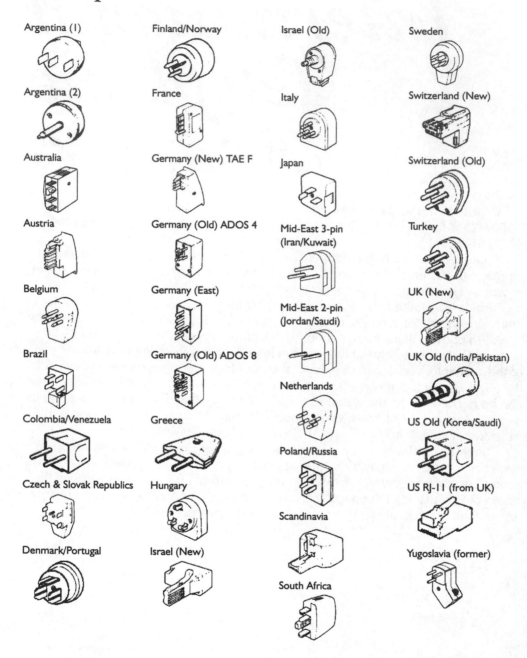

Argentina (1)

Argentina (2)

Australia

Austria

Belgium

Brazil

Colombia/Venezuela

Czech & Slovak Republics

Denmark/Portugal

Finland/Norway

France

Germany (New) TAE F

Germany (Old) ADOS 4

Germany (East)

Germany (Old) ADOS 8

Greece

Hungary

Israel (New)

Israel (Old)

Italy

Japan

Mid-East 3-pin
(Iran/Kuwait)

Mid-East 2-pin
(Jordan/Saudi)

Netherlands

Poland/Russia

Scandinavia

South Africa

Sweden

Switzerland (New)

Switzerland (Old)

Turkey

UK (New)

UK Old (India/Pakistan)

US Old (Korea/Saudi)

US RJ-11 (from UK)

Yugoslavia (former)

Wise travelers who rely on their modems to transmit important data from around the world also take along "patch cord kits" (available from the same sources that sell foreign telephone adaptors). These kits include such tools as a small screwdriver for removing wall plates, "alligator clips" for attaching to telephone wires, a compact line tester to check that correct connections have been made, etc. These "road warrior" kits are valuable should non-modular ("hard-wired") telephones be encountered.

Equivalents

Unit	Metric Equivalent	US Equivalent
acre	0.404 685 64 hectares	43,560 feet^2
acre	4,046,856 4 meters^2	4,840 yards^2
acre	0.004 046 856 4 kilometers^2	0.001 562 5 miles2, statute
acre	100 meters^2	119.599 yards^2
barrell (petroleum, US)	158.987 29 liters	42 gallons
(proof spirits, US)	151.416 47 liters	40 gallons
(beer, US)	117.347 77 liters	31 gallons
bushel	35.239 07 liters	4 pecks
cable	219.456 meters	120 fathoms
chain (surveyor's)	20.116 8 meters	66 feet
cord (wood)	3.624 556 meters^3	128 feet^3
cup	0.236 588 2 liters	8 ounces, liquid (US)
degrees, celsius	(water boils at 100°C, freezes at 0°C)	multiply by 1.8 and add 32 to obtain °F
degrees, fahrenheit	subtract 32 and divide by 1.8 to obtain C°	(water boils at 212°F, freezes at 32°F)
dram, avoirdupois	1.771 845 2 grams	0.0625 5 ounces, avoirdupois
dram, troy	3.887 934 6 grams	0.125 ounces, troy
dram, liquid (US)	3.696 69 milliliters	0.125 ounces, liquid
fathom	1.828 8 meters	6 feet
foot	30.48 centimeters	12 inches
foot	0.304 8 meters	0.333 333 3 yards
foot	0.000 304 8 kilometers	0.000 189 39 miles, statute
foot^2	929.030 4 centimeters^2	144 inches^2
foot	2 0.092 903 04 meters^2	0.111 111 1 yards^2
foot^3	28.316 846 592 liters	7.480 519 gallons
foot^3	0.028 316 847 meters^3	1,728 inches^3
furlong	201.168 meters	220 yards
gallon, liquid (US)	3.785 411 784 liters	4 quarts, liquid
gill (US)	118.294 118 milliliters	4 ounces, liquid
grain	64.798 91 milligrams	0.002 285 71 ounces, advp.
gram	1,000 milligrams	0.035 273 96 ounces, advp.
hand (height of horse)	10.16 centimeters	4 inches
hectare	10,000 meters^2	2.471 053 8 acres
hundredweight, long	50.802 345 kilograms	112 pounds, avoirdupois
hundredweight, short	45.359 237 kilograms	100 pounds, avoirdupois
inch	2.54 centimeters	0.083 333 33 feet
inch^2	6.451 6 centimeters2	0.006 944 44 feet^2
inch^3	16.387 064 milliliters	0.000 578 7 feet^3
inch^3	16.387 064 milliliters	0.029 761 6 pints, dry
inch^3	16.387.064 milliliters	0.034 632 0 pints, liquid
kilogram	0.001 tons, metric	2.204 626 pounds, avoirdupois
kilometer	1,000 meters	0.621 371 19 miles, statue
kilometer^2	100 hectares	247.105 38 acres
kilometer^2	1,000,000 meters^2	0.386 102 16 miles^2, statue
knot (1 nautical mi/hr)	1.852 kilometers/hour	1.151 statue miles/hour
league, nautical	5.559 552 kilometers	3 miles, nautical
league, statute	4.828.032 kilometers	3 miles, statute
link (surveyor's)	20.116 8 centimeters	7.92 inches
liter	0.001 meters^3	61.023 74 inches^3
liter	0.1 dekaliter	0.908 083 quarts, dry
liter	1,000 milliliters	1.056 688 quarts, liquid
meter	100 centimeters	1.093 613 yards
meter^2	10,000 centimeters^2	1.195 990 yards^2
meter^3	1,000 liters	1.307 951 yards^3
micron	0.000 001 meter	0.000 039 4 inches
mil	0.025 4 millimeters	0.001 inch

Unit	Metric Equivalent	US Equivalent
mile, nautical	1.852 kilometers	1.150 779 4 miles, statute
mile^2, nautical	3.429 904 kilometers^2	1.325 miles^2, statute
mile, statute	1.609 344 kilometers	5,280 feet or 8 furlongs
mile^2, statute	258.998 811 hectares	640 acres or 1 section
mile^2, statute	2.589 988 11 kilometers^2	0.755 miles^2, nautical
minim (US)	0.061 611 52 milliliters	0.002 083 33 ounces, liquid
ounce, avoirdupois	28.349 523 125 grams	437.5 grains
ounce, liquid (US)	29.573 53 milliliters	0.062 5 pints, liquid
ounce, troy	31.103 476 8 grams	480 grains
pace	76.2 centimeters	30 inches
peck	8.809 767 5 liters	8 quarts, dry
pennyweight	1.555 173 84 grams	24 grains
pint, dry (US)	0.550 610 47 liters	0.5 quarts, dry
pint, liquid (US)	0.473 176 473	0.5 quarts, liquid
point (typographical)	0.351 459 8 milliliters	0.013 837 inches
pound, avoirdupois	453.592 37 grams	16 ounces, avourdupois
pound, troy	373.241 721 6 grams	12 ounces, troy
quart, dry (US)	1.101 221 liters	2 pints, dry
quart, liquid (US)	0.946 352 946 liters	2 pints, liquid
quintal	100 kilograms	220.462 26 pounds, avdp.
rod	5.029 2 meters	505 yards
scruple	1.295 978 2 grams	20 grains
section (US)	2.589 988 1 kilometers^2	1 mile^2, statute or 640 acres
span	22.86 centimeters	9 inches
stere	1 meter^3	1.307 95 yards^3
tablespoon	14.786 76 milliliters	3 teaspoons
teaspoon	4.928 922 milliliters	0.333 333 tablespoons
ton, long or deadweight	1,016.046.909 kilograms	2,240 pounds, avoirdupois
ton, metric	1,000 kilograms	2,204.623 pounds, avoirdupois
ton, register	2.831 684 7 meters^3	100 feet^3
ton, short	907.184 74 kilograms	2,000 pounds, avoirdupois
township (US)	93.239 572 kilometers^2	36 miles^2, statute
yard	0.914 4 meters	3 feet
yard^2	0.836 127 36 meters^2	9 feet^2
yard^3	0.764 554 86 meters^3	27 feet^3
yard^3	764.554 857 984 liters	201.974 gallons

Index

Also Available from Adams Publishing

The Adams Business Advisors
All books are $10.95, trade paperback, 5 1/2" x 8 1/2", 300 pages, unless otherwise noted.

- *Accounting for the Small Business*: How to do your own accounting simply, easily, and accurately. Christopher R. Malburg

- *The All-in-One Business Planning Guide*: How to create cohesive plans for marketing, sales, operations, finance, and cash flow. Christopher R. Malburg

- *Entrepreneurial Growth Strategies*: Strategic planning, restructuring alternatives, marketing tactics, financing options, acquisitions, and other ways to propel the new venture forward. Lawrence W. Tuller

- *Exporting, Importing, and Beyond*: A handbook for growing businesses selling products and services in global markets. Lawrence W. Tuller

- *Marketing Magic*: Innovative and proven ideas for finding customers, making sales, and growing your business. Don Debelak

- *The Personnel Policy Handbook for Growing Companies*: How to create comprehensive guidelines, procedures, and checklists. Darien McWhirter

- *Service, Service, Service*: The growing business' secret weapon; innovative and proven ideas for getting and keeping customers. Steve Albrecht

- *The Small Business Valuation Book*: Easy-to-use techniques for determining fair price, resolving disputes, and minimizing taxes. Lawrence W. Tuller

- *Winning the Entrepreneur's Game*: How to start, operate, and be successful in a new or growing business. David E. Rye

And coming in May 1995:

- *Managing People*: Creating the team-based organization; guidelines for total group participation, employee empowerment, and organization development. Darien McWhirter
- *The Total Quality Handbook for Small Companies*: Strategies for products, people, and processes. John Woods
- *Do-It-Yourself Advertising, Direct Mail, and Publicity*: Ready-to-use templates, worksheets, and samples for creating ads, direct mail pieces, press releases, and other promotional items. Sarah White and John Woods. $15.95, 8 1/2" x 11", 300 pages.
- *The Small Business Legal Kit*: 300 forms, agreements, and contracts for any small business. J.W. Dicks. $15.95, 8 1/2" x 11", 300 pages.

The authors of this book wish to express their appreciation to Getting Through Customs of Newtown Square, Pennsylvania. Getting Through Customs specializes in teaching executives how to do busines globally, providing customized research reports, seminars, language training and translations, and the online database, PASSPORT. The authors augmented their own research and experience with Getting Through Customs' online PASSPORT database.

The PASSPORT online database contains up-to-date business and cultural data on more than seventy countries, in greater detail than could be included in this book. Numerous corporations and institutions—including AT&T, DuPont, and the Wharton Export Network of the University of Pennsylvania—have found the PASS-PORT System to be a valuable tool for facilitating globalization.

PASSPORT can be accessed via modem through various online networks, installed in-house on PCs, or purchased as country printouts.

The study of intercultural communication represents a lifelong interest for the authors of *Kiss, Bow, or Shake Hands*. By way of continuing that research, the authors invite your comments. Whether your own experience confirms or diverges from the data in this book, they would like to hear from you. Your comments may be sent to the following address:

Kiss, Bow, or Shake Hands
c/o Getting Through Customs
Box 136, Newtown Square, PA 19073
Tel: (610) 353-9894
Fax: (610) 353-6994